In the volume *African Industrial Development and European Union Co-operation: reflections for a reengineered partnership*, Francis Matambalya and the contributors offer in-depth analyses of the industrial development issues in Africa. They shed light on missed opportunities in view of the longstanding Africa–European cooperation, which if properly leveraged, could have produced completely different results. The book offers food for thought for development planners in Africa, the European Union, and the international economic community as a whole. The raised issues should be taken seriously, if the partnership between these two groups of the countries – one of the oldest in the world – is not to go down in history as a botched enterprise.

Ludovico Alcorta, *Director, Development Policy, Statistics, and Strategic Research, United Nations Industrial Development Organization, Vienna, Austria*

As the global economic landscape is shifting through the erosion of the clout of the West, coupled with the emergence of new countries, as key players in African economic affairs, the volume *African Industrial Development and European Union Co-operation: reflections for a reengineered partnership* could not be more timely. The book takes the reader through a *Zeitreise* of international economic partnership. In careful analyses blending theory and practice, including practical lessons from numerous Africa–European Union development co-operation arrangements thus far hardly encouraging for African industrialisation, the volume provides scholars and policy-makers alike with exhilarating views on what international economic partnership can achieve in terms of instilling industrial development. It is a 'MUST-READ' for well-wishers of international partnership as a model for sustainable industry-led economic growth.

Helmut Asche, *Director, German Institute for Development Evaluation, Bonn, Germany*

The economic relations between the African states and their European partners have evolved over a long period of time. Indeed, there are many who would consider the European Union model of development co-operation, from which the African countries ought to have benefited, to have generally served its purpose well. This is also the line of argument followed by 'official' Africa and Europe. Yet, the on-going changes in the international economic system, which have become the hallmark of our time, are invariably connected with great uncertainties for the future for African–European Union co-operation. The shift in the constellation of the international economic system, away from 'North–South' partnerships towards 'South–South' partnerships is inconspicuous. New players from the South dominate new investments in Africa, and are the continent's key trade partners. This trend of events is, at least in part, attributable to the disillusionment with 'North–South' partnership as a model of development, including the numerous regimes linking Africa and the European Union. In the 14 chapters making up the volume *African Industrial Development and European Union Co-operation: reflections for a reengineered partnership*, Francis Matambalya and the contributors have expertly put in context the health and future prospects of African–European Union partnership. The book is a good reference for those who wish to salvage African–European Union partnership in a dynamic world.

Gerrishon Ikiara, *Associate Director, Institute of Diplomatic and International Studies, University of Nairobi; and former Permanent Secretary, Government of Kenya*

T0331393

African Industrial Development and European Union Co-operation

Of the 54 African states, only South Africa is categorised by the United Nations Industrial Development Organization (UNIDO) amongst industrialised countries. The economic activities in Africa are still dominated by the production and trade of agricultural and mineral commodities. This situation is in spite of the long-standing Africa–European Union (EU) co-operation, which intends, among other things, to support Africa's industrialisation endeavours.

Imperatively, a long road to substantive levels of industrialisation still lies ahead of the African countries. This raises the question as to what role the international community could and should play in the twenty-first century to provide the support needed to expedite Africa's industrial transformation.

This book argues that to supplement the initiatives of each African country, international partnerships, of both a 'North–South' and 'South–South' nature, will serve better purposes if they are leveraged to develop productive capacities in African economies. In order to enable the African countries to leverage their traditional partnership with the EU for industrialisation, a paradigm shift is obligatory. A feasible model should emulate the Japanese-led 'flying geese' model and the Chinese-led 'bamboo capitalism' model.

Francis A.S.T. Matambalya is Professor of International Trade and Marketing and Senior Researcher at the Nordic Africa Institute (NAI) in Uppsala, Sweden.

Routledge studies in development economics

African Industrial Development and European Union Co-operation

Prospects for a reengineered partnership

Edited by Francis A.S.T. Matambalya

Routledge
Taylor & Francis Group

LONDON AND NEW YORK

First published 2015
by Routledge

2 Park Square, Milton Park, Abingdon, Oxfordshire OX14 4RN
52 Vanderbilt Avenue, New York, NY 10017

Routledge is an imprint of the Taylor & Francis Group, an informa business

First issued in paperback 2019

British Library Cataloguing in Publication Data
A catalogue record for this book is available from the British Library

Library of Congress Cataloging in Publication Data
African industrial development and EU cooperation/edited by Francis Shasha Matambalya.
    pages cm. – (Routledge studies in development economics)
    1. Industrialization–Africa. 2. Industrial policy–Africa.
    3. Africa–Foreign economic relations–European Union countries.
    4. European Union countries–Foreign economic relations–Africa.
    I. Matambalya, Francis A.S.T.
    HC800.Z9I532 2014
    338.96–dc23   2013048254

ISBN: 978-0-415-67127-9 (hbk)
ISBN: 978-0-367-86613-6 (pbk)

Typeset in Times New Roman
by Wearset Ltd, Boldon, Tyne and Wear

Contents

Figures

Tables

Contributors

Kibre Moges Belete received his BA in Economics from Addis Ababa University in 1983, and a postgraduate diploma and MA in Economics and Social Statistics from Manchester University, UK, in 1986 and 1988 respectively. He was also a visiting study fellow to Oxford University, Food Studies Group, UK during 1990–1991. His professional work focused largely on macroeconomic modelling, trade, and industry. He has provided a number of consultancy services to national and international organisations such as McGill University of Montreal, Canada (1995), United Nations Economic Commission for Africa (1995 and 1996), the World Bank (2003), Center for International Private Enterprise – an affiliate of the US Chamber of Commerce (2006), Swedish International Development Agency (2007), and Friedrich Ebert Stiftung of Germany (2008), and for consulting firms such as PADCO, a Washington based international consulting firm sponsored by UNDP (1996), and KUAB, a local consulting firm sponsored by UNDP and World Bank (1999 and 2001). Since 2001, he has also written and published several chapters in edited volumes, working papers, and articles for international conferences.

Imen Belhadj is a Tunisian national and holder of a PhD from the Centre for African Studies of Peking University, Beijing, China. Ms Belhadj's PhD research project focused on China–Maghreb Relations, but her research interests cover also China–Africa Co-operation as a whole. She also holds a Master Degree in Chinese Contemporary Literature from Peking University, Beijing, China. She got her Bachelor Degree in Chinese Language and Literature from L'Institut Supérieur des Langues de Tunis, Tunisia. From 2 April to 29 June 2012, Ms Belhadj was invited as a Guest Researcher at the Nordic Africa Institute. Ms Belhadj has participated in many academic activities related to China–Africa co-operation in China. She published two academic works on Tunisia in Chinese in core academic review in China, and currently is teaching Arabic in the School of Foreign Languages of Peking University.

Tommaso Ciarli is Senior Research Fellow at the Science and Technology Policy Research (SPRU) at Sussex University where he is currently involved in several research projects: entrepreneurship and conflict, the evolution of rice technological trajectories, modelling the effects of different dimensions of structural change on long-run growth, development and technological change in agriculture, and on inclusive growth and innovation. Tommaso's main research interests are in the overlapping areas of technological change, institutional change, and economic development. Some of his work has focussed on international trade and the globalisation of agriculture, firm organisation, and environmental innovation. He has a PhD in Economics and Industrial Development from the University of Birmingham and the University of Ferrara (Italy). Before the PhD Tommaso worked for the United Nations Industrial Development Organization (UNIDO) and Economic Commission for Latin America and the Caribbean (ECLAC). From 2008 to 2011, he worked as a researcher at the Max Planck Institute of Economics.

Massata Cissé is a Senegalese national and former Chief of the Africa Programme at the United Nations Industrial Organization (UNIDO) Headquarters in Vienna, Austria. Prior to that he served as Primary Administrator in charge of the UNIDO field operations, based at the Head Office in Vienna (2006–2008), UNIDO Representative for Côte d'Ivoire, Burkina Faso, Mali, and Niger, with residence in Abidjan (2000–2006), UNIDO Representative for the Mano River Union Countries, i.e. Guinea, Liberia, and Sierra Leone with residence in Conakry (1988–2000), and UNIDO Representative for Guinea and Mali, with residence in Conakry (1995–2008). He holds a Master of Economic Sciences (major: Private Economy and Management from the University of Dakar, Senegal).

Michele Di Maio is Assistant Professor in Economics at the University of Naples 'Parthenope' (Italy). He is Senior Affiliate of the Household in Conflict Network (HiCN) and member of the Network of European Peace Scientists (NEPS). He holds a BA from Bocconi University (Italy) and an MA and PhD from the University of Siena (Italy). He has held several visiting positions (UN-CEPAL, Santa Fe Institute, CESPRI-Bocconi, Sant'Anna School for Advanced Research). He has been part of a number of Italian and international research groups and projects such as PRIN, FIRB, IPD (Initiative for Policy Dialogue). Trained as an international trade economist, his research interests focus on the effect of trade liberalisation in developing countries and the effects of industrial policies on economic growth. He has extensively published in international journals such as *Journal of Development Economics, Journal of Population Economics, Journal of International Trade and Economic Development, Journal of Economics, American Journal of Economics and Sociology, Structural Change and Economic Dynamics* and contributed to collective books such as *International Development: ideas, experience, and prospects* (Oxford University Press) and *The Political Economy of Capabilities Accumulation: the past and future of policies for industrial development* (Oxford University Press).

Francis A.S.T. Matambalya is a Professor of International Trade and Marketing, and currently works as a Senior Researcher at the Nordic Africa Institute

(NAI) in Uppsala, Sweden. From 2008 to 2010, he worked as a Senior Development Consultant at the Headquarters of the United Nations Industrial Development Organization (UNIDO) in Vienna. In his earlier career, from 1987 Mr Matambalya was a member of academic staff of the Faculty of Commerce and Management of the University of Dar es Salaam in Tanzania (now University of Dar es Salaam Business School), with which he is still associated. He is also a facilitator of several capacity development programmes of the United Nations Institute for Planning and Economic Development (IDEP), including the IDEP Specialised Training Course on Industrial Development Policy for Senior African Officials. Mr Matambalya holds a PhD (International Economic Relations – major in International Trade) from the Ruhr University Bochum (Germany), an MSc (Business Administration; majors in Marketing and Business Informatics) from Johannes Kepler University Linz (Austria), and a Bachelor of Commerce (major in Marketing) from the University of Dar es Salaam, Tanzania.

Henning Melber is Professor and Senior Adviser/Director Emeritus of The Dag Hammarskjöld Foundation in Uppsala, Sweden, and Extraordinary Professor at the Department of Political Sciences/University of Pretoria and the Centre for Africa Studies/University of the Free State. He was Director of The Namibian Economic Policy Research Unit (NEPRU) in Windhoek (1992–2000) and Research Director at The Nordic Africa Institute in Uppsala (2000–2006).

Acknowledgements

This book is the result of hard work on the part of the authors, the editor, and the publisher. The book carries on the debates about industrialisation, the European Union (EU) co-operation model with developing countries, and the political economy and international economic relations. It reflects the reality of the processes surrounding industrial transformation, and economic growth and development over the period that spans the time during and after the cold war.

The urge to contribute towards informing policy formulation through an analysis using policy-relevant information and data was a key motivation to write this book. To that purpose, the chapters in this book use different indicators to provide breakdowns, which illustrate the diversity of developments of importance for the development of industrial competitiveness.

The editor got the inspiration for writing this book when he was Senior Industrial Development Consultant at the United Nations Industrial Development Organization (UNIDO) Headquarters in Vienna, Austria. During the three-year period spent at this United Nations Agency with a mandate to oversee industrialisation efforts, from 2008 to 2010, the editor worked in various capacities. First, he worked as *Senior Development Programme Expert/Senior Expert on Least Developed Countries* (LDCs), in the Special Programmes Group. Later, he worked as *Senior International Industrial Development Expert*, in the Africa Bureau/Africa Programme. Among the many key documents produced for the Special Programmes Group is the Concept of the 'Aid for Trade: An Industrial Agenda for LDCs', which guided the 'LDCs Ministerial Conference', which was held at Siem Reap, Cambodia, in 2008. Among the major documents produced for the Africa Programme are three Annexes to the 'The implementation strategy of the African Union's action plan for the accelerated industrial development of Africa (AIDA)': The Financing and Resource Mobilisation Strategy, The Monitoring and Evaluation (M&E) System, and The Steering Committee (for steering the process of implementation of AIDA).

Apart from getting invaluable insights about industrial development initiatives for Africa, the editor established contacts with several of the contributors to this volume and exchanged ideas with them about the prospects for writing a book on Africa's industrialisation in a fashion that is novel and provocative. Eventually, it was agreed to write a book that focuses its discussion on re-aligning the EU development co-operation agenda, to support African industrial transformation. The focus on African countries perhaps made it markedly more difficult to write, as industrial development is evidently not a priority research area in the context of Africa's development, and attracts hardly any research funding. Even so, the contributors committed themselves to work on this theme on an *extra mural* basis, out of conviction and academics' allure and inquisitiveness.

To be able to produce this volume, I, in my dual role as editor and author, needed a conducive institutional setting. The Nordic Africa Institute provided me with such an opportunity and an ideal working environment for the endeavours. In this connection, I would like to dedicate special gratitude to my very best friend Dr Yenkong Ngajoh-Hodu (currently at Manchester University Law School, and formerly at the Nordic Africa Institute) for recommending the Institute to me.

As the production of this book is very much a joint effort of all the contributors and our publishing house, I acknowledge the great sacrifices by the authors, and the grand indulgence by the publishers. Our gratitude goes out also to the institutions we are affiliated to, for this possibility: The Nordic Africa Institute (Uppsala, Sweden), Dag Hammarkjöld Foundation (Uppsala, Sweden), University of Naples 'Parthenope' (Italy), Sussex University (Sussex, The United Kingdom), and Peking University (Beijing, China).

On behalf of the team of authors, I also wish to express our thanks to Mr Massata Cissé, the immediate former Chief of the Africa Programme at UNIDO Head Office in Vienna, for the encouragement to continue with the mission, even when it looked like we might not be able to mobilise enough contributors to write the volume.

We have tried to create something that reflects our shared thoughts on explanations of past and current EU development co-operation with the African countries, and its relevance for industrialisation. As we have written, these entrenched relationships have developed beyond a simple *co-operation model*, into a de facto *co-operation symbol*. However, African–EU relations have not been evolving in isolation, but within the context of broader international economic relationships. Hence, we have also evaluated them in the context of the disillusionment about their limited dividends vis-à-vis delivering industrialisation and overall economic transformation, when compared to other parallel schemes of international economic co-operation.

Nevertheless, the editor and his team of authors do not claim to be faultless, or to have covered everything of interest to the reader in just this one book volume. Besides, even with regard to what we have addressed in this book, some things might have passed us by, and we apologise for any such errors or omissions. In any case, the views expressed in this book are those of the editor and the authors, and do not necessarily express the official positions of the institutions to which they are affiliated.

The editor had significant distractions on the way to finishing this edited book volume, and it is to this duo that he dedicates this book: the new-born distraction, *Andreas Shasha Keplinger Matambalya* and his older sibling *Alexander Junior Lambert Wambura Matambalya*.

Abbreviations and acronyms

3ADI	African Agribusiness and Agro-industry Development Initiative
AA	Association Agreements
ACF	African Cohesion Fund
ACP	African, Caribbean and Pacific (group of nations associated with the EU)
ADLI	Agriculture Development Led Industrialisation
AEC	African Economic Community
AERC	African Economic Research Consortium
AIA	Alliance for Industrialisation in Africa
AIDA	Accelerated Industrial Development of Africa
AMU	Arab Maghreb Union
APCF	African Productive Capacity Facilities
APCI	Africa Productive Capacity Initiative
ARDF	African Regional Development Fund
ARIPO	Africa Regional Industrial Property Organisation
AS	Advanced Status
ASEAN	Association of South East Asian Nations
AU	African Union
AUC	Africa Union Commission
AWEEPA	Association of West European Parliamentarians for Action Against Apartheid
BEE	Black Economic Empowerment
BDSP	Business Development Service Providers
BLS	Botswana, Lesotho, Swaziland
BWI	Bretton Woods Institutions
CAA	Cairo Agenda of Action
CAMI	Conference of African Ministers of Industry
CDE	Centre for the Development of Enterprise
CDI	Centre for the Development of Industry
CEMAC	*Communauté Économique et Monétaire de l'Afrique Centrale*
CEN-SAD	Community of Sahel-Saharan States
CEPGL	*Communauté Économique des Pays des Grand Lacs*

CET	Common External Tariff
CIC	Committee on Industrial Co-operation
CID	Centre for Industrial Development
CIP Index	Competitive Industrial Performance Index
COMESA	Common Market for Eastern and Southern Africa
CU	Customs Union
DBs	Development Banks
DFI	Development Finance Institutions
DMI	Domestic Market Integration
DSM	Dispute Settlement Mechanism
EAAS	East African Air Aviation Services
EAC	East African Community
EACSO	East African Common Services Organisation
EADB	East African Development Bank
EAP	East Asia and Pacific
EAPT	East African Posts and Telecommunications
EARH	East African Railways and Harbours
EC	European Commission
ECCAS	Economic Community of Central African States
ECOSOC	Economic and Social Council (of the United Nations)
ECU	European Currency Unit
EDF	European Development Fund
EEC	European Economic Community
EIB	European Investment Bank
ELI	Export-Led Industrialisation; also referred to as Export-Oriented Industrialisation (EOI) or Export-Substitution Industrialisation (ESI)
EMP	Euro-Mediterranean Partnership (also called the 'The Barcelona Process')
ENP	European Neighbourhood Policy
ENPI	European Neighbourhood and Partnership Instrument
EOI	Export-Oriented Industrialisation; also referred to as Export Substitution Industrialisation (ESI) or Export-Led Industrialisation (ELI)
EPA	Economic Partnership Agreement
EPP	Economic Policy Philosophy
EPZ	Export Processing Zone
ESI	Export Substitution Industrialisation; also referred to as Export-Led Industrialisation (ELI) or Export-Oriented Industrialisation (EOI)
ETCZ	Economic and Trade Co-operation Zone
EU	European Union
FDI	Foreign Direct Investments
FiR	Financial Resources
FRMS	Financing and Resource Mobilisation Strategy

GAFTA	Greater Arab Free Trade Area
GATS	General Agreement on Trade in Services
GATT	General Agreements on Tariffs and Trade
GDP	Gross Domestic Product
GFCF	Gross Fixed Capital Formation
GNI	Gross National Income
HCTs	High Commission Territories
HT	High Technology
ICTs	Information and Communication Technologies
IDDA	Industrial Development Decade for Africa
IDPOs	Industrial Development Promotion Organisations
IDR	Industrial Development Report (published by UNIDO annually since 2002/2003)
IIDA	Integrated Industrial Development Agenda
IIDGF	Integrated Industrial Development Governance Framework
IMF	International Monetary Fund
IOC	Indian Ocean Commission
IPOs	Intellectual Property Offices
ISI	Import Substitution Industrialisation
ISS	Import Substitution Strategy
ITC	International Trade Centre
LAC	Latin America and the Caribbean
LDCs	Least Developed Countries
LED	Local Economic Development
LPA	Lagos Plan of Action
LSIEs	Large Scale Industrial Enterprises
LT	Low Technology
MA	Market Access
MDGs	Millennium Development Goals
MENA	Middle East and North Africa
MFCF	Manufacturing Fixed Capital Formation
MFN	Most Favoured Nation
MRU	Mano River Union
MSMEs	Micro, Small and Medium Enterprises
MT	Medium Technology
MTER	Manufactured Good to Total Export Ratio
MTIR	Manufactured Good to Total Import Ratio
MVA	Manufactured Value Added
NBFIs	Non-Bank Financial Institutions
NCDI	National Centre for the Development of Industry
NDCs	Newly Developed Countries
NEPAD	New Partnership for Africa's Development
NFiR	Non-Financial Resources
NGT	New Growth Theory
NHIES	National Household Income and Expenditure Survey

NIC	Newly Industrialising Country
NTBs	Non-Tariff Barriers
OAPI	*Organisation Africaine de la Propriété Intellectuelle*
OECD	Organisation for Economic Co-operation and Development
PAFTA	Pan Arab Free Trade Area
PRC	People's Republic of China
PSD	Private Sector Development
RECs	Regional Economic Communities
RFZs	Regional Free Zones
RoO	Rules of Origin
RTAs	Regional Trade Agreements
SACU	Southern African Customs Union
SADC	Southern African Development Community
SAP	Structural Adjustment Programme
SAS	South Asia
SEA	South East Asia
SEDOM	Small Enterprise Development Organisation
SEZs	Special Economic Zones
SMEs	Small and Medium Scale Enterprises
SMSIEs	Small and Medium Scale Industrial Enterprises
SoEs	State-owned Enterprises
SRCU	Southern Rhodesia Customs Union
SSA	Sub-Saharan Africa
STABEX	System for the Stabilisation of Exports
SWAPO	South West Africa Peoples' Organisation
SYSMIN	Systéme Minerais (i.e. system for stabilising minerals)
TDCA	Trade and Development Co-operation Agreement
TIPEEG	Targeted Intervention Programme for Employment and Economic Growth
TNCs	Transnational Corporations
TVET	Technical and Vacational Education and Training
UEMOA	*Union Économique et Monétaire Ouest Africaine* (English abbreviation: WAEMU)
UfM	Union for the Mediterranean
UMA	Union du Maghreb Arabe
UMOA	*Union Monétaire Ouest Africaine*
UN	United Nations
UN-NADAF	United Nations New Agenda for the Development of Africa
UN-PAAERD	United Nations Program of Action for the African Economic Recovery and Development
UNCTAD	United Nations Conference on Trade and Development
UNECA	United Nations Economic Commission for Africa
UNIDO	United Nations Industrial Development Organization
UNIDEP	United Nations Institute for Planning and Economic Development

UNIN	United Nations Institute for Namibia
UNTACDA	United Nations Transport and Communications Decade for Africa
VAT	Value Added Tax
WACIP	West African Common Industrial Policy
WAEMU	West African Economic and Monetary Union (French abbreviation: UEMOA)
WAMU	West African Monetary Union (French abbreviation: UMOA)
WB	World Bank
WTO	World Trade Organization

Notations and variables used in various estimations

δRP	Change in relative price
CIP Index	Global average Competitive Industrial Performance Index
CNME	Country's number of manufacturing establishments per 100,000 people
Em	Elasticity of import demand
EMPMsh	Country's number of employees in manufacturing sector as a percentage of total number of employees
Es	Elasticity of substitution between imports from a partner economy and the rest of the world
IMP_t	Index (number) of Manufacturing Production in year t
imWIGFCF	Country's Industry Gross Fixed Capital Formation as a share of World Gross Fixed Capital Formation
imWINVM	Country's Investments in manufacturing sector as a share of World Investments in Manufacturing
imWINVMHM	Country's Investments in Medium- and High-tech manufacturing sub-sector as a share of World Investments Medium- and High-tech manufacturing sub-sector
imWME	Country's number of manufacturing employment per 100,000 people as a ratio of World Manufacturing employment per 100,000 people
ImWMT	Country's Manufactured Exports as a share of World Manufactured Trade
ImWMVA	Country's Manufacturing Value Added as a share of World Manufacturing Value Added
INVMpc	Country's total investments in Manufacturing sector per capita
MFDIpc	Country's FDI inflows in Manufacturing sector per capita
MFDIsh	Country's FDI inflows in manufacturing sector as share of total FDI inflows
MHMFDIpc	Country's FDI inflows in Medium- and High-tech manufacturing sub-sector per capita
MHMFDIsh	Country's FDI inflows in Medium- and High-tech manufacturing sub-sector as a share in total FDI inflows

$MHVAsh$	Country's Medium- and High-Tech Manufacturing Value Added share in total Manufacturing Value Added
$MHXsh$	Country's Medium- and High-tech manufactured Exports share in total manufactured exports
M^O	Imports before liberalisation
MP_t	Country's manufacturing Production in year t
M^{TP}	Current volume of imports from current commercial partners, given domestic price P and tariff T
MVA	Average Manufacturing Value Added as a percentage of Gross Domestic Product
$MVApc$	Manufacturing Value Added per capita
$MVAsh$	Manufacturing Value Added share in total Gross Domestic Product
$MXpc$	Country's Manufacturing Exports per capita
$MXsh$	Country's Manufactured Exports share in total exports
P	Domestic price
$POPsh$	Country's share of World population
RP	Relative price
T	Tariff
TC	Trade Creation
TD	Trade Diversion
T_0	Pre-liberalisation tariff rate
T_1	Post-liberalisation tariff rate
$\left(\dfrac{T_1 - T_0}{T_0}\right)$	change in tariff, given the pre- and post-liberalisation rates of T_0 and T_1
$WEMPMsh$	World number of employees in manufacturing sector as a percentage of total number of employees
$WINVMpc$	World investments in Manufacturing sector per capita
$WMFDIpc$	FDI inflows in Manufacturing sector per capita
$WMFDIsh$	World FDI inflows in Manufacturing sector as share of total FDI inflows
$WMHMFDIpc$	World FDI inflows in Medium- and High-tech manufacturing sub-sector per capita
$WMHMFDIsh$	World FDI inflows in Medium- and High-tech manufacturing sub-sector as a share in total FDI inflows
$WMHVAsh$	World's Medium- and High-tech manufacturing Value Added share in total Manufacturing Value Added
$WMHXsh$	World's Medium- and High-tech Manufactured Exports share in total manufactured exports
$WMVAp.c$	World Manufactured Value Added per capita
$WMVAsh$	World's Manufacturing Value Added share in total GDP
$WMXpc$	World Manufactured Exports per capita
$WMXsh$	World's Manufactured Exports share in total exports
$WNME$	World number of manufacturing establishments per 100,000 people

Part I

Contextualising industrialisation

1 Leveraging African–European Union co-operation for Africa's industrialisation

An introduction

Francis A.S.T. Matambalya and Massata Cissé

The detailed objectives for economic development may differ across countries. However, they tend to have a common denominator in the form of a focus on the creation of wealth through the growth of (aggregate national, household, and individual) incomes, and the reduction of poverty through the redressing of income inequalities in the society. Industrialisation can contribute to the achievement of all these goals. Wherever it has happened, the industrial revolution has been momentous in terms of inexplicably increasing the output of the economy, improving the quality of products, raising the incomes (of individuals, households, and institutions), uplifting the living standards of the people, and increasing the momentum of further economic transformation.

1.1 Conceptualising industrialisation

Several formal definitions of industrialisation exist. Inter alia, it has been defined as:

a   The process in which a society or country (or world) transforms itself from a primarily agricultural society into one based on the manufacturing of goods and services. Individual manual labor is often replaced by mechanized mass production and craftsmen are replaced by assembly lines. Characteristics of industrialization include the use of technological innovation to solve problems as opposed to superstition or dependency upon conditions outside human control such as the weather, as well as more efficient division of labor and economic growth.
                         (cf. Investopedia, available at: www.investopedia.com/
                                                terms/i/industrialization.asp)
b   'A development path based on expanding a country's capacity to process raw materials and manufacture products for consumers, businesses, and export' (cf. www.frontierassoc.net/greenaffordablehousing/tools/Chemical Terms.sht).

Delineated further, industrialisation in an economic sense can be understood to mean a process in which a human society is transformed from a lower level of development (pre-industrial) to a higher level of development (industrial). This process is characterised by two key changes:

a   Change in the organisation of economic production from 'artisanal' and 'subsistence' modes of production (with minimal or no automation, and therefore minimal or no use of automated machinery and equipment, reliance on non-skilled labour) towards 'industrial modes of production' (i.e. with more automation, and therefore more use of machinery, equipment, and skilled and specialised labour);
b   Re-orienting the structure of the various dimensions of the economy (investments, production, trade), from activities at the lower end of the value chain with minimal or no value addition (e.g. such primary activities as agriculture, quarrying, mining) towards activities at the higher stages of the value chain through value addition (e.g. agribusiness and agro-industries, mineral beneficiation, manufacturing, etc.). In a typical industrial economy, manufacturing activities attract a significant share of investments, and make a significant contribution to economic production in general, and to trade in particular.

Therefore, industrialisation is, in essence, a generic name for expressing economic processes (or industrial activities) which are characterised by more efficient ways for the creation of value.

1.2 Industrial activities and industrialisation

Industrial activities play a central role in an industrial economy. In national accounts statistics, industrial activities are broadly defined to include construction, generation, and supply of utilities (energy, gas, water), manufacturing, mining, and quarrying. To give a practical impression of industrial activities, Box 1.1 summarises the term's legal meaning basing on Australian INCOME TAX ASSESSMENT ACT 1997 – SECT 43.150.

Manufacturing stays at the centre of industrialisation. By producing such goods as machines and equipments, it transforms industrial activities in all sectors of the economy (i.e. primary, secondary, and tertiary) from 'pre-industrial' to the 'industrial' modes of production.

1.3 Industrialisation and development

Industry constitutes an important driver of economic transformation and growth. Industry-driven growth is the key to unlock the development potential of a country. In practical terms, industrialisation is synonymous with development. Invariably, international disparities in levels of industrial transformation conspicuously mirror international disparities in the levels of development. Rich countries are more industrialised than poor ones, and all developed economies have essentially followed the industrialisation route to prosperity. The

Box 1.1 Meaning of industrial activities

'Industrial activities' means:

(a) Any of the following activities (*core activities*):

    (i) Operations where manufactured items are derived from other goods even if those manufactured items are themselves used as parts or materials in the manufacture of other items;

    (ii) Operations (other than packing, placing in containers, or labelling) by which manufactured items are brought into or maintained in the form or condition in which they are sold or used, even if they are for sale or use as parts or materials in the manufacture of other items;

    (iii) The separation of a metal or a compound of a metal from its ore (not including crushing, grinding, breaking, screening, or sizing to facilitate that separation) or the treatment or processing of a metal or a compound of a metal after its separation;

    (iv) For a metal or a compound of a metal not requiring separation – applying to the metal or compound a treatment or process which, if the metal or compound had required separation, would not have been applied until after the separation;

    (v) Refining petroleum;

    (vi) Scouring or carbonising wool;

    (vii) Milling timber;

    (viii) Freezing primary products;

    (ix) Printing, lithographing, or engraving, or a similar process, in the course of carrying on a business as a publisher, printer, lithographer, or engraver;

    (x) Curing meat or fish;

    (xi) Producing chilled or frozen meat;

    (xii) Pasteurising milk;

    (xiii) Canning or bottling foodstuffs;

    (xiv) Producing electric current, hydraulic power, steam, compressed air or gases (other than natural gas) for the purpose of sale, or use wholly or mainly in carrying on another activity mentioned in this paragraph; or

(b) Any of the following activities:

    (i) The packing, placing in containers or labelling of any goods resulting from the carrying on of core activities;

    (ii) The disposal of waste substances resulting from the carrying on of core activities;

    (iii) The cleansing or sterilising of bottles, vats, or other containers used by the entity to store goods to be used in carrying on core activities or goods resulting from the carrying on of core activities;

    (iv) The assembly, maintenance, cleansing, sterilising, or repair of property used in carrying on core activities;

    (v) The storage, within premises in which core activities are carried out on, or premises contiguous to those premises, of goods in carrying on core activities, goods in relation to which core activities have commenced

> but not finally been completed or goods resulting from core activities;
> but does not include the preparation of food or drink (whether for con-
> sumption on the premises where it is prepared or elsewhere) in, or in
> premises occupied in connection with, a hotel, motel, boarding house,
> catering establishment, restaurant, cafe, milk-bar, coffee shop, retail
> shop, or similar establishment.
>
> > Source: Based on Australian INCOME TAX ASSESSMENT
> > ACT 1997 – SECT 43.150 (available online at: www.austlii.
> > edu.au/au/legis/cth/consol_act/itaa1997240/s43.150.html).

level of socio-economic development and standards of living of a country's
citizens are highest in industrialised States, while at the other end of the spectrum, the Least Developed Countries (LDCs) are those where manufacturing
value-added (MVA) accounts for less than 10 per cent of Gross Domestic
Product (GDP).

Apart from the practical observations cited in the previous paragraph, generally, that industrialisation is a *sine qua non* for development is underlined by
empirical research, which shows strong causality running from industrial production to GDP. (Using indexes of GDP and MVA as proxies, in which the year
2005 = 100), Figure 1.1 portrays the evolutionary relationship between industrial
production (IP) and (economic output) GDP, for the period 2000 to 2010. MVA
is used as a proxy for IP. Notably, the portrayed progression seems to be in line

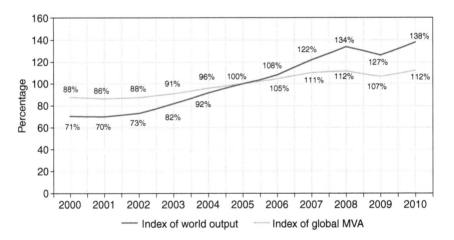

Figure 1.1 Evolution of the indices of global economic output and global MVA,
2000–2010 (source: Author. Based on (1) UNCTADstat (available at: http://
unctadstat.unctad.org/UnctadStatMetadata/Documentation/UNCTADstatCon-
tent.htm), and (2) UNIDO (2011), *Industrial Development Report 2011:
Industrial energy efficiency for sustainable wealth creation*. United Nations
Industrial Development Organization, Vienna).

with the general postulation (i.e. the two variables move in tandem). The picture seems to be in line with the proposition of some empirical studies, that generally, 1 per cent GDP growth requires more than 1 per cent growth of industry. Thus, ideally, industry should grow faster than GDP to achieve economic transformation. To give a more detailed overview, Chapter 3 of this book summarises a selection of useful empirical evidences of the linkages that exist between industrialisation and development.

Moreover, among the economic activities categorised under industry, manufacturing activities embody the strongest catalysts for the development of the fundamentals of sustainable and self-propelled economic transformation. Indeed, the achievement of prosperity in advanced countries and regions of the world is closely associated with the development of robust industrial sectors, in which the manufacturing sector predominates. The roles of manufactured production and manufactured trade in the generation of wealth and stimulation of socio-economic advancement underline the significance of industrialisation. Among other things, the manufacturing sector generates economy-wide spill-over effects by promoting intra-sectoral linkages, and backward and forward inter-sectoral linkages. The economic opportunities provided by industry stimulate entrepreneurship and enterprise development, development of knowledge and skills, emergence of strong institutions to oversee and support the economic development process, and technological dynamism; all of which lead to higher levels of efficiency and productivity.

Drawing from the arguments in the previous paragraphs, it is imperative that in order to realise its socio-economic development ambitions and ascertain decent socio-economic life for its people, Africa must undertake urgent measures to expedite its industrial development. Indeed, efforts towards this end can be traced through the various periods of Africa's development: pre-colonial era, colonial era, and post-colonial era.

1.4 Industrial development activities in Africa from the pre-colonial era to date

Inasmuch as industrialisation is a process, efforts to transform African communities have been going on for thousands of years. Table 1.1 attempts to characterise Africa's industrialisation trajectory, from the traditional (pre-colonial) industrial development activities, through to colonial models of industrial development, through to post-colonial models of industrial development. The analysis captures also international initiatives, some of which were purely African with international support, while others were multilateral.

In this regard, Africa's evolution of industrialisation agenda is introduced and discussed in the subsequent subsections. Moreover, the multitude of schemes, which have been designed to support the continent's industrialisation from the late 1970s to date, is discussed in detail in Chapter 6 of this book (on 'Pan-African and multilateral schemes and Africa's industrialisation: synthesis of substance and legacy').

Table 1.1 Evolution of industrial development schemes for Africa

Scheme	Up to late 1800s	Late 1800 to early 1960s	Early 1960s to late 1970s	Late 1970s to 1990	1990 to 2000	2000 onward	
						From 1st half of 1st decade	From 2nd half of 1st decade
1 Traditional models of industrial development	▓						
2 Colonial models of industrial development		▓					
3 Early post-colonial models of industrial development			▓				
4 UNTACDA I				▓			
5 UN-PAAERD				▓			
6 IDDA I				▓			
7 UNTACDA II					▓		
8 SAP					▓		
9 UN-NADAF					▓		
10 IDDA II					▓		
11 CAA						▓	
12 AIA						▓	
13 MDGs						▓	
14 APCI						▓	
15 AIDA							▓
16 3ADI							▓

Sources: Based on diverse sources.

Notes

AIA = Alliance for Industrialization in Africa; AIDA = Accelerated Industrial Development of Africa; PAAERDP = Program for Action for African Economic Recovery and Development Programme; CAA = Cairo Agenda of Action; IDDA = Industrial Development Decade for Africa; MDGs = Millennium Development Goals; NADAF = New Agenda for the Development of Africa; SAP = Structural Adjustment Programme; UN = United Nations; UNTACDA = United Nations Transport and Communications Decade in Africa; 3ADI = African (Accelerated) Agribusiness and Agro-industries Development Initiative.

1.4.1 Africa's industrial development efforts during the pre-colonial era

1.4.1.1 Mineral processing in pre-colonial Africa

As evidenced by empirical studies, mineral processing was done for thousands of years in pre-colonial Africa, as was the use of metals. Box 1.2 uses selected evidences to highlight mineral processing in pre-colonial Africa (de Kun 1987; Schmidt 1996; Alemayehu 2000).

1.4.1.2 General status of industrialisation in pre-colonial Africa

Presumably due to the continent's current industrialisation status, it is commonly assumed and generally argued that the circumstances which prevailed in pre-colonial Africa did not favour industrialisation. Among other things, it is argued that Africa was then characterised by land-abundant territories, with shortages of labour and capital, and lack of or existence of low levels of technology not sufficient to support industrialisation, and very low levels of political centralisation that exacerbated the situation (Gareth 2010).

In contrast, as evidences in Box 1.3 (alongside those in Boxes 1.1 and 1.2) show, in reality, industrialisation in Africa was possible and, indeed, Africans did experiment with industrialisation. The pre-colonial industrial development efforts produced different results in different parts of the continent, with comparatively high progress in certain types of industrial activities and in some parts (regions), and little progress in others.

Nonetheless, the general verdict is that most pre-colonial societies in Africa were also pre-industrial societies. As a result, literally all African countries

---

Box 1.2 Selected evidences of mineral processing in pre-colonial Africa

*c.*3,000 years ago • People in Bomvu Ridge, in today's Swaziland, recovered iron oxide

400 to 500 BC
• Iron mining in *Akjout*, in today's Mauritania
• Iron mining in *Nok*, in today's central Nigeria
• Iron mining in the vicinity of today's *Lake Victoria* in East Africa
• Iron ore smelting by Nubians in today's Sudan
• Copper mining in *In Gall*, in today's Niger
• Copper smelting in *Tsumeb*, in today's Namibia
• Brass work in present day Nigeria and neighbouring countries
• Widespread use of coins (brass, gold, silver) and metal spears in Africa
• Use of metal crosses and crowns in Ethiopia
Source: Based on Alemayehu (2000).

Box 1.3 An industrial experiment in pre-colonial Africa

This experiment occurred in Merina, a central province of Madagascar, between 1825 and 1861, in an overwhelmingly rural society. The experiment was based on irrigated *riziculture* and possessing a small number of full-time artisans. The Merina state initiated the drive to industrialise, on the basis initially of textile manufacture but later on the production of armaments, and on the processing of raw materials, notably sugar, tobacco, and animal products.

By the mid nineteenth century, many of the preconditions for successful industrialisation had been met. Lacking capital, the Merina crown promoted industry through labour-intensive means, organising and directing its labour resources through the institutions of *fanompoana*, for the 'free' population, and through slavery. It formed both skilled and unspecialised, full- and part-time labour units.

Education, considered vital in moulding an efficient industrial workforce from a rural agricultural population, was promoted by the crown to the degree that possibly 7 per cent of the adult Merina population were literate. At the same time, wage costs, critical to the competitiveness of industrial products, were minimised. Malagasy workers were unremunerated whilst the salaries of foreign workers were met through extraordinary taxation.

By 1950 the Merina state had succeeded in creating several industrial sites, the largest of which, Mantasoa, comprised five factories with blast furnaces, plus numerous workshops, employing 5,000 workers and producing a wide range of manufactured goods including cannon, muskets, glass, tiles, clothes, and leather. Nevertheless, the industrial experiment failed. In the first instance, low wage costs were largely cancelled out by high transport costs due to the Merina state's deliberate neglect of roads and its refusal to implement transport innovations – a policy aimed at deterring possible invaders. More important were the opportunity costs of transferring possibly 35 per cent of the Merina work force from agriculture to unremunerated industrial employment. Minimal earnings for this workforce shrank domestic demand for the products of Merina industry already barred from international markets by exorbitant transport costs. In addition, the lack of material incentive resulted in large numbers of workers abandoning through flight from the industrial sites and employment, as well as in industrial sabotage. Such action effectively paralysed the industrial experiment. Of greater consequence was the long-term damage this inflicted upon the Merina economy as, in the attempt to avoid the intolerably harsh *fanompoana* regime, artisans abandoned their trade and petty farmers abandoned the land, thus undermining the rural economy, the very strength of which, at the start of the nineteenth century, had made feasible the attempt to industrialise.

Source: Extracted from Campbell (1991).

started the period of colonial subjugation as subsistence agrarian economies. Indeed, that external forces from such places as the Arabian Peninsula, and in particular from Western Europe, could make an 'easy prey' of Africa, is at least in part attributed to the fact at this time African communities were essentially pre-industrial communities, using simple pre-industrial (artisanal) tools including weapons of war.

1.4.2 Africa's industrialisation under colonialism

1.4.2.1 General rule: propagation of the non-industrial development model

Under colonial rule, Africa, as was the case in most other colonised territories, followed a non-industrial model of development. During this period, home-grown industrial development initiatives were largely, *de jure* and de facto suppressed and replaced with models that propagated dependence to colonial centres. The prime goal of colonialism was to integrate the colonies into the international capitalist economic system, managed by the colonial powers. Concerning industrial development, the main characteristics of the economy could be characterised as follows:

a *Dominance of extractive entrepreneurship.* Though present in significant proportions, enterprises owned by entrepreneurs from the European colonial centres were largely restricted to the extraction of natural resources and provision of commercial services. In order to commercially exploit Africa's resources, the development of the primary sector was vigorously promoted. Hence, Africa's mineral resources were intensely commercially exploited on a large-scale basis, using modern scientific mining methods. Also, the commercialisation of agriculture began during this period, with plantation production of diverse crops such as cocoa, coffee, cotton, sisal, and tea. This mostly resulted in monoculture and, indeed, the 'extraversion' and 'monoculture' of African economies are widely seen as a victory of colonial interests over African interests. Also, commercial outlets for such crops like groundnuts, peanuts, palm, etc., were introduced, although the crops themselves were largely produced by small-scale holders (see Kilby 1975).

b *Conscious discouragement of indigenous industrial entrepreneurship.* In line with the philosophy of colonialism, home-grown industrial development initiatives were largely *de jure* and de facto suppressed and replaced with models that propagated dependence to colonial centres. In a colonial economic system, African countries were not supposed to build industrial productive bases of their own. Therefore, even where there were realistic opportunities for industrial production, colonial governments were rarely interested in upsetting the *status quo* in which colonial markets for manufactured goods were supplied largely by monopsonistic European merchants, selling goods produced in the European metropolitan economy concerned (Kilby 1975; Brett 1978: 266–282). In literally all colonial territories in Africa, colonial government laws prohibited indigenous manufacturing entrepreneurship, and severely punished 'offenders'. The consequence was that, in most African countries, little progress was achieved in terms of industrialisation, and in many cases there was even retrogression.

1.4.2.2 Exceptions to the rule: emergence of some industries

However, there were exceptions to the general rule. Generally, some industry developed in the colonial (urban) centres of gravity, as well as in some countries.

Thus, South Africa, followed on a smaller scale by Southern Rhodesia, and Belgian Congo, acquired a substantial manufacturing sector by the time most of the rest of Africa achieved independence. The 'artificially' low cost of black labour helped, but only in unskilled jobs because the skilled ones were anyway reserved for whites and the choice of technique was generally capital-intensive. Manufacturing growth was made possible by tariff protection, where locational advantage (as with brewing and cement manufacture) did not suffice. Thus, the government's programme in 1924 based on promoting import substitutions industrialisation (ISI) through high tariffs and state investments in electricity and steel. Similar programmes were adopted in South Rhodesia in the 1930s. Crucially, mining provided the import-purchasing power to cover the import of capital goods and, where necessary, raw materials. It was also the direct or indirect source of much of the revenue used by governments to invest in manufacturing, whether directly or through the provision of infrastructure (Kilby 1975; Feinstein 2005; Gareth 2010).

Other countries that had achieved substantial developments of the industrial sectors at the end of the colonial period were Kenya and Senegal (due to their privileged positions as key seats of power of the French-ruled territories in West Africa and British-ruled territories in East Africa respectively), and Nigeria (due to the overall large size of the economy).

Overall, different results were achieved in different parts of the continent, with some parts making comparatively high progress, while most were left behind and were actually falling back.

1.4.3 Post-colonial initiatives to promote Africa's industrial development

1.4.3.1 Initiatives in the early post-colonial period

In most African countries, industrial development initiatives in the post-colonial period fall into two main phases, i.e. the period immediately after independence to around 1980, and the period afterward. Accordingly, in the context of this book, the former is referred to as the *early post-colonial period*, while the later is referred to as the *late post-colonial period*.

If we take 1960 as the departure point of the analysis, during this time, the manufacturing sector was in its infancy stage, as shown in Table 1.2 for a sample of 18 African countries. Overall, the manufacturing sector in Africa could be characterised as follows:

a   Modern manufacturing in most African countries was quite small, with the exception of South Africa. Moreover, even in the case of South Africa, the manufacturing sector was not competitive internationally.

Table 1.2 Population, income, and manufacturing output in selected African countries in 1960

Country	Population (million)	GDP (US$m)	Per capita income (US$)	Manufacturing production (US$m)	Share of manufacturing in GDP (%)	Manufacturing production per capita US$	Deviation of manufacturing production per capita from average (US$)[g]
1 Nigeria	40.0	3,500	88	157.5	4.5	3.94	−5.36
2 Ethiopia	20.7	1,021	49	161.3	6.0	7.79	−1.51
3 Belgian Congo[a]	14.1	910	58	127.4	14.0	9.04	−0.26
4 Sudan	11.8	909	77	43.6	4.8	3.69	−5.61
5 Tanganyika[b]	9.6	671	67	20.1	3.0	2.09	−7.21
6 Kenya	8.1	641	79	60.9	9.5	7.52	−1.78
7 Gold Coast[c]	6.8	1,503	222	94.7	6.3	13.93	4.63
8 Uganda	6.7	583	87	37.9	6.5	5.66	−3.64
9 Angola	4.8	726	151	31.2	4.3	6.50	−2.80
10 Cameroun	4.7	511	109	30.6	6.0	6.51	−2.79
11 Southern Rhodesia[d]	3.6	751	206	120.2	16.0	33.39	24.09
12 Northern Rhodesia[e]	3.2	511	155	28.1	5.5	8.78	−0.52
13 Ivory Coast	3.2	584	181	31.0	5.3	9.69	0.39
14 Senegal	3.1	678	218	64.4	9.5	20.77	11.47
15 Dahomey[f]	2.4	175	74	4.6	2.6	1.92	−7.38
16 Sierra Leone	2.3	316	133	19.9	6.3	8.65	−0.65
17 Togo	1.6	150	92	6.2	4.1	3.88	−5.43
18 Gabon	0.6	131	294	8.2	6.1	13.67	4.37

Source: Author. Based on Kilby (1975: 489).

Notes

a …current Democratic Republic of Congo.
b …now part of the United Republic of Tanzania.
c …current Ghana.
d …current Zimbabwe.

e …current Malawi.
f …current Benin.
g …based on the average of the 18 sample countries.

b   During the period in question, there were only three countries in Africa, in
    which manufacturing accounted for more than 7 per cent of GDP – and two
    of the three, i.e. South Africa and Rhodesia, were full-scale 'settler eco-
    nomies'. The only other two countries that approached the 10 per cent mark
    were the 'semi-settler' economies of Kenya and Senegal, which coinciden-
    tally also served as administrative and commercial centres of gravity of
    British East Africa, and of French West Africa respectively (Kilby 1975:
    472). Though Senegal was essentially still a 'peasant' colony, as the admin-
    istrative and commercial centre of French West Africa, it had also a remark-
    ably large resident European population, which increased the supply of
    people with managerial experience, technical expertise, and access to capital
    (Kilby 1975: 473, 488–490). Moreover, generally, in West Africa even these
    low levels of manufacturing in 1960 represented a surge, propelled by post-
    war development (government subsidies for manufacturing in the case of
    Senegal) and decolonisation, which led European firms to establish local
    factories to protect their existing markets (Kilby 1975: 475, 490–507; Boone
    1992: 65–77).

c   The manufacturing production per capita was very low, amounting to
    US$9.3. Moreover, only in 5 of the 18 sample countries, i.e. Southern Rho-
    desia (US$33.39), Senegal (US$20.77), Gold Coast (US$13.93), Gabon
    (US$13.67), and Ivory Coast (US$9.69), was manufacturing per capita
    above this average (cf. Figure 1.2);

d   In most African countries, the number of industrial firms was quite small, as
    portrayed in anecdotal evidence presented in Table 1.3. Thus, by 1960, there

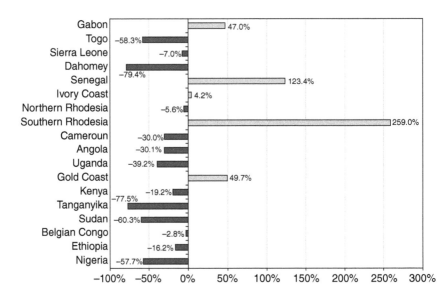

Figure 1.2 Deviation of manufacturing per capita from the average in the sample African
economies (source: Author. Based on data from Kilby (1975)).

Table 1.3 Senegalese industrial firms with 50 or more employees, pre-1925 to 1965

Year of start-up	Groundnut oil	Food	Textile and shoes	Metal engineering	Chemicals	Constructional materials	Miscellaneous	Cumulative total
Pre 1925	1	–	–	–	–	–	–	**1**
1926–30	2	1	–	–	1	2	–	**7**
1931–35	–	1	–	–	–	–	–	**8**
1936–40	1	–	2	1	–	–	1	**13**
1941–45	2	2	–	1	1	–	–	**19**
1946–50	–	–	1	2	2	5	5	**34**
1951–55	1	2	2	2	–	1	2	**44**
1956–60	1	5	3	2	1	–	1	**55**
1961–65	1	2	1	2	1	–	–	**61**
Total	**7**	**13**	**9**	**10**	**5**	**8**	**9**	**61**

Source: Author. Based on data from Kilby (1975: 472).

were only 55 manufacturing establishments in Senegal. The number of firms had marginally grown to 61 in 1965, of which 47.5 per cent were in the production of groundnut oil, food, and shoes and textiles (cf. Kilby 1975: 489).

In most African countries, industrial development initiatives in the post-colonial period fall into two main phases, i.e. the period immediately after independence to around 1980, and the period afterward. Accordingly, in the context of this book, the former is referred to as the *early post-colonial period*, while the later is referred to as the *late post-colonial period*.

The early post-colonial period covers largely the time frame ranging from the early 1960s to the late 1970s. In a post-colonial Africa, moving up the value chain became a key issue of interest. During this period, industrial policy development initiatives were dominated by the economic policy philosophy (EPP) of import-substitution strategy (ISS). The root of the argument for ISS is that nascent industries often do not have the economies of scale and scope that their older competitors from other countries may have, and thus need to be protected until they can attain similar economies of scale and scope. The argument was given credibility by the fact that, in economic history, almost all Newly Developed Countries (NDCs) had adopted some form of infant industry promotion strategy when they were in catching-up positions.

ISS was largely achieved through tariff barriers and non-tariff barriers (NTBs) to trade, and Africa was no exception. In Africa, the strategy was widely used by capitalist-oriented and socialist-oriented countries alike.

1.4.3.2 Initiatives in the late post-colonial period

The late post-colonial period can be divided into two distinct phases: the first phase, which covers the time frame ranging from the early 1980s to early 1990s, and the second phase that comprises programmes initiated from the early 1990s onward. Specifically:

a   The first phase was a time of major reforms across the African continent. During this phase, several overlapping (and partly still ongoing) programmes were initiated, including the IDDA I and SAP (cf. Table 1.1).
b   In the second phase, further reforms were undertaken, largely in response to the subdued developmental impact of the initiatives launched earlier. Among the new initiatives coinciding with this phase are CAA, AIA, UN-PAAERD, MDGs, and AIDA (cf. Table 1.1).

1.4.3.4 Efforts at leveraging international co-operation for Africa's industrialisation

Cognisant of the essence of industrialisation, literally all governments in post-colonial Africa and their development partners have prioritised industrial development, and initiated measures to realise this goal. Complementary to initiatives undertaken at the national level, the African Union (AU), in collaboration with the United Nations Industrial Organization (UNIDO) and other development partners, have intended to advance industrial transformation in African countries.

Table 1.1 shows the evolution of the most notable initiatives, some of which were purely African with international support, while others were multilateral. They include: United Nations Transport and Communications Decade in Africa (UNTACDA) I and II, Industrial Development Decade for Africa (IDDA) I and II, Structural Adjustment Programmes (SAP), Cairo Agenda of Action (CAA), Alliance for Industrialization in Africa (AIA), United Nations Economic system-wide programmes for Africa, Millennium Development Goals (MDGs), Africa Productive Capacity Initiative (APCI), Implementation Strategy of the Accelerated Industrial Development of Africa (AIDA), and African Agribusiness and Agro-industry Development Initiative (3ADI).

1.5 Overall legacy of the past and ongoing industrialisation initiatives in Africa

Globally, there are many success stories of industrialisation initiatives. The most recent success stories include the South East Asian (SEA) Tigers. Moreover, the achievements of the SEA tigers are being successfully emulated by such countries as Brazil, China, and India.

In most African countries, industrialisation initiatives have so far failed to deliver the expected results. Figure 1.3, which portrays comparable industrial performance ratios of Indonesia and Tanzania, bears witness to the legacy of industrialisation initiatives in African countries. Notably, while Indonesia's economic activities have systematically changed from a situation of dominance of agricultural activities to dominance of manufacturing services activities, in Tanzania the economy has retained its agrarian nature over the observation period of 40 years.

To give some more insights, Figure 1.4 compares the manufacturing to GDP ratios of selected groups to that of the best performers, i.e. East Asia and Pacific in 2008. The plotted points indicate the manufacturing to GDP ratio of selected groups of countries: LDCs, Sub-Saharan Africa (SSA), Middle East and North Africa (MENA), South Asia, World, Latin America and the Caribbean (LAC), Countries with economies in transition, and Developing countries; each one of them divided by the manufacturing to GDP ratio in East Asia and Pacific (vertical axis).

Notably, Africa has the worst performance, lying second (SSA) and third (MENA) from the bottom respectively. It should also be noted that the LDCs, which are the worst performers in this comparison, are dominated by African countries (which make up 34 out of the 49 LDCs as of 24 January 2014).

Further clues of stagnation in industrial development in Africa, compared to other developing regions, are shown in Figure 1.5. For instance, the share of Asian developing countries in global manufacturing doubled between 1995 and

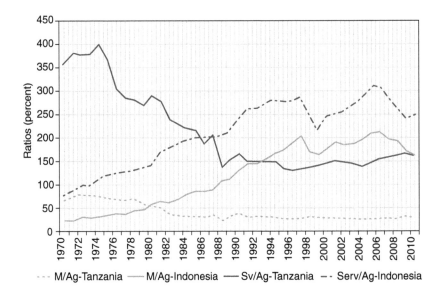

- - - M/Ag-Tanzania   ——— M/Ag-Indonesia   —— Sv/Ag-Tanzania   – – Serv/Ag-Indonesia

Figure 1.3 Evolution of industrial performance in Indonesia and Tanzania, 1970–2010 (source: Author. Based on UNTADstats (available at: http://unctadstat.unctad. org/TableViewer/tableView.aspx)).

Notes
M/Ag = Manufacturing GDP/Agricultural GDP, while Sv/Ag is computed as Services GDP/ Agricultural GDP

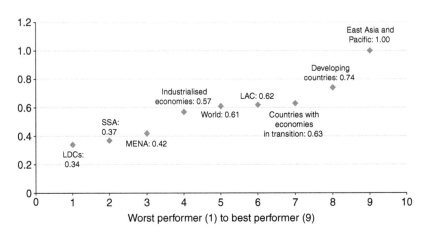

Figure 1.4 Manufacturing to GDP ratio of country group in 2008/manufacturing to GDP ratio in East Asia and Pacific in 2008 (source: Author. Based on data from UNIDO (2009)).

Notes
GDP = Gross Domestic Product; LAC = Latin America and the Caribbean; LDCs = Least Developed Countries; MENA = Middle East and North Africa; SSA = Sub-Saharan Africa.

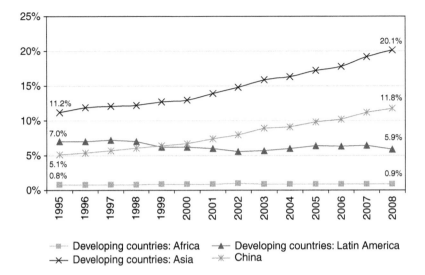

Figure 1.5 Evolution of the shares of global MVA (in %) of selected developing regions of the world (source: Author. Based on data from UN (2008)).

2008, rising from 11.2 per cent to 20.1 per cent. During the same period, the comparable share of developing countries in Africa marginally changed from 0.8 per cent to 0.9 per cent!

1.6 Looking forward

1.6.1 Contemporary initiatives to promote Africa's industrial development

Currently, the main initiative to promote Africa's industrial transformation in a co-ordinated manner is enshrined in the implementation strategy of the action plan for the *Accelerated Industrial Development of Africa* (AIDA). This initiative, which was also developed by the AU with assistance of UNIDO and in collaboration with other development partners, was endorsed by the Conference of African Ministers of Industry (CAMI) at its 18th ordinary session, which was held 24–28 October 2008 in Durban, South Africa. Among other things, AIDA stresses the need for Africa to mobilise technological capacities, as a precondition for its industrial development (cf. AUC 2008; AUC and UNIDO 2010).

1.6.2 Feasibility of leveraging co-operation with the EU for Africa's industrialisation

The Economic Partnership Agreements (EPAs) between the European Union (EU) and the African Caribbean and Pacific (ACP) group of nations offer nominal opportunities for Africa's economic development. Building on a long tradition of development co-operation, they seek to, among other things, strengthen intra-African regional integration, and enhance a trade-driven integration of African economies into the global economy through greater access to the EU market.

However, the achievement of these ambitions will depend on substantial increase of the trading capacities of the African and all ACP countries, which in return underscore the need to develop their productive capacities. Notably, intra-regional trade among the ACP states is just 11 per cent, and even lower among African countries. This situation can be attributed to the existence of a multitude of factors that restrain the quantities, qualities, and diversification of production. The pertinent retraining factors, which are accountable to the limited productive capacities in most African economies, include lack of adequate physical infra-structure, human capital gaps, gaps in technological capacities, gaps of capa-cities in terms of essential skills, etc. The basic challenges caused by these capacity limitations are compounded by the international production and trade structures, which usually trigger import surges, thereby stifling the development of productive capacities in Africa. To complete the round of restraining factors, tariff barriers as well as non-tariff barriers (NTBs) still substantially hinder trade between ACP blocs.

1.7 Objective of the book

Industry constitutes an important driver of economic transformation and growth. Indeed, the achievement of prosperity and a decent economic socio-economic life for the citizens of advanced countries and regions of the world is closely associated with the development of robust industrial sectors in the concerned countries and regions, in which typically manufacturing dominates. Thus, according to the UN *UNCTAD Handbook of Statistics 2008*, in 2005 the shares of global industrial production of developed countries, all developing countries, and African countries were 65.9 per cent, 44.5 per cent and 9.3 per cent respec-tively. The comparable shares of global manufacturing production of developed countries, all developing countries, and African countries were 66.9 per cent, 44.2 per cent and 4.9 per cent (cf. UN 2008).

The significance of industrialisation in the generation of wealth and stimu-lation of socio-economic advancement is underlined by the role of manufactured production and trade in both processes. Among other things, the manufacturing sector generates economy-wide spill-over effects by promoting intra-sectoral linkages, and backward and forward inter-sectoral linkages. The economic opportunities provided by industry stimulate entrepreneurship and enterprise development, technological dynamism, and higher efficiency and productivity. In essence, overall, manufacturing activities embody the strongest catalysts for the development of the fundamentals for sustainable and self-propelled eco-nomic transformation.

Thus, industrialisation is a prime objective of development strategy. Through industrialisation, countries aspire to achieve higher levels of investments, economic output, economic growth rates, accumulation of wealth, and, eventually, higher status of human development.

Moreover, a long road to substantive levels of industrialisation still lies ahead of most African countries. The challenges facing policy-makers, industrialists, industrial development activists, and all other actors in these countries are enormous. This raises the question as to which role should the international community play in the twenty-first century to provide support intended to expedite Africa's industrial development?

Therefore, arguments in this books are predicated on the philosophy that Africa is poised to maximise the development impact of its international development co-operation partnerships, if its co-operation arrangements with the EU are leveraged to promote industrial transformation on the continent. These co-operation agreements in question include the Trade and Development Co-operation Agreement (TDCA) for South Africa, EPAs for the rest of the Sub-Saharan African Economies (SSA), and the EU–Maghreb Agreements for the Arab African countries (AAC). Invariably, the various EU–African economic development co-operation arrangements should be tuned to promote trade-driven industrialisation in Africa.

Hence, beginning with the contextualisation of industrialisation, the 14 chapters in this edited volume logically argue the case for leveraging African–EU co-operation arrangements for Africa's industrialisation, and show the way towards the achievement of this objective. In this context, the book seeks to establish the elements of a comprehensive agenda to leverage African–EU co-operation for industrial transformation of African economies, as part of a broader 'enabling framework' to support Africa's industrialisation efforts. This should be placed within the context of multi-track efforts to achieve the goal of Africa's industrialisation.

1.8 Perspectives of the debate and structure of the book

This book has drawn on the lessons learned from the various national, sub-regional, and pan-African industrialisation initiatives in Africa. Moreover, the authors draw partly on the experiences and insights gained in working in various capacities for various institutions that are engaged in the industrial development agenda in Africa, such as the national governments, African Union, Regional Economic Communities (RECs) like the East African Community (EAC), United Nations Institute for Economic Development and Planning (UNIDEP), UNIDO.[1]

The comprehensive volume is divided into six parts and 14 chapters. Part I contextualises industrialisation. It puts the theme of the book into perspective. Also, the authors use theoretical explications and empirical evidences to introduce the subject matter of industrial transformation and highlight its essence for the overall socio-economic development. Accordingly, this part is divided into four chapters, including this one.

Chapter 2 carries the title 'Theoretical arguments for industrialisation-driven development'. It is co-authored by Dr Tommaso Ciarli (Sussex University, UK) and Prof. Michele di Maio (University of Naples 'Parthenope'). The authors review the theories of economic development and growth in which the industrial sector plays some role. They discuss briefly the theoretical arguments that have been put forward in each of them, and summarise the explanation of how industrialisation promotes growth and economic development. The authors follow a (sometimes overlapping) chronological order and find it convenient to distinguish three main periods in development thinking: the *theories of the stages of economic development*; the *classical theories of economic development*; and the *modern views*. Furthermore, the authors abstract from context specificities and rely on the terminology used by the theories to solve for the differential between growth and economic development.

The analysis in the chapter shows that, with very few exceptions, industrialisation has always been considered the driver of economic growth in economic theory. However, for a good part of this literature the superiority of industry is assumed, or observed, rather than explained, suggesting that there are a number of unresolved issues behind the different theoretical arguments for industrialisation-led economic development. Any development policy that focuses on industrialisation should consider these arguments in relation to specific objectives and contexts, rather than taking them for granted.

Both Chapter 3, on 'The urge to industrialise African countries' and Chapter 4 on 'Integration in the global industrial economy of the African and comparator regions' are also authored by Prof. Francis Shasha Matambalya (Nordic Africa Institute).

Chapter 3 is dedicated to the examination of the practical manifestations of the evolution of the industrialisation process, and to deriving lessons from the findings of empirical studies about the phenomenon. Notably, starting in England in 1760, industrialisation spread systematically to various parts of the world. The early history of its proliferation was marked by systematic spread of the 'industrial state' from Britain to the United States, to Europe (north-west Europe, and then central Europe, and then Eastern Europe particularly Russia), to Asia (particularly Japan).

Overseas offshoots of European powers (e.g. settler states, colonial states), benefited to some extent from this early episode of industrialisation though in most cases, the markedly low degree of industrialisation (e.g. in African states with the exception of South Africa, in Asia, in Latin America and the Caribbean, in the Middle East) did not transform them into industrial states. Up till the 1950s with the exception of Japan, there was no significant industrial power that was not a European country, or a country in the 'new world' or elsewhere conquered and settled by Europeans, or an overseas territory under the control of European power.

Then, from the second half of the 1900s, industrialisation permeated to other parts of the world, with several East Asian countries (e.g. Malaysia, South Korea, Taiwan, Thailand) sequentially becoming late industrialisers (cf. Xing 2007). Consequently, there are now industrial countries in all major regions of the world. Today, the United Nations Industrial Development Organization (UNIDO) categorises many countries as being industrialised (mostly from

Europe, North America, East Asia, and Oceania). However, the list includes also South Africa, although it is the only country from the African continent to be included in it (cf. UNIDO 2013).

Considering the significance of the industrialisation phenomenon, it is not surprising that many scholars have examined its history. The scrutiny has attempted to identify the characteristics that have contributed to the success of the process.

In order to highlight the patterns of the process, Section 3.1 of this chapter recounts the industrialisation experiences of selected countries, starting with the pioneer role of the UK, followed by the spread of the process to Europe and North America, and Asia, and touching the newly industrialising countries. Then Section 3.2 reviews selected econometric studies, to extract lessons about the relationship between industrialisation and economic growth and development.

The analysis in Chapter 4 has been prompted by the fact that the health of Africa's industrial economy has long been a subject of great concern for development policy-makers and activists. This arises from the fact that one of the manifestations of Africa's economic underdevelopment is its backwardness in industrial development. That the continent lags behind the rest of the world is evidenced by several economic development indicators related to industrial investments, industrial production, and industrial trade.

From this backdrop, with assistance of empirical comparisons of the performance of Africa and other regions in the international economic system, the author relates Africa's position in the global industrial economy, using several simple indicators. The chapter explores and compares the performance of Africa and other developing regions in the global industrial economy. The used indicators gauge the status of industrial development – relating them to investments in the industrial sector, output of the industrial sector, and industrial trade. Also, an overall ranking according to UNIDO's Competitive Industrial Performance (CIP) Index is presented and assessed.

The main purpose is to assess Africa's position in the global industrial economy, by presenting crucial issues of industrial performance at aggregate economic levels (regional, global). Several graphical presentations give an informative perspective of international benchmarking.

Overall, the chapter sheds light on the question of whether industrialisation is, today, still a necessary and reliable propeller of growth that it has been since the industrial revolution.

A further analysis of the CIP Index proposes its improvement, in order to make it a more comprehensive and reliable instrument.

Part II dwells on the issues of integration of the industrialisation agenda in the African sub-regional as well as in the pan-African development process. Hence, apart from assessments of selected regional economic communities (RECs) and their member states, pan-African initiatives in this direction (e.g. IDDA I, IDDA II, APCI, AIDA) are analysed in detail. Selected benchmarks are used to get an impression of the extent to which the industrial development agenda has been mainstreamed in the sub-regional and pan-African development agenda.

To highlight the point, the author traces the rise of regional integration as a model of development and its evolution in Africa, revisits the key documents containing the industrialisation provisions of the continent's RECs, examines saliencies of the industrial economies of African RECs, and synthesises the pan-African industrial development schemes. This part is divided into two chapters.

The title of Chapter 5 is 'Integration of industrialisation in sub-regional development agendas'. It is authored by Prof. Francis Shasha Matambalya (Nordic Africa Institute). Using selected RECs, the author assesses the extent to which the industrialisation agenda has been integrated into the development agenda at the sub-regional level. This is because, arguably, industrialisation plays a vital role in economic growth and development. Cognisant of these virtues, literally all governments in post-colonial Africa and their development partners have prioritised industrial development, and initiated measures to realise this goal. Complementary initiatives have been undertaken at regional levels, within the framework of Regional Economic Communities (RECs).

Using the Competitive Industrial Performance (CIP) Index, the chapter also sheds light on the industrial competitiveness of the member countries of the sampled RECs.

Chapter 6 addresses the theme 'Pan-African and multilateral schemes and Africa's industrialisation', and is authored by Prof. Francis Shasha Matambalya (Nordic Africa Institute). The author revisits many instructive facts. *Inter alia*, cognisant of the essence of industrialisation, literally all governments in post-colonial Africa and their international development partners have prioritised industrial development, and initiated measures to realise this goal. Thus, in tandem with efforts undertaken at national and sub-regional levels, complementary initiatives were carried out at the pan-African level, usually based on international economic co-operation efforts.

Though the Organization of African Unity (OAU) and later the African Union (AU) was the main advocate of these initiatives, their architecture and implementation involved UN institutions such as the United Nations Industrial Development Organization (UNIDO), United Nations Economic Commission for Africa (UNECA), International Trade Centre (ITC), etc. The concrete initiatives in this category include: Africa Agribusiness and Agro-industries Development Initiative (3ADI), African Productive Capacity Initiative (APCI), Alliance for Industrialization of Africa (AIA), Cairo Agenda of Action (CAA), First Industrial Development Decade for Africa (IDDA I), Second Industrial Development Decade for Africa (IDDA II), Plan of Action for Accelerated Industrial Development of Africa (AIDA), etc.

Also, in addition to Structural Adjustment Programmes (SAP), usually prescribed by the Bretton Woods institutions (BWI), the African countries have been eligible for multilateral initiatives, usually driven by UN agencies, some of which targeted all developing countries. In this category are such schemes as: The First and Second United Nations Transport and Communications Decade in Africa (UNTACDA I and UNTACDA II), United Nations New Agenda for the Development of Africa (UNNADAF), United Nations Program of Action for the

African Economic Recovery and Development (UN-PAEERD), The Lima Dec-
laration and Plan of Action on Industrial Development, The 1980 New Delhi
Declaration and Plan of Action on Industrialization of Developing Countries,
The Millennium Development Goals (MDGs) of 2000, etc.

Therefore, this chapter reviews the substance and legacy of role of these
schemes in the industrial transformation of African countries, in order to derive
lessons for future action.

Part III examines the integration of the industrial development agenda in the
national development agenda. It uses different benchmarks to assess whether,
how, and the extent to which the industrial development agenda has been mainstreamed in the national development agenda. Two country case studies are presented in the two chapters that make up this part.

The country case study of Ethiopia is presented in Chapter 7, which is
authored by Kibre Moges Belete (formerly with the Ethiopian Economic
Research Institute). The chapter addresses the broadly drawn 'Industrial Development Strategy of Ethiopia' which has been in place for almost a decade. It discusses the soundness of the strategy, particularly at the early stage of the
industrialisation programme, in an economy that is predominantly agrarian and
where the bulk of the population depends on subsistence agriculture for its
livelihood.

It also portrays the existing state and structure of the economy, including agriculture, industry, and infrastructure. Besides, it raises issues on the challenge of
industrialisation in such a least developed economy and draws relevant lessons
from recently industrialising Asian economies, particularly on the state of agriculture during the early phase of their industrialisation period. The chapter
includes also suggestions on the way forward.

This is followed by Chapter 8, a country case study of Namibia, which is
authored by Prof. Henning Melber (Dag Hamarskjöeld Foundation, Uppsala,
Sweden). The chapter introduces Namibia as a case study for a resource rich but
structurally underdeveloped economy with a so far failed industrialisation
strategy and major socio-economic disparities. After an overview on the
historical-colonial legacy of resource exploitation without local investment it
summarises the initiatives taken and results achieved with regard to the aspirations to turn the relative natural wealth into assets for an industrialisation of the
economy. It shows that such wealth in combination with other limiting factors
and constraints is no guarantee for a sustainable industrial policy or the establishment of a vibrant manufacturing sector. The missed opportunities are
reflected in the continued unequal distribution of wealth, high rates of unemployment and poverty, and misleading aggregated per capita figures of income con-
trasting the sober realities of extreme socio-economic disparities.

The focus of this chapter is on purely domestic policy and economic issues. It
deliberately ignores to a large extent the impact and effects of external factors
and foreign interests. These do of course set limitations, reinforce the structural
constraints, and limit the manoeuvring space for a government and its policy
rationale. But there remain choices. A case in point is the ongoing process of

contentious negotiations with the European Commission (EC) over the ratification of an Economic Partnership Agreement (EPA). Suffice to say, that this particular matter as well as other limiting factors rooted more in the global trade regime and related economic limitations would be of similar importance to balance the picture, but would go beyond the this chapter. Instead, separate analytical efforts beyond the scope of this case study would be required.

Part IV is dedicated to the assessment of the industrial development agenda in the African–EU co-operation arrangements, which in essence means pledges by the EU to support industrialisation endeavours in SSA and the Maghreb. It is divided in two chapters. In Chapter 9, Prof. Francis Shasha Matambalya (The Nordic Africa Institute) explores the evolution of the industrial development agenda in SSA–EU co-operation arrangements. The author sheds light on the main issues in co-operation (i.e. institutions involved in promoting industrial co-operation, types of resources dedicated to promote industrial co-operation, industrial co-operation financing instruments, institutional beneficiaries of the industrial co-operation programmes, and the channels used to deploy the resources to foster industrial development).

Then, in Chapter 10, Prof. Francis Matambalya (The Nordic Africa Institute) and Dr Imen Belhadj (Peking University) analyse industrial development in the African Maghreb–EU co-operation arrangements. The context in which the analysis is made is the sheer underdevelopment of the industrial economies of the Maghreb countries, in spite of longstanding engagement in relationship with EU – a region that is truly an 'industrial pioneer and giant'! These countries are namely linked to the EU through special arrangements between the EU and the Maghreb countries, as well as through the arrangements linking the EU to the ACP states (for Mauritania).

Therefore, the chapter makes a broad assessment about the industrial co-operation between Maghreb and the EU, by focusing on the impact of the Maghreb–EU industrial co-operation on the development of the Maghrebi industrial sectors. Using selected evidences, the authors probe the practical impact, achievements, and limitations of the evolving co-operation vis-à-vis industrial development. On the basis of the analysis, they derive lessons and propose the way forward.

Part V turns the attention to the architecture of a feasible strategy for leveraging Africa–EU partnership for industrialisation. It outlines the key lessons that have emerged from past practices, and proposes the fundamental issues to consider, in the re-engineering of African–EU partnership, to make it deliver the anticipated dividends in terms of Africa's industrial transformation. This part is also divided into two chapters, both of which are authored by Prof. Francis Matambalya (The Nordic Africa Institute).

Chapter 11 carries the title 'Pathways to Africa's industrialisation and economic growth and development: a digest of stylised ideas and facts'. This is in recognition of the fact that industrialisation is widely acknowledged to be a pathway to sustainable economic growth and development. It is also a response to the realities on the ground: for literally all African economies, a long way still lies ahead to the achievement of competitive levels of industrial development. Imperatively, determining the appropriate pathways to achieving substantive industrialisation is one of the key challenges facing the stakeholders involved in the search for a formula for sustainable economic growth and development in Africa. Therefore, the author highlights the essential considerations – what should be the de facto leitmotif for the architecture of a feasible strategy for leveraging African–EU development co-operation arrangements for the industrialisation of the SSA economies and African Maghreb countries.

The title of Chapter 12 is 'Pathways to industrialisation in Africa: key considerations and elements of a hybrid strategy'. It is authored by Prof. Francis Shasha Matambalya (The Nordic Africa Institute). The background to the reflections in this chapter is that Africa is, irrefutably, the least industrialised of the world's major regions. This well-known fact is also evidenced by the analysis in Chapter 4 of this book. Thus, for many African countries, the basic premise for charting the way forward is that without transforming their industrial sectors, and in particular developing their manufacturing sub-sectors, they cannot harness their resources and other potentialities to achieve the *ex ante* development ambitions. Neither can they exploit the opportunities associated with being part of an integrated global economy to achieve this goal.

Moreover, the architecture of a feasible industrial development agenda[2] would ideally attempt to answer several pertinent questions for industrialisation in African countries, including:

a   Which entrepreneurial capacities, knowledge and skills capacities, organisational or institutional capacities, physical infrastructural capacities, and technological capacities are needed to facilitate the process of industrialisation?
b   How can international entrepreneurship be harnessed for national industrialisation?
c   Which role(s) should the state play in the industrialisation process: in relation to the development of specific capacities (e.g. entrepreneurship and enterprise development, financial resources, knowledge and skills, organisations or institutions, physical infrastructure, technology, etc.) and in relation to providing the right policy guidance?

These questions suggest that numerous considerations are necessary in designing a feasible framework for leveraging African–EU partnership for industrialisation. The author discusses the relevant considerations, which relate to: a feasible country-focused industrialisation agenda, diverse types of productive capacities, access to and leveraging of natural resources, and a pragmatic approach that refrains from ideologising and politicising the recipe for industrialisation.

Part VI dwells on the policy implications and way forward, arising from the need to harness Africa–EU partnership for Africa's industrialisation. It is divided into two chapters. Deriving from the reflections contained in the previous chapters on the frameworks and practical impacts of Africa–EU development co-operation, Chapter 13 is authored by Prof. Francis Shasha Matambalya (The Nordic Africa Institute). Speeding up industrialisation is essential in order to achieve integrated and sustainable development processes in African countries. The author considers the central features of the industrialisation process, and reflects in this chapter on the beacons of a strategy that would lead the efforts to harness African–EU development co-operation to promote and achieve tangible and competitive industrial transformation in both the SSA countries and African Maghreb countries.

Chapter 14, which is the last chapter of this book, summarises the implications for the management of the development policy agenda in future and charts the way forward in harnessing Africa–EU partnership for Africa's industrialisation. It is also authored by Prof. Francis Shasha Matambalya (The Nordic Africa Institute). The main argument in the chapter is that the adoption of new approaches to Africa's industrialisation-driven economic growth and development would entail changes in the management of the development agenda. Hence, the author briefly outlines the implications for the management of the development agenda, which include the following: broadening the agenda to guide industrial transformation, the lead roles of African countries in their industrialisation processes, changing of mindsets by Africa's development partners, and broadening international partnership for Africa's industrial development.

Notes

1   For instance, from 2008 to 2010, Prof. Francis Matambalya worked as a Senior Consultant at UNIDO's Head Office in Vienna, where he was directly involved in developing projects and programmes related to the action plan for AIDA. Prof. Michele di Maio has been a Consultant of the AU on industrial development matters. Both Prof. Matambalya and Prof. di Maio have participated in the process of the generation of the industrial policy and industrial strategy of the EAC.
2   The Integrated Industrial Development Agenda (IIDA) is proposed in Chapter 13.

References

Alemayehu, M. (2000). *Industrializing Africa*. Africa World Press Inc Trenton/NJ and Asmara/Eritrea.
AUC (2008). *Strategy for the implementation of the action plan for accelerated industrial development of Africa*. Addis Ababa.
AUC and UNIDO (2010). *Financing and resource mobilisation strategy and monitoring and evaluation framework for the implementation strategy of the AU action plan for the accelerated industrial development of Africa*. Background Paper. Vienna.
Boone, C. (1992). *Merchant capital and the roots of state power in Senegal 1930–1985*. Cambridge University Press. Cambridge.
Brett, E. (1978). *Colonialism and underdevelopment in East Africa: the politics of economic change 1919 to 1939*. Heinemann. London.
Campbell, G (1991). An industrial experiment in pre-colonial Africa: the case of Imperial Madagascar, 1825–1861. *Journal of Southern Africa*. Vol. 17, No. 3.

de Kun, N. (1987). *Mineral economics of Africa*. Elsevier Science Publishers BV. Amsterdam.

Feinstein, C. (2005). *An economic history of South Africa: conquest, discrimination, and development*. Cambridge University Press. Cambridge.

Gareth, A. (2010). *African economic development and colonial legacies*. International Development Policy Series. The Graduate Institute. Geneva.

Kilby, P. (1975). Manufacturing in colonial Africa. In Gan, H. and Duignan, P. (eds), *Colonialism in Africa 1870–1960, Vol. 4, The economics of colonialism 1870–1960*. Cambridge University Press. Cambridge, pp. 470–520.

Schmidt, P. (1996) (ed.). *The culture and technology of African iron production*. University Press of Florida. Gainsville.

UN (2008). *UNCTAD handbook of statistics 2008*. United Nations Conference on Trade and Development.

UN (2013). *UNCTADstat* (available at: http://unctadstat.unctad.org/UnctadStatMetadata/Documentation/UNCTADstatContent.htm).

UNIDO (2009). *Breaking-in and moving up: new industrial challenges for the bottom billion and middle income countries*. Industrial Development Report 2009. Vienna.

UNIDO (2011). *Industrial energy efficiency for sustainable wealth creation*. Industrial Development Report 2011. Vienna.

UNIDO (2013). *Competitive industrial performance report 2012/2013*. United Nations Industrial Development Organization. Vienna.

Xing, L. (2007). *East Asian regional integration: from Japan-led 'flying-geese' to China-centred 'bamboo capitalism'*. Centre for Comparative Integration Studies. CCIS Research Series. Working Paper No. 3.

2 Theoretical arguments for industrialisation-driven economic growth and development[1]

Tommaso Ciarli and Michele Di Maio

2.1 Introduction

At the beginning of the twenty-first century, the role of Sub-Saharan African countries (SSA) in world trade is that of suppliers of primary commodities used for production taking place elsewhere (Abdon and Felipe, 2011; Hidalgo and Hausmann, 2009): metals and materials for manufacturing; land used for bio-fuel production; agricultural products such as coffee, bananas and flowers, to name but a few, used in agro-industries.

This raises a number of questions. Is it possible for a country to enter a pattern of sustained growth based on the production and export of primary resources? More to the point, can a country experience long-run growth without developing a vibrant and growing manufacturing sector? If the answer is no, why and how is industrialisation key to sustained growth?

Growth and economic development theory have devoted much effort to understand the role of manufacturing and industrialisation in income growth and economic development in the last six decades.

In this chapter, we give an overview of the main answers to the above questions trying to understand why manufacturing is key to income growth. We review the different theories of growth and economic development in which the industrial sector, or more specifically manufacturing, plays a role, and we briefly discuss the theoretical arguments that have been put forward by these theories in support of industry-driven growth. In doing so, we follow an (occasionally over-lapping) chronological order, finding it expedient to distinguish three main periods of development thinking: the theories of the stages of economic development; the classical theories of economic development; and the modern views, which include a variety of theories, among them the New Growth Theory (NGT), the evolutionary growth theories and the new structural economic models.

We briefly summarise the way in which each theory explains how industrialisation promotes growth and economic development. Where a reference to the manufacturing sector is only implicit, we describe how the theory uses this implicit assumption and the way in which it implies that industrialisation promotes growth.

The chapter shows that, with few exceptions, industrialisation has always been considered the driver of economic growth in economic theory, even if in many cases this is not at all made explicit.

For this review we need to cut through a highly heterogeneous literature with a heterogeneous terminology. In this respect, two related aspects are crucial: the definition of industrialisation and the relation between income growth and economic development.

First, the industrial sector usually includes manufacturing, mining and construction. For the sake of clarity, given the implicit focus of most of the literature on the primary, secondary and tertiary sectors, we restrict ourselves to industrialisation referred to manufacturing. In turn, a common definition of manufacturing is any physical or chemical transformation of materials, substances or components into new products, where materials, substances or components are products of agriculture, forestry, fishing and mining, or other manufacturing output. Substantial alteration, renovation or reconstruction of goods is generally considered to be manufacturing (UNIDO and UNCTAD, 2011).

Second, in contrast with economic development, where the focus is on change, growth is often seen as the 'idealization of economic dynamics in which things simply get bigger or smaller or stay the same size' (Dosi *et al.*, 1994a, p. 1) (citing Nelson, 1994). Here we privilege those theories that consider growth as change and not only as expansion (Wood, 1994), but we do not exclude growth theories that, although they do not refer to structural change, have an implicit say on manufacturing.

In this chapter, we will abstract from the difference between economic development and income growth and mainly stick to the terminology used in the theories under review.

Third and last, the evolution of theories was driven by, among other things, the issues perceived as the most crucial in a given period by the scientific elite, the general advance in knowledge, as well as the passing trends. Therefore, there is limited scope for the generalisability of any of the reviewed theories across time and space. Nonetheless, here we need to abstract from context specificity. This is not to say that it is irrelevant. Accordingly, we conclude this chapter with a caveat that any serious consideration of the role of industrialisation should take into account at least the objective (e.g. GDP growth, income distribution or cultural freedom) and the specific setting (e.g. geographical, historical and cultural) in which it takes place. Even when we look at apparently homogeneous countries such as continental Europe, we observe immense differences in the process of industrialisation through the three main waves. This is equally true for any particular region of SSA – even more so in view of the mainly exogenous way in which geographic boundaries were designed. It follows that one should always keep in mind the distinction between the predictions and mechanisms described in theoretical models as well as the experiences of real world people.

Before proceeding further we must apologise for the injustice made to many theories. We could not include all of them in one single chapter, and those included must be highly stylised, leaving out aspects that might be crucial to the theory/model, but not to this chapter.

The chapter proceeds as follows. In the next section, we provide a brief summary of the main theoretical reasons for the relevance of manufacturing in income growth and economic development (Section 2.2.). In Section 2.3, we discuss the theories that interpret economic development as a sequence of development stages. In Section 2.4, we present the classical theories of economic development and the discussions on the role of the economic structure in income growth and economic development. In Section 2.5, we address a number of different theories that, since the 1980s, have employed different concepts of economic development, income growth and analytical frameworks. We pick some of the main contributions from each literature to highlight their main stance with respect to the role of industrialisation. Section 2.6 concludes with some final remarks.

2.2 Why is manufacturing important?

It is a historical regularity that sustained economic growth and modernisation is associated with industrialisation, i.e. higher growth in production, value added and employment in the manufacturing relative to other sectors (Maddison, 2001, 2007; Szirmai, 2012).

This strategic role of manufacturing in modern economic growth is usually ascribed to a variety of sector-specific characteristics such as: (1) increasing returns, technology and spillover effects; (2) high capital intensity; (3) forward and backward linkages; (4) demand consideration; (5) employment potential (UNIDO and UNCTAD, 2011).

2.2.1 Increasing returns, technology and spillover effects

It is now commonly recognised that manufacturing is less likely to experience decreasing returns to scale than land-based activities, which are subject to the fixed supply of land of different qualities (e.g. Collier and Venables, 2007). Moreover, several authors have argued that manufacturing is the main source of innovation and technological change in modern economies (e.g. Gault and Zhang, 2010; Lall, 2005), for example as an outcome of research and development activities undertaken by manufacturing firms, especially in industrialised countries (Shen *et al.*, 2007). In turn, innovation and technological change have been shown to be crucial ingredients of economic growth and transformation; see, for example, the evidence collected on the industrial revolution in England (e.g. Mokyr, 2010; von Tunzelmann, 1995). The manufacturing sector also contributes to the diffusion of new technologies to other sectors of the economy (Cornwall, 1977) in the form of embodied knowledge.

2.2.2 Capital intensity

Manufacturing is usually[2] assumed to be more capital intensive than agriculture and services, one reason being that capital can be accumulated more easily in spatially concentrated manufacturing than, for instance, in spatially dispersed agriculture. Another reason is that manufacturing is more prone to escape decreasing returns to investment. It follows that an increasing share of manufacturing determines an increase in capital accumulation.

2.2.3 Backward and forward linkages

Manufacturing is also assumed to be characterised by strong backward and forward linkages with other sectors, which are an important source of their demand: manufacturing firms are larger consumers of services (such as banking, transportation and insurance) and raw materials (such as energy and agriculture) than the other way around. Moreover, backward and forward linkages are also assumed to be more dense within manufacturing than within other sectors. As a consequence, an investment in manufacturing is likely to generate demand for investment in a related (sub)sector rather than in agriculture or services. It follows that manufacturing can also be a major source for employment and output growth.

2.2.4 Demand: Engel's Law and elasticity of demand

Engel's law states that the share of basic products, e.g. food and shelter, in household expenditure falls with an increase in per capita income. It follows that as world income increases, countries specialising in basic goods will profit less from expanding world markets than countries exporting manufactured goods. In fact, recent research shows that what matters in terms of growth is not only how much is exported but also what is exported (Hausmann *et al.*, 2007). The countries that in the last three decades have benefited most from world income growth are those that have specialised in products for which the demand has increased with income, such as high-tech manufacturing goods, i.e. goods with a high-income elasticity of demand.

2.2.5 Employment potential

Manufacturing is usually believed to have a higher potential for employment creation relative to agriculture and traditional services.The higher employment multiplier of manufacturing vis-à-vis agriculture depends on the above-mentioned difference in returns to scale, which limits the opportunities for employment growth in agriculture. In fact, in manufacturing output expansion can take place without a reduction in workers' productivity.[3] It has been noted that the importance of services in terms of employment shares has been increasing in the last decades, particularly in high-income industrialised countries

(Rowthorn and Ramaswamy, 1997). However, the quality of employment in the service sector is very heterogeneous: some activities show high levels of productivity, while others entail levels of productivity and income much lower than in manufacturing. Moreover, it seems that high-productivity services are related to the production of services for the manufacturing sector (e.g. Ciarli *et al.*, 2012). Therefore, the importance of manufacturing goes beyond its direct effect in creating direct employment.

The potential for the increasing division of labour is one the reasons why manufacturing was considered by Adam Smith (1776) as the engine of economic growth. In fact since the beginning of the economic theory economists attributed to the manufacturing sectors some peculiar features, namely the fact that the division of labour was more likely in those activities rather than in agriculture.

The above-mentioned factors have been used, in a variety of combinations in economic models, to justify the mechanisms behind the industrialisation-led theories of economic growth and development and to support the view of industrialisation as a necessary stage of economic development and an objective per se. The question whether manufacturing continues to be the engine of growth that it has been since the industrial revolution – with large differences in the process and results in different parts of the world – needs to be resolved empirically (see Chapter 3 in this book).

In the next section, we outline some of the theories that originated at the outset of the Second World War and share the notion that development is a process characterised by linear[4] stages which all countries have to pass through before achieving modern industrialisation. We present two of the most influential views.

2.3 Stages of economic development

The idea that manufacturing (and industrialisation in general) is the key to economic development has a long history. For instance, economic historians largely agree on the importance of the industrial revolution and the manufacturing growth as one of the key elements that made England the economic world power of the nineteenth century. The evidence on the industrial revolutions has translated into the view of economic development as a linear process comprised of well-defined consecutive stages.[5] For instance, Marx identifies four different stages in his analysis of growth (von Tunzelmann, 1995): (1) pure labour economy producing subsistence goods; (2) early capitalism based on handicraft technologies; (3) emergence of manufacture based on merchants and initial accumulation of capital; (4) modern industry ('machinofacture') based on the capitalist mode of production. Probably the most influential proponent of the stages-of-growth model of development is the American historian Walt W. Rostow.[6]

In *The Stages of Economic Growth*, Rostow (1960) uses evidence from Kuznets to propose the occurrence of economic development in five stages: (1) traditional society; (2) preconditions for take-off; (3) take-off; (4) drive to maturity; (5) the age of mass consumption. He suggests that as they develop, all countries necessarily pass through these five stages. Countries in the stage of a traditional society or in a condition prior to take-off only need to fulfil three pre-conditions: (1) the rise of investment to 10 per cent (!) of national income; (2) the advance of one or more 'leading' manufacturing sectors[7]; (3) the existence or emergence of a political, social and institutional framework able to support the growth of the modern sector, i.e. favouring the mobilisation of capital from domestic resources. Investment and the increase in capital supply are key to these preconditions and in Rostow's view can be achieved by mobilising domestic and foreign savings.[8]

Once the leading sectors are established, they will implement (pull) the sub-sequent developments through backward and forward linkages (intermediate demand). Interestingly, Rostow differentiates between *social overhead capital* or *infrastructures* and *capital* used in production. For instance, roads and railroads differ from factory machinery in that the payback period is much longer and that it is society as a whole, and not an individual investor, that enjoys the returns to investment. In other words, investment in infrastructures has large positive exter-nalities, therefore requiring an involvement of the government. Rostow also sug-gests that one important characteristic of successful industrialisation is the simultaneous development of a number of sectors. For example, England experi-enced take-off because banking, trade, shipping and manufacturing all made pro-gress and because this was backed by military power to defend the country's interests. In sum, the main characteristics of a take-off are an increased effective demand for the output of new sectors capable of a rapid expansion of capacity; new methods of production; availability of financial capital to support the process and a high rate of reinvestment of profits; and the growth of leading sectors that induce increased demand for the products of other sectors in the domestic economy.

While Rostow's view was highly influential, it also drew several criticisms. In attempting to offer a general model of economic growth, Rostow discussed many non-typical cases, making it difficult to conclude that there was in fact a typical case. His theory points us towards issues of investment and capital and the idea that industrialisation will automatically follow if investment is chan-nelled towards/to the 'right' sectors.

With few exceptions,[9] this view of economic development through stages of growth was in full accordance with the predominant view among economists of a mechanical positive effect of industrialisation on growth. For instance, Kaldor (1966) established four stages of economic growth, which characterise any coun-try's industrial development. As in Rostow (1960), the transition from one stage to the next is deterministic.[10] In the first stage, the emergence of a domestic con-sumer goods industry reduces the dependence on imported goods; the equipment to manufacture these goods is either produced domestically or imported. Subse-quently, industrialisation must enter the second stage, in which the domestic pro-duction of consumer goods provides the basis for positive net exports, sustaining demand and division of labour through export. In the third stage (which may occur simultaneously with the second), domestic production substitutes also for the import of capital goods. In the fourth stage, a country becomes an exporter of capital goods. In this stage, a fast external demand growth for capital goods is coupled with the domestic demand growth supported by the expansion of the capital goods sector (Kaldor, 1966). The main features of the Kaldorian four-stage model are the identified sources for the expansion of demand and its auto-catalytic character that works through the division of labour and the demand for capital goods. There are three crucial assumptions: the initial exogenous demand growth, the higher learning associated with manufacturing and an increase in productivity in the capital sector.

In sum, the stages of economic growth imply a process of industrialisation. One element common to all these stages is the importance investment has in all the different types of capital required to sustain industries, i.e. infrastructures, consumer goods and capital goods, and the growth of manufacturing, substituting for imported goods. To be sure, implicit in the stages is a process of modernisation that leads to wealth increase. In Rostow, this is mainly related to the goods produced and consumed and to socio-political status. In Kaldor (as will be seen more clearly in the next section), it is the productivity of different technologies that constitutes the implicit leverage in the progress by successive stages.

We now turn to the main classical theories of growth and economic development that have been strongly influenced by the idea of stages and have, in turn, greatly influenced the modern view of economic development, as will become clear in Section 2.5.

2.4 Classical theories of growth and economic development

Immediately after the Second World War, research on the causes of growth gained much attention. We distinguish three main strands: balanced and unbalanced growth, Keynesian and neoclassical growth models and theories of international trade and growth.

2.4.1 Balanced and unbalanced growth and development theories

We begin discussing a set of theories, involving very different strategies of development as a result of the investment in modern manufacturing sectors. At one extreme, there is the theory of the 'big push' and balanced industrialisation (cf. Rosenstein-Rodan, 1943).[11] At the other extreme,[12] there is the theory of unbalanced industrialisation (cf. Hirschman, 1958).[13]

The idea that development consists mainly in a process of structural change led by the expansion of the manufacturing sector was first exposed theoretically in Rosenstein-Rodan's work (cf. Rosensten-Roden, 1943). The author suggested that the virtuous cycle of development depends essentially on the relations between the firm's economies of scale and the size of the market.[14] In an economy with a traditional and a modern sector, the latter has the potential to be more productive and pays higher wages. However, for the productivity advantage of the modern sector to be large enough to pay higher wages, the sector requires a minimum scale and, hence, a sufficiently large market. It follows that the modern sector requires a market of workers who earn a wage high enough to cover the higher prices of the modern sectors goods: these are the workers in the modern sector. Therefore, unless a sufficiently large modern sector is already in place, the economy is stuck in a trap in which nobody has an incentive to invest in the modern sector if there is no demand, and demand is not created because nobody invests.

The solution of the Rosenstein-Rodan model is to kick off modernisation by providing the resources to invest on a sufficiently large scale, after which the economy becomes self-sustaining. In essence, Rosenstein-Rodan calls for a 'Big Push' industrialisation, co-ordinated by the state to overcome the co-ordination failures in exploiting network effects of industrial linkages that characterise the decentralised market and lead to underdevelopment traps.

Hirschman (1958) also analyses the relation between manufacturing sectors as a key to growth and economic development but takes an opposite position with respect to the 'Big Push'. Starting from the same interaction between economies of scale in manufacturing sectors and the size of the market, Hirschman argues that the opportunities for growth are endogenous to a developing economy: one needs to find the sectors that have a comparative advantage, where there are opportunities for investment. Backward linkages with providers of intermediate inputs, and forward linkages with buyers of intermediate inputs can generate a self-reinforcing growth (increasing returns to investment at the aggregate level).

In Hirschman's definition, a backward linkage exists when a sector's demand enables an upstream sector to be established at least at the minimum efficient scale. This means the demand of a strategic sector is large enough for an investment in at least one upstream sector to be profitable. Similarly, a forward linkage exists when the increase in productivity due to sector growth is sufficient to reduce the cost of its output so that, for producers in a downstream sector, it is profitable to use it as an input and to increase investment. It follows that a new upstream or downstream sector can generate the same dynamics, creating linkages with new sectors, and so on, following an unbalanced pattern of growth through different phases of investment and creation of imbalances. The imbalance is crucial here as it represents the period of excess demand (supply), which increases (reduces) the price (cost) of an intermediate good to make it profitable for a provider (buyer) to invest in its production. Moreover, the differences between sectors is strengthened by the fact that each sector has its own system of linkages, thus exerting push and pull forces on the rest of the economy with different intensity. In Hirschman (1958), it is the manufacturing sector that is characterised by stronger backward and forward linkages with respect to agriculture and service.[15]

However, it is important to note that the phenomena of backward and forward linkages are not practical in all circumstances: notably, many developing countries like those in Africa are primarily agrarian, with the agricultural sector however highly underdeveloped. Under these circumstances, there are few link-ages, as most output goes for consumption or exports. Invariably, African coun-tries are lacking in interdependence and linkages.

Kaldor also privileges an unbalanced interpretation of the growth mechanism and, similarly to Rosenstein-Rodan and Hirschman, puts manufacturing (and particularly capital goods) at centre stage. As mentioned above, it is the interac-tions between (different sources of) demand and the division of labour that explain an autocatalytic process of cumulative causation in which growth breeds growth:[16] on the one hand, the increase in the demand for intermediate goods, on the other, the increase in productivity due to learning in specialised activities.[17] Therefore, the process kick-starts with an increase in exogenous demand, which is the precondition for a minimum scale that induces specialisation. Second, learning by doing increases productivity. In the manufacturing sector, this mech-anism is usually referred to as Kaldor's first law. When, through specialisation, the economy also produces capital goods, then technological advance (that increases their embedded productivity) percolates in the economy, having an effect on growth that is more than proportional.

> It is the rate of growth of manufacturing production (together with the ancil-lary activities of public utilities and construction) which is likely to exert a dominating influence on the overall rate of economic growth: partly on account of its influence on the rate of growth of productivity in the indi-vidual sector itself, and partly also because it will tend, indirectly, to raise the rate of productivity growth in other sectors. And of course it is more generally true that industrialisation accelerates the rate of technological change throughout the economy.
>
> (Kaldor, 1966, p. 112)

This diffuse increase in productivity reduces output prices which is likely to lead to an increase in demand (also on foreign markets where domestic production is more competitive due to an increase in productivity), production, and again learning, via the second Kaldor Law, namely the Kaldor–Verdoorn Law: the 'positive causal relationship between the growth of manufacturing output and the growth of labour productivity in manufacturing'.

It should be noted that Kaldor's interpretation of Verdoorn's Law (causal positive relation between manufacturing output and manufacturing productivity growth) is related to his perception that economic growth is demand determined rather than resource constrained. The alternative interpretation of the positive relationship between output growth and productivity growth would be to con-sider manufacturing output growth as a consequence of manufacturing produc-tivity growth, where the latter could take place once constraints on the supply side are removed. In other words, the constraint would be on the supply side and not on the demand side. It is this self-reinforcing mechanism that leads to the cumulative causation of a virtuous growth cycle. In summary, it can be said that once an economy gains a growth advantage, it will tend to maintain it through increasing returns of the most advanced manufacturing (capital) activities and the competitive gains induced by demand growth. It is important to emphasise that in Kaldor's view, the growth of manufacturing is determined by the growth of effective demand which has both an exogenous and an endogenous component (triggered by the Kaldor–Verdoorn Law), while both productivity growth and employment growth are endogenous. Two factors are the main sources of effective demand: the rural sector in the early stages of development and export in its later stages (Kaldor, 1966, 1975).

The two leitmotivs of the discussion on balanced vs unbalanced growth and economic development are the centrality of industrialisation (manufacturing sectors) and the presence of non-linearities requiring some form of intervention to avoid the trap of non-development. In the case of balanced growth, the scope for intervention is clear: due to the low level of demand for 'modern' goods, there is no incentive for private investment in modern manufacturing sectors, and planned co-ordination is needed. In the case of unbalanced growth, what is needed is an identification of the sectors that have strong linkages, both backward and forward, and can be competitive in the short term. Once the manufacturing engine is set in motion, there will be small incentives to substitute locally produced capital goods for imported ones as this sector is the core of an economy's competitiveness. Therefore, although industrialisation is considered to invariably lead (more or less automatically) to growth, some kind of state intervention is needed to start this process.[18] These theories have posed novel and complex issues for economic research. If investment and growth are not automatic and depend on what a country produces, choices have to be made concerning both the specialisation pattern and the type of investments. Unfortunately, these issues were left unresolved for a long time because of the economic discipline's change of direction towards growth models that could not easily deal with the non-linearities and multiple equilibria underlying structural change (Krugman, 1994).

2.4.2 Growth theories

The first mathematical models of economic growth were developed by Harrod (1939) and Domar (1946) in a Keynesian framework. The Solow (1957) and Swan (1956) models instead initiated the tradition of Neoclassical growth theories. The common objective of all these models was to understand the mechanics of growth in order to identify its main determinants from both a theoretical and empirical point of view.

In the Harrod–Domar framework, growth is a function of capital accumulation only, characterised by constant returns to scale. In turn, capital accumulation is determined by a number of exogenous variables, such as population growth and saving rate. A central role is played by savings (that allow the increase in the amount of capital): a country with low saving rates (where consumers need to allocate all income to consumption) can kick off income growth with an exogenous increase in savings/capital. However, savings indicate the growth potentials, but are not sufficient for the realisation of growth. In Harrod-Domar savings need to be transformed into investments, which in a Keynesian fashion is function of animal spirits, the expected returns on investment. An initial condition of high savings and low investment, on the contrary, may induce low consumption, and therefore low investment and growth.

The Solow model (Solow, 1957) is the seminal contribution to the Neoclassical theory of growth. It expanded on Harrod–Domar, adding a second factor, labour, and introducing a third exogenous variable, technology, to the growth equation. Unlike the fixed-coefficient and the constant-returns-to-scale assumptions of the Harrod–Domar model, Solow's model exhibits diminishing returns to labour and capital and constant returns to both factors. Consequently, capital investment alone is then no longer sufficient for sustained growth. Instead, technological progress becomes the main factor explaining long-term growth. As for savings in Harrod–Domar, they are determined exogenously, that is, independently of all other factors. Investment per se is then no longer sufficient for growth, but acquisition of technology is. One important prediction of this model is the convergence to an income level given by technology, *ceteris paribus*: poorer economies with lower capital per worker (relative to their long-run or steady-state capital per worker) grow faster due to the decreasing returns to capital, *ceteris paribus*.

Notably the idea that growth needs structural change was absent in these early theories of economic growth. The reason is that formal models were usually one-sector growth models.[19] The mathematical formalisation of the basic mechanics of growth came at the cost of a reduction of the complexity of the economic structure to one single sector, implying no transformation. The attention to industrialisation and the role of manufacturing are thus implicitly lost in these initial theories of growth. However, in the Harrod–Domar model it is quite clear that it is capital accumulation that drives growth, and this is fully in line with the idea of investment in infrastructures and capital-intensive sectors. Indeed, the policy prescription of the 'Big Push' is very similar to that of the savings gap implicit in the Harrod–Domar model, as is witnessed by decades of World Bank policies (cf. Easterly, 2002). The case of the Solow model is different, where convergence assures that capital investment has a more limited scope (though it is still required for convergence). Another difference between the two models is the need for policies. On the one hand, in the Solow model competitive markets (via wages and profit rates) will automatically provide the incentives required to invest whatever is needed for (conditional) convergence. On the other hand, in Harrod–Domar, as savings are exogenous, there is no automatic mechanism that ensures that investment will occur: domestic investments must be complemented by foreign investments. In other words, for Solow, policy is irrelevant (beyond securing competitive markets), while for Harrod–Domar governments should induce the necessary capital investment (and hence policies are critical). The importance of public investment is underlined by the risks of an ever decreasing rate of investment.

2.4.3 International trade and growth

Since the dawn of economics, the relation between international trade and economic growth has been strongly disputed. One relevant aspect of the debate – which was particularly heated during the post-colonial period – considered in this section is the structure of trade: the question whether international trade benefits all economies or only those with a particular sectoral specialisation of production. Indeed, net export is a relevant source of demand, which may lead to growth.

According to the standard theory of comparative advantage, a country always improves its (aggregate) welfare by increasing trade integration and specialising in the production of goods where the opportunity cost of production is relatively lower than in other countries.

However, other theories have emphasised that exporting agricultural products and raw materials is not equal to exporting manufactured goods. For example, in stark contrast with the theory of comparative advantage, Prebish (1950) and Singer (1950) showed that in the 1960s the trade specialisation of developing countries had an adverse effect on their economic development. They observed that the relative terms of trade of primary products, which were exported mainly by countries in the periphery, with respect to manufacturing goods followed a negative trend (possibly secular). They explained this price divergence with the differences in market structure between the primary and the manufacturing sectors. For instance, the supply of agricultural products is rather inelastic with respect to manufacturing.

A reduction in global demand is therefore reflected in a reduction in the supply of manufactured goods to clear the market, with some decrease in price, while agricultural production usually does not adapt to demand and the only variable that might change, thereby clearing the market, is price. Similar observations can be made with respect to market power. The manufacturing sectors are often characterised by an oligopolistic market structure while the agricultural sector is usually assumed to be characterised by perfect competition. The different mechanism for price determination in the two sectors implies that prices for manufacturing products are expected to be more stable than those for agriculture products (cf. also Kalecki, 1990).

The labour market also plays a role in the deterioration of the terms of trade: more organised unions in the centre allow workers to transform part of productivity growth into higher wages, rather than into lower prices. Inversely, informality and the elasticity of labour supply in developing economies imply that workers do not have the bargaining power required to avoid that productivity gains are entirely transferred to prices. Moreover, these modes are closely related to production patterns and barriers to entry related to technology and learning. Interestingly, the appropriation by workers in the centre of increases in productivity is viable solely in the case in which high barriers to entry prevent prices from falling. This implicitly assumes the existence of some sort of (Schumpeterian) dynamic comparative advantages that are recreated and which are not easily eroded by imitation.

Under the circumstance that for several developing countries export is largely represented by primary products, it follows that the pattern of specialisation negatively affects their growth.[20]

It follows that countries in an early stage of development should attempt to produce and export manufacturing goods with increasing terms of trade despite the comparative advantages.[21] The picture becomes even more interesting when the distinction between static and dynamic comparative advantages is introduced. Dynamic comparative advantages refer to the fact that factor costs evolve over time – also due to trade – and that some sectors may yield longer-term benefits which are overlooked when only present factor costs are considered (for a discussion, see Redding, 1999). Exporting a good with a higher value added, requiring an investment in skills even when the country has not a comparative advantage in producing it, will under certain circumstances benefit the economy in terms of an increase in skills, higher wages, higher domestic demand and a higher balance of trade. Traditional theories of trade are static in nature and thus do not consider differences among sectors since trade always brings in static efficiency gains. It will be shown in Section 2.5.2 how this may change in dynamic terms.[22] The bottom line is that what matters is not only how much but also what a country exports (Hausmann *et al.*, 2007), due to terms of trade, the productivity growth of capital and manufacturing, learning and dynamic comparative advantages, market power, value added appropriation, and so forth. The basic idea is that sectors differ from the point of view of the potential for productivity growth and creation of externalities for the rest of the economy: in some sectors this potential is higher than in others because their sector-specific technological opportunities are higher (Dosi, 1988). In this context, specialisation according to existing comparative advantages may be welfare decreasing, while active trade policies may be welfare increasing (typically by favouring entry into high-tech sectors or protecting strategic sectors).

2.5 The modern views

The contributions to the theories of growth and development since the 1980s have taken a number of different directions. Two common traits characterise the theorising change concerning growth and economic development: the microeconomic foundations in terms of the actors involved, the institutions in which they act and their inherent heterogeneity as well as the increased focus on the specifics, such as context, region, country, stage and even culture, as opposed to broad generalisations. Such trends become even more pronounced following the dissatisfaction with the Washington Consensus doctrine around the turn of the twenty-first century.

In this section, we will mainly focus on growth theories and the recent revisiting of the relation between trade and growth. Without any claim to doing justice to a huge and still growing body of literature, we only concentrate on one or two focal contributions to briefly summarise the main works of each theory relevant to this chapter. In particular, we summarise the main theoretical arguments (or lack of) in support of industrialisation as a source of income growth (and economic development).

2.5.1 Growth theories

We distinguish three main waves of growth theorising in modern times. The first wave merges economic development and income growth under the same label of income growth, leaving on one side the analysis of change. For example Lucas (1988, p. 3):

> By the problem of economic development I mean simply the problem of accounting for the observed pattern, across countries and across time, in levels and rates of growth of per capita income. This may seem too narrow a definition, and perhaps it is, but thinking about income patterns will necessarily involve us in thinking about many other aspects of development of societies too, so I would suggest that we withhold judgement on the scope of this definition until we have a clearer idea of where it leads us.

A second wave emerged from a group of structuralist and evolutionary economists who focus on the changes that accompany economic growth, particularly those in the structure of the economy, explicitly referring to the relations between sectors, industrial dynamics, changes in product composition, and the like. This group of theories usually assimilates economic development with those structural changes.

The third wave is comprised of a group of theories that focus, in different ways, on the changes in the institutions that govern economic activities. In their analysis, some of the theories merge various transformational aspects of growth and economic development, such as institutional changes, sectoral changes and the changing patterns of people skills and demand.

2.5.1.1 New growth theory

The lack of evidence on the convergence of the per capita income across countries with an initially different income, as predicted by the then prevailing theory of growth (Solow, 1957), has motivated the research on models that, building on Solow, could endogenously represent diverging economies (Lucas, 1988; Romer, 1986). This required the models to represent an element of endogenous growth that allowed an economy to escape the law of decreasing returns to capital (investment). In this way, economies can grow infinitely, and unconditional convergence need not occur, as empirically observed (e.g. Mankiw *et al.*, 1992). The endogenous mechanisms also improve the understanding of growth, in particular by focusing on endogenous changes in the technology of production (which, in turn, affects the productivity of inputs to production). For a comprehensive review of the large number of models we address the reader to Aghion and Howitt (1998). Furthermore, in the previous models in which population and technology change were exogenous, there was no scope for any development policy (Romer, 1994), and industrialisation could play a role only through a non-sector-specific capital accumulation (up to the point where marginal returns to capital are non-zero).

Within the NGT, we can distinguish four different basic mechanisms of endogenous growth: (i) investment in one factor of production, capital, that cumulates at the aggregate (national) level; (ii) the introduction of public goods, again in terms of investment at the economy level; (iii) accumulation of a different type of capital, human capital; and (iv) technological innovation as a systematic activity of Research and Development (R&D) (Amable and Guellec, 1992). The relevance of the manufacturing sector thus follows from the assumption that this is where the benefits of the endogenous change in technology occur, independently from their sources.

Romer (1986) explicitly refers to the learning process that occurs in production at the aggregate level. He uses Marshallian externalities to explain increasing returns of firm investment at the aggregate level, assuming some of this investment spills over to other firms. The basic assumption in Romer's model is that capital investment at the firm level increases the firm's production with the usual diminishing returns, but still increases the technological level of the country. Although Romer does not tie the analysis to any specific sector – as is true for all the NGT – reference to spillovers and Marshallian externalities are usually found with respect to the manufacturing sector, where most of the technological investment occurs.

Alternatively, Lucas (1988) introduces a different source of aggregate increasing returns via the investment in the human capital employed in firms. Although firms' production function still represents constant returns to capital, the productivity now also depends on the investment in human capital applied to production. As a consequence, it is not capital per se that increases income growth (*à la* Kaldor) but its use coupled with high skills. As in the previous case Lucas' model considers one representative sector. The relevance of industry for growth then depends on the relative relevance of human capital for industry's productivity with respect to other sectors.

Finally, a series of models have concentrated on the role of firms' R&D activities, thus internalising the gains of research instead of accounting for them as externalities cumulating at the aggregate level. These models provide a disaggregated view of the growth process in terms of both firms and sectors. The base version of these models considers two sectors: the intermediate good sector that produces differentiated intermediate goods using raw inputs and a final sector that produces goods for consumption using intermediate goods.

Models in this tradition differ in the way in which they represent the output of R&D. Some models focus on the variety (in term of their number) of goods (Romer, 1990), either in the final goods sector or in the intermediate sector, keeping constant the quality of the new goods (e.g. respectively Grossman and Helpman, 1989a, 1989b). Because the inputs used by firms in the final goods market are subject to decreasing returns to scale, it is the increase in the number of inputs invented in the intermediate sector that sustains growth. Because these models are strictly supply driven (no role for demand of technology) it is the rate of innovation in this sector which is the crucial engine of growth. Other models focus on the quality of goods – with no change in their variety – in the commodity market or in the capital sector (e.g. Aghion and Howitt, 1992; Grossman and Helpman, 1989c, respectively). In particular, Aghion and Howitt (1992) consider actual innovation in the production of new intermediate goods that offset the old ones, inducing a sequence of capital vintages. The higher productivity of the new capital vintages is thus what offsets the decreasing returns to capital, putting emphasis on the research activity of an intermediate sector. Because this innovation is characterised as a random event, the growth rate of the economy also follows a stochastic process. In these models, growth therefore depends on the incentives to innovate such as the demand by firms in the commodity market, an increase in monopoly power or an increase in innovation cost (or an increase in the productivity of innovation).

How do these models give grounds for manufacturing and industrialisation as the source of growth? The positive effects of industrialisation are realised when we observe either increasing returns due to externalities from investment, or employment of human capital that increases productivity, or active efforts to improve the quality of intermediate goods. Although there is no explicit mention in the above NGT models, de facto manufacturing is the sector where technological externalities from investment are likely to occur, where there is also a higher incentive to absorb high-skilled workers (with higher wages) and where R&D expenditure is a formal part of business activity. This view is reinforced by the fact that these models represent income growth as a supply-side question: the goods that most likely create their own demand are produced in the manufacturing sector. Thus, with reference to NGT, industrialisation is the main engine of growth only under the condition that manufacturing has the technological properties summarised above.

2.5.1.2 Structural change growth models

Since the beginning of the 1980s, a number of growth models have sought to analyse the relation between income growth and sectoral dynamics with the focus on the changes taking place at the microeconomic and sectoral levels. Differently from the Solow model and the two-sector NGT models, in these models the share of sectors in an economy – measured as employment or output – changes endogenously as an outcome of the competition among sectors, their technical relations and the composition of demand. Structural change models thus provide some insights into the effect of the sectoral composition on income growth, when such a composition changes over time (e.g. when an economy makes the transition from primary goods and commodities to producing manufacturing goods). Under the particular condition that all sectors follow the same dynamics, we are back to the Solow-NGT framework, and an analysis at the sectoral level would not add any new insights.

Pasinetti (1981) considers an economic system composed of different, vertically related sectors, each with an autonomous production process. Output is produced through capital goods and labour. Assuming that the sectors can be ordered along a vertical structure, the final sector constitutes the final demand, and simultaneously provides the labour input to all other sectors. An equilibrium is reached only when all sectors produce at full capacity and when there is full employment, which is not assumed at the outset. The contribution of each sector to aggregate production depends on its technical efficiency and on the demand for its output. Technical change is exogenous but heterogeneous across sectors. Each sector may also be characterised by a specific demand elasticity, which changes following the aggregation of individual Engel curves. These are consumer specific and thus change with the change in income, as consumers learn about the new goods made available. As a result, changes in demand are uniform across sectors. These changes generate imbalances between sectors. Ultimately, the relation between techniques of production and changes in demand determines the long-term quantity and prices in the economy. In each specific time period, demand concentrates on specific sectors, depending on the dynamics of technology, on how gains from increased productivity are distributed, and on how this affects the demand pattern. Pasinetti assumes that consumers first satisfy their need for essential goods (high priority wants) and then move to the next good in the hierarchy of needs. Pasinetti distinguishes three main possible growth dynamics: population driven, technology driven and demand driven. In the latter dynamics, which is the most important here, changes in sector-specific technology and demand mean a reshuffle in employment across sectors, requiring changes in the use of inputs and investment, in turn implying changes in the sectoral composition of the economy. Without making any a priori assumption on how to map sectors of the model onto real sectors, it is the interplay between technical change and demand that is crucial in the model and the sequential way in which sectors contribute to the growth of the economy. In other words, new products and sectors need to emerge, following changes in demand induced by technical change, as the demand for one particular good is becoming exhausted and generates decreasing returns. The structure of Pasinetti's model provides important hints on the composition of an economic system and its influence on growth, which are explored in a number of models that followed his contribution.

In line with Pasinetti's approach, different models conceive of the sector as the unit of observation and relate the growth patterns of the economy to the sectoral restructuring and a country's trade specialisation (Cimoli, 1994; Cimoli and Porcile, 2009; Cimoli et al., 2010; Los and Verspagen, 2003; Verspagen, 1993, 2002). These models bridge the structuralist (discussed in Section 2.4.3) and the evolutionary tradition (discussed below) in a number of different ways. Without doing full justice to the rich diversity of contributions, it can be said that these models are an attempt to merge an explicit account of technological change in the evolutionary Schumpeterian tradition (Nelson and Winter, 1982) with the main features of the structuralist approach.[23] The main general result of these models is that a country that specialises in sectors with a low elasticity of demand, i.e. with a stagnant international demand, has little opportunity to grow: domestic income, as well as wages and investment, do not grow with world income. Therefore dynamic economies, producing goods for which demand increases are closer in magnitude to world income increases, diverge from stagnant ones for which the likelihood of changing specialisation becomes increasingly difficult, thus ending in a poverty trap.

Due to the large differences in the treatment of technology, sectors and trade across these models, we briefly describe their main features with reference to one of the seminal contributions (Verspagen, 1993). These models aim at explaining long-run dynamics, paying particular attention to countries' trade specialisations. Very much in the spirit of the post-Keynesian approach, demand is a fundamental determinant of growth. The macro framework is often based on the balance of payments constraint (Thirlwall, 1992). Thus, the 'global' economic system is constituted of different open economies, comprising different sectors, each of which produces a different good, each exhibiting a different demand elasticity (in national or international markets) and labour productivity. Wages are endogenised as a function of productivity and the relation between demand and supply (unemployment rate). Given the difference in the cost structure across sectors with unchanged consumer preferences, sectors across countries are selected by international demand on the basis of the technology of the goods produced. Moreover, similarly to Pasinetti (1981), consumer preferences are often non-homothetic (they change with income), adding another element of selection. In this way, the models usually reproduce the cumulative causation dynamics stressed by Kaldor. Technology is usually simplified with respect to the more micro-based approach (see below), and technological change is a function of learning in the spirit of the 'Kaldor–Verdoorn' law. This means that productivity changes endogenously through investment (capital embodied technical change), learning, economies of scale and capital renovation (vintage capital) as in some of the NGT models, although modelled in a different way.

The bottom line here is that a country that exhibits specialisation in sectors with increasing demand elasticity on the international market and has invested sufficiently to increase productivity with respect to competing countries will experience a further increase both in sectoral demand and investment and thus in future productivity. A further increase in productivity makes the country even more competitive. On the contrary, countries that are specialised in sectors with low demand elasticity experience few export gains and little investment. They will therefore not increase productivity and are bound to stagnate in the long run. In line with Kaldor's view the dynamic sectors are the manufacturing sectors with an intense use of capital, while the primary sectors are likely to stagnate. In these models of structural change, more explicitly than in the NGT models, it is by assumption (or with reference to empirical evidence) that it is not agriculture but manufacturing, particularly the sectors with high content of knowledge and technology, that ignites the cumulative causation process of growth.

Another group of models build on the NGT framework and introduce structuralist features, thereby highlighting the relevance of the structure of the economy for representing growth dynamics. Leaving aside methodological and conceptual distinctions – which are considerable across the models discussed in this section but are outside the scope of this chapter – these models mainly focus their analysis on the relation between income distribution and growth through the change in demand for differentiated goods (assuming away homothetic preferences) in closed economies. (Aoki and Yoshikawa, 2002; Föllmi and Zweimüller, 2008; Matsuyama, 2002). The main difference with respect to the NGT models surveyed above is that here product innovation occurs solely in the consumables sector and is directly related to changes in the structure of demand where preferences change with income. In the typical model, a new good is produced only when an initial demand exists, and it diffuses only when there is sufficient demand for firms to invest in its production and to reduce its production cost via learning (such that an increasing number of consumers with different incomes can access it). In a model in which the consumer decides with respect to both price and quality of the good Zweimüller and Brunner (2005) show, for example, that high-income inequality reduces the incentives to product innovation because the low-income classes keep buying low-quality goods. In other words, the upgrading in the manufacturing sector occurs only in established firms that target the high-income class.

In the Aoki and Yoshikawa (2002) model, the growth of income of a country depends on the rate of invention and diffusion of new goods that emerge as the demand of incumbent goods reaches satiation. The important difference in this model is that 'upgrading', or an increase in quality, is not sufficient here as the demand is saturated, irrespective of the goods' quality. Instead, the creation of new markets is the main engine of growth. Improvement in quality increases demand and production but only to a limited extent. When saturation is reached, the endogenous engine of growth disappears. In other words, the invention of new products may create a new demand, and under the condition of product diffusion, income increases in a logistic fashion. The results implicitly point to the need of a manufacturing sector (or services) capable of creating new goods that satisfy new consumer wants – which is less conceivable for the primary sector. The authors refer to such a dynamics to explain the extent of the 'Asian miracle'.

All these models add important insights to the mechanics of the relation between industrialisation and growth, in which domestic demand is highly relevant for growth and needs to be stimulated by the creation of new markets. A grossly unequal income distribution does not provide any incentive to innovate and increase the quality of goods, let alone create new goods. This aspect was quite clear to some of the traditional development scholars discussed in Section 2.4.1 above, particularly in the structuralist and *dependencia* schools: to satisfy the demand arising from a grossly unequal distribution, high-income classes import luxury goods of good quality, and local production can focus on a limited number of standard, low-quality goods. As we have seen in the models discussed above, this structure backlashes on trade dynamics and international competition, suppressing even more the ability of a relatively poor and unequal country to produce new and good quality goods to drive industrialisation.

2.5.1.3 Evolutionary growth models

Both demand and structural change are of great relevance in the evolutionary theory of growth. Having discussed more aggregated models in the evolutionary tradition in the previous section, we now refer to the models that focus on the micro behaviour of production, consumption, or both, in the tradition of Nelson and Winter (1982). The Nelson and Winter (1982) model largely draws on the Schumpeterian view of innovation processes and places the firm as the main agent of technical change. Nelson and Winter use an appreciative understanding of firms' 'regular' behaviour and model firm innovation and investment decisions as a response to market conditions. Thus, firms innovate and imitate when they have the resources and are required to. In doing so, firms follow a satisfying, rather than maximising behaviour. Moreover, firms cannot choose a technique but need to move in the neighbourhood of their current technology. The model also represents industrial dynamics, with the fittest firms surviving and new firms entering. Features such as selection, firms' heterogeneity, non-equilibrium and industrial dynamics are at the core of most of the following evolutionary models of economic growth. It should also be noted that almost all these models focus on manufacturing sector, and by referring to firm dynamics, they implicitly refer to a corporation of an industry.

The first wave of evolutionary growth models focuses mainly on process innovation as a source of endogenous growth based on one or two sectors (capital and commodities). Some contributions model technical change as 'quasi-vintages' (capital differs in terms of the technologies embodied, not in terms of its vintage as time in use) (Silverberg and Verspagen, 1994a, 1994b). Other contributions consider disembodied technical change and variation in labour productivity (Chiaromonte and Dosi, 1993; Dosi *et al.*, 1994b), which represent a two-sector economy where both sectors are manufacturing: capital goods and consumer goods.

With the focus on the resources to invest in finding new technologies, on the hiring of skilled labour or scientists for the R&D process (as in Chiaromonte and Dosi, 1993), on the imitation of firms that try to be more successful in the choice of techniques with respect to competitors, emphasis is once more placed on the industrial sector where the use of capital is more intensive. In other words, although innovation, imitation, learning and selection are found in all sectors of the economy, the evolutionary growth models assume that these factors are stronger in the manufacturing sector which is why industrialisation is essential to growth in these models. It could easily be argued that these models mainly address industrialised economies.

A more recent wave of evolutionary models places more weight on the sectoral transformation of economies and the changes in demand so as to better account for the processes of transformation that have been observed in the long-run dynamics of development (Metcalfe *et al.*, 2006; Saviotti and Pyka, 2004, 2008). Some of them integrate Schumpeterian and Keynesian features, thus modelling structural change on both the demand and supply side (Ciarli *et al.*,

2010; Dosi *et al.*, 2010). Saviotti and Pyka propose several models in which they interpret development as the creation of new sectors. In their models, an entrepreneur has an incentive to invest in a sector in view of the monopolistic profits that can be made initially. Once the sector is established, imitating entrepreneurs have an easier access to the sector (with uncertainty becoming lower) so that investment and production increase. As production increases with competition, demand is eventually saturated, technology becomes mature and firms are selected out of the market. This gives them a further incentive to innovate and eventually create new sectors. Thus, the more innovative entrepreneurs are, the larger is the number of new sectors and the larger the production, i.e. growth. The final result also depends on the pace at which consumers become knowledgeable for the new goods/sectors incorporating new service characteristics.[24] The authors' final conclusion is that a larger variety (more sectors) determines higher economic growth. The term variety can be interpreted in a highly general sense, including the change from an agriculture-based economy to the production of manufactured goods and services as well as the number of manufacturing goods; ultimately the interpretation will depend on the sectoral aggregation assumed.

Ciarli and Lorentz (2010) and Ciarli *et al.* (2010) are novel attempts to represent different dimensions of structural change of the type occurring in a process of long-run growth, namely the emergence of new sectors, the change in production technology, the growth of firm size leading to corporate production and the related changes in the demand side regarding the distribution of income and consumption patterns. One of the main results of Ciarli and Lorentz (2010) is that the shift from pre-Malthusian to post-Malthusian growth[25] strongly depends on related aspects of the transformation of an economy – rather than on one aspect at a time, *ceteris paribus*. Take-off occurs only when, in the economy, there is an increase in firm size sufficient to introduce demand heterogeneity, but at the same time the increase in firm size is not characterised by an oversized increase in inequality (wage differences between different levels of a firm's organisational layers). Similarly, a faster transformation of the product composition of an economy (increasing product variety) increases overall demand only if there is a change in the demand structure (consumption patterns also change in the process). However, a too-fast change in consumption shares has a negative effect on growth because firms, in keeping up with the rapid changes in demand, do not have sufficient time to build competitive industries.

The bottom line here is that a change in sectoral/product composition has a number of positive effects in terms of increasing demand, allowing firms to escape satiation and increasing investment and labour. However, this should be accompanied by a number of complementary structural changes that generate enough demand for new sectors. Otherwise, we face the case discussed above, where an overly unequal society with a too-low demand for new goods does not induce product innovation and sectoral transformation of the economy. Finally, the model replicates the evidence that changes in demand have, from a historical perspective, been accompanied by radical changes in the organisation of production.

2.5.1.4 Unified growth theory

Recently, a number of models have been set up explicitly to study the transformation from a stagnant economy to that of rapid growth, with particular reference to the experience of the industrial revolution in Britain (Desmet and Parente, 2009; Galor, 2010; Lagerlöf, 2006; Stokey, 2001; Voigtländer and Voth, 2006). These models (subsumed under the general heading of Unified Growth Theory) explain the take-off of an economy and the transition from an agricultural to an industrialised economy.

In Galor (2010), the transition is explained by the interaction between population growth, the availability of technology and the incentives to invest in offsprings' education. During the Malthusian period population growth increases the demand for technology, the supply of inventions, their faster diffusion, the 'Smithian' specialisation of production and trade. The initial establishment of industrial production then increases the demand for educated workers, who have an incentive to invest more in the formation of human capital, reducing fertility. Subsequently, these changes in education give way to the transition to a growth process in which the increase in productivity is larger than the increase in population. These changes can be considered to follow a dynamics *à la* Nelson and Phelps (1966), who showed that an increase in skills does not only affect (the productivity of) current production but mainly the capability to adapt to technological changes and adopt new production techniques, thus speeding up their diffusion.[26] Initial differences in technological progress can therefore be explained by a number of factors such as property rights, Enlightenment, the application of knowledge to production (as, e.g. in Mokyr, 2010) or cultural traits (more on these aspects below). Similarly, different patterns of change in human capital can be explained by institutions, access to finance, inequality, and so on.

In a different model, Desmet and Parente (2009) also introduce changes in product innovation which are related to changes in demand. The transition to sustained growth occurs when, due to a population increase, industrial firms in urban areas start process innovation and attract labour from rural areas. Migration then changes consumer preferences towards industrial goods. This, in turn, generates an increase in firm size and competition and a decrease in markups, providing an incentive for product innovation, which appeals to the increasing urban population.

In these models, industrialisation is not assumed to start from scratch but emerges as an interaction between technology, population and education. However, it is the manufacturing sector and its technology that demands skilled labour, thus providing an incentive for investment in education or migration to urban areas. This then triggers more technology and gives way to take-off, a transition from Malthusian growth to modern, sustained growth. The different timing of this transition readily explains the increasing divergence between different economies.

2.5.1.5 Political economy models

Since the work of North (1981) on the relation between economic change and institutional change, a large set of models (and empirical analysis) has been developed to interpret different aspects of institutional change related to growth and development (Acemoglu and Johnson, 2005; Acemoglu and Robinson, 2006; Adam and Dercon, 2009; Bourguignon and Verdier, 2000; Greif, 2006). As we did for previous theories, we discuss only a group of examples and model features that we believe are general enough to represent this set.[27] The focus of this literature is on how economic institutions shape economic incentives. These institutions are usually identified and defined as the rules of the game in a fairly broad sense from property rights to the rule of law.[28] The main aspect of these rules is that they allow to reduce variability in human interactions, thus reducing transaction costs in a New Institutional Economics framework. Moreover, different rules of the game shape economic incentives differently and provide important political economy outcomes. What is the incentive to respect a contract if there is no mechanism to enforce it? What is the incentive to give a good or money in exchange for a good or service when this is available at no cost? Or more to the point, what is the incentive to invest in an industry, if most of the investment value added goes to someone else such as, for example, an exporter or retailer with strong contractual power?

In more systematic terms, following Acemoglu *et al.* (2005), institutions determine the incentives to invest and organise production efficiently and determine the way in which gains from the increase in efficiency are redistributed among the population. Political institutions determine the *de jure* political power while the distribution of resources defines the de facto political power. These need not be aligned, and often they are not. However, both political powers determine political institutions (in the future) and economic institutions. The economic institutions, in turn, determine economic performance and the distribution of resources (in the future). Many contributions in this literature analyse the conditions under which those variables change over time and how these changes affect economic performance. Let us focus on a couple of examples.

A number of models study the transition from medieval societies with large landholdings to societies in which democracy goes hand in hand with industrialisation. For example, Acemoglu and Robinson (2006) show the relevance of a political elite in blocking innovation. The main argument here is that the elite's power is eroded by innovation, decreasing the share of the future distribution of gains. The political elite prefers to maintain the status quo, inducing a social loss – and retarding any process of technological change and industrialisation – rather than use the opportunity to increase societal wealth, which would increase the risk of losing political power and of having to forgo the distribution of wealth in its favour. This also shows that, when a technology requires a small redistribution of de facto political power in order for it to be adopted, its adoption may, in turn, have a significant impact on the future change of political institutions, also accelerating future changes in technology and the increase and distribution of wealth. If, on the other hand, industrialisation is led by the same elite that holds political power and leaves this power unaltered, the contribution of technology and industrialisation to an increase in wealth is likely to be limited.

Other theories focus more on the role of institutions in determining the organisation of production. They show how, as a result of the historical heritage, cultures and past events, societies organise themselves differently and establish political power either based on kinship ties or on more formal rules of law. The main thesis of these theories is that societies organised by a rule of law have a much larger space for the division of labour and specialisation of production. This is because transaction costs are low throughout the society and not only within a limited kinship group. For example, Greif (2006) shows how two societies that successfully trade in the Mediterranean Sea, the Maghribis and the Genoese, develop in a highly different way, with the Genoese succeeding earlier in the process of modernisation. Though simplifying a rich analysis, one can state that this difference is due to the fact that the Maghribis successfully reduced transaction costs through their strong and widespread kinship ties. Given the relative uniformity of their society, they did not need a formal rule of law. At the other end of the spectrum, Genoa attracted a large number of migrants from different societies with no kinship ties, thus requiring the establishment of a formal rule of law. The existence of formal rules did not put up a limit to trade and hence to the extent of the division of labour and specialisation, which are at the core of the industrialisation process.

To summarise, the relation between institutions and industry is bi-directional. Institutions, through rules and incentives, define the way to accumulate wealth, while changes in the accumulation of wealth have potentially disruptive effects on political institutions and the distribution of power. On the one hand, the literature on political economy models seems to suggest that the process of industrialisation may be held back not only by unfavourable trade relations or poverty traps but also by the system of institutions that defines the distribution of power. Although most of this literature refers to a closed system, we should not leave out the distribution of international power, of political organisations and corporations.[29] On the other hand, this literature suggests that initial steps towards industrialisation may have a strong effect on institutional change by redistributing political power and access to resources more equitably.

2.5.2 Trade and growth revisited

Recent evidence seems to concur on the strong relevance of trade specialisation for income growth. Funke and Ruhwedel (2001) show that product variety (as measured relative to the US) is correlated with countries' relative per capita income level. Saviotti and Frenken (2008) find that related variety (goods that are close in the product space) in export is a significant predictor for short-run growth across OECD countries, while the effect of unrelated variety (goods that are distant in the product space) is positive only in the long run. Hausmann and Rodrik (2003) show that for most economies (excluding those that have a relatively sophisticated production mix) a successful industrialisation requires concentration on a small number of sectors with high productivity. In seeming contrast to this result, recent works by Hidalgo and Hausmann (Hidalgo and Hausmann, 2008, 2009; Hidalgo *et al.*, 2007), which have gained increasing attention,[30] show that the complexity of a country's export is a crucial determinant of income growth (and divergence across countries). Complexity is simply measured in terms of export diversification (export variety) and relative specialisation with respect to competitors. A complex country is one with a large variety in export, in goods that are exported by a low number of/by few other countries (Hidalgo and Hausmann, 2009). Felipe *et al.* (2012) use the same measure to rank products according to their complexity and find that their export share is positively correlated with income levels.

It has been discussed earlier how some models explicitly predict the relevance of increased variety for growth (Aoki and Yoshikawa, 2002; Ciarli and Lorentz, 2010; Saviotti and Pyka, 2004, 2008). However, these results were valid for closed economies. Yet Hidalgo and Hausmann (2009) show that it is not only the variety of goods that is related to growth but also how many other countries produce those goods that explains the divergence in economic development across countries.[31] Hausmann and Hidalgo (2011) go one step further to explain why a diversified production of goods that are produced only in a few other countries is positively related to development. In their model, the production of each good is associated with the existence of necessary capabilities within the country, which are non-tradable. The higher the capability content of a good, the larger is the capability endowment required for a country to produce it. But countries with an initial low endowment also have little incentive to invest in new capabilities because one new capability is of little use if the country produces a limited number of goods (as is the case when the diversity of goods produced is low). That country then finds itself in a 'low quiescence' trap and will continue to produce a small number of low capability goods. The more capabilities increase at the global level, the more complex becomes the production of differentiated goods, and the less likely a low capability country is to catch up.

The relation between trade specialisation and growth differs when uncertainty is introduced. A number of studies have explored how diversification and variety in industrial structure determine the relation between trade specialisation and growth. In particular, diversification of exports (an increased complexity) acts as a growth-enhancing insurance device in the context of uncertain (trade) environments (Di Maio, 2008; Di Maio and Valente, 2013).

Galor and Mountford (2006), explicitly referring to the shift from agriculture to industry, postulate that it is the increase in trade relations after the industrialisation of one part of the world that determines the subsequent divergence in income growth. In fact, countries that started an industrialisation process increased per capita income, while countries with the largest part of their population working in agriculture experienced a growth in population. This is explained by the fact that returns from trade in industrialising countries were mainly used for investment in physical and human capital, while these were used for population growth in agriculture-based economies.[32] This argument is hardly different from other arguments that for long have denied that comparative advantages are the best trade policy – including the recent call by the World Bank for more active industrial policies (Lin, 2011).[33] An economy that specialises by investing in a nascent industry also needs skilled labour and can devote the increased income (from trade) to capture changes in knowledge and transform them into technology: usually, this also induces a demographic transition towards urbanisation and higher education. On the contrary, a country that has a comparative advantage in exporting raw materials to industrialising economies has no incentive to change and finds itself competing with no gains from trade in the short run.

> Thus, the historical patterns of international trade reinforced the initial patterns of comparative advantage and generated a persistent effect on the distribution of population in the world economy and a great divergence in income per capita across countries and regions.
>
> Galor and Mountford (2006, p. 299)

The implications for the relation between industrialisation and growth are instructive, though not surprising, and are largely already known. Some exported products produce more income than others, and few countries develop the capability to produce them (e.g. because of the greater availability of required labour skills). These products also generate positive externalities, inducing more products to emerge (more innovative activity) and promoting the accumulation of skills and capabilities to match ongoing production and invent new products. This, in turn, expands the export basket, raising overall output and contributing to an increase in positive externalities.

2.6 Summary and final remarks

In this chapter, we have discussed a large set of theoretical arguments for industrialisation-driven development. We started off with the stage theories of growth and development, which postulate that all economies need to go through relatively well-defined stages of development. Interestingly, all stage theories indicate that all countries will eventually, more or less linearly, industrialise and reach the final stage of a modern high-income economy. But how to achieve this goal is a matter of disagreement among scholars. For instance, in the case of Rostow, industrialisation automatically follows from an increase in investment with no or little need for intervention, while for Kaldor more targeted policies are needed to converge the investment in high-productive industrial sectors.

Similarly, when we consider balanced and unbalanced theories of economic development, the discussion dwells on how to make industrialisation happen and on the constraints that hold back the economy in a non-industrialised backward state. The bottom line is that industry breeds industry through intermediate demand, and intermediate demand gives way to a virtuous growth cycle.

Although industrialisation is considered to lead more or less automatically to growth, some kind of state intervention is needed to kick off this process.

The first contributions to growth theory suggest that it is increased savings for capital investment that lead to a higher growth rate (when investments are realised), in absolute or relative terms, together with the technology determining the productivity of capital. In these models there is no explicit mention of a manufacturing sector, but the introduction of a general technology indicator as a determinant of growth, together with the focus on capital investment, suggest that technological change in sectors with higher productivity is the main engine of growth.

The requirement for investment in sectors in which a country may not have a comparative advantage but which have higher terms of trade and high-income elasticities is also regarded as a crucial aspect in the process of economic development by a large number of trade theories (and policies such as import substitution).

At the turn of last century, both growth and economic development theories started to investigate the sources of productivity and the role of intermediate good producers. In the New Growth Theory there is no mention of the role of manufacturing with respect to other sectors. However, it is manufacturing which is more likely to gain from various sources of increasing returns: investment externalities, human capital or improved intermediate goods. Ultimately, manufacturing is conducive to growth because it is assumed to benefit from the positive externalities.

When we turn to theories that explicitly model structural change, the assumption is that manufacturing – with a higher content of skills and knowledge – is more competitive on the international market than agriculture, which justifies the role of manufacturing as a source of growth. Some of these models add valuable insights on the demand side effect, that is, on the relation between the initial distribution of income and growth through new, modern products: an unequal society does not provide any incentive to innovate and increase the quality of goods, much less create new goods. Such a society is thus less likely to industrialise.

In the evolutionary tradition, on the other hand, it is firms' technological behaviour that plays the central role in growth dynamics. There is an implicit assumption that innovative firms are present mainly in the manufacturing sector and that it is therefore the manufacturing and high-tech activities that enable a sustainable growth pattern. Some of these models also show that a change in the sectoral composition of an economy enables an increase in demand and thus in investment and employment. They also show that these sectoral changes need to be accompanied by changes in the organisation of production structure, namely the transformation from workshops to corporate firms, which is again mainly a feature of the manufacturing sector. Moreover, sectoral changes require a relatively equal distribution of income in order to ensure sustainable growth, which is in many cases a feature of industrialised rather than rural (feudal) societies.

Unified Growth Theory models do not assume industrialisation to start from scratch but to emerge as an interaction between technology, population and education. However, it is assumed that it is the industrial sector that uses the technology that, in turn, requires educated labour, thus providing an incentive to invest in education or urbanisation. In other words, these models are interesting devices to explain how the transition from agriculture to industry occurred, and under which assumptions, ultimately, industry sustains growth.

Political economy models provide important insights on the relation between institutions and industrialisation. For example, institutions that favour the vested interests of a ruling elite may hold back any form of innovation likely to redistribute economic and political power, including technological change and industrialisation. Cimoli and Rovira (2008) show evidence on the vicious cycle between rent seeking behaviour of elites and a country's specialisation in primary resources.[34] However, small steps towards a new system of the distribution of resources and de facto political power, possibly along with small investments in industry, may have a large impact on institutional change and lead to sustained growth. Institutions are also seen as a fundamental explanatory variable of the emergence of trade and division of labour, without which industrialisation does not take place. The political economy models explain differences in the growth rate as differences in the division of labour, which are an outcome of the institutional context.

Finally, the implications of the modern theories of trade, growth and development are conceptually similar to the old structuralist theories of trade: income growth of a country gains from producing a large number of products that are more competitive than others on the international market. These theories also imply that a country develops capabilities to produce these goods, which have a positive effect on future innovation (an autocatalytic process). The product space that is more conducive to such dynamics is manufacturing.

This summary shows that, once accounted for the large differences in methodology, assumptions and the more or less explicit reference to sectors, the manufacturing and capital sectors are assumed to be central to growth and economic development across a large set of theories proposed during six decades. As we have highlighted on a number of occasions, in many cases the reference to manufacturing can only be induced by the correlation between empirical evidence and model assumptions; in a number of other cases, instead, manufacturing is explicitly modelled as the sector explaining growth. However, at least three crucial aspects of growth and economic development should be discussed further before any conclusions can be drawn from this theoretical excursus. Below, we only mention them, leaving a fully fledged discussion for future research.

First, the *objective*. All theories reviewed here are well grounded in the assumption that income growth is the only policy objective, and most of them do not make any particular distinction between income growth and economic development. However, development is a broad term that may or may not include income growth (see, e.g. Sen, 1979, 1994 or more recently Stiglitz, 2009), but it can certainly not be equalised to income growth. In other words, if growth and development constitute two sets, growth may be fully included in development; they may intersect; or be completely disjointed.

Moreover, structural change does not happen exclusively in terms of a change in the sectoral composition of an economy, leaving the rest equal. Some of the contributions reviewed here have made clear that structural change occurs in several dimensions: demand, organisation of labour, education supply and demand as well as massive urbanisation, distribution of political and economic power and opportunities, job displacements and changes in the prices of primary commodities and goods. Most of these changes are related to income distribution – which may have effects that hold back growth – or to the displacement of masses replaced by a dam or an industrial investment.

In our review, we have mentioned no theory that endorses manufacturing and also addresses the collateral aspects of industrialisation.[35] These crucial aspects should not be taken for granted. In particular, what needs to be considered first is the objective for a specific country, or region, which aspect of development should be and which effects this might have. A policy that aims to tackle inequality is probably different from a policy that has income growth as its sole objective.

Second, the *conditions*. Each theoretical argument in favour of industrialisation-driven development identifies different conditions for this to happen. We have shown that institutions may play a significant role in promoting or hindering industrialisation. We have also shown that one explanation for income divergence across countries in the last couple of centuries may lie in trade patterns linked to the positive feedback loops between trade specialisation and the formation of domestic capabilities. Inequality, or access to resources, is another relevant dimension here.

The bottom line is that even when the final objective is industrialisation-led growth, increasing capital investment will not be sufficient to achieve this objective. A large body of literature, particularly in the evolutionary tradition, has underlined the need to build the capabilities necessary to change, learn, acquire and understand radically different technologies such as manufacturing for an agricultural economy, production using the new technologies and innovation to increase the variety of the product space (e.g. Abramovitz, 1986; Amsden, 1991; Bell and Pavitt, 1993; Katz, 2001; Kim, 1997).

This capability dynamics is related to the institutional setting, probably going beyond the institutions that shape economic incentives, and crucially to the activity of entrepreneurs, social or business, who take the risk of investing in and adopting new technologies (Naudé, 2010; Nelson and Pack, 1999; Stiglitz, 2011), as well as to the role of macroeconomic uncertainty (e.g. Cimoli and Katz, 2003; Katz, 2001).

Third, *increasing returns*. The results of most theories reviewed here depend on an a priori assumption that manufacturing is the one sector that shows increasing returns to investment due to externalities, technological change and human capital, as opposed to agriculture. However, it should be carefully considered which are the sources of increasing returns in an economy. Knowledge, beyond technological capabilities, is certainly one of these sources: there are sources of knowledge that are extinguished by the sudden transformation of an economy, giving way to a new productive regime. Other sources of increasing returns are related to the clustering of economic activity due to agglomeration dynamics, social capital, spillovers or fragmentation of production. A further exercise for future work in this area is to analyse whether increasing returns continue to be the exclusive feature of manufacturing, and to look more deeply at different patterns of sectoral of innovation and positive externalities at different stages of growth and development.

With this chapter we have aimed at providing a systematic, though selective, review of a rich literature on growth and economic development, highlighting the different understandings with respect to the relevance of industry as a source of growth. We have also shown that in many parts of this literature, the superiority of industry is implicitly assumed or observed rather than explained. Our hope is that by clarifying these assumptions, we have placed more emphasis on the unresolved issues that form the basis of the different theoretical arguments for industrialisation-led economic development. Any development policy that focuses on industrialisation should weigh these arguments in relation to specific objectives and contexts rather than taking them for granted. The large array of literatures surveyed here should serve as an initial menu of ingredients. The recipes (if any) require much more analysis in the line of the work done by Rodrik (2007, 2010), which must, however, be left for future research. By focussing on manufacturing we have explicitly decided to leave out the role of the service sector, which is crucial in the process of growth and structural change. We suggest that another review is needed to analyse the different ways in which services are assumed to sustain growth and economic development in the respective theories.

Notes

1 This chapter has benefited from discussions with colleagues and friends who have spent years working on issues related to structural change and growth. However, we are particularly indebted to Alberto Botta, Nelson Correa, Gabriel Porcile, Stefano Vannuccini and Ulrich Witt, whose comments on a first version of the chapter have helped us to radically improve it. We are also grateful to Francis Matambalya for commissioning this work to us. All errors, omissions, misinterpretations are due to our own imprecision in stylising together so many decades of theories. Tommaso Ciarli also gratefully acknowledges financial support by the Max Planck Institute of Economics in Jena, where he has conducted a substantial part of the present research as a research fellow in the Evolutionary Economics group.

2 Capital intensity is a feature of the overall industrial sector: manufacturing can also be labour intensive, particularly in the initial stages of development. The capital-intensive nature of the manufacturing sector is an empirical issue: sectors characterised by lower capital intensity like light-manufacturing may result in more growth inducing than heavy-manufacturing capital intensive sectors.

3 Empirical evidence on the employment elasticity of manufacturing seems to support this argument (Szirmai, 2012). Note, however, that the problem may well be the opposite, with increases in labour productivity due to technological change in manufacturing that reduce the demand for workers, as is usually the case with skill-biased technical change.

4 '*Linearity*' is based on the assumption that for each Independent Variable (IV) X, the amount of change in the mean value of Dependent Variable (DP) Y *associated* with a unit increase in the X (*ceteris paribus*, i.e. holding all other variables constant) is the same regardless of the level of X. For instance, increasing X from *10 to 11* will produce the same amount of increase in Expected value of Y; $E(Y)$; as increasing X from *20 to 21*. Put another way, the effect on Y of a 1 unit increase in X does not depend on the value or level of X.

5 This tradition goes back to Mill (1848) and Smith (1961).

6 Interestingly, Rostow (1960) develops his analysis as an antithesis to Marx's analysis of the stages. Indeed, the subtitle of Rostow's book is 'A Non-Communist Manifesto'.

7 Which historically differed across countries.

8 Note that this is clearly a different view with respect to the Keynesian one in term of relation between savings and investments.

9 For instance, Gerschenkron questioned Rostow's proposition that all developing countries go through a similar series of levels and stages and its implication that it is possible to generalise the growth trajectory of different countries.

10 Note that Kaldor did not imply that the transition was smooth or that it occurred in the same way in the different countries. His analysis (Kaldor, 1966) is indeed based on the observation that the process of vertical specialisation, as suggested by Young, did not occur evenly and that it was not always based on the same source of demand (Argyrous, 1996).

11 Nurkse (1961) shares with Rosenstein-Rodan several theoretical elements.

12 These authors are conveniently regarded as being opposed to one another, although in practice they agreed on a large number of points (Alacevich, 2007), particularly with reference to the need for industrialisation programmes.

13 Another important contributor to this approach is Fleming (1955).

14 See Murphy *et al.* (1989) for a later reappraisal of the Rosenstein-Rodan theory in the economic growth modelling literature.

15 According to Hirschman (1958):

   i Forward linkages are created when investment in a particular project encourages investment in subsequent stages of production.
   ii Backward linkages are created when a project encourages investment in facilities that enable the project to succeed.

   Typically, projects create both forward and backward linkages. Investment should be made in those projects that have the greatest total number of linkages. Projects with many linkages will vary from country to country; knowledge about project linkages can be obtained through input and output studies.

16 See also Argyrous (1996) and Myrdal (1968) for a discussion on its different uses.

17 This idea is inspired by Young (1928) who argues that the development of mass production and the application of heavy machinery mean that processes which were once undertaken within the same craft shop became the bases for entirely separate industries.

18 The term 'state' as used in this context refers to 'a set of organisations, including the administrative and legislative order, with the authority to make and implement binding rules over all people and all action in a particular territory, using force if necessary' (Evans *et al.* 1985, pp. 46–47).

19 One exception is Uzawa (1961), but the objective there is to determine the steady-state solution in a two-sector version of the Solow model.

20 While the Prebisch–Singer (PS) hypothesis is very appealing, one should note that recent evidence casts some doubt on the secular negative trend of the terms of trade and on its deterministic nature (see Blattman *et al.*, 2007). However, even if the PS hypothesis is not verified and the secular trend is not negative, it could be argued that

being specialised in primary commodities generates another dependence: primary commodity prices are more volatile than manufacturing goods prices. Yet, as a final counter-argument, there is evidence that if insurance and precautionary savings are possible, the volatility problem disappears. To summarise, theoretical arguments for industrialisation based on the PS hypothesis are now less strong than when this was formulated in the 1950s.

21 Please note that those recommendations are hardly different from those discussed in relation to the stages of development in Section 2.3 or the balanced growth debate in Section 2.4.1.

22 In particular, diversification may work as a welfare and growth enhancing insurance device in the context of uncertain environments (Di Maio, 2008; Di Maio and Valente, 2013).

23 Schumpeter put technological change at the centre of economic analysis and sought to explain a number of economic phenomena focussing on innovation dynamics. These phenomena imply changes in different aspects of the structure of an economy such as sectors, firms within sectors, firm size and organisation. With reference to the long run, Schumpeter related innovation dynamics and the emergence of periodical radical innovations to the unbalanced dynamics of the business cycle. Central to his analysis were the concepts of innovation, the innovative entrepreneur (both in technical and social terms), the large corporation with access to innovation funding and the increases in efficiency due to the replacement of incumbent old technologies with new ones (creative destruction), all of which seem to point to the focal role that industry plays in a country's growth.

24 Similar to Aoki and Yoshikawa (2002), the main driver of growth here is to escape satiation. Although Saviotti and Pyka somewhat simplify the demand side and avoid meddling with income distribution, they describe an endogenous Schumpeterian mechanism for the emergence of new sectors.

25 Here pre-Malthusian growth refers to an increase in income that is mainly linked to the population growth, and negatively related to real wages growth. While post-Malthusian growth occurs when the Malthusian trap is escaped and the increase in productivity allows for a much larger increase in income than in the population: population change is positively related with real wages.

26 It may be relevant to note, though, that Nelson and Phelps (1966), for an empirical validation of the main hypothesis of the model, refer to the adoption of new technologies in agriculture: the adoption of more productive technologies in the US occurred relatively faster among relatively more educated farmers.

27 The interested reader is referred to a number of excellent reviews and discussions describing this literature in more detail: Acemoglu *et al.* (2005); Adam and Dercon (2009); Bertocchi (2006); Casson *et al.* (2010).

28 This is relevant for at least two reasons. First, it allows economists to provide a reasonably bounded definition of a rather indeterminate concept. Second, and related to the first reason, it allows to limit the analysis to the direct relation between institutions and economic behaviour through economic incentives.

29 See, e.g., the question of preferential trade agreements with SSA that are linked to countries' governance dimensions, the biased trade relations despite governance concerns, when primary resources are needed (Grauwe *et al.*, 2010), the changes in agri-food market governance with the increase in private standards (Fuchs *et al.*, 2011), and the biased impact of contract farming on producers (von Hagen and Gabriela, 2011).

30 A few scholars have started to investigate the properties of trade networks, e.g. Barigozzi *et al.* (2010).

31 See also the discussion in Hausmann and Hidalgo (2011) on how their complexity measure differs from more traditional measures of product concentration such as the entropy index (Saviotti and Frenken, 2008), which does not distinguish between different products and how many countries produce them.

32 See also Galor and Mountford (2008) for an empirical confirmation.
33 See, for instance, Lin and Chang (2009) for a recent development in a debate that has been ongoing for many decades.
34 See also Auty (2001) for a wider discussion on the natural resources curse.
35 The economic development literature does not lack discussion on urban bias, agricultural development, distribution of land, poverty, inequality, migration, basic needs, and the like.

References

Abdon, A. and J. Felipe (2011). *The product space: What does it say about the opportunities for growth and structural transformation of Sub-Saharan Africa?* Economics Working Paper Archive 670, Levy Economics Institute, Annandale-on-Hudson, NY.

Abramovitz, M. (1986). Catching up, forging ahead, and falling behind. *Journal of Economic History* 66, 385–406.

Acemoglu, D. and S. Johnson (2005). Unbundling institutions. *Journal of Political Economy* 113(5), 949–995.

Acemoglu, D. and J.A. Robinson (2006). Economic backwardness in political perspective. *American Political Science Review* 100(01), 115–131.

Acemoglu, D., S. Johnson and J.A. Robinson (2005). Institutions as a fundamental cause of long–run growth. In P. Aghion and S.N. Durlauf (eds), *Handbook of Economic Growth*, Volume 1A of *Economic Handbooks*, Chapter 6, pp. 385–472. Amsterdam: Elsevier.

Adam, C. and S. Dercon (2009). The political economy of development: An assessment. *Oxford Review of Economic Policy* 25(2), 173–189.

Aghion, P. and P. Howitt (1992). A model of growth through creative destruction. *Econometrica* 60(2), 322–352.

Aghion, P. and P. Howitt (1998). *Endogenous Growth Theory*. Cambridge, MA: MIT Press.

Alacevich, M. (2007). *Early development economics debates revisited*. Policy Research Working Paper Series 4441, The World Bank.

Amable, B. and D. Guellec (1992). Les théories de la croissance endogène. *Revue d'Economie Politique* 102(3), 313–377.

Amsden, A.H. (1991). Diffusion of development: The late–industrializing model and greater East Asia. *American Economic Review* 81(2), Papers and Proceedings of the Hundred and Third Annual Meeting of the American Economic Association, 282–286.

Aoki, M. and H. Yoshikawa (2002). Demand saturation–creation and economic growth. *Journal of Economic Behavior & Organization* 48, 127–154.

Argyrous, G. (1996). Cumulative causation and industrial evolution: Kaldor's four stages of industrialization as an evolutionary model. *Journal of Economic Issues* 30(1), 97–119.

Auty, R. (ed.) (2001). *Resource Abundance and Economic Development*. WIDER Studies in Development Economics. Oxford: Oxford University Press.

Barigozzi, M., G. Fagiolo and D. Garlaschelli (2010). Multinetwork of international trade: A commodity-specific analysis. *Physical Review* E 81, 046104.

Bell, M. and K. Pavitt (1993). Technological accumulation and industrial growth: Contrast between developed and developing countries. *Industrial and Corporate Change* 2(2), 157–210.

Bertocchi, G. (2006). Growth, history and institutions. In N. Salvadori (ed.), *Economic Growth and Distribution: On the Nature and Causes of the Wealth of Nations*, Chapter 14, pp. 331–349. Cheltenham, UK, Northampton, USA: Edward Elgar.

Blattman, C., J. Hwang and J.G. Williamson (2007). Winners and losers in the commodity lottery: The impact of terms of trade growth and volatility in the periphery 1870–1939. *Journal of Development Economics* 82(1), 156–179.

Bourguignon, F. and T. Verdier (2000). Oligarchy, democracy, inequality and growth. *Journal of Development Economics* 62(2), 285–313.

Casson, M.C., M. Della Giusta and U.S. Kambhampati (2010). Formal and informal institutions and development. *World Development* 38(2), 137–141.

Chiaromonte, F. and G. Dosi (1993). Heterogeneity, competition, and macroeconomic dynamics. *Structural Change and Economic Dynamics* 4, 39–63.

Ciarli, T. and A. Lorentz (2010). *Product variety and changes in consumption patterns: The effects of structural change on growth.* Working paper mimeo, Max Planck Institute of Economics.

Ciarli, T., A. Lorentz, M. Savona and M. Valente (2010). The effect of consumption and production structure on growth and distribution. A micro to macro model. *Metroeconomica* 61(1), 180–218.

Ciarli, T., V. Meliciani and M. Savona (2012). Knowledge dynamics, structural change and the geography of business services. *Journal of Economic Surveys* 26(3), 445–467.

Cimoli, M. (1994). Lock-in specialization (dis)advantages in a structuralist growth model. In J. Fagerberg, B. Verspagen and N. von Tunzelmann (eds), *The Dynamics of Technology Trade and Growth*. Aldershot: Edward Elgar.

Cimoli, M. and J. Katz (2003). Structural reforms, technological gaps and economic development: A Latin American perspective. *Industrial and Corporate Change* 12(2), 387–411.

Cimoli, M. and G. Porcile (2009). Sources of learning paths and technological capabilities: An introductory roadmap of development processes. *Economics of Innovation and New Technology* 18(7), 675–694.

Cimoli, M. and S. Rovira (2008). Elites and structural inertia in Latin America: An introductory note on the political economy of development. *Journal of Economic Issues* XLII(2), 327–347.

Cimoli, M., G. Porcile and S. Rovira (2010). Structural change and the BOP-constraint: Why did Latin America fail to converge? *Cambridge Journal of Economics* 34(2), 389–411.

Collier, P. and A.J. Venables (2007). Rethinking trade preferences: How Africa can diversify its exports. *World Economy* 30(8), 1326–1345.

Cornwall, J. (1977). *Modern Capitalism: Its Growth and Transformation*. New York: St. Martin's Press.

Desmet, K. and S.L. Parente (2009). *The evolution of markets and the revolution of industry: A quantitative model of England's development, 1300–2000*. Working Papers 2009–06, Instituto Madrileño de Estudios Avanzados (IMDEA) Ciencias Sociales.

Di Maio, M. (2008). Uncertainty, trade integration and the optimal level of protection in a Ricardian model with a continuum of goods. *Structural Change and Economic Dynamics* 19(4), 315–329.

Di Maio, M. and M. Valente (2013). Uncertainty, specialization and government intervention. *Metroeconomica* 64(2), 215–243.

Domar, E. (1946). Capital expansion, rate of growth, and employment. *Econometrica* 14(April), 137–147.

Dosi, G. (1988). Sources, procedures and microeconomic effects of innovation. *Journal of Economic Literature* 26, 1120–1171.

Dosi, G., C. Freeman and S. Fabiani (1994a). The process of economic development: Introducing some stylized facts and theories on technologies, firms and institutions. *Industrial and Corporate Chance* 3(1), 1–45.

Dosi, G., S. Fabiani, R. Aversi and M. Meacci (1994b). The dynamics of international differentiation: A multi–country evolutionary model. *Industrial and Corporate Chance* 3(1), 225–241.

Dosi, G., G. Fagiolo and A. Roventini (2010). Schumpeter meeting Keynes: A policy–friendly model of endogenous growth and business cycles. *Journal of Economic Dynamics and Control* 34, 1748–1767.

Easterly, W. (2002). *The Elusive Quest for Growth. Economists' Adventures and Misadventures in the Tropics*. Cambridge, MA: MIT Press.

Evans, P., R. Dietrich and S. Theda (eds) (1985). *Bringing the State Back In*. Cambridge: Cambridge University Press, pp. 46–47.

Felipe, J., U. Kumar, A. Abdon and M. Bacate (2012). Product complexity and economic development. *Structural Change and Economic Dynamics* 23(1), 33–68.

Fleming, J. (1955). External economies and the doctrine of balanced growth. *Economic Journal* 65, 241–256.

Föllmi, R. and J. Zweimüller (2008). Structural change, Engel's consumption cycles and Kaldor's facts of economic growth. *Journal of Monetary Economics* 55(7), 1317–1328.

Fuchs, D., A. Kalfagianni, J. Clapp and L. Busch (2011). Introduction to symposium on private agrifood governance: Values, shortcomings and strategies. *Agriculture and Human Values* 28, 335–344.

Funke, M. and R. Ruhwedel (2001). Product variety and economic growth: Empirical evidence for the OECD countries. *IMF Staff Papers* 48(2), 225–242.

Galor, O. (2010). The 2008 Lawrence R. Klein lecture comparative economic development: Insights from unified growth theory. *International Economic Review* 51(1), 1–44.

Galor, O. and A. Mountford (2006). Trade and the great divergence: The family connection. *American Economic Review* 96(2), 299–303.

Galor, O. and A. Mountford (2008). Trading population for productivity: Theory and evidence. *Review of Economic Studies* 75(4), 1143–1179.

Gault, F. and G. Zhang (2010). The role of innovation in the area of development. In E. Kraemer-Mbula and W. Wamae (eds), *Innovation and the Development Agenda*. Paris: OECD/IDRC.

Grauwe, P.D., R. Houssay and G. Piccillo (2010). *China Africa relationship: good for both parts?* Working Paper mimeo, CES, University of Leuven.

Greif, A. (2006). *Institutions and the Path to the Modern Economy: Lessons from Medieval Trade*. Political Economy of Institutions and Decisions series. Cambridge: Cambridge University Press.

Grossman, G.M. and E. Helpman (1989a). *Comparative advantage and long run growth*. NBER WP 2970, National Bureau of Economic Research.

Grossman, G.M. and E. Helpman (1989b). Product development and international trade. *Journal of Political Economy* 97, 1261–1283.

Grossman, G.M. and E. Helpman (1989c). *Quality ladders and product cycles*. NBER WP 3201, National Bureau of Economic Research.

Harrod, R.F. (1939). An essay in dynamic theory. *Economic Journal* 49(1).

Hausmann, R. and C. Hidalgo (2011). The network structure of economic output. *Journal of Economic Growth* 16, 309–342.

Hausmann, R. and D. Rodrik (2003). Economic development as self discovery. *Journal of Development Economics* 72(8952), 603–633.

Hausmann, R., J. Hwang and D. Rodrik (2007). What you export matters. *Journal of Economic Growth* 12(1), 1–25.

Hidalgo, C.A. and R. Hausmann (2008). A network view of economic development. *Developing Alternatives* 12(1), 5–10.

Hidalgo, C.A. and R. Hausmann (2009). The building blocks of economic complexity. *Proceedings of the National Academy of Sciences* 106(26), 10570–10575.

Hidalgo, C.A., B. Klinger, A.-L. Barabási and R. Hausmann (2007). The product space conditions the development of nations. *Science* 317(5837), 482–487.

Hirschman, A.O. (1958). *The Strategy of Economic Development*. New Haven: Yale University Press.

Kaldor, N. (1966). *Causes of the Slow Rate of Economic Growth in the United Kingdom*. Cambridge: Cambridge University Press.

Kaldor, N. (1975). Economic growth and the Verdoorn law: A comment on Mr. Rowthorn's Article. *Economic Journal* 85(340), 891–896.

Kalecki, M. (1990). Consequences of dumping. In J. Osiatynski (ed.), *Collected Works of Michael Kalecki, Volume I, Capitalism: Business Cycles and Full Employment*, pp. 26–34. Oxford: Oxford University Press.

Katz, J. (2001). Structural reforms and technological behaviour: The sources and nature of technological change in Latin America in the 1990s. *Research Policy* 30, 1–19.

Kim, L. (1997). *Imitation to Innovation: The Dynamics of Korea's Technological Learning*. Boston: Harvard Business School Press.

Krugman, P. (1994). The fall and rise of development economics. In L. Rodwin and D.A. Schoen (eds), *Rethinking the Development Experience: Essays Provoked by the Work of Albert O. Hirschman*, Chapter 3, pp. 39–58. Washington, DC: The Brooking Institution.

Lagerlöf, N.-P. (2006). The Galor-Weil model revisited: A quantitative exercise. *Review of Economic Dynamics* 9(1), 116–142.

Lall, S. (2005). *Is African industry competing?* QEH working papers, Queen Elizabeth House, University of Oxford.

Lin, J. and H.-J. Chang (2009). Should industrial policy in developing countries conform to comparative advantage or defy it? A debate between Justin Lin and Ha-Joon Chang. *Development Policy Review* 27(5), 483–502.

Lin, J.Y. (2011). New structural economics: A framework for rethinking development. *The World Bank Research Observer* 26(2), 1–29.

Los, B. and B. Verspagen (2003). *The evolution of productivity gaps and specialisation patterns*. Working Paper mimeo, University of Groningen.

Lucas, R.E. (1988). On the mechanics of economic development. *Journal of Monetary Economics* 22(1), 3–42.

Maddison, A. (2001). *The World Economy: A Millennial Perspective*. Paris: OECD.

Maddison, A. (2007). *Contours of the World Economy 1–2030 AD: Essays in Macro-Economic History*. Oxford: Oxford University Press.

Mankiw, N.G., D. Romer and D. Weil (1992). A contribution to the empirics of economic growth. *Quarterly Journal of Economics* 107, 407–437.

Matsuyama, K. (2002). The rise of mass consumption societies. *Journal of Political Economy* 110(5), 1035–1070.

Metcalfe, J.S., J. Foster and R. Ramlogan (2006). Adaptive economic growth. *Camb. J. Econ.* 30(1), 7–32.

Mill, J.S. (1848). *Principles of Political Economy, with Some of Their Applications to Social Philosophy*. London: Parker and Co.

Mokyr, J. (2010). The contribution of economic history to the study of innovation and technical change: 1750–1914. In B.H. Hall and N. Rosenberg (eds), *Handbook of The Economics of Innovation, Vol. 1*, Volume 1 of *Handbook of the Economics of Innovation*, pp. 11–50. Amsterdam: North-Holland.

Murphy, K., A. Shleifer and R. Vishny (1989). Industrialization and the big push. *Journal of Political Economy* 97, 1003–1026.

Myrdal, G. (1968). *Asian Drama. An Inquiry into the Poverty of Nations*, Volume 3. New York: Twentieth Century Fund.

Naudé, W. (2010). *New challanges for industrial policy*. Working Papers 2010–107, World Institute for Development Economic Research (UNU-WIDER).

Nelson, R. and S. Winter (1982). *An Evolutionary Theory of Economic Change*. Cambridge, MA: Harvard University Press.

Nelson, R.R. (1994). The co-evolution of technology, industrial structure, and supporting institutions. *Industrial and Corporate Change* 3(1), 47–63.

Nelson, R.R. and H. Pack (1999). The Asian miracle and modern growth theory. *The Economic Journal* 109(457), 416–436.

Nelson, R.R. and E.S. Phelps (1966). Investment in humans, technological diffusion and economic growth. *American Economic Review* 61(2), 69–75.

North, D.C. (1981). *Structure and Change in Economic History*. New York: Norton.

Nurkse, R. (1961). *Problems of Capital Formation in Underdeveloped Countries*. New York: Oxford University Press.

Pasinetti, L.L. (1981). *Structural Change and Economic Growth. A Theoretical Essay on the Dynamics of the Wealth of Nations*. Cambridge: Cambridge University Press.

Prebish, R. (1950). *The Economic Development of Latin America and its Principal Problems*. United Nations Department of Economics Affairs, Lake Success, NY: United Nations Publications.

Redding, S. (1999). Dynamic comparative advantage and the welfare effects of trade. *Oxford Economic Papers* 51(1), 15–39.

Rodrik, D. (2007). *One Economics, Many Recipes: Globalization, Institutions, and Economic Growth*. Princeton, NJ: Princeton University Press.

Rodrik, D. (2010). Diagnostics before prescription. *Journal of Economic Perspectives* 24(3), 33–44.

Romer, P.M. (1986). Increasing returns and long run growth. *Journal of Political Economy* 94(5), 1002–1037.

Romer, P.M. (1990). Endogenous technological change. *Journal of Political Economy* 98(5, Part 2: The Problem of Development: A Conference of the Institute for the Study of Free Enterprise Systems), S71–S102.

Romer, P.M. (1994). The origins of endogenous growth. *Journal of Economic Perspectives* 8(1), 3–22.

Rosenstein-Rodan, P.N. (1943, June–September). Problems of industrialisation of eastern and South–Eastern Europe. *The Economic Journal* 53(210/211), 202–211.

Rostow, W.W. (1960). *The Stages of Economic Growth: A Non Communist Manifesto*. Cambridge: Cambridge University Press.

Rowthorn, B. and R. Ramaswamy (1997). *Deindustrialization: Causes and implications*. IMF Working Papers 97/42, International Monetary Fund.

Saviotti, P. and K. Frenken (2008). Export variety and the economic performance of countries. *Journal of Evolutionary Economics* 18, 201–218.

Saviotti, P.P. and A. Pyka (2004). Economic development by the creation of new sectors. *Journal of Evolutionary Economics* 14(1), 1–35.

Saviotti, P.P. and A. Pyka (2008). Technological change, product variety and economic growth. *Journal of Evolutionary Economics* 18(3–4), 323–347.

Sen, A. (1979). The welfare basis of national income comparison. *Journal of Economic Literature* 17, 1–45.

Sen, A. (1994). Growth and economics: What and why? In L.L. Pasinetti and R.M. Solow (eds), *Economic Growth and the Structure of Long-Term Development. Proceedings of the IEA Conference*, Volume IEA Conference 112, Varenna, Italy, pp. 363–368. St. Martin's Press.

Shen, J., D. Dunn and Y. Shen (2007). Challenges facing US manufacturing and strategies. *Journal of Industrial Technology* 23(2), 2–10.

Silverberg, G. and B. Verspagen (1994a). Collective learning, innovation and growth in a boundedly rational, evolutionary world. *Journal of Evolutionary Economics* 4, 207–226.

Silverberg, G. and B. Verspagen (1994b). Learning, innovation and economic growth: A long–run model of industrial dynamics. *Industrial and Corporate Chance* 3(1), 199–223.

Singer, H. (1950). The distribution of gains between investing and borrowing countries. *American Economic Review* 40, 473–485.

Smith, A. (1961). *An Inquiry into the Nature and Causes of the Wealth of Nations* (Edwin Cannan (1904), in 2 vols. ed.). London: Methuen.

Solow, R. (1957). Technical change and the aggregate production function. *Review of Economics and Statistics* 39(3), 312–320.

Stiglitz, J.E. (2009). GDP fetishism. *The Economists' Voice* 6(8), Article 5.

Stiglitz, J.E. (2011). Rethinking development economics. *The World Bank Research Observer* 26(2), 230–236.

Stokey, N.L. (2001). A quantitative model of the British industrial revolution, 1780–1850. *Carnegie-Rochester Conference Series on Public Policy* 55(1), 55–109.

Swan, T.W. (1956). Economic growth and capital accumulation. *Economic Record* 32, 334–361.

Szirmai, A. (2012). Industrialisation as an engine of growth in developing countries, 1950–2005. *Structural Change and Economic Dynamics* 23(4), 406–420.

Thirlwall, A.P. (1992). A Kaldorian model of growth and development revisited: A rejoinder to Dutt. *Oxford Economic Papers* 44(1), 169–172.

UNIDO and UNCTAD (2011). *Fostering industrial development in Africa in the new global environment*. Economic Development in Africa report. New York and Geneva: UNIDO and UNCTAD.

Uzawa, H. (1961). On a two-sector model of economic growth. *The Review of Economic Studies* 29(1), 40–47.

Verspagen, B. (1993). *Uneven Growth Between Interdependent Economies. The Evolutionary Dynamics of Growth and Technology*. Aldershot: Avebury.

Verspagen, B. (2002). Evolutionary macroeconomics: A synthesis between neo–Schumpeterian and post-Keynesians lines of thought. *Electronic Journal of Evolutionary Modelling and Economic Dynamics* (1007).

Voigtländer, N. and H.-J. Voth (2006). Why England? Demographic factors, structural change and physical capital accumulation during the industrial revolution. *Journal of Economic Growth* 11(4), 319–361.

von Hagen, O. and A. Gabriela (2011). The impacts of private standards on producers in developing countries. *Literature Review Series on the Impacts of Private Standards Part II*, ITC, Geneva.

von Tunzelmann, G.N. (1995). *Technology and Industrial Progress: The Foundations of Economic Growth*. Aldershot: Edward Elgar.

Wood, A. (1994). Comment on 'Part i: Empirical evidence'. In L. Pasinetti and R.M. Solow (eds), *Economic Growth and the Structure of Long-Term Development. Proceedings of the IEA Conference*, Volume IEA Conference 112, Varenna, Italy, pp. 65–70. St. Martin's Press.

Young, A.A. (1928). Increasing returns and economic progress. *History of Economic Thought Articles* 38, 527–542.

Zweimüller, J. and J.K. Brunner (2005*)*. Innovation and growth with rich and poor countries. *Metroeconomica* 56(2), 233–262.

3 The urge to industrialise African countries

Which lessons can be learnt from the empirics of the process?

Francis A.S.T. Matambalya

3.1 Drivers of industrialisation: lessons from the industrialisation experiences of countries

Starting in England in 1760, industralisation spread systematically to various parts of the world. The early history of its proliferation was marked by systematic spread of the 'industrial state' from England to the United States, to Europe (north-west Europe, and then central Europe, and then Eastern Europe particularly Russia). The overseas offshoots of European powers benefited to some extent from these early episodes of industrialisation, although significant achievements did not happen beyond North America (Canada and USA) and Oceania (Australia and New Zealand).

Then, starting with Japan in the second half of the 1950s, major waves of industrialisation spread to East Asia, where arguably the phenomenon took a highly successful sequential development path (Xing 2007).

To get some insights into the process, this sub-section reviews the industrialisation experiences of selected countries, including the UK, two other European countries (Germany, Finland), USA, East Asia, and emerging emerging economies from outside East Asia (Brazil and Turkey).

3.1.1 Lessons from pioneer industrial evolution in the United Kingdom

England was the first country to experience industrial transformation. The achievement of this feat was preceded by remarkable developments, which became popularly known as reformation. One of the manifestations of the process was that the King of England declared 'independence' from the Vatican in 1534. The break-up with the Pope also meant that the Majesty (at that time the King) become also the head of the church (of England). Revenues hitherto paid to the Vatican were now paid to the King.

Judged using today's knowledge of how economies work, the reformation process unleashed several changes that facilitated the emergence of an industrial society: creating a conducive environment for learning and the generation of knowledge and development of skills, strengthening national identity and unity (economic, political, social and cultural), smoothening the progress of domestic market integration (DMI), agricultural revolution, improvement of infrastructure, securing access to abundant supplies of mineral raw materials, technological evolution.

3.1.1.1 National identity, unity vs security

The reformation unleashed a development process, which profoundly trans-formed the primordial forms of the nation-state by strengthening further the pillars of national unity. It inspired a development process, which was character-ised by internal changes that strengthened national consciousness and unity, and the appreciation of the symbolism of English culture. In this connection, the Protestant movement did, *inter alia*, defragment political authority and power, by taking away loyalty to feudal lords in favour of concentration of such author-ity and power in the hands of the King of England (cf. Hobsbawm 1968; Hill 1969; Thomson 1973).

Other important observations related to the role of entrepreneurship and national security. Evidently, entrepreneurship has contributed towards driving industrial transformation in the past, and continues to do so today. Strong entre-preneurial societies have led to the evolution of strong economies, typically aligned with the evolution of strong nations generally. However, English indus-trialisation occurred in a world still dominated by less-law abiding societies, wars and conquests, which constantly threatened the interests of individuals, entrepreneurial ventures and whole nations. Imperatively, entrepreneurs like industrialists and merchants needed strong government for the maintenance of internal peace, law and order, and for protection from foreign rivals. Thus, equally important for an emergence of England as an industrial state and strong economy, were the strengthening of internal law and order and rule of law through the establishment of internal police, and the building and maintenance of strong armies that could demonstrate military superiority over key rivals and thereby protect English interests – where necessary by force (cf. Hobsbawm 1968; Hill 1969; Thomson 1973).

3.1.1.2 Domestic market integration

The national unity provided the basic ingredients for primordial domestic market integration.

As highlighted in the previous subsection, reformation led to the enhanced fusion of fragmented communities into a strong nation-state. Imperatively, English communities were integrated into a single country, and a single national market. Moreover, the cumulation of these previously fractionalised populations ensured the existence and growth of demand for basic industrial commodities, such as cloths, foods, fishing and fuel (cf. Hobsbawm 1968; Hill 1969; Thomson 1973).

Furthermore, by centralising tax collection in the mandate of the King (as opposed to medieval times, when traders had to pay tax to local lords, whose land they traversed), national unification facilitated trade, and had effects reminiscent to those of contemporary trade liberalisation.

The combined effects of these measures were the creation of, what will, using today terminology, be called 'single market' all over the country, thereby lowering market access transaction costs. The existence of a unified national market provided a secure basis for the germination of capitalist entrepreneurship, and was strengthened further by a systematic political unification that in the seventeenth and eighteenth centuries established London and other urban centres as England's industrial and commercial centres of gravity (cf. Birnie 1953; Hill 1969; Thomson 1973).

3.1.1.3 Access to foreign markets

Access to foreign markets, akin to what in today's world is negotiated for in various *fora*, such as the World Trade Organization (WTO), Regional Trade Agreements (RTAs), etc., did also aid the English industrial revolution process. A major difference however is that the English Market Access (MA) was not negotiated for, but was forcefully obtained through colonial mode of international economic relations. Eventually, colonial expansion provided significant markets for England's manufactured goods (Birnie 1953; Blanqui 1968; Hobsbawm 1968; Hill 1969).

Overall, the model of metropolis-colony relationship, which was first created by England and later copied by other imperial powers, was not a kind of free trade, rather the colony was appended to the metropolis through legislation that granted privileges to certain companies, and prohibited any external relations of the colony (Blanqui 1968).

3.1.1.4 Betterment of conditions for generation of knowledge and development of skills

The new, freer educational system, which was characteristic of the reformation, stimulated immense scientific transformation. The dissolution of monasteries and chantries led to the creation of a national educational system, which stimulated not only individualism, but also in the long run fundamentally influenced the scientific outlook (cf. Hill 1969; Thomson 1973; Koenigsberger 1987). The generation of knowledge and skills in various sciences (e.g. natural sciences, economic sciences, etc.) eventually provided the ammo for the country's industrialisation, by creating an educated and skilled labour force essential for industrial transformation. Higher levels of literacy precipitated the generation and diffusion of knowledge and skills.

3.1.1.5 Agriculture as a source of agricultural raw materials

Agricultural revolution, through its capitalisation and commercialisation (of agriculture), opened up the possibility for feeding the large populations, including the growing urban population that provided both home market and labour force for newly emerging industrial sector (Hill 1969; Wallerstein 1974). Concretely, the Enclosure Act transformed the lands of monasteries and common lands into self-contained private land-units and brought waste lands under cultivation (Hobsbawm 1968). The foundation for large-scale commercial farming, which eventually was manifested by plantation farming, was laid down. Furthermore, colonies served as important sources of agricultural raw materials (e.g. cotton, sugar, tobacco, etc.), for processing in England and eventual export to the world (Birnie 1953; Blanqui 1968, Hobsbawm 1968; Hill 1969), including back to the colonies.

3.1.1.6 Infrastructure

The expansion of the economy which is spurred by industrialisation, cannot happen in the absence of supporting infrastructure. Therefore, throughout history, industrialisation has been greatly aided by the development of diverse infrastructural capacities. This is because both backward and forward linkages in the economic production system depend on the existence of diverse types of physical infrastructures: energy, telecommunication, transport, water supply, etc.

For instance, the development of transport infrastructure in industrialising England not only made the waters navigable, but also contributed towards the reduction of transport costs. In this context, it was a major contributing factor to English industrialisation transformation (Hobsbawm 1968: 24), a fact that remains true for countries that industrialised later.

3.1.1.7 Securing abundant supplies of mineral raw materials

A healthy industrial economy relies heavily on reliable supplies of different types of agricultural and mineral raw materials. In this context, it is also imperative that the mineral raw materials (including precious metals) which were locally available in England or were brought in from colonies (e.g. Africa, Oceania, the Americas, etc.) did feed and sustain the country's industrial transformation process (cf. Wallerstein 1974).

3.1.1.8 Technological evolution

The industrial revolution was also propelled by profound technological advancements of the time. For instance, in the early sixteenth century, there was a changing energy usage from wood to coal. Eventually, coal became the major source of energy for several industries such as sugar refining, armament, paper production (Hill 1969).

3.1.1.9 Slave trade as a source of capital accumulation

Important sources of capital accumulation included slaves, both as a tradable commodity, as well as sources of free labour. The significance of the slave trade as an important source of capital accumulation for industrial revolution has been underscored by several authors. In a triangular trade, slaves were carried from Africa to the Americas by ships owned or chartered by English merchants, and mineral raw materials (such as gold and raw materials) were imported to England from the Americas (Birnie 1953; Blanqui 1968, Hobsbawm 1968; Hill 1969). This underlines further the contribution of the colonies in the industrial transformation of England.

3.1.2 Lessons from selected cases of industrial revolution in continental Europe

England's pioneer industrialisation role was followed by industrial revolution in continental Europe. This process gained strength after the 1830s, and comparatively evolved at much faster rates than even in the case of the UK (Birnie 1953:1). The following subsections highlight the dynamics of industrial transformation in continental Europe, using two country case studies: Germany and Finland.

3.1.2.1 Lessons from the industrial transformation of Germany

At the beginning of the nineteenth century, present day Germany was divided into many small states, which had their own independent economic policies. Progress towards industrialisation was hampered by the absence of a bigger entity – economically and politically.

Expressed in the language of this book, Germany's industrialisation was driven by, *inter alia*:

a   *Market integration.* The establishment in 1834 of *Zollvereign*, i.e. Customs Union (CU) of German states removed a key obstacle against the realisation of a broader market, and thereby created one of the pillars for eventual industrialisation (Henderson 1961:11). It created a conducive governance framework.

b   *Enhancement of infrastructural capacities.* Most notably, the German economy benefited from the construction of a railway system. The improved transport infrastructure and network facilitated the utilisation of the natural resource endowment, and spurred the expansion of the manufacturing sector. It also fostered rapid transformation towards a unity state (including but not restricted to the establishment of a railway system).

c   *Capital accumulation*, which was associated with strengthening Financial Resources (FiR) capacities. Thus, reminiscent of the situation in England before, joint-stock companies began to be established first among railway companies, contributing to capital accumulation (Henderson 1961:30). Also, to be sincere, it must be mentioned that at least three other ingredients provided input into industrial production and positively contributed to capital accumulation: cheap labour (including both domestic labour, and slave-like colonial labour in later years), the slave trade and cheap raw materials acquired from colonised territories free of charge.

d   *Enhancement of technological capacities.* From a technological perspective, in the 1830s, Germany saw the improvement of machines, some driven by steam, and the transformation from *workshops* to *factories.* Overall, the production methods were improved through the increased use of better machines. Through this change, industrial productivity, with such industries as coal, for instance, was substantially strengthened by the use of improved methods of production (Henderson 1961).

Overall, though Germany was a late starter, it systematically caught up with England, and by the end of the nineteenth century had become a major pole of industrial development.

3.1.2.2   Lessons from the industrial transformation of Finland

Jäntti and Vartiainen (2009) offer a useful account of Finland's ability to achieve transformation from an agrarian to an industrial economy. The view presented by the authors is that the country is an excellent example of a very successful state-led industrialisation. Finland was a late industrialising nation – the country's industrial transformation did not take off before the Second World War. As soon as the 1930s, the economy was predominantly agrarian. Even by the 1950s, more than 50 per cent of the population were employed in the primary sector. Likewise, in the 1950s, more than 40 per cent of economic output still came from the primary sector. Also, in the 1950s, the country's Gross Domestic Product (GDP) per capita was only half of that of Sweden.

What was the country's industrialisation trajectory? The departure point is that Finland's model of broad development philosophy is deeply anchored into capitalism. The country's constitution underscores the protection of the basic property rights in accordance with capitalist ideology. Therefore, the actual approach used to manage the industrial transformation process was a multi-pronged one, involving a careful blending of *heavy governmental interventions* and *incentives for the private sector,* while preserving the capitalist nature of the country's development ideology.

The interventions by the government sought and contributed to the accumulation of industrial capital, which in turn ensured the establishment of a solid manufacturing base within a capitalist economic setting. Hence, vigorous accumulation of capital became the most important engine for growth. It was mirrored in outstandingly high investment rates.

Politically, the process was guided by long-standing political coalition of the centre-left parties, which emerged as the strongest political bloc after the Second World War. Within the broad ambit of capitalism, the state cooperated with the private sector, and from the 1950s onwards also with the labour movement (through trade unions) in a de facto tripartite social contract.

The core elements of Finland's strategy for attaining industrial competitiveness and profitability can be summed up as follows:

a   A *high rate of capital accumulation* in particular sustained by a high public saving rate. The public savings accounted for as much as 30 per cent of aggregate savings during the 1950s and 1960s. This surplus was channelled partly to:

    i   support private investments in capital equipment throughout the country

    ii Start *state owned enterprises* (SoEs) in some key sectors of the economy, such as basic metal industries, chemical-fertiliser industries and the energy sector. As late as in the 1980s, they contributed about 18 per cent of the total industry value-added in Finland.

b   *High rates of Gross Fixed Capital Formation (GFCF).* For instance, from 1960 to 1984, it was 26.3 per cent of GDP, meaning that among the Organisation for Economic Cooperation and Development (OECD) member states only Norway had a higher rate.

c   *Low interest rates.* The very low interest rates, which were administratively set (through government interventions) created conducive credit conditions for businesses. The other presumably less palatable side of the coin is that, in practice, this meant that the savings individuals and households subsidised the business sector borrowers.

d   *Priority areas of business investment.* This was achieved through (administratively guided) rationing of credit to preferred sectors.

e   *Tripartite social contract.* This involved:

    i   What we would now call Public-Private Partnership (PPP) in the form of pragmatic co-operation between the government and private business sector agents (bankers and business leaders).

    ii Integration of the working class in the decision-making process. This translated the PPP into a tripartite partnership of the public sector, the private sector, and the working class.

The narrated combination of measures over a long period of time helped to mobilise financial resources which, through high rates of investments, were deployed to support a process of sustainable industrial transformation. It should be noted that the policy space that existed during the material time allowed Finland to undertake many measures, to guide and protect its industrial development. Considering the major changes in international economic relations, which have apparently affected also the scope of policy space, some of the pertinent questions for development planners in non-industrialised countries are: Can the measures still be used? Has any country been able to use them, in later periods?

3.1.3 Lessons from East Asia

Many useful lessons that are related to industrialisation experiences of East Asia are captured in several other studies (Lal 1983; Corbo *et al.* 1985; Krueger 1985; Balassa 1988; Harberger 1988; Harvie and Lee 2003, etc.). The emerging picture suggests that success cannot be traced back to a single factor, but to a melange of factors, including conducive policies, 'developmental states' that practiced careful blending of liberalisation and protectionism, which ostensibly led to the creation of the necessary conditions for industrialisation.

For instance, in simplified arguments, it is usually presumed that Korea pursued an EOI (i.e. adoption of outward-oriented industry-led strategy). However, it must be emphasised that in actual fact, the country followed a hybrid strategy, in which the state was also very active. For instance, the state played a key role in the development of large-scale industrial conglomerates, particularly in the 1970s. The resultant (de facto entrepreneurial capacities) enabled the country to attain economies of scale, as well as the essential techno-logical capacities – two very important preconditions for international competitiveness.

Chapter 11 discusses in detail issues related to the industrialisation experience of East Asia, under the leadership of Japan.

3.1.4 Contemporary experiences of emerging economies from outside East Asia

The East Asia economies in general, and China in particular, are often held up as models for other developing countries to emulate in their aspirations to achieve industrial transformation. However, considering the broad context of industrial development (historical, theoretical and practical), it is worthwhile examining the situation in other success stories, and seeing whether Africa can draw lessons from them as well. As such, broadening the review to embrace emerging markets outside of South Asia may be instructive given that the economic development trajectory in, say, Latin America or South-East Asia more closely resembles that of Africa.

3.1.4.1 Turkey's industrial development experience

The 1960s and 1970s saw a shift in economic policy towards state-led national development and strategies based on import-substitution industrialisation (ISI) to move Turkey away from a producer and exporter of agricultural goods. In successive five-year plans, the state used protectionist policies to shield the domestic market and support nascent industrial firms.

As was often the case in many developing countries at the time, policies aimed to foster industrial development protected domestic firms from external competition, but did not necessarily lead to greater incentives for technological upgrading or to higher rates of investment, more generally. Growing pressure from fiscal and balance of payments deficits in the late 1970s led to the adoption of IMF/WB structural adjustment programmes and a shift to export-oriented industrialisation (EOI) overseen by an interim military government from 1980 to 1983 that further opened the economy and reduced the size of the public sector.

In 1989 Turkey experimented significantly with liberalising its capital account, culminating in financial crisis in the mid-1990s and early 2000s. This period also witnessed a wave of Turkish democratic reforms to prepare for EU membership, starting with the Customs Union (CU) in the mid-1990s. Today, manufactured products (such as transport equipment, clothing, iron and steel and electrical machines) contribute a significant portion to Turkey's export basket, but also to the country's import basket, resulting in increasing trade deficits (Memis and Montes 2008; WTO 2008; Onis 2010). The expression is also particularly important, considering that countries from other regions are recording achievements similar to those observed in East Asia.

For example, the Turkish economy grew by 10.2 per cent in the first half of 2011, on the back of consumption-led growth that created a current account deficit of 9 per cent. To cover this shortfall, Turkey attracted roughly US$75bn in foreign capital inflows, of which only US$10–12 billion was in the form of Foreign Direct Investment (FDI). Roughly US$50 billion came in the form of borrowing and portfolio inflows, which raises questions over the sustainability of growth since such flows make the country more vulnerable to destabilising external shocks.

Though the cited factors do not present an exhaustive list, they convey essential experiences of emerging markets outside East Asia, and the way they have influenced industrialisation.

3.1.4.2 Brazil's industrial transformation experience

Brazil's setting on the industrial path did not begin at the end of the 1930s and the beginning of the 1940s, when the country started recording substantial and sustainable positive changes in the sectoral composition of GDP (Baer 1978), with a clear shift towards the secondary sector. However, the first major achievements were recorded in the 1950s, when the secondary sector's share of GDP for the first time overtook the share of the primary sector. This change can be partly deduced from Figure 3.1

In order to understand the factors behind Brazil's industrial transformation, it is instructive to revisit the overall economic policy stance, and the evolvement of the various capacities that actually drove the industrialisation process.

A ECONOMIC POLICY STANCE

Brazil's economic policy stances at different periods give useful clues about the policies that drove its industrial transformation. Luna (2013) broadly identifies three models of economic development, attempting in this manner to match them with specific dates: *export-oriented model* (from 1901 to 1942) during which an average annual growth rate of 4.3 per cent was achieved, *import-substitution model* (from 1943 to 1980) with a growth rate of 7.4 per cent, and *neoliberal model* (ongoing since 1981) during which a growth rate of 2.6 per cent has been recorded.

During the pursuance of the export-oriented model of economic development, agriculture continued to constitute a big share of the country's GDP (see Figure 3.2) and make the biggest contribution to its export economy. However, during

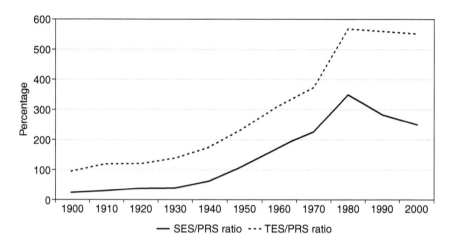

Figure 3.1 Evolution of Brazil's industrial performance, 1900–2000 (source: Author, using data based on Luna (2013). The cited source further quotes Boneli (2003)).

Notes
SES = Secondary Sector; TES = Tertiary Sector; PRS = Primary Sector.

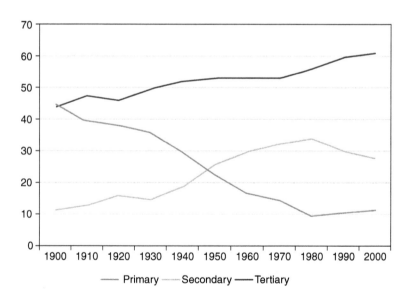

Figure 3.2 Evolution of sectoral composition of Brazil's GDP, 1900–2000, constant 1949 prices (source: Author, using data based on Luna (2013). The cited source further quotes Boneli (2003)).

this period, private banks did also systematically invest substantially in infrastructure, and selected industrial sectors, such as food and textile industries (cf. Furtado 1962; Luna 2013). The modest growth rate of 4.3 per cent is commensurate with an economy still predominated by agriculture (which enjoyed government support), and in which actual industrial transformation was still lacking.

The contribution of the primary sector to the economy declined fast from 44.57 per cent in 1900 to 29.42 per cent in 1940. However, the secondary sector did not perform much better – its GDP share grew slowly from 11.59 per cent in 1900 to 13.08 per cent in 1920, and then to 15.72 per cent in 1930, before declining to 14.81 per cent in 1940 (cf. Luna 2013).

The period guided by the import-substitution model of economic development (1943–1980) was characterised by markedly faster industrialisation. The country produced substantial amounts of both consumer and durable goods, which went beyond the demand and the needs of the domestic primary sector.

The ongoing neoliberal model of economic development (ongoing since 1981) has been characterised by market reforms, embracing the financial market and labour markets (cf. Guth 2006; Hermann 2010; Marquetti *et al.* 2010). By comparison, the average annual growth rate that has been recorded during this period has been less impressive, just 2.6 per cent (cf. Luna 2013).

B CAPACITIES DRIVING INDUSTRIALISATION

Again using the language of this book, actual industrial transformation can be attributed to deliberate measures that developed both FiR capacities and NFR capacities. Notably, the government did among other things develop:

a   *Public industrial enterprises.* For instance, Volta Redonda (steel) and Petrobras (oil) were created at the beginnings of the 1940s (cf. Luna 2013).
b   *Financial institutions.* For instance, the *Superintendência de Moeda e do Crédito* (SMC) which co-ordinated the monetary issuing was created in 1945. Also, *Banco Nacional de Desenvolvimento Econômico e Social* (BNDES) was established in 1952. This development bank provided long-term financing. Indeed, empirical research shows that BNDES made important contribution to industrialisation from 1952 until the 1970s (cf. Luna 2013).

It is therefore not surprising that by the end of the 1970s, Brazil was the most industrialised country in Latin America (Baddini 1998; Guth 2006; Luna 2013).

3.1.4.3 Summary

More generally the similarities of the factors that have shaped the contemporary development process of the key non-East Asian emerging markets embrace:

a   Economic policy framework. This is characterised by comprehensive and speedy liberalisation of the economic policy space.

b   Democratisation pressure. This is characterised by demands for greater civil liberties.
c   Regional integration. This is associated with the increasing role regional economic communities (RECs) play in policy design and management of the implementation of the same.
d   Economic management practices. These mirror the capacity differences among the governments of the individual economies.
e   Inward globalisation of industry. This is characterised by greater degrees of influence held by outside actors.

3.2 Links between industrialisation and economic growth and development: lessons from reviews of selected empirical econometric studies

The findings of a relatively large body of empirical studies support the argument that industrialisation is an engine of growth. Among the scholars who have addressed the subject and come to this conclusion are Fagersberg and Verspagen (1999, 2002), Guardano (2005), Tregenna (2007), Rodrik (2008), Szirmai and Verspagen (2010), Timmer and de Vries (2009), Szirmai (2011).

3.2.1 Studies by Szirmai (2011)

Szirmai (2011) in the study 'Industrialisation as an engine of growth in developing countries, 1950–2005' examined the emergence of manufacturing in developing countries in the given period. The aim of the study was to explore the theoretical postulations and empirics of industrialisation as an engine of growth. The sample used for the study included 63 developing countries and 16 advanced economies.

The author finds that manufacturing tends to be more important as an engine of growth in developing countries than in advanced economies. During the observation period, manufacturing was more important from 1950 to 1973 than after 1973. However, in spite of statistical evidence of the importance of manufacturing for growth in developing countries, not all expectations of the 'engine of growth' hypothesis are clearly demonstrated. Conversely, the author observes that the more general historical evidence provides more solid support for the 'industrialisation as engine of growth' hypothesis.

Overall, the author argues that industrialisation is essential for a successful catch-up in developing countries. In this context, industrialisation is characterised as a 'single global process of structural change, in which separate countries follow different paths depending on their initial conditions and moment of their entry into the industrial race' (Szirmai 2011:1). This underlines the centrality of country particularities, as key considerations in specifying a feasible industrial development agenda.

3.2.2 *Study by Szirmai and Verspagen (2010)*

In the comprehensive study 'Is manufacturing still an engine of growth in developing countries?', Szirmai and Verspagen (2010) conducted an econometric analysis of the role of manufacturing as a driver of growth in developing countries in the period 1950–2005. They used a panel data set for a sample of 90 countries: 21 advanced countries and 69 developing countries. For part of the analyses, they split the sample into four groups: Asia, Latin America, Africa and advanced countries. For similar reasons, they split the observation period into three distinct periods: 1950–1970, 1970–1990 and 1990–2005. The data included series of value-added shares (in current prices) for manufacturing, industry, agriculture and services for covering the observation period.

Regression analysis is used to analyse the relationships between sectoral shares and per capita GDP growth for different time periods and different groups of countries. The dimensions analysed include the contribution of manufacturing to growth, as well as the contribution of manufacturing and services to growth accelerations. Hausman and Rodrik definitions of growth accelerations are used. The focus of the analysis was the 'Engine of Growth Hypothesis' which posits that manufacturing is the key sector in economic development.

Specifically, the authors sought to answer the following research questions:

a   Is there a positive relationship between the value-added share of manufacturing and growth of GDP per capita? Their hypothesis is that there is a positive relationship for the 90 countries in the period 1950–2005.

b   Is the relationship between the value-added share of manufacturing and per capita GDP growth stronger than that between the value-added share of services and growth of per capita GDP? Their hypothesis is that the relationship between manufacturing and growth is stronger than the relationship between services and growth.

c   Does the relationship between the share of manufacturing and growth of GDP per capita become weaker over time? Their working hypothesis is that the relationship between manufacturing and growth will be stronger in the period 1950–1975 than in the period 1975–2005.

d   Is there a positive relationship between the share of manufacturing and the rate of growth during growth accelerations? Their working hypothesis is that the impact of manufacturing on growth is stronger during growth accelerations.

e   Is the relationship between the share of manufacturing and growth during growth accelerations stronger or weaker than that between the share of services and growth? Their working hypothesis is that the coefficient of manufacturing share is higher than that of services in general and that the difference between the coefficients is greater in acceleration periods than in non-acceleration periods.

f   Are there systematic differences between the role of manufacturing in countries with different characteristics (e.g. level of GDP per capita, human capital and region)?

Accordingly, the analyses were guided by two hypotheses:

a   The relationship between share of manufacturing and growth is weaker at higher levels of GDP per capita than at lower levels (i.e. more advanced economies are less dependent on manufacturing for their growth).
b   The relationship between the share of manufacturing and growth will be stronger in countries with high levels of human capital.

The findings of the empirical analysis corroborated the postulations made by the engine of growth hypothesis. For the whole sample, the share of manufacturing was found to be positively related to economic growth and this effect was more pronounced for the poorer countries. No such effects were found for services. These results are consistent with their first two hypotheses on the importance of manufacturing. The role of manufacturing seems of particular importance during growth accelerations. Services also play a role in growth accelerations, but are less important than manufacturing.

The impact of manufacturing is more important in the middle period (1970–1990) than in the early period (1950–1970) and then becomes less important in the final period (1990–2005). With regard to services, they find significant effects in the first two periods (1950–1970 and 1970–1990) and hardly any effects in the final period (1990–2005) – which contrasts the predictions concerning the increasing significance of services and of service-driven growth.

There are also curious differences among country groupings, when the sample is broken down. Hence, manufacturing seem to impact growth in Latin America, but the same could not be proved for the other groupings of developing countries. Besides, while manufacturing continues to be important in the advanced economies, its effects decreases as the concerned countries come closer to US income levels, but the effects of services increase.

3.2.3 *Rodrik (2008)*

Structural change is essential for economic growth. However, rather than being an automatic process, it is stimulated by certain factors, including those related to the right policy stance. In this connection, in the paper 'The real exchange rate and economic growth', Rodrik (2008) offers some useful insights about the relationship between industrialisation and economic growth. Apparently, countries that pursue a policy stance in favour of competitive or undervalued currencies tend to experience more growth-enhancing structural change. These findings are in keeping with other studies, which have documented positive effects of undervaluation on modern tradable industries. Arguably, undervaluation acts as a subsidy on those industries and facilitates their expansion.

3.2.4 *Study by Timmer and de Vries (2009)*

Another insightful study in this connection, 'Structural change and growth accelerations in Asia and Latin America: A new sectoral dataset', is attributed to Timmer and de Vries (2009). Using growth accounting techniques, they examine the contributions of different sectors in periods of growth accelerations, in periods of normal growth and in periods of deceleration. In periods of normal growth they find that manufacturing contributes most. In periods of acceleration, this leading role is taken over by the service sector, though manufacturing continues to have an important positive contribution. Thus, while affirming the role of the manufacturing sector, they also confirm the increasing importance of the service sector in driving economic growth.

3.2.5 *Study by Tregenna (2007)*

In the study 'Which sectors can be engines of growth and employment in South Africa?: An analysis of manufacturing and services' by Tregenna (2007), the author examines the linkages between the manufacturing and services sectors in South Africa, and between each of them and the rest of the domestic economy, based on analysis of input-output tables and employment trends. The study reveals that manufacturing is particularly important as a source of demand for the services sector as well as the rest of the economy through its strong backward linkages, which suggests that in this respect a decline in manufacturing could negatively affect future growth. Services are especially important in terms of employment creation, both direct and indirect.

3.2.6 *Study by Guardano (2005)*

In a study on the 'The determinants of industrialization in developing countries, 1960–2005', Guardano (2005) estimated the equation for explaining manufacturing growth and its role in economic growth, based on the model developed by Cornwall (1977). The estimations used a mixed sample of 74 developed and developing countries for the period 1960–2005.

The author came to the following conclusions:

a   Industrialisation is faster for larger countries with an undeveloped industrial base and development strategies based on trade openness, undervaluation, skills and knowledge accumulation.
b   From 1970 to the mid 1990s technological backwardness and undervaluation were the main drivers of industrialisation.
c   Since 1995 investments in knowledge accumulation have become increasingly crucial for industrialisation.

3.2.7 Studies by Fagersberg and Verspagen

Two studies conducted by Fagersberg and Verspagen are among empirical work whose findings concur with the hypothesis that manufacturing is an engine of growth. Accordingly, both offer useful insights about the impact of industrialisation on development.

In the study 'Technology-gaps, Innovation-diffusion and Transformation: an Evolutionary Interpretation', Fagersberg and Verspagen (2002) examine the impact of the shares of manufacturing and services in three periods: 1966–1972, 1973–1983 and 1984–1995 for a sample of 76 countries. They find that manufacturing has much more positive contribution before 1973 than after.

In an earlier study 'Modern capitalism in the 1970s and 1980s' the same authors (Fagerberg and Verspagen 1999) did a regression of real economic growth rates on growth rates of manufacturing. If the coefficient of manufacturing growth is higher than the share of manufacturing in GDP, this is interpreted as supporting the engine of growth hypothesis. The authors find that manufacturing was typically an engine of growth in developing countries in East Asia and Latin America, but that there was no significant effect of manufacturing in the advanced economies.

The interpretation in both papers is that the period 1950–1973 offered special opportunities for catch-up through the absorption of mass production techniques in manufacturing from the USA. After 1973, Information and Communication Technologies (ICTs) started to become more important as a source of productivity growth, especially in the 1990s. These technologies are no longer within the exclusive domain of manufacturing, but operate in the service sector.

References

Baddini, C. (1998). *A atuacão do sistema BNDES como instituição financeira no período 1952/1996.* Master Dissertation. Universidade Estadual de Campinas.

Baer, W. (1978). Evaluating the impact of Brazilian industrialization. *Luso – Brazilian Review* 2: 178–190.

Balassa, B. (1988). The lessons of East Asian development: An overview. *Economic Development and Cultural Change* 36 (3): S273–S290.

Birnie, A. (1953). *An Economic History of Europe.* London: Methuen and Company Ltd.

Blanqui, J. (1968). *History of Political Economy in Europe.* New York: Augustus M. Kelley (Translation by Emily J. Leonard of the fourth edition of the book published in French in 1882 by G.P. Putnam's Sons, New York).

Boneli, R. (2003). Nível de actividade e mudança estrutural. In IBGE (ed.) *Estadisticas do século.* Brasil: IBGE, pp. 228–278.

Corbo, V., Krueger, A. and Ossa, F. (eds) (1985). *Export Oriented Development Strategies: The Success of Five Newly Industrializing Countries.* Boulder, CO: Westview Press.

Cornwall, J. (1977). *Modern Capitalism: Its Growth and Transformation.* New York: St. Martin's Press.

Fagerberg, J. and Verspagen, B. (1999). Modern capitalism in the 1970s and 1980s. In M. Setterfield (ed.) *Growth, Employment and Inflation.* Houndmills, Basingstoke: Macmillan.

Fagerberg, J. and Verspagen, B. (2002). Technology-gaps, innovation-diffusion and transformation: An evolutionary interpretation. *Research Policy* 31: 1291–1304.

Furtado, C. (1962). *A Pré-Revolução Brasileira* (The Brazilian Pre-Revolution). Rio: Fundo de Cultura.

Guardano, F. (2005). *The determinants of industrialization in developing countries, 1960–2005.* Unpublished paper. UNU-MERIT and Maastricht University.

Guth, F. (2006). *O BNDES nos anos 1990: uma análise keynesia.* Master Dissertation. UFRJ.

Harberger, A. (1988). *Growth, Industrialization, and Economic Structure: Latin America and East Asia Compared: Reflections on Social Project Evaluation.* Nankang, Taipei, Taiwan, Republic of China: Institute of Economics, Academia Sinica.

Harvie, C. and Lee, K. (2003). *Export led industrialisation and growth – Korea's economic miracle 1962–89.* Faculty of Commerce – Economics Working Papers. University of Wollongong.

Henderson, W. (1961). *Industrial Revolution on the Continent.* London: Frank Cass & Co. Ltd.

Hermann, J. (2010). *Los bancos de desarrollo en la era de la liberalización financiera* (Development Banks in the era of financial liberalisation). Santiago: CEPAL.

Hill, C. (1969). *Reformation to Industrial Revolution.* Harmondsworth, UK: Penguin Books.

Hobsbawm, E. (1968). *Industry and Empire.* New York: Pantheon Books.

Jäntti, M. and Vartiainen, J. (2009). *What can developing countries learn from Finland's industrial transformation?* WIDER *Angle* Newsletter. United Nations University World Institute for Development Economics Research.

Koenigsberger, H. (1987). *Early Modern Europe.* New York: Longman.

Krueger, A. (1985). The experiences and lessons of Asia's super exporters. In V. Corbo, A. Krueger and F. Ossa (eds), *Export Oriented Development Strategies: The Success of Five Newly Industrialized Countries.* Boulder, CO: Westview Press, pp. 187–212.

Lal, D. (1983). *The Poverty of Development Economics.* London: Institute of Economic Affairs. Hobart Paperback No. 16.

Luna, V. (2013). *BNDES' contribution to Brazilian industrialization from 1952 to present day.* Research on money and finance. Economics Department. University of Utah. Discussion Paper No. 42. July.

Marquetti, A., Filho, E. and Lautert, V. (2010). The profit rate of Brazil: 1953 to 2003. *Review of Radical Political Economics* XX(X): 1–20.

Memis, E. and Montes, M. (2008). *Who's afraid of industrial policy?* UNDP Discussion Paper. July 2008, UNDP Regional Center Colombo.

Onis, Z. (2010). Crises and transformations in Turkish political economy. *Turkish Policy Quarterly* 9 (3): 46–61.

Rodrik, D. (2008). The real exchange rate and economic growth. *Brookings Papers on Economic Activity.* Fall. pp. 365–412.

Szirmai, A. (2011). Industrialisation as an engine of growth in developing countries, 1950–2005. *Structural Change and Economic Dynamics* (6 February 2011).

Szirmai, A. and Verspagen, B. (2010). *Is manufacturing still an engine of growth in developing countries?* Paper prepared for the 31st General Conference of The International Association for Research in Income and Wealth, St Gallen, Switzerland, 22–28 August.

Timmer, M. and de Vries, G. (2009). Structural change and growth accelerations in Asia and Latin America: A new sectoral dataset. *Cliometrica* 3(2): 165–190.

Thomson, A. (1973). *The Dynamics of Industrial Revolution*. London: Edward Arnold.

Tregenna, F. (2007). *Which sectors can be engines of growth and employment in South Africa?: An analysis of manufacturing and services*. Paper presented at the UNU-WIDER CIBS Conference.

Wallerstein, I. (1974). *The Modern World-System*, vol. I: Capitalist Agriculture and the Origins of the European World-Economy in the Sixteenth Century. New York and London: Academic Press.

WTO (2008). *Trade Policy Review: Turkey 2007*. Geneva: World Trade Organization.

Xing, L. (2007). *East Asian regional integration: From Japan-led 'flying-geese' to China-centred 'bamboo capitalism'*. Centre for Comparative Integration Studies. CCIS Research Series. Working Paper No. 3.

4 Integration in the global industrial economy of the African and comparator regions

Francis A.S.T. Matambalya

4.1 Precursor: comparative overview of integration in the global economy

Effective participation in the global economy is a multi-dimensional under-taking, of which a country's or region's performance vis-à-vis industrial activ-ities is a crucial element. Pertinent industrial activities embrace the entire value chain, from investments, to production, to trade.

Moreover, a process of gargantuan proportions, as industrial transformation, would be revealed in a country's or region's economic data. In essence, such a process would be revealed by accelerated growth of many dimensions of the economy along the entire economic value chain: from the way resources are mobilised and deployed (invested), to production, and to trade.

Bearing these considerations in mind, a preliminary review of Africa's parti-cipation in the global economy offers useful insights about the character of its industrial economy. Therefore, as a precursor to the discussions in Section 4.2, which is focused on the industrial sector, this section broadly portrays Africa's performance in three important dimensions of the global economic value chain: Africa in total international investments, aggregate economic output, and trade.

4.1.1 Africa's investments landscape in an international perspective

Several indicators can be used to indicate the magnitude and direction of change of Africa's investments, in comparison to other regions of the world. In the following subsections, Africa's position in the global investment landscape is analysed with assistance of developments related to Gross Fixed Capital Formation (GFCF),[1] and international investments particularly Foreign Direct Investments (FDI).

4.1.1.1 Gross investments in Africa and comparator regions

The GFCF provides a good proxy for gross investments. The term refers to the increase in the capital stock resulting from investment spending. It denotes the net increase in physical assets (investment minus disposals). Concretely, it captures investments for land improvements (fences, ditches, drain, and so on);

plant, machinery, and equipment purchases. It further includes investments in the construction of transport infrastructure (e.g. roads, railways, etc.), physical educational infrastructure (e.g. schools, universities, etc.), office premises, physical health infrastructure (e.g. hospitals), private residential dwellings, and commercial and industrial buildings. However, it does not account for the consumption (depreciation) of fixed capital, and also does not include land purchases.

Understanding the GFCF is important, because it explicitly touches many areas in which investments are needed in order to propel industrial transformation. Empirical evidences reveal that the growth in the size of capital stock of industry is an important co-driver of the industrialisation process, alongside other factors, and that its significance is particularly high during the early stages of industrialisation (Jäntti and Vartiainen 2009; Kahan 1978).

Table 4.1 shows comparable values of aggregate Gross Domestic Product (GDP) and GFCF data for the world, Africa, and other groups of countries from 1970 to 2010. For each group of country, it also presents the group's GFCF as a ratio of group's GDP, and the group's GFCF as a ratio of World GFCF.

Two important observations can be made from the picture portrayed in Table 4.1:

a   During the 40-year period from 1970 to 2010, Africa's share of global GFCF was only 1.9 per cent, compared to Asia's 15.7 per cent. Certainly, Africa's share is very low, even if population differences among the groups of countries are taken into account.
b   From conventional wisdom, as well as from observation of the performance of countries, we can deduce that, during the industrial transformation phase, a country would invest around 25 per cent of its GDP into capital formation. When the developing countries groups are taken, it appears that only Asia (at 27.3 per cent) is fulfilling this condition, while Africa (at 18.4 per cent) is very far off-target.

The observations suggest that gross investments do not reach the threshold needed in order to set Africa on an industrial transformation path. The annual average of GFCF per capita in US$ from 1970 to 2010, which are presented in Figure 4.1, underline this gloomy outlook.

4.1.1.2 Total international investments in Africa and comparator regions

FDI plays a key role in integrating countries in the global economy, by creating international production chains. In this regard, by making investment resources available in financial resource deficient countries, FDI contributes towards a geographical wide-spreading of production (or invariably: de-concentration of production from a few areas).

Figure 4.2 depicts FDI inflows to various country groups (developed, developing) and developing regions (Africa, America, Asia, and Oceania). As evidenced by the graphic, the trend of FDI flows to developing countries as a group is encouraging, starting to pick up in the 1990s and their values literally

Table 4.1 Comparable GDP and GFCF for groups of countries from 1970 to 2010

	Aggregate values at constant prices (2005) and constant exchange rates (2005)		Group GFCF as a % of	
	GDP trillion USD	GFCF trillion USD	Group GDP	World GFCF
World	1,272.472199	265.9702426	20.9	100
Developing economies	258.5887492	62.47622268	24.2	23.5
Developed economies	976.5995137	190.3620608	19.5	71.6
Developing economies: Africa	27.304784	5.016098333	18.4	1.9
Developing economies: America	77.42566558	15.44768743	20.0	5.8
Developing economies: Asia	153.2259885	41.88291399	27.3	15.7
Developing economies: Oceania	0.6323110807	0.1295229189	20.5	0.049
Least developed countries	7.942726685	1.419020858	17.9	0.534

Source: Author. Based on UNCTAD (2013).

Notes
GDP = Gross Domestic Product; GFCF = Gross Fixed Capital Formation.

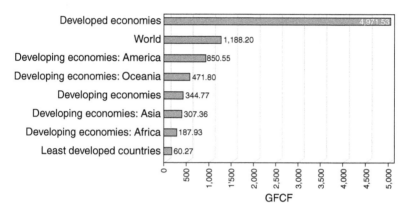

Figure 4.1 Annual average of GFCF per capita in US$, 1970–2010 (source: Author. Based on UNCTAD (2013)).

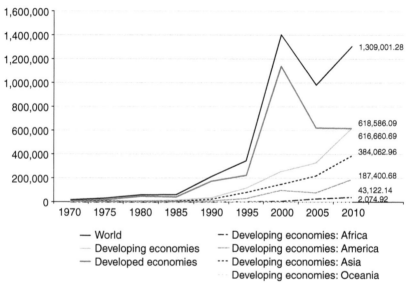

Figure 4.2 Total FDI inflows in US$ million, 1970–2010, selected regions and years (source: Author. Based on UNCTAD (2013)).

converging with the value of comparable flows to developed countries by 2010. According to data from *UNCTADstat* database, in 2010, developed countries recorded FDI inflows worth US$618,586.09 million, while the comparable value for developing countries was US$616,660.69 million (equivalent to 99.7 per cent of inflows into developed countries).

However, it is also visible that not all developing regions play similar roles in the evolution of global FDI: significant improvements in inflows to Asia and

America are contrasted by subdued performances by Africa and Oceania. Africa's poor performance is alarming, bearing in mind the continent's huge size both geographically and in terms of share of global population:

a   With an area of 30,221,512 square kilometres (equalling 6 per cent of the Earth's total surface area and 20.4 per cent of the total land area), Africa is the second largest continent. It is surpassed only by Asia, which covers 44,579,000 square kilometres (equal to 8.7 per cent of the Earth's total surface area and 30 per cent of total land area).
b   In 2011, Africa's population stood at 994,527,534, compared to the world's 6,974,036,375. Hence, Africa's population was equivalent to 14.3 per cent of the global population. Again, only Asia is more populous, with a population of 4,140,336,501 in the same year, which is equivalent to 59.4 per cent of the world population.

Furthermore, Africa's FDI inflows increased only 34-fold,[2] when its US dollar values for 1970 and 2010 are compared. This is inferior when compared with Asia's increase of 450-fold, and the developing economies' 160-fold increase. This performance was only better than the performance of the developing countries in Oceania, which are largely small island states (Figure 4.3).

The growth trends demonstrated further in Figure 4.4 show that the share of total global FDI flowing to developing countries has over time risen from 28.1 per cent in 1970 to reach 47.1 per cent in 2010, literally converging with the share of developed countries (which dropped from 71.9 per cent in 1970 to 47.3 per cent in 2010; and has been decreasing since 2000).

However, when data of the developing country group is evaluated separately for each region, the dispersion in FDI performance across the regions of the world remains quite remarkable. In this regard, Africa's miserable performance becomes clear, as shown in Figures 4.5 and 4.6. The continent's share of aggregate global FDI inflows declined from 9.5 per cent in 1970 to 3.3 per cent in 2010. In contrast, Asia's share grew from 6.1 per cent in 1970 to 29.3 per cent in 2010. In fact, Africa's average share of global FDI inflows during the observation years (1970, 1975, 1980, 1985, 1990, 1995, 2000, 2005, and 2010) was only 3.1 per cent (Figure 4.5).

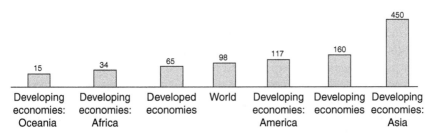

Figure 4.3 Number of times FDI inflows increased between 1970 and 2010 (source: Author. Based on UNCTAD (2013)).

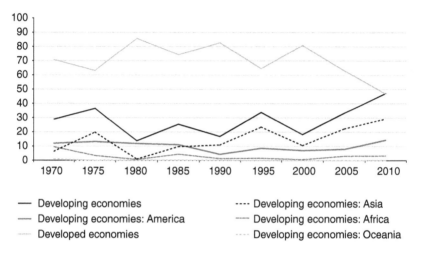

Figure 4.4 Regional shares (in %) of global inward FDI inflows, 1970–2010, selected years (source: Author. Based on UNCTAD (2013)).

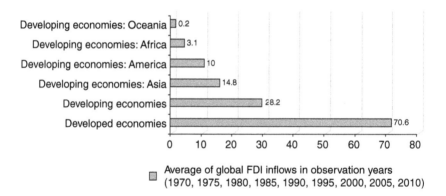

Figure 4.5 Average shares (in %) of global FDI inflows for various country groups (source: Author. Based on UNCTAD (2013)).

Figure 4.6 gives further insights about Africa's integration into global investments by comparing the continent's FDI per capita inflows and deviation of FDI per capita inflows from the global average of US$218.59 (in 2011) with that of other regions. Notably, Africa received the lowest per capita in that year, transforming into a deviation of US$177.78 from the global average. Also at US$188, Africa received the lowest FDI per capita from 1970 to 2010. By comparison, per capita inflows for the world, developed economies, developing economies, American developing economies, Asian developing economies, and Oceania's developing economies were US$1,188, US$4,972, US$345, US$851, US$307, and US$60 respectively.

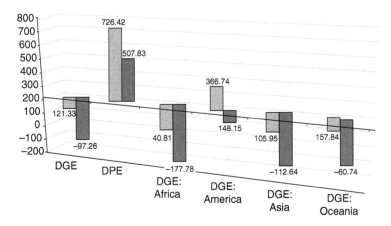

□ Country group average   ■ Deviation of country group average from world average

Figure 4.6 Integration into global investment: characteristics of per capita FDI inflows in 2011 (source: Author. Based on UNCTAD (2013)).

Notes
DGE = developing economies; DPE = developed economies.

Also important are the relations implied in Figure 4.7, which shows FDI as a percentage of GFCF from 1990 to 2012. In addition to what is portrayed in the figure, a direct comparison of the years 1990 and 2012 shows 1.99-fold, 1.69-fold, 2.29-fold, *4.05-fold*, 3.91-fold, 4.9-fold, and 1.85-fold increase of FDI to GFCF ratio for the world, developed economies, developing economies, *African developing economies*, Asian developing economies, American developing economies, and Oceania's developing economies respectively.

The overall verdict is that Africa is more dependent on FDI for its capital formation than the global average as well as the average of the developing countries. Imperatively, if it is to emulate Asia's example, Africa must mobilise and deploy more resources from its own sources.

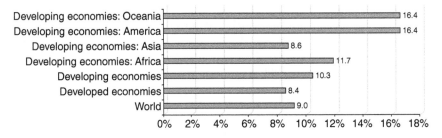

Figure 4.7 FDI inflows as a percentage of GFCF, average of 1990–2012 (source: Based on UNCTAD, FDI/TNC (available at: www.unctadstat.org/fdistatistics)).

4.1.2 Contribution of Africa and comparator regions to global economic output

The global economy is in a constant forward motion. From its 1960 level (expressed in constant 2000 US$), the global economy measured in GDP had grown 5.9-fold (or by 590 per cent) by 2011: increasing from US$7.229 trillion in 1960 to US$42.567 trillion in 2010. The matching changes in GDP per capita were from US$2,378 in 1960 to US$6,105 in 2011, marking an increase of 257 per cent (cf. knoema.com/mhrzolg#World).[3]

Therefore, a systematic improvement of economic output at various levels of aggregation is a necessary (even though not a sufficient) condition for economic development and betterment of welfare, as well as competitive integration of a given country or region in the global economy.

This subsection uses statistics related to economic output, to assess Africa's position in the global economy. In this connection, Africa is compared with other major regions of the world. The statistics used provide important information about the size, structure, and dynamics of the world's economies. Viewed over time, these statistics show the health of an economy and the quality of macroeconomic management. Viewed across countries and regions, they reveal the variations in the patterns of development achieved.

Overall, they inform different interest groups about the results of economic development initiatives, and thereby guide them in making choices about alternative development strategies. In this connection, increasing shares of global economic output, changing structure of economic output away from primary commodities towards value-added products, and faster growth rates of outputs would be indications of the healthy evolution of the economies of developing countries. Needless to say, this kind of transformation is essential, because developing countries need to systematically close the gap with richer economies with a view to catching up. Moreover, achieving these performance targets (i.e. narrowing the gap to advanced economies) will be a good measure of the adequacy of investments in physical capital, human capital, etc.

4.1.2.1 Shares of global output

Africa's ambiguous economic development picture is captured in the following narrative, which is extracted from Leke *et al.* (2010)

> Africa's economic pulse has quickened infusing the continent with new economic life. Real GDP rose by 4.9 percent a year from 2000 through 2008, more than twice its pace in the 1980s and 1990s.... Yet Africa's collective GDP at $1.6 trillion in 2008, is now roughly equal to Brazil's or Russia's...

Indeed, a sombre view of Africa's economic performance is that the continent has still got a long way to go. Its share of Gross World Output (GWO) is a good indirect indicator of the continent's poor integration in global industrial production. As shown in Table 4.2, which uses real GDP as a proxy for GWO, while the share of developing countries as a group has been rising, the continent's

Table 4.2 Evolution of country group or regional shares of global output at constant prices and constant exchange rates (2005) (%)

Country or regional group	1970	1975	1980	1985	1990	1995	2000	2005	2010	Average of observation years
Developing economies	13.8	15.5	16.8	16.9	17.3	20.0	21.1	23.7	28.6	19.3
Developed economies	82.8	81.0	79.4	79.1	78.5	77.8	76.9	73.9	68.8	77.6
Developing economies: Africa	2.2	2.2	2.3	2.2	2.0	2.0	2.0	2.2	2.4	2.2
Developing economies: America	5.4	6.2	6.8	6.3	5.8	6.0	6.0	5.9	6.4	6.1
Developing economies: Asia	6.1	7.0	7.6	8.4	9.5	12.0	13.1	15.6	19.7	11.0
Developing economies: Oceania	0.052	0.053	0.047	0.047	0.050	0.054	0.049	0.048	0.050	0.050

Source: Author. Based on UNCTAD (2013).

share has been stagnating over time. The rise of the share of developing countries from 13.8 per cent in 1970 to 28.6 per cent in 2010 was substantially driven by the developing countries from Asia, whose share grew by 13.6 percentage points during the observation period.

More recent observations show that the average annual percentage change of output of *emerging and developing countries*[4] taken as a group from 2004 to 2011 was 6.78 per cent (Table 4.3). The comparable growth rates for developing countries Asia, Sub-Saharan Africa (SSA), Middle East and North Africa (MENA), and Latin America and the Caribbean (LAC) were 9.0 per cent, 5.7 per cent, 4.9 per cent, and 4.4 per cent respectively (IMF 2012).

Hence, SSA deviated by −1.08 from the cited average of the emerging and developing countries. Notably, only Asian developing countries recorded positive deviation of the magnitude of 2.2 per cent. The comparable deviations for MENA and LAC were −1.88 and −2.38 respectively.

4.1.2.2 Simple estimates of economic productivity

There is a general consensus that GDP per capita is a rough indicator of a nation's prosperity, while the GDP per employed person provides a general picture of a country's productivity. The GDP per person employed is obtained by dividing GDP by total employment in the economy.

Figure 4.8 depicts the GDP per employed person index, computed as a ratio of the world average (at 1980 constant prices and exchange rates). The values of GDP per capita employed are averages of the years 1990 to 2005. As is clearly notable, African countries (which are grouped either in SSA and MENA), are below the world average. The implicit productivity gap that Africa has in comparison to other regions of the world explains, at least in part, why the continent's share of global economic output is so small and under-proportionate.

Table 4.3 Comparison of the changes in total economic output (%)

Year	2004	2005	2006	2007	2008	2009	2010	2011
Annual change of output of emerging and developing countries								
	7.5	7.30	8.20	8.70	6.0	2.8	7.5	6.2
Country group's deviation from the annual change of output of emerging and developing countries								
Developing countries: Asia	1.0	2.2	2.1	2.7	1.8	4.3	2.2	1.6
Sub-Saharan Africa	−0.4	−1.1	−1.8	−1.6	−0.4	0.0	−2.2	−1.1
Middle East and North Africa	−1.3	−1.7	−2.1	−3.1	−1.3	−0.1	−2.6	−2.7
Latin America and the Caribbean	−1.5	−2.6	−2.5	−2.9	−1.8	−4.4	−1.3	−1.7

Source: Author. Based on IMF (2012).

Notes
The 'emerging and developing economies' include: emerging economies from central and Eastern Europe as well as the Commonwealth of Independent States (CIS); and developing countries from Sub-Saharan Africa (SSA), Middle East and North Africa (MENA), Latin America and the Caribbean (LAC), and Asia (for detailed description, see IMF (2012)).

Figure 4.8 further demonstrates that in contrast, GDP per employed person index for the other groups of developing countries included in the assessment (i.e. South Asia, and East Asia and the Pacific) are substantially above the world average.

4.1.2.3 Structure of economic output

A survey of the structure of the output of most mature industrialised countries show that their manufacturing to GDP ratio are rather high, though of late they have been eroded by the ever-increasing share of services. Hence, in 1990, the ratios were 28 per cent for Germany, 26 per cent for Japan, and 18.3 for the USA. In 2009, these changed to 19.1 per cent for Germany, 20.2 per cent for Japan, and 10.1 for the USA (UN 2011).

Moreover, a scrutiny of the comparable structures of output of dynamically industrialising economies show that they maintain very high manufacturing to GDP ratios over an extended time period, usually well in the excess of 20 per cent. The phenomenal figures for China were 35.5 per cent, 40.6 per cent, 40.5 per cent, and 42.1 per cent in 1990, 2000, 2005, and 2009 respectively (UN 2011).

These observations appear to be consistent with empirical studies, which found manufacturing to be more important as an engine of growth in developing countries than in advanced economies. Thus, during the industrialisation push, countries customarily achieve very high rates of manufacturing to GDP ratios (cf. Chapter 3 of this book).

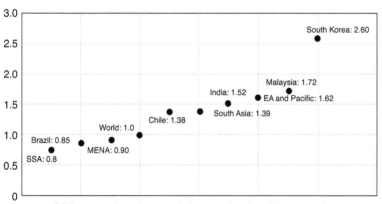

● GDP per employed person index as ratio of world average (averages of 1990 to 2005, at constant 1980 exchange rates and prices)

Positioning compared to world average (herewith: 1.0)

Figure 4.8 GDP per employed person index as ratio of world average (source: Author. Based on World Bank (2008)).

Notes
EA = East Asia; MENA = Middle East and North Africa; SSA = Sub-Saharan Africa.

Bearing these facts in mind, let us look at Table 4.4, which shows the structures of GDP of the world and groups of countries (developed economies, developing economies, developing countries in Africa, developing countries in America, developing countries in Asia, and developing countries in Oceania) by kind of economic activity, as reported by UNCTAD (cf. UN 2011). The structural differences underscore Africa's gap from the rest of the world in terms of the development of manufacturing. Notably, not only does the continent have the relatively smallest share of manufacturing to GDP ratio among the major regions of the world, but also this ratio consistently declined during the observation of years without ever having critical levels.

Moreover, of the major regions of the world, Africa has the highest share of agriculture to GDP ratio, which in 2009 was 3.4 fold, 6.5 fold and 1.3 fold of that of the world average, average of developed countries, and average of developing countries respectively.

Invariably, Africa's economies are largely at the pre-industrial levels of development. Also, at this rate of transformation of the GDP, Africa's dream of catching up with the rest of the world in terms of the development of the industrial sector seems to be unrealistic, unless something dramatic happens.

4.1.2.4 Growth and drivers of economic output

The rate of growth of GDP gives useful hints about the performance of the economy. Because of the need to catch up, African countries must grow faster than other economies. Using data from *UNCTADstat* (UNCTAD 2013), Figures 4.9

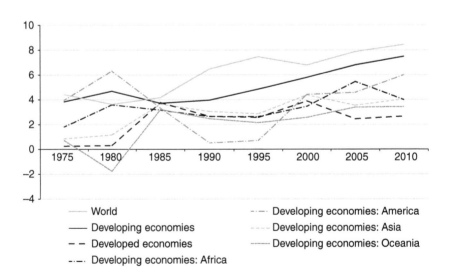

Figure 4.9 Comparative growth rates of real GDP (at constant 2005 prices and exchange rates) in selected country groupings (source: Author. Based on UNCTAD (2013)).

Table 4.4 Structures of GDP of selected groups of countries and years: sectoral shares of GDP

Sector		Year	Economy		Developing				
			World	Developed	All	Africa	America	Asia	Oceania
Agriculture		1990	5.4	2.8	14.2	18.3	7.2	17.0	15.5
		1995	4.3	2.2	11.9	17.0	6.7	13.8	17.4
		2000	3.6	1.7	10.3	15.4	5.7	11.7	16.2
		2009	4.0	1.4	9.7	16.8	5.7	10.2	14.7
Industry	Manufacturing	1990	21.7	21.4	21.7	15.0	20.6	23.8	7.9
		1995	20.4	19.8	22.5	14.8	18.6	25.7	7.9
		2000	19.2	18.2	22.6	12.6	18.4	26.1	10.0
		2009	17.6	14.7	24.3	10.1	16.4	28.7	10.5
	Other	1990	11.1	10.5	13.9	20.2	12.2	13.4	14.9
		1995	10.2	9.5	12.7	18.1	11.5	12.4	14.7
		2000	9.9	8.8	13.7	22.7	13.3	12.6	15.4
		2009	11.4	9.6	14.9	27.8	16.4	12.8	16.8
Services		1990	61.9	65.4	50.3	46.7	60.0	45.8	61.6
		1995	65.1	68.5	52.9	50.2	63.1	48.1	60.0
		2000	67.2	71.3	53.4	49.3	62.6	49.6	58.5
		2009	67.0	74.3	51.1	45.2	61.5	48.3	58.1

Source: Based on UN (2011). UNCTAD Statistical Year Book 2011. United Nations Conference on Trade and Development. New York and Geneva. Pages 424, 428, 432 and 435.

and 4.10 present comparative overviews of the rates of growth of total GDP as well as GDP per capita for Africa and comparator regions.

The long-term growth trend (1975 to 2010) presented in Figure 4.9 reveals that throughout the observation period, Africa's growth rate remained below the developing country average, as well as the average of the Asian developing countries, despite being above the global average for some time. Moreover, after it peaked in 2005, it has been growing much slower than almost all the developing regions, except Oceania, and tending towards convergence with the average global growth rate.

Further scrutiny of data reveals two further important facts. First, as demonstrated in Figure 4.10, the growth rates of Africa's GDP per capita have consistently remained below of those of Asia; and since the second half of the 1980s, also below the average growth rate of developing countries.

In fact, if the average growth rates of GDP per capita for the sample years (i.e. 1975, 1980, 1985, 1990, 1995, 2000, 2005, and 2010) of the different country groups are computed and compared, Africa's poor performance is illuminated from another perspective. Then, the growth rates of the developing economies, and Asian developing countries were 3.73 times and 4.46 times of that of Africa. Of all the developing country groups, Africa's performance was only better than that of Oceania's developing economies (Figure 4.11).

A key question here is: what did actually drive growth in the different country groups? *A simple indication of the driver of growth is obtained by examining*

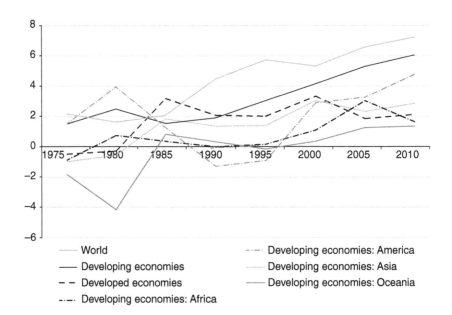

Figure 4.10 Comparative growth rates of real GDP per capita in selected country groupings (source: Author. Based on UNCTAD (2013)).

Figure 4.11 Average growth rate of country group/average growth rate of Africa (source: Author. Based on UNCTAD (2013)).

how the GDP growth rate moved in comparisons to the growth rates of its component sectors, i.e. agriculture, industry, and services. Appendixes 1a to 1g present the relevant graphs for the world, developing economies, developed economies, African developing economies, American developing economies, Asian developing economies, and Oceania developing economies. Notably:

a   When the two sectors that play a lead role in international economic integration through merchandise trade (i.e. industry and agriculture) are taken, the graphs reveal *a greater role of industry* for all country groups (world, developed countries, all developing countries, American developing counties, Asian developing countries), except developing African and Oceanian countries.

b   When all three major sectors (services, industry, and agriculture) are taken, the graphs contained in appendixes 1a to 1g reveal the following:

   i   Substantial gap between services and industry at the global level;

   ii   Smaller gap between services and industry for developing economies as a group as well as for individual groups of developing countries.

   iii   In Africa and Oceania, agriculture is still a more important driver of the economy than industry.

4.1.3 Contribution of Africa and comparator regions to world trade

In order to highlight Africa's participation in global trade (i.e. exports and imports), the following subsections examine the continent's shares of world trade, structure of international trade, and growth trends of international trade. The comparative analyses help to position Africa vis-à-vis other regions, which are both its competitors and partners in the global economy.

4.1.3.1 Shares of world trade

That the integration of the world economy through the international trade channel continues unabatedly is demonstrated by evolution of the global exports and imports by the meteoric rise of their share when the values of 1950 and 2010 are compared. A notable development associated with this phenomenon is that the role of developing countries in global trade is growing. Their relative weight has grown enormously, as shown in Figure 4.12.

Hence, overall, the value of global exports in 2010 was US$15.258 trillion, up from US$61,835.3 million in 1950. The 1950 values for the developed and developing countries groups were US$38.830 trillion and US$21.051 trillion respectively. This means that in 1950, the value of exports by developing countries were just 52.2 per cent of the value of exports of developed countries. By 2010 the value of exports by developing countries were almost 78 per cent of the value of exports of developed countries.

As further revealed in Table 4.5, the developing countries as a group accounted for roughly a third of global trade over the observation years (i.e. 1950, 1955, 1960, 1965, 1970, 1975, 1980, 1985, 1990, 1995, 2000, 2005, and 2010). Africa's shares of exports and imports are markedly small, which also mirrors the fact that the growth of the continent's trade was lower compared to other developing regions.

Overall, it should be noted that the integration of the developing regions of the world in international trade is far from even. The Asian countries, driven by China and India, are clearly driving the process, while other developing regions lag behind.

Africa's situation is particularly precarious, because the continent is falling back in real terms. Overall, the following features sum up its position in international trade:

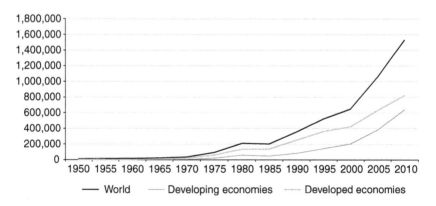

Figure 4.12 Exports in US$ million at current prices and exchange rates in millions, 1950–2010 (source: Author. Based on UNCTAD (2013)).

Table 4.5 International trade geographically decomposed: shares of regions in global exports* (%)

Country group	Shares of global exports	Shares of global imports
Developing economies	34.5	31.6
Developed economies	62.0	65.5
Developing economies: Africa	3.2	4.3
Developing economies: America	5.4	5.3
Developing economies: Asia	25.8	23.3
Developing economies: Oceania	0.07	0.47
Least developed countries	0.81	0.9

Source. Author. Based on UNCTAD (2013).

Notes
* …shares computed based sums of the years 1950, 1955, 1960, 1965, 1970, 1975, 1980, 1985, 1990, 1995, 2000, 2005, and 2010.

a Its share of global trade is both small and declining. It declined from 7.2 per cent in 1950 to 3.3 per cent in 2010 (cf. also Figure 4.13).
b It exports mainly agricultural and mineral commodities (cf. next subsection).
c It imports most of the value-added products that it needs (cf. next subsection).

4.1.3.2 Structures of international trade

Overall, international trade is dominated by goods, of which manufactured goods make up the lion's share for all country groups, with the exception of the developing countries from Africa. Even Oceania's developing countries get most

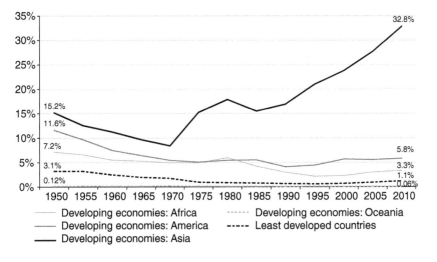

Figure 4.13 Developing country groups' shares of global exports, selected years, 1950–2010 (source: Author. Based on UNCTAD (2013)).

of their revenue from merchandise exports from manufactured goods. In contrast, Africa gets most of its revenue from merchandise exports from fuels. Table 4.6, Figure 4.19 (cf. subsection 4.2.4), and Appendix 2 underline these scenarios.

4.2 Comparative overview of integration in the global industrial economy

Diverse industrial activities give a good indication of the integration of a given country or region in the global industrial economy. Accordingly, when the developing countries are taken as a group, the process of their integration in the global economy appears to be evolving quite well. They have achieved impressive performances in terms of GFCF – Table 4.1, Figure 4.1), FDI (Figures 4.2–4.7), economic output (Tables 4.2–4.4, and Figures 4.8–4.11), and international trade (Tables 4.5 and 4.6, and Figures 4.12 and 4.13).

However, as may already be deduced from the analysis in the preceding sections, there are noticeable interregional industrial performance differences. Certain groups of developing countries are performing quite astoundingly, and propelling the integration of developing countries in the global economy. In this connection, the Asian countries have done particularly well, but positive trends are observable also for American countries. In contrast, the analysis has also verified that the African economies, excluding South Africa, while part of the international economic system, are obviously not meaningfully participating in global economic activities. The continent is performing badly across the entire spectrum of industrial activities: investments, production, and trade.

Moreover, notable characteristics of Africa's growth are that, where remarkable growth rates were recorded, such growths were most likely driven by either new mineral discoveries or commodity booms or both. A key feature of this growth is that it has not been uniform, and instead, the resource-rich countries have been leading the pace. The desired structural change has conspicuously not yet set in (Arbache and Page 2010; Arbache *et al.* 2008).

Table 4.6 Comparable drivers of international trade

Country group	Leading merchandise export product group	Average share in merchandise exports (1995, 2000, 2005, 2010) (%)
World	Manufactured goods	70.52
Developed countries	Manufactured goods	75.63
Developing countries	Manufactured goods	62.84
Developing countries: Africa	Fuels	51.36
Developing countries: America	Manufactured goods	49.98
Developing countries: Asia	Manufactured goods	72.6
Developing countries: Oceania	Manufactured goods	24.27

Source: Author. Based on UNCTAD (2013).

4.2.1 *Ideal scope of analysis of industrial competitiveness*

A thorough analysis of a country's or region's performance should embrace the entire value chain. To begin with, it should employ appropriate indicators to conduct interregional comparisons of investments in the industrial sector. Thus, for a better understanding of Africa's role in the global industrial economy, pertinent indicators should be ideally, among other things: a region's or a country's share of the global Manufacturing Fixed Capital Formation (MFCF), share of industrial investments in total investments, total industrial investments per capita, proportion of FDI that flows into the manufacturing sector, industrial FDI inflows per capita, etc. Then, it should use appropriate indicators to analyse the performance in industrial production, and industrial trade (cf. subsections 4.2.3 and 4.2.4).

However, due to data availability limitations, most indicators related to investments could be used to compare the performances of Africa and other regions. In this case, only limited anecdotal evidences could be presented. Nevertheless, the analyses in subsections 4.2.2–4.2.4 do still offer very useful insights into the continent's industrial performance in a global context.

4.2.2 *Debunking Africa's industrial investments: issues for analysis*

A better understanding of Africa's role in the global industrial economy would require the use of such pertinent indicators as a region's or a country's share of the global MFCF, share of industrial investments in total investments, total industrial investments per capita, proportion of FDI that flows into the manufacturing sector, industrial FDI inflows per capita, etc.

However, economic activities in Africa are also the least documented of any regions in the world. Due to the explicit data availability limitations, none of the pertinent indicators could be used to compare the performances of Africa and other regions.

Though comprehensive data to support a more rigorous interregional comparison is not available, some anecdotes give useful clues of industrial investments. Table 4.7 depicts some industrial statistics for selected African and comparator countries. Notably, though both Mauritius and South Africa count as the most industrialised countries on the continent, the numbers of their industrial establishments per 100,000 people (61 for Mauritius) and manufacturing employees per 100,000 people (6422 and 2449 for Mauritius and South Africa respectively) are very small compared to the only highly industrialised country in the sample, i.e. Germany. It is also worthwhile to note that South Africa, the only African country classified by UNIDO as industrialised, has the second lowest number of manufacturing employees per 100,000 people, beating only another African country, i.e. Morocco.

Overall, Africa's contribution to global industrial activities mirrors its overall performance in global investments, global production, and global trade, which have been highlighted in the previous sections. A brief period of industrial

Table 4.7 Selected industrial statistics for African and comparator countries

Country (year)	Population divided by 100,000	No. of industrial establishments per 100,000 people	No. of manufacturing employees per 100,000 people
China (2009)	13,118	31	5,885
Chile (2008)	168	25	2,599
Germany (2008)	825	237	8,410
Fiji (2008)	8	83	3,033
India (2008)	11,909	12	Data not available
Mauritius (2009)	13	61	6,422
Morocco (2009)	316	25	1,547
South Africa (2009)	498	Data not available	2,449

Source: Author. Based on UNIDO (2012).

growth following independence – chiefly triggered by state investment and import substitution (i.e. the IS model) – was followed by industrial decline and de-industrialisation. Today on average manufacturing in Africa's low-income countries is smaller as a percentage of GDP than it was in 1985. Moreover, unlike in other developing countries, the tradable services economy has not quite taken off. This is demonstrated by, among other things, the values and sectoral distribution of investments, values and structure of production, values and structural composition of trade, dependencies, etc.

Thus, the general verdict is that the continent has experienced inadequate growth enhancing structural change, and consequently failed to industrialise. This has resulted into a lopsided integration in the global economy. Moreover, as a result of its lopsided integration in the global economic activities, Africa is falling back even behind other developing regions, which are systematically narrowing the gap between themselves and the developed world.

4.2.3 Interregional comparisons of industrial production

The Index of Industrial Production (IIP) is used to provide insight into short-term changes in economic activity. The compilation of such indices for purpose of international comparisons dates back to at least the 1920s. Depending on available data, relevant indices can be computed for the whole industrial sector, for subsectors of the industrial sector (i.e. manufacturing, mining, quarrying, and construction). Also, bearing in mind that industrialisation broadly interpreted means transformation from the pre-industrial to industrial modes of production (in all sectors of the economy), the IIP can be computed for other sectors and their subsectors.

In order to get some clues about the industrial economic activity, this subsection explores the saliencies of manufacturing production, and aggregate manufacturing value added.

4.2.3.1 Saliencies of manufacturing

Three simple indicators are used to highlight Africa's position in the global manufacturing economy vis-à-vis comparator regions: index of manufacturing production, Manufacturing Value Added (MVA) as a share of aggregate regional output, and shares of regions in global MVA.

A INDEX OF MANUFACTURING PRODUCTION

Figure 4.14 uses the Index (numbers) of Manufacturing Production (IMP) to highlight the trends of growth of the manufacturing sector for the period 1970–2010. Taking 2000 as the base year, the computations[5] are based on data from UNCTAD (see *UNCTADstat* available at: http://unctadstat.unctad.org/UnctadStatMetadata/Documentation/UNCTADstatContent.htm).

Africa's performance is compared with the performances of the world as a whole, (all) developing countries, developed countries, Asian developing countries, American developing countries, and Oceania's developing countries.

In this case as well, manufacturing production should logically grow faster in developing countries than in developed countries, as the former need to catch up. The IMP shows that the Asian developing countries are clearly achieving this target. In contrast, Africa is clearly incapable of keeping pace with both Asian developing countries and the developing countries as a whole. Overall the index numbers depicted in Figure 4.14 show that, from comparing 1970 and 2010,

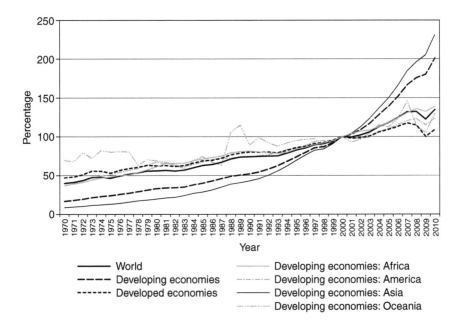

Figure 4.14 Evolution of the index numbers of manufacturing production for Africa and comparator regions, 1970–2010 (source: UNIDO (2011b, 2012)).

manufacturing production increases 3-fold, 12-fold, 2-fold, 4-fold, 3-fold, 27-fold, and 2-fold for the world, developing economies, developed economies, developing economies Africa, developing economies America, developing economies Asia, and developing economies Oceania respectively. The overall implication is that Africa is poorly integrated in global manufacturing production.

Furthermore, Figure 4.15 depicts the IMP for a sample of countries, using total manufacturing production as a proxy for the Index of Industrial Production (IIP). The index numbers used are those computed by UNIDO and the observation period is 1998–2008 (where base 2000 = 100). Since these figures are given per country, rather than per region, a sample of African and comparator countries has been used as follows: developed country (Germany), developing SSA country (Senegal), developing North African country (Morocco), developing American country (Chile), developing Asian country (India), and developing Oceania country (Fiji).

In interpreting the picture portrayed in Figure 4.15, logic dictates that industrial production should grow faster in developing countries than in developed countries, because the former's need to catch up. The IIP shows that, among the sample developing countries, India is clearly achieving this catching-up requirement. By comparison, though South Africa and Mauritius are amongst the best industrial performers in the African continent, they cannot keep pace and their growths remain far behind that of India. These evidences further strengthen the observations that Africa is poorly integrated in global manufacturing. The overall implication is that Africa is poorly integrated in global production as a whole.

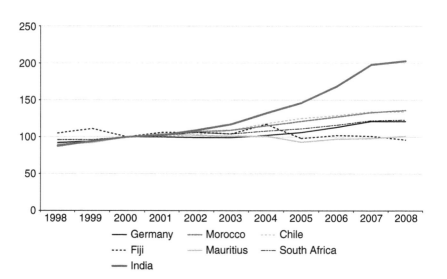

Figure 4.15 Evolution of the index numbers of manufacturing production for selected African and comparator countries, 1998–2008 (source: UNIDO (2011b, 2012)).

B REGIONAL MVA AS SHARES OF AGGREGATE REGIONAL ECONOMIC
OUTPUT

MVA as shares of aggregate economic output is an important indicator of the manufacturing development of an economic entity. Figure 4.16 shows MVA as shares of aggregate economic output, for Africa and other major regions of the world.[6] In the case of OECD, most of which are highly industrialised economies, the computed figure for the observation period is around 18.7 per cent.

Also, the developing economies that are catching up are recording very high values as reflected in the aggregate average of East Asia and Pacific (at around 31 per cent). In contrast, both the sub-regions that cover African countries remain below 16 per cent; with SSA having a figure of 14.9 per cent while MENA has a figure of 13.2 per cent during the observation period. Hence, both SSA and MENA remain below the world average of around 19.2 per cent.

To complement the observations in Figures 4.14–4.16, Appendix 3 shows the trend of MVA to GDP ratio for the period of 1991–2007 for Africa and comparator groups of countries – which is essentially an indicator of the *manufacturing development path* of the relevant country groups. In the Appendix, the catching-up process by East Asia and Pacific is vivid. Indeed, by 2010, China, South Korea, and Taiwan accounted for ca. 25 per cent of world MVA. To characterise Africa's industrial production further, only South Africa is classified by UNIDO as an industrialised economy (UNIDO 2012, 2013).

From previous empirical analyses, we know that generally, in the case of industrialised economies, the share of MVA in output has stabilised at around 17 per cent. On the contrary, with a single exception of South Africa, the MVA to GDP ratios of African countries are very low (UNIDO 2009).

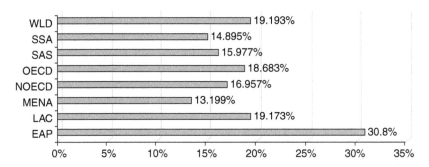

Figure 4.16 Share of MVA in output in Africa and comparators, averages of 1991–2007 (source: Based on ECONSTAT (available at: www.econstats.com/wdi/wdiv_717.htm). The cited source further cites 'World Bank national accounts data and OECD National Accounts data files').

Notes
EAP = East Asia and Pacific; LAC = Latin America and the Caribbean; MENA = Middle East and North and North Africa; NOECD = Non-OECD high income countries; OECD = Organisation for Economic Co-operation and Development; SSA = Sub-Saharan Africa; SAS = South Asia; WLD = World.

The implications of these scenarios of the manufacturing sector should be understood in a broader context. While MVA gives clues about the level of industrialisation, the manufacturing economy itself has extended linkages with other sectors that depend heavily on a manufacturing base: they include the basic sectors (i.e. agriculture and mining), and a wide range of services such as finance, telecommunication, commerce, etc. The degree of mechanisation and therefore productivity of these sectors, which occupy lower or higher positions in the sectoral pyramid (or value chain), depends on the level of development and performance of the manufacturing sector.

C REGIONAL SHARES OF GLOBAL MVA

Generally, worldwide, manufacturing production is at the highest point in history and has maintained this trend for several years. Table 4.8 shows the evolution of the shares of global MVA over the period 2005–2010 for groups of countries/ regions. However, as is clearly notable, compared to other regions of the world, Africa's performance in terms of MVA is quite weak. UNIDO data further shows that during the period 2001–2005, Africa's MVA grew by an average annual rate of just 3.2 per cent, compared to 6.2 per cent for the entire developing country group. For the period 2006–2010, Africa's average growth rate declined to 3.0 per cent, while that of the developing countries as a group climbed to 7.1 per cent (UNIDO 2011a: 16).

Moreover, even in the aftermath of the world economic crisis from which some countries are still suffering, industrial production is on the rise again. As reported by UNIDO, world manufacturing output grew by 6.5 per cent in the first quarter of 2011 compared to the same period the year before, partly due to strong performance of newly industrialised countries: Turkey, Mexico, and India recorded growth rates of 13.8 per cent, 7.4 per cent growth rate, and 5.1 per cent respectively.

Table 4.8 Shares (in %) of global MVA in Africa and comparators, selected years

Year	2005	2006	2007	2008	2009	2010	*Average of 2005–2010*
Developed economies	71.7	70.7	69.4	68.2	65.5	64.4	68.3
Developing economies	28.5	29.3	30.6	31.8	34.3	35.6	31.7
Sub-Saharan Africa	0.72	0.71	0.70	0.72	0.74	0.73	0.72
South Africa	0.41	0.41	0.40	0.41	0.40	0.38	0.40
East Asia and the Pacific	14.7	15.4	16.5	17.6	19.8	20.8	17.5
Latin America and the Caribbean	5.68	5.68	5.66	5.76	5.66	5.72	5.7
Middle East and North Africa	2.0	2.87	2.89	2.95	3.08	3.10	2.9
South and Central Asia	2.0	2.41	2.47	2.52	2.76	2.84	2.5
Least developed countries	0.3	0.38	0.39	0.41	0.46	0.46	0.4

Source: Author. Based on UNIDO (2011a).

Notes
MVA = Manufactured Value Added.

4.2.3.2 Aggregate industrial value added

In this estimation, the ratio of industrial GDP to total GDP is used as a proxy for aggregate industrial value added. Figure 4.17 depicts the trends for Africa and comparator regions.

The compared regions are: world, developed countries, (all) developing countries, developing countries Africa, developing countries Asia, developing countries from America, and developing countries from Oceania. Also, it is important to note that since around 1994, manufacturing has effectively shifted to developing countries, which accordingly as a group have the highest industrial to total GDP ratio. Presumably driven by mining, Africa is performing quite well with regard to this index, ranking second behind Asia among the major developing countries. However, this situation is still alarming, considering that Africa still remains behind the average of the developing countries as a group. Apparently, it is Asia which is driving the good overall performance of the developing countries.

4.2.4 Africa in the interregional comparisons of industrial trade

As Figure 4.18 establishes, while international trade is consistently rising, the phenomenon is driven by manufactured exports. Manufactured goods clearly dominate that trade – followed distantly by trade in primary goods and trade in services, which are roughly at the same levels. During the observation period

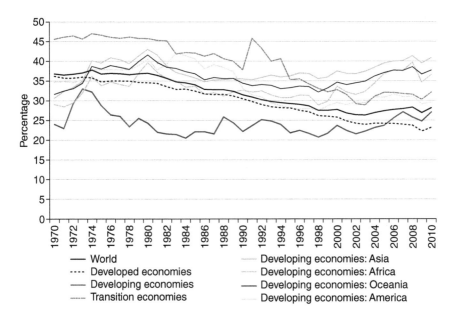

Figure 4.17 Industrial GDP as a ratio of total GDP for Africa and comparator regions (source: Author. Based on UNCTAD (2013)).

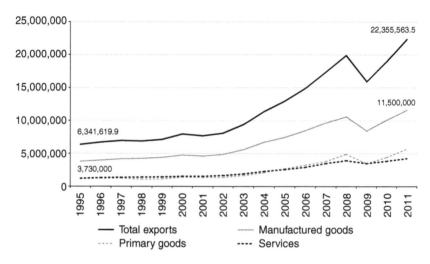

Figure 4.18 Evolution of world exports by main product categories, US$ million, 1995–2011 (source: Based on UNCTAD (2013)).

(1995–2011), manufactured goods accounted for 56 per cent of global exports and generally tended to move in tandem with total exports (cf. also Appendix 4).

Moreover, apart from consistently rising, trade in manufactured goods has been recording faster growth rates than MVA. For instance, from 1995 to 2011, manufactured exports grew by over 300 per cent. By comparison, from 1995 to 2010, MVA grew by only 170 per cent (cf. *index mundi*, available at: www. indexmundi.com/facts/world/manufacturing).

Some of the key reasons advanced to explain the situation, where trade grows faster than output include Trade Creation (TC) through falling costs of trade, as well as through growth of productivity vis-à-vis tradable goods[7] (cf. Chapter 11 of this book for the computation of TC). Lesser but also important reasons include increased demand due to growing disposable incomes, reduction of exchange distortions though falling exchange rate volatility, convergence of country shares of world output triggered by the growing significance of developing countries in global economic production (Dean and Sebastian-Barriel 2004). The last point underlines the fact that production competitiveness (which mirrors production capacities) is essential for trade competitiveness.

This section uses more evidences to show that industrial trade participation of the various regions mirror their industrial production capacities. Among other things, it uses the following simple indicators for interregional comparisons of the saliencies of manufactured trade:

a   *Shares of trade in manufactured goods*. The following indicators are used: shares of manufactured goods in total exports of regions, shares of manufactured goods in total imports of regions, regional shares of aggregated global manufactured exports, regional shares of aggregated global manufactured exports by category of manufactured goods (e.g. high-tech, low-tech, etc.), regional shares of aggregated global manufactured imports, regional shares of aggregated global manufactured imports by category of manufactured goods (e.g. high-tech, low-tech, etc.)

b   *Structure of trade in manufactured goods.* The used indicators include the following: structure of manufactured exports by level of production techno- logy, structure of manufactured imports by level of production technology.

c   *Trade in manufactured goods per capita.* The indicators used include the following: exports of manufactured goods per capita, and imports of manu- factured goods per capita.

4.2.4.1 Shares of manufactured goods in total exports and imports of regions

Table 4.9 shows the computed value of the Manufactured Goods to Total Export Ratio (MTER) and Manufactured Goods to Total Import Ratio (MTIR) for Africa and comparator regions – averages of 1995–2011.

Generally, MTER indicate the relative capacity of a given economic entity to interact competitively with the global economy through the manufacturing channel. In this connection, MTER provide invaluable clues about the economic entity's international standing in terms of value added. Equally, they give a good indication of the extent to which the exporting economic entity keeps abreast of changing technologies. A high value for MTER is particularly important, for an economy which needs to catch up.

Nevertheless, Africa has notably, the lowest values in the cases of both MTER and MTIR. This stresses its generally marginal role in the global indus- trial economy.

To explore the situation further, Africa's lacklustre performance is underlined by the fact that the continent has the smallest share of manufactured to merchandise

Table 4.9 Manufactured exports to total export ratio and manufactured imports to total import ratio for Africa and comparator regions – averages of 1995–2011

Country group	MTER	MTIR
World	0.569831682	0.581855
Developed countries	0.595925695	0.59461
Developing countries	0.546225865	0.569834
Developing countries: Africa	0.179690852	0.50591
Developing countries: Asia	0.610879468	0.558859
Developing countries: America	0.426530714	0.651765
Developing countries: Oceania	0.217456673	0.67009

Source: Author. Based on UNCTAD (2013).

Notes
MTER = Manufactured Goods to Total Export Ratio; MTIR = Manufactured Goods to Total Import Ratio.

export ratio, which in 2006 for instance was 17.8 per cent. The comparable ratios for other developing economies (American, Asian, and all) in the same year were 46.6 per cent, 70.4 per cent, and 62.8 per cent respectively. The ratio for developed economies and the global average ratios were 76.3 per cent and 69.3 per cent respectively (cf. UN 2008: 72, 76, 84, 88, 92, and 96).

4.2.4.2 Regional shares of global manufactured exports

Table 4.10 demonstrates that the shares of the various regions in the global Manufactured Exports (ME) differ significantly. In this connection, Africa has the smallest share of global ME among the regions depicted in the table. The best performing group is East Asia and the Pacific, which accounted for an annual average of 22 per cent of global ME during the observation period.

Digging deeper into data reveals that from 2000 to 2004, the growth rate of SSA's share of global ME of 14.4 per cent compared favourably with that of all developing countries as a group that stood at 14 per cent. However, from 2005 to 2009, SSA's average growth rate wilted to 3.8 per cent, compared to a drop to 9 per cent for the developing countries group (UNIDO 2009: 17).

Another interesting feature of ME is that they have been growing faster than MVA in all regions of the world. This manifests the increasing internationalisation. Also, East Asia dominates ME from developing country goods even more than it does with regard to MVA.

4.2.4.3 Global structure of trade in manufactured goods by level of production technology

In order to fully understand trade competitiveness of a country or region, it is also essential to assess the manufactured trade performance by level of production technology (i.e. high-tech, low-tech, etc.). Useful indicators include global

Table 4.10 Shares (in %) of global manufactured exports for Africa and comparators, averages, selected years

Year	2004	2005	2006	2007	2008	2009	Average of selected years
Developed economies	67.4	65.5	64.2	63.5	62.4	61.0	64.0
Developing economies	32.6	34.5	35.8	36.5	37.7	39.0	36.0
Sub-Saharan Africa	0.65	0.68	0.68	0.64	0.69	0.61	0.7
South Africa	0.37	0.40	0.37	0.39	0.42	0.38	0.4
East Asia and the Pacific	19.9	21.0	22.0	22.6	22.6	24.3	22.1
Latin America and the Caribbean	4.31	4.58	4.43	4.20	4.42	4.37	4.4
Middle East and North Africa	3.0	2.9	3.2	3.3	3.6	3.5	3.2
South and Central Asia	1.4	1.6	1.6	1.6	1.6	1.9	1.6
Least developed countries	0.26	0.23	0.23	0.19	0.12	NA	0.21

Source: Author. Based on UNIDO (2011a).

shares of manufactured exports by level of production technology, manufactured exports per capita by level of production technology, etc.

The picture portrayed in Table 4.11 is quite clear: one factor that differentiates Africa from the rest of the major regions of the world is that it is still largely relies on exports of primary products. Moreover, to the extent that the continent exports manufactured goods, most of them are basic manufactured goods, which belong to the Low Technology (LT) category. Clearly, this shows that Africa has not been part of the industrial transformation.

4.2.4.4 Trade in manufactured goods per capita

Table 4.12 shows the evolution of per capita exports in manufactured goods for the period 2005–2009 for groups of countries/regions. If the averages of the observation years are taken, the worst performers are Central and South Asia, Sub-Saharan Africa, and the Middle East and Northern Africa, in that order. In absolute terms, Sub-Saharan African performance, alongside that of Central and South Asia is quite alarming, showing no significant improvements over time. Again, this is an indication that industrial policy in Africa is not delivering.

4.3 International comparisons of the Competitive Industrial Performance Index

4.3.1 Antecedents

The structures and dynamics of industrial production compared to competitors offers useful clues about a country's or a region's industrial competitiveness. Therefore, the Competitive Industrial Performance (CIP) Index is used to provide

Table 4.11 Global trade by level of production technology, averages of 2006–2009

Country group	Manufactured exports		
	HT	*MT*	*LT*
World (US$ billions)	2,366	4,049	1,896.25
Shares in %			
Developed countries	46.82	72.14	51.71
Developing countries	41.02	27.87	48.29
Developing countries: Sub-Saharan Africa	0.14	0.55	0.55
Developing countries: Middle East & North Africa	1.02	2.41	3.81
Developing countries: Central & South Asia	0.53	0.74	3.43
Developing countries: East Asia & Pacific	35.77	15.59	32.10
Developing countries: Latin American & the Caribbean	2.41	4.56	3.27

Source: Author. Based on UNIDO (2011a).

Notes
HT = High Technology; MT = Medium Technology; LT = Low Technology.

Table 4.12 Evolution of manufactured exports per capita in US$, current prices

	2005	2006	2007	2008	2009	Average of 2005 to 2009	Deviation from world average
World	1,356	1,535	1,740	1,917	1,490	1,607.6	4,943.2
Developed countries	5,650	6,302	7,120	7,755	5,927	6,550.8	–5,875.4
Developing countries	534	629	725	824	665	675.4	–562.6
Developing countries: Sub-Saharan Africa	99	113	116	138	98	112.8	539
Developing countries: Middle East & North Africa	458	585	697	880	639	651.8	–556.2
Developing countries: Central & South Asia	78	91	98	109	102	95.6	1,105.4
Developing countries: East Asia & Pacific	938	1,115	1,301	1,442	1,209	1,201	–369.6
Developing countries: Latin American & the Caribbean	726	803	861	1,000	767	831.4	

Source: Author. Based on UNIDO (2011a).

Notes

HT = High Technology; MT = Medium Technology; LT = Low Technology.

an overall picture of country's or region's industrial sector competitiveness, in the international context (i.e. relating the performances of comparator countries or regions).

The CIP Index was developed and used by UNIDO for the first time in its Industrial Development Report (IDR) 2002/3. The Index, which has since been revised and improved, assesses an economy's ability to produce and export manufactured goods. It is a composite index, which in its current conceptualisation, is obtained through a geometric aggregation of eight equally weighted sub-indicators.[8] As a tool for tracking and benchmarking the industrial performance of an economic entity, and therefore ranking it against comparator entities (usually countries), it is particularly useful for policymakers and for industrial development activists.

The CIP is a still evolving index, with modellers still testing the estimation methods.[9] As shown in Figure 4.19, currently, the Index's eight sub-indicators are grouped in three dimensions of industrial competitiveness as follows:

a   The first dimension relates to a *country's capacity to produce and export manufactured goods*. It is captured by two indicators, (i) Manufacturing Value Added per capita (denoted as *MVApc*)[10], and (ii) Manufactured Exports per capita (denoted as *MXpc*).

b   The second dimension covers a *country's level of technological deepening and upgrading*. It is also captured by four indicators, generated as follows:

   i   *A country's degree of industrialisation intensity* (INDint), which is computed as a linear aggregation of two indicators:

      i   Medium- and High-tech manufacturing Value Added share in total Manufacturing Value Added (denoted as *MHVAsh*).[11]
      ii Manufacturing Value Added share in total GDP (denoted as *MVAsh*).[12]

   ii A *country's export quality* (MXQual), which is a composite indicator obtained as an average of the linear aggregation of the Medium- and High-tech Manufactured Exports share in total Manufactured Exports (denoted as *MHXsh*),[13] and the Manufactured Exports share in total exports (denoted as *MXsh*).

c   The third dimension relates to a *country's impact on world manufacturing*. It is captured by two indicators, i.e. a country's:

   i   MVA as a share of World MVA (denoted as *ImWMVA*).
   ii Manufactured Exports as a share of World Manufactured trade (denoted as *ImWMT*).

The CIP Indices are standardised in the range of [0, 1], i.e. the highest value is mapped to the value of 1 and the lowest value is mapped to 0. The higher the industrial competitiveness of a given economic entity, the higher the

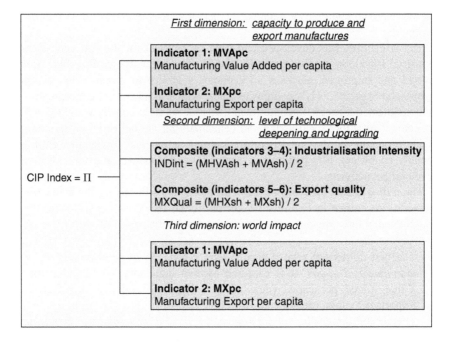

Figure 4.19 The CIP Index.

value of its CIP Index. Thus, the Index enables industrial development analysts, policymakers, and activists, to get a very clear impression of the industrial competitiveness of a given economic entity.

4.3.2 Incidence of global industrial competitiveness

Table 4.13 compares African countries with the top ten and bottom ten ranked countries in terms of the CIP Index. Overall, when the major regions of the world are compared, two seem to dominate industrial competitiveness: Europe, and East Asia and the Pacific. While 50 per cent of the countries with top ten CIP indices come from East Asia and the Pacific, 16 European countries belong to the top quintile of the CIP ranking (cf. UNIDO 2013).

However, as is also visible, African countries record very low CIP indices, with the continent's best performer, South Africa, ranking 41 overall, among the 135 compared countries worldwide. Most notably, all African countries, including South Africa, remain below the global average CIP Index (i.e. *CIP Index*), which as computed and presented in Table 4.13, is 0.084635.

Besides, nine African countries belong to the bottom ten performers (cf. UNIDO 2013). The nudging question here is whether the African countries are catching up or falling behind in terms of industrial competitiveness. The answer appears to be: they are not catching up but rather falling back!

Table 4.13 Competitive Industrial Performance Index, 2010

CIP ranking	Country	CIP Index	CIP ranking	Country	CIP Index
Top 10 countries			*Ranks occupied by African Countries*		
1	Japan	0.5409	41	South Africa	0.0722
2	Germany	0.5176	58	Tunisia	0.0476
3	USA	0.4822	62	Egypt	0.0450
4	RoK	0.4044	66	Morocco	0.0374
5	CTP	0.3649	79	Mauritius	0.0240
6	Singapore	0.3459	82	Algeria	0.0220
7	China	0.3293	85	Swaziland	0.0212
8	Switzerland	0.3118	86	Botswana	0.0206
9	Belgium	0.3114	89	Côte d'Ivoire	0.0166
10	France	0.3095	95	Nigeria	0.0143
			97	Cameroon	0.0121
Bottom 10 countries			100	Congo	0.0108
124	Cape Verde	0.0032	101	Senegal	0.0100
125	Malawi	0.0031	102	Kenya	0.0100
126	Sudan	0.0030	103	Gabon	0.0095
127	Haiti	0.0030	106	Tanzania	0.0085
128	Niger	0.0027	111	Zambia	0.0077
129	Rwanda	0.0022	116	Madagascar	0.0055
130	Ethiopia	0.0019	118	Ghana	0.0043
131	CAR	0.0011	120	Uganda	0.0040
132	Burundi	0.0006	122	Mozambique	0.0034
133	Eritrea	0.0000	124	Cape Verde	0.0032
133	Gambia	0.0000	125	Malawi	0.0031
133	Iraq	0.0000	126	Sudan	0.0030
			128	Niger	0.0027
			129	Rwanda	0.0022
			130	Ethiopia	0.0019
			131	CAR	0.0011
			132	Burundi	0.0006
			133	Eritrea	0.0000
			133	Gambia	0.0000

Source: Based on UNIDO (2013).

Notes
CAR = Central African Republic; CTP = China, Taiwan Province; RoK = Republic of Korea; USA = United States of America.

The descriptive statistics of the CIP indices presented in Table 4.14, as well as the histogram and skewness graph of the CIP indices depicted in Figure 4.20, provide further clues about the incidence of industrial competitiveness among the sample countries.

Notably, the distribution of the CIP Indices presented in Table 4.14 and Figure 4.20 is highly skewed, i.e. *skewness > +1*. Moreover, the distribution is skewed right (i.e. skewness is positive): the right tail of the distribution is longer and most of the distribution is at the left. What this kind distribution of the CIP indices tells us is that most CIP Index values are concentrated on left of the Mean CIP Index

Table 4.14 Descriptive statistics of the CIP Index for all sample countries in 2010

N	Mean	Median	Std. Deviation	Variance	Skewness	
Statistic	Statistic	Statistic	Statistic	Statistic	Statistic	Std. Error
135	0.084635	0.0367	0.1142679	0.013	1.985	0.209

Source: Author. Based on UNIDO (2013). Competitive Industrial Performance Report 2012/2013. United Nations Industrial Development Organization. Vienna.

Notes
N = Number of observations; Std. Deviation = Standard Deviation; Std. Error = Standard error.

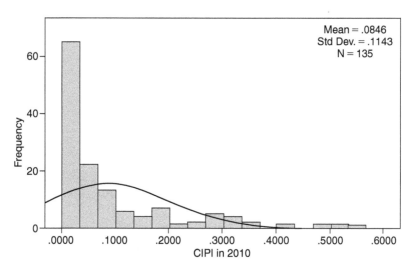

Figure 4.20 Histogram of CIP Indices for all 135 sample countries in 2010 (source: Author. Based on UNIDO (2013)).

(with extreme values to the right). To be precise, the CIP Indices of 98 countries (equivalent to 72.6 per cent of the sample countries) are below the global Mean CIP Index of 0.084635. These observations concur with the real world reality that industrial competitiveness is not balanced among the countries: a few countries are industrially highly competitive, while most are not.

Overall, incidence of global industrial competitiveness is as exciting as at it is worrisome. On the positive side, the developing countries as a group are systematically increasing their role in global industrial economic activity. Nonetheless, the picture is worrying because industrial performance is diverging rather than converging, with success confined to a few countries.

If the observed drivers of the success in industrial transformation are anything to go by, then much of the underperformance in developing countries can be attributed to structural factors that – first, develop cumulatively, and second may not be so easily addressed by economic liberalisation. Imperatively, in order to achieve long-term, sustainable industrial development, the backward countries need an *Integrated Industrial Development Agenda* (IIDA) – centred around three dimensions: *Integrated Industrial Development Governance Framework (IIDGF)* that transcend policies and strategies, *development of Financial Resource (FiR) capacities for industrial finance, development of diverse Non-Financial Resource (NFiR) capacities*. This agenda is developed further in Chapter 13 of this book. Moreover, reference to and clarification of the term governance framework is also contained in Chapters 5, 6, 11, 12, and 14.

4.3.3 Distribution of Competitive Industrial Performance Index among African countries

For the 32 African countries, whose CIP Index was estimated in UNIDO's Competitive Industrial Performance Report 2012/2013, further clues about the incidence of industrial competitiveness are given by the descriptive statistics of the CIP indices (Table 4.15), and by the histogram and skewness graph of the CIP indices (Figure 4.21).

Table 4.15 Descriptive statistics of the CIP Index for all sample African countries in 2010

N	Mean	Median	Std. Deviation	Variance	Skewness	
Statistic	Statistic	Statistic	Statistic	Statistic	Statistic	Std. Error
32	0.0135	0.0081	0.0170632	0.000	2.241	0.414

Source: Author. Based on UNIDO (2013).

Notes
N = Number of observations; Std. deviation = Standard deviation; Std. error = Standard error.

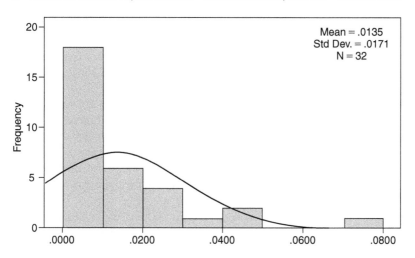

Figure 4.21 Histogram of CIP Indices for all 32 sample African countries in 2010 (source: Author. Based on UNIDO (2013)).

In this case as well, the distribution of the CIP indices is highly skewed to the right (i.e. *skewness* > +*1*). Thus, most CIP Index values are concentrated on left of the Mean CIP Index for the group of African countries. To be precise, the CIP indices of ten countries (equivalent to 68.8 per cent of the sample African countries) are below the (very low!) sample Mean CIP Index. This implies that, even among African countries, industrial development and competitiveness is highly lop-sided: a handful of countries have developed some relative industrial competitiveness, while most have not. Therefore, it is not surprising that UNIDO's *Handbook of Industrial Statistics* categorises only one African country, i.e. South Africa, as being industrialised.

4.4 Summarising remarks

The evidences presented in the discussions in the previous sections show close associations between industrialisation and development. Also, the pattern of global industrial activity is changing systematically. Industrial investments, production, and trade are shifting across activities and countries/regions. In this regard, the developing countries are becoming ever-more important locations of industrial activity. Overall, today's map of global industrial activity is characterised by a systematic shift of the centre of gravity of industrial activities from developed to developing countries. In this connection, Africa's marginal role in global industrial activities is both vivid and distressing. In order to increase its prospects for industrial transformation, Africa and its international partners need to chart new ways.

4.4.1 Systematic shift of the centre of gravity of industrial activities to developing regions

In explicit terms, to date, manufacturing activity remains heavily concentrated in industrialised countries. This is evidenced by MVA per capita (which is a good indicator of *intensity of industrialisation*[14]) and other indicators (e.g. ME per capita). However, this cannot conceal the fact that the centre of gravity of industrial activity is shifting towards developing countries.

Also, despite the fact that developing countries as a group are catching up rapidly, the performances of countries and regions are diverging rather than converging. Success is still confined to a few regions; and in many developing regions, to a few countries within those regions. Much of the divergence can still be traced back to *structural factors*[15] (which mirror a long-term phenomenon, since such factors can only develop cumulatively). Implicitly, a structural solution is needed in order to address them.

Among developing regions, East Asia (including China) is the best industrial performer in most respects, though it still lags slightly in manufacturing value added per capita. It has the highest growth rates in manufacturing production and exports. It is far more export oriented than other developing regions. It has a more technologically advanced structure and is rapidly improving all the main drivers of industrial performance. It is advancing well in skill creation, and research and development (R&D).

4.4.2 Africa's marginal role in global industrial activities

As highlighted by the many examples in this chapter, the developing countries as a group have achieved impressive performance in terms of GFCF (Table 4.1, Figure 4.1), FDI (Figures 4.2–4.6), economic output (Tables 4.2–4.4, and Figures 4.7–4.10), and international trade (Tables 4.5 and 4.6, and Figures 4.11 and 4.12). Asian countries have performed particularly well.

In contrast, the analysis in this chapter has also demonstrated that the African economies, excluding South Africa, while part of the international economic system, are obviously not meaningfully participating in the global economic activities. Indeed, the vulnerability of the African economies is directly associated with their poor performance across the entire spectrum of industrial activities: investments, production, and trade.

Africa's performance in global industrial activities mirrors its overall performance in investments, global production, and trade. This is demonstrated by, among other things, the values and sectoral distribution of investments, values and structure of production, values and structural composition of trade, etc. Overall, the industrial development trajectory – which is mirrored by investments, production, and trade – suggests that African countries are not becoming significantly less commodity-dependent than before.

Every student of business or economic studies knows that an entity's economic performance is influenced by the products it produces and trades. Specialisation in one or other product category would have a significant influence on its performance. Generally, countries whose production, and eventually trade portfolio is dominated by manufactured goods, tend to perform better. In straight terms, African economies are suffering from their uncompetitive production structures.

While contemplating the future of industry in Africa, it should be borne in mind that achieving industrial transformation requires mobilising and deploying sufficient investments. Without critical masses of industrial investments, particularly in the manufacturing sector, African countries are unable to derive maximum potential embedded in them. This has resulted further in their lopsided integration in global economic activities, in which case they tend to be falling back even behind other developing regions. Most of the developing regions of the world are namely systematically narrowing the gap between them and the developed world.

Invariably, one of the main challenges facing almost all African countries today is how to improve their development prospects through substantially improved performance in the global economy. Therefore, to the extent that Africa's feeble performance is associated with the status of development of its industrial sector, there is an apparent and urgent need to improve their development prospects through more effective industrial development strategy.

4.4.3 Prospects for Africa industrial transformation

4.4.3.1 The context

When analysing the prospects for Africa's industrialisation, it is important to recall how the other economies, most recently the emerging economies of Asia and Latin America, achieved their own industrialisation. None of them achieved this without developing the necessary capacities to invest, to produce, and to trade competitively. The explicit message is that industrial transformation needs capacities along all stages of the value chain.

In addition, literally all countries which have experienced the industrial transformation, from the pioneers (like the UK), to the early and late followers (like Germany, USA, Japan Korea, etc.), to the emerging economies of our contemporary world (e.g. Brazil, China, India), have benefited from protective economic regimes. Important spheres of the economy, such as intellectual property, investment, and trade, were substantially insulated from competition. In this connection, each of the resultant industrial policy could essentially be seen as a mélange of Import Substitution Industrialisation (ISI) measures and Export-Led Industrialisation (ELI) measures, although in each case one or the other (i.e. ISI and ELI) carried more weight.

Africa's industrialisation, however, has to take place at a time when some of the policy instruments that have been proven to work in history (protections, promotion through subsidies) have largely become redundant through regional and multilateral liberalisation. However, measures related to developing the necessary capacities to invest, to produce, and to trade competitively, which are more fundamental for industrial and economic transformation as well as for economic transformation in general, are still available to African economies.

4.4.3.2 The pathway

So, how will Africa industrialise under these conditions? As we can derive from experience, there are huge economies of scale in industry, with required capacities to mobilise and deploy:

a   Lumpy investments, in order to *transform the qualities of locations*. The target of the location transformation is enabling it to harness its own Financial Resource (FiR) capacities, as well as to attract FiR and diverse Non-Financial Resource (NFiR) capacities, from other sources (e.g. countries, regions). For corporate investors, a related locational quality that emerges from this process of improving the quality of location is the spillovers emanating from belongingness to clusters of complementary or interdependent economic activities.

b   Lumpy investments to *produce diverse goods and services* (even if the involvement in the production value chain is restricted only to task components of the product in question).

African countries would benefit from serious international co-operation in developing FiR capacities (involving mobilising and deploying both local financial resources, as well as levering international investment) and NFiR capacities (involving mobilising from both internal and external sources, and deploying entrepreneurial capacities, knowledge and skills, organisational/institutional capacities, physical infrastructural capacities, and technological capacities).

4.4.3.3 Leveraging African–EU co-operation for industrialisation

Development agendas, as embedded in strategies, policies, and other elements of a governance framework, need time to show their effect in changing economic structures. However, given the time that has elapsed, a necessary conclusion emerging from the observed scenario is that the industrial development agendas of most African economies have been faltering and unable to deliver the expected results. After around 50 years of independence for most African countries, and several development co-operation arrangements with the EU – with provisions on industry – there is little to show in terms of changes in economic structure. This underlines the need for a re-drafting of the industrial development agenda, including a very fundamental reengineering of the Africa–EU co-operation agenda, in order to make it deliver the industrial transformation.

True, the EU offers good trading opportunities for Africa. However, for Africa to leverage those opportunities for its competitive participation in the global economy, it must not only increase the volume of its trade very significantly, but perhaps even more importantly, it must transform the structure of its trade. Transforming the structure of Africa's trade will not happen, unless changes happen in the earlier stages of the value chain: in the structure and volumes of investments, and in the structure and volumes of economic production. In this connection, the diversification of investments and production towards manufactured goods is indispensable.

The question here is: can the African–EU co-operation be geared towards achieving the transformation of the quality of Africa as an investment destination, and actually undertaking competitive corporate investments in the continent? Is there a political will to achieve this?

The co-operation with the EU has all the potential that is needed to achieve Africa's industrial transformation. However, in order for Africa–EU co-operation to have a chance for becoming the right catalyst for Africa's industrial transformation, a major reengineering of the Economic Partnership Agreement (EPA) development model is absolutely necessary. The departure point for the reengineering should be the recognition that a development agenda has been most effective in fostering industrial transformation, when it has created the necessary conditions for the structural transformation of the domestic economy. In this connection, the essence of *productive capacities* for a transformative process cannot be overstated, since African economies are generally characterised by many gaps in relation to those capacities. As highlighted above, to use simple and straight language, Africa's capacity gaps can be clustered into two broad groups as follows:

a   *FiR capacity gaps*. Thus, the development of FiR capacities is vital, to enable the African economies to be able to reliably finance investments at all stages of the value chain.
b   *NFiR capacity gaps*. Therefore, the pertinent capacities must be developed, because they are essential ingredients of any sustainable development process. They include entrepreneurial capacities, knowledge and skills capacities, institutional or organisational capacities, physical infrastructural capacities, and technological capacities.

Imperatively, when reflecting about the essential considerations in the re-engineering of the Africa–EU co-operation agenda, the FiR capacities and NFiR capacities should be recognised as key ingredients that will drive the industrial transformation of the African economies.

In addition to the largely Market Access (MA) issues addressed in the EPAs, the other key elements of the agenda for leveraging African–EU co-operation for Africa's industrial transformation should include the improvement of the quality and quantity of investments in Africa's economies along the entire value chain, as well as improving Africa's production of goods and services through comprehensive diversification programme (also along the entire value chain). Ostensibly, the achievement of the latter requirement depends on the achievement of the former. Only a realistic investment regime will unleash Africa's potential and make it capable of taking advantage of the MA opportunities in the various global markets, not necessary the EU. A diversified investment portfolio will result in a diversified production portfolio, which in turn will result in a diversified trade portfolio. The other merits of diversity are that it is the only reliable basis for socio-economic stability, and for the sustainability of its development.

Notes

1 GFCF was formally referred to as Gross Domestic Fixed Capital Formation (GDFCF).
2 Authors have attributed Africa's miserable performance largely to a lack of conducive environment. However, more critical analysis should recognise the undervaluation of Africa's natural and other assets, which have made the continent become short-changed in FDI deals; largely because of corruption – a line which few authors dare to take when discussing FDI in Africa. An apparently equally important set of factors, which are also scantly researched, is the fact that, in contrast to other regions of the world, there is hardly any meaningful intra-African FDI. Despite being an interesting subject, a thorough discussion of the reasons why the figures for FDI into Africa are so low, goes beyond the objective of this chapter and book volume.
3 The cited data source (i.e. knoema.com/mhrzolg#World) cites further the GDP statistics from the World Bank.
4 The group includes: emerging economies from Central and Eastern Europe as well as the Commonwealth of Independent States (CIS); and developing countries from Sub-Saharan Africa (SSA), Middle East and North Africa (MENA), Latin America and the Caribbean (LAC), and Asia (for detailed description, see IMF 2012).

5 Invariably, this simple but informative index is computed as follows for a specific year:

$$IMP_t = MP_t \, / \, MP_{2000},$$

where MP_t = Manufacturing Production in year t, while MP_{2000} = Manufacturing Production in the year 2000.

6 This simple ratio has been computed as follows:

$$\overline{MVA} = \sum\nolimits_{1997}^{2007} (MVA \, / \, 17),$$

where $\overline{MVA}$ is the average MVA as a percentage of GDP for the observation period.

7 In the cited study by Dean and Sebastian-Barriel (2004), the two factors – falling costs of trade productivity growth of tradable goods – accounted for *c*.65 per cent of the observed increase in global trade to total expenditure ratio from 1984 and 2004.

8 Accordingly, under the weighted aggregation method, the CIP is computed as a weighted geometric mean as the q sub-indicators as follows:

$$CIP_{jt} = \prod\nolimits_{i=1}^{q} I_{ijt}^{w_i},$$

in which q is the number of sub-indicators, w_i is the weight of the indicator i. A further requirement is that all the weights should be positive and add up to one (cf. UNIDO 2013: 133).

9 The CIP can also be computed as a weighted linear mean as the q sub-indicators as follows:

$$CIP_{jt} = \sum\nolimits_{i=1}^{q} w_i I_{ijt},$$

in which q is the number of sub-indicators, w_i is the weight of the indicator i. In this case as well, all the weights should be positive and add up to one (cf. UNIDO 2013: 133).

10 The *MVA p.c.* (which by definition is deflated by population to adjust for the size of the country or region), is a useful indicator of a country's or region's relative level of industrialisation.

11 *MHVAsh* captures the technological complexity of the manufacturing within the economy. Capturing the *technological structure of production* is of particular importance. This is because the trajectory to the maturity of the industrial economy involves a shift from relatively simple to production activities that need low technology, to complex ones that need complex technologies. The importance to complex activities is that they are desirable for long-term competitive performance and growth. In this connection, technologically complex production activities are associated with several externalities (i.e. benefits): economies of scale, economies of scope, learning, higher technological absorptive capacities.

12 *MVA as share of GDP* is a good proxy of the capability of a given economic entity to mobilise and leverage knowledge and skills to transform the base of the economy, away from primary economic activities.

13 *MHXsh* captures technological complexity of manufactured exports of a given economic entity. It reflects the ability of the economy to leverage economies of scale and economies of scope to move towards more dynamic and competitive export structure.

14 *The intensity of industrialisation* is measured by the simple average of two indicators: the share of manufactured goods in GDP, and the share of medium- and high-technology activities in MVA.

15 The key structural factors, which hinder industrialisation include: (i) lack of technological capabilities to support industrialisation, (ii) lack of proper infrastructure to support industrialisation, (iii) lack of industrial entrepreneurial capacities, (iii) lack of institutional (i.e. organisational) capacities to support industrialisation, and (iv) lack of knowledge and skills for industrialisation.

References

Arbache, J. and Page, J. (2008). *Is Africa's Recent Growth Robust?* Africa Region Working Paper Series No. 111. World Bank. Washington DC. January.

Arbache, J. and Page, J. (2010). How fragile is Africa's recent growth? *Journal of African Economies.* Vol. 19, Issue 1, pp. 1–24. January.

Arbache, J., Go, D., and Page, J. (2008). *Is Africa at a Turning Point?* Policy Researching Paper No. 4519. World Bank. Washington DC.

Dean, M. and Sebastian-Barriel, M. (2004). Why has world trade grown faster than world output? *Bank of England Quarterly Bulletin.* Autumn, pp. 310–320.

IMF (2012). *World Economic Outlook April 2012: Growth Resuming, Dangers Remain.* International Monetary Fund. Washington DC.

Jäntti, M. and Vartiainen, J. (2009). *What Can Developing Countries Learn From Finland's Industrial Transformation?* WIDER *Angle* Newsletter. United Nations University World Institute for Development Economics Research.

Kahan, A. (1978). Capital formation during the period of early industrialization in Russia, 1890–1913. In Mathias, P. and Postan, M. (eds). *The Cambridge Economic History of Europe. Volume 7 Part 2: The Industrial Economies Capital, Labour, and Enterprise.* Chapter VI. Cambridge University Press. Cambridge.

Knoema (accessed in 2013). *GDP Statistics from the World Bank.* Knoemabeta Knowledge Platform. Available at: knoema.com/mhrzolg#World.

Leke, A., Lund, S., Roxburgh, C., and Wamelen, A. (2010). *What is Driving Africa's Growth.* www.mckinsey.com/insights/economic_studies/whats_driving_africas_growth.

UN (2008). *UNCTAD Handbook of Statistics 2008.* United Nations Conference on Trade and Development. New York and Geneva.

UN (2011). *UNCTAD Statistical Year Book 2011.* United Nations Conference on Trade and Development. New York and Geneva.

UNCTAD (2013). *UNCTADstat.* Available at: http://unctadstat.unctad.org/UnctadStat-Metadata/Documentation/UNCTADstatContent.htm. United Nations Conference on Trade and Development.

UNIDO (2003). *Industrial Development Report 2002/2003.* United Nations Industrial Development Organization. Vienna.

UNIDO (2008). *Industrial Development in a Changing Global Landscape.* United Nations Industrial Development Organization. Vienna.

UNIDO (2009). *Financing and Resource Mobilisation Strategy and Monitoring and Evaluation Framework for the Implementation Strategy of the Plan of Action for Accelerated Industrial Development of Africa.* United Nations Industrial Development Organization. Vienna.

UNIDO (2011a). *Industrial Development Report 2011: Industrial Energy Efficiency for Sustainable Wealth Creation.* United Nations Industrial Development Organization. Vienna.

UNIDO (2011b). *International Yearbook of Industrial Statistics.* United Nations Industrial Development Organization. Vienna.

UNIDO (2012). *International Yearbook of Industrial Statistics.* United Nations Industrial Development Organization. Vienna.

UNIDO (2013). *Competitive Industrial Performance Report 2012/2013.* United Nations Industrial Development Organization. Vienna.

World Bank (2008). World Development Indicators CD-ROM. World Bank. Washington DC.

Part II

Integration of industrialisation in the regional and pan-African development agenda

5 Integration of industrialisation in sub-regional development agendas

Overviews of African Regional Economic Communities

Francis A.S.T. Matambalya

Arguably, industrialisation plays a vital role in economic growth and development. Empirical facts reveal that all the developed countries of the world broke the vicious circle of underdevelopment through industrialisation. The transformation experiences of countries from pre-industrial to industrial levels of economic status show close associations between industrialisation, and economic growth and development. Indeed, from classical development economics theory, manufacturing – which is at the core of industrial activity – was touted as the engine of growth in the industrialisation era due to its ability to facilitate economies of scale (with increasing returns to scale) and economies of scope.

A point for further emphasis is that, where it is properly developed, the manufacturing sector clearly serves as a central joint, linking economic activities at the lower levels of the value chain (i.e. economic activities in the primary sector) with those at the higher levels of the value chain (i.e. economic activities in the tertiary sector, quaternary sector, quinary sector, etc.).

Also, as alluded to in Chapter 2, the strategic role of industrialisation for economic growth and development is usually associated with the impact it has on various factors that signify development. These include: higher economic productivity and increasing returns to scale, technology and spill-over effects; high capital intensity; diversification through forward and backward linkages of the various sectors of the economy; demand consideration; and creation and diversification of employment. Accordingly, these factors have been used – in a variety of combinations – to explain the mechanisms behind the industrialisation-led theories of growth and economic development, and to justify industrialisation as a necessary stage of economic development and an objective parse.

Cognisant of the essence of industrialisation, literally all governments in postcolonial Africa and their development partners have prioritised industrial development, and initiated measures to realise this goal. Complementary initiatives have been undertaken at regional levels, within the framework of Regional Economic Communities (RECs).

Using two RECs, i.e. the East African community (EAC) and Southern African Development Community (SADC), this chapter assesses the extent to which the industrialisation has been integrated into the development agenda at the sub-regional level. It also examines the saliencies of the industrial economy in the two RECs.

5.1 Regional integration and industrialisation

How can trade-driven regional integration schemes influence industrialisation processes of member countries? Seemingly, trading arrangements can have a major impact on this development process. Therefore, expressed in simple terms, the answer to the question is that by changing (improving) the attractiveness of a country as a base for manufacturing production (e.g. because of belongingness and provision of access to a larger market), regional integration schemes can potentially trigger investments, which are necessary for industrialisation.

Following this line of argument, the degree to which a country's participation in a regional economic bloc can improve its chances for industrialisation, is closely associated with *market size* and the *locational qualities*. Under the right circumstances, including the existence of appropriate governance framework (see Chapters 4, 11, 12 and 13 of this book) to give direction to industrial and overall economic growth and development, and socio and political stability; these two factors (i.e. market size and locational qualities) act as magnets for increased industrial investments. They contribute to the creation of sustainable patterns of competitive advantages, as well as to the inducement of critical mass of concentration of industrial activity in a country.

In connection with market size, as succinctly expressed by Harris (1980: 76): 'Wider markets are seen especially as incentives to new investments in manufacturing activity, and therefore as stimulus to industrialization and diversification of production structure'. In this chapter, the locational qualities are understood to be manifested by the level of development of Financial Resources (FiR) capacities, and non-Financial Resource (NFiR) capacities (cf. Chapters 4, 12, 13, and 14 of this book). Thus, a location with high concentration of FiR capacities and NFiR capacities to support industrial economic activities will be a high quality location.

Also, distance from major markets and economic centres of gravity influences a location's quality, to the extent that they influence the transaction costs associated with accessing these major markets (cf. Ernits 2003).

5.2 The rise of regional integration as a model of development

Regional integration agreements have been around for hundreds of years. For example, from the emergency of colonialism in the fifteenth century, the relationships between the colonised territories, as well as between those territories and the centre of the empire, were based on preferential schemes reminiscent of regional trade agreements. Moreover, the idea of a Customs Union (CU) preceded the emergency of theory to explain the phenomenon. Hence, in practices, CUs were precursors to or embodied in the creation of several of today's States, including Germany (which started as a 'Zollverein'), Italy, South Africa and the United States of America (USA) just to mention a few.

A survey of the evolution of international economic interactions in subsequent years, particularly since the end of the Second World War, reveals that concerted efforts through the formation of regional economic blocs has become a very popular and tested model of international economic co-operation. Consequently, today, there are many regional groupings, and most countries belong to at least one such grouping.

Most contemporary regional groupings are driven by trade development agendas and are accordingly referred to as Regional Trading Agreements (RTAs). From 1948 to 2008, the total number of RTAs notified to the General Agreements on Tariffs and Trade (GATT), and from 1995 upward to the World Trade Organization (WTO), is at least 230 (cf. Table 5.1).

However, the actual number of regional blocs is much smaller, and most notifications refer to trade arrangements between RTAs and a single beneficiary[1] or group of beneficiaries.[2] Also, movements from one stage of integration to another (deeper) stage of integration are notified to the WTO.

The theoretical explanation of why countries choose to participate in regional integration schemes include gains associated with Trade Creation (TC) through the post-liberalisation reduction of prices (cf. Chapter 11 of this book for the computation of TC), dynamic restructuring of the economy due to competition and the inducement to lock-in policy reforms (cf. Checchini *et al.* 1990; Cornett 1999; DeRosa 1998; Viner 1950).

Table 5.1 Regional Trade Agreements notified to the GATT/WTO and in force as of 15 December 2008

Status	Related provisions			
	Enabling clause	GATS Art. V	GATT Art. XXIV	Grand total
FA in preparation	11	21	24	56
FP distributed	1	14	22	37
FP on hold	3	6	36	45
FP to be done	3	17	27	47
Report adopted	1		17	18
No report	8			8
FA distributed			19	19
Grand Total	27	58	145	230

Source: Based on WTO, available at: www.wto.org/english/tratop_e/region_e/summary_e.xls.

Notes
FA = Factual Abstract; FP = Factual Presentation; GATS = General Agreements on Trade in Services; GATT = General Agreements on Tariffs and Trade.

5.3 Africa and the phenomenon of regional integration

5.3.1 Africa an early seedbed for regional integration

Regional integration is not a new phenomenon in Africa – on the contrary the continent has been home to some of the oldest schemes in the world. Partly through the accident of colonialism and the urge by colonial authorities to streamline the managements of their colonial territories, the continent became one of the pioneers in experimenting with integration initiatives[3] with several concrete schemes: Congo Basin Treaty, first iteration of the EAC, CU of the Cape Colony of Good Hope and Orange Free State, Southern African CU (i.e. SACU) and Southern Rhodesia CU. Table 5.2 provides overviews of these early initiatives, all of which came long before GATT and WTO, and were accordingly not notified to either of them.

5.3.1.1 Relevance of developments during the colonial period

Although at the time not guided by any well-developed integration theory, it is obvious that the early regionalisation schemes involving colonial territories had several benefits. The implied benefits arising from these schemes included:

a   *The creation of larger markets.* This could allow the colonial rulers to locate some manufacturing industries in the region, whose products targeted largely the local regional markets. Thus, as pointed out in Chapter 1 of this book, some countries became de facto centres of gravity of the colonial territories, thereby benefitting from the development of a substantial manufacturing sector. These countries included: Kenya (as centre of gravity of British-ruled member states of the first iteration EAC), Belgian Congo, Nigeria (which attracted special attention due to the sheer size of the market), Senegal (as the centre of gravity of French colonial states in West Africa), South Africa, Rhodesia (cf. Feinstein 2005; Gareth 2010; Kilby 1975).

b   *The harmonisation of trade policy and simplification of customs administration.* The creation of a CU involving the colonial territories of Kenya and Uganda (in 1917), which was later joined by Trustee Territory of Tanganyika (in 1922), served this purpose. In line with the viewpoint taken by this book, this was an important step towards the creation of a conducive *governance framework* (cf. also Chapters 4, 6, 11, 12 and 14 for further clarification of this term) to guide development of the region.

c   *The establishment of joint infrastructural projects.* For instance, the Uganda–Kenya Railway was a major infrastructural undertaking, linking two British colonial territories (cf. Table 5.2). In line with the philosophy of argument in this book, it contributed towards the development of an essential component of NFiR capacities in the region.

d   *The simplification of political administration.* The British colonial rulers of East Africa, for instance, largely harmonised the administrative procedures in Kenya and Uganda, and later, also in what is today's Tanzania.

Table 5.2 Pre-independence integration experiments in Africa

Scheme	Description	Parties
Congo Basin Treaty	• Emerged from the Berlin conference of 1884–1885 • Secured freedom of trade and navigation into the Congo River basin and its adjoining regions for all interested external powers	Austria–Hungary, Belgium, Britain, France, Germany, Denmark, Italy, Netherlands, the Ottoman Empire, Portugal, Russia, Spain, Sweden–Norway, USA
EAC	• Its seed sown in 1894 through a decision by the British authorities to construct the Uganda–Kenya railway, to link the two major territories it administered in east Africa • In 1900, Kenya established in Mombasa a Customs Collection centre for Uganda • In 1917, CU of Kenya and Uganda created • Tanganyika (= present day Tanzania Mainland) joined CU in 1922 • By 1967, the co-operation had gone through several stages of integration (most notably: High Commission in 1948, and Common Services Organisation in 1961) and became one of the most advanced integration schemes in the world, culminating in the first EAC CU • Collapsed in 1977 due to adverse economic and political factors	Kenya, Tanzania, Uganda
CU of the Cape Colony of Good Hope and Orange Free State	Created in 1989 by two colonial territories in present-day South Africa	Cape Colony of Good Hope, and Orange Free State
SACU	• First signed at Potchefstroomon 29 July 1910 • Is one of the oldest CUs in the world • Is the oldest still surviving CU in the world	Cape Colony, Orange River Colony, Transvaal, Natal (in present day South Africa), Basutoland Protectorate (now Lesotho), Swaziland, Bechuanaland Protectorate (now Botswana) Southern Rhodesia, North-Western Rhodesia
SRCU	• Formed in 1949	Present day South Africa and present day Zimbabwe

Source: Different sources.

Notes
CU = Customs Union; EAC = First iteration of the East African Community; SACU = Southern African Customs Union; SRCU = Southern Rhodesia Customs Union; USA = United States of America.

e   *The establishment of joint services organisations.* The first iteration of the
EAC, for instance, involved the creation of a Common Services Organisation
(EACSO) in 1961. The services, which were jointly administered, included:
East African Posts and Telecommunications (EAPT), East African Railways
& Harbours (EARH), East African Airways, East African Air Aviation Services (EAAS), East African Development Bank (EADB). In line with the line
of argument in this book, the creation of several organisations (EAPT, EARH,
regional airlines, EAAS and EADB) addressed another important gap in NFiR
capacities, i.e. institutions. In addition, the EADB was an essential component
of FiR capacities, which needed to be developed in the region.

5.3.1.2 Developments during the post-colonial period

The seed of regional integration that was planted in colonial Africa resonated
well amongst post-colonial African leaders, who time and again, reiterated its
importance for development, and went ahead to establish several schemes to that
effect. Hence, the post-colonial period saw many activities, in a process that
resulted in the dissolution of some earlier experiments (in some cases, only to be
resurrected later), while other schemes were transformed, and new ones were
initiated. Amongst the noteworthy early attempts at regionalisation include the
Trade Agreement between Ghana and Upper Volta (now Burkina Faso) of 1962
and the 1962 Equatorial Customs Union (ECU) that linked Cameroon, Central
African Republic, Chad, Congo and Gabon (see UNECA 2004).[4] Overall, integration schemes proliferated.

On the whole, there have, arguably, been more integration schemes in Africa
than on any other continent with no fewer than 24 schemes being created or resurrected in the post-colonial era, of which six trade-driven RTAs were also notified to the WTO (cf. Table 5.3).

Besides, the enthusiasm for regional integration appears to persist in Africa,
despite the fact that such initiatives have neither translated into the integration of
the real economies, nor contributed significantly to economic growth and development. To date, the African economies have largely maintained their colonial
structure in terms of production and trade links, and are the least developed. Of
the 54 African countries, none is developed, and 34 are least developed (equivalent to 63 per cent). Another comparison: of the world's 48 Least Developed
Countries (LDCs) as of 14 January 2014, 34 are African (equivalent to 70 per
cent), and this is after two African countries graduated from the group, i.e. Botswana (in 1994) and Cape Verde (in 2007).

5.3.2 Reinvigoration of regional integration as a model of development in Africa

In contemporary terms, the seed of Regional Economic Communities (RECs) as
a framework for the governance of the economic development agenda in Africa
was sawn by the 1980 Lagos Plan of Action (LPA). According to the 'Final

Table 5.3 Notifications to GATT/WTO of RTAs involving African countries

Agreement	Date of entry into force	Date of notification	Related provisions	Type of agreement
ECOWAS	1993	26 September 2005	Enabling Clause	PA
SADC	1 September 2000	9 August 2004	GATT Art. XXIV	FTA
TDCA	1 January 2000	21 November 2000	GATT Art. XXIV	FTA
EAC	7 July 2000	11 Oct 2000	Enabling Clause	PA
CEMAC/ECCAS	24 June 199	29 September 2000	Enabling Clause	PA
WAEMU/UEMOA	1 January 2000	3 February 2000	Enabling Clause	PA
COMESA	8 December 1994	29 June 1995	Enabling Clause	PA
SACU	15 July 2004	25 June 2007	Article XXIV	CU

Source: Based on information from WTO.

Notes

CEMAC = Communauté Économique des États de l'Afrique Centrale; COMESA = Common Market for Eastern and Southern Africa; CU = Customs Union; EAC = East African Community; ECCAS = Economic Community of Central African States; ECOWAS = Economic Community for West African States; GATT = General Agreements on Tariffs and Trade; SADC = Southern African Development Community; TDCA = Trade and Development Co-operation Agreement between the EU and South Africa; UEMOA = Union Economique et Monétaire Ouest Africaine; WAEMU = West African Economic and Monetary Union.

Acts' of the Lagos Plan of Action (LPA) of 1980, which are contained in Appendix 1, the 53 African countries committed themselves to being fully integrated into a single African Economic Community (AEC) by 2000. Trade integration, which is outlined in §249 to §251, should play a key role in that process (see AU 2001: 65–66 and 98–100).

Further provisions to strengthen the resolve for a systematic pan-African integration through regional integration have been included in several subsequent pan-African Frameworks, most notably the *Treaty Establishing the African Economic Community* (popularly known as the Abuja Treaty of 1981), and the Constitutive Act of the African Union (AU) of 2000. Table 5.4 shows the various documents related to the evolution of the pan-African integration agenda.

Subsequently, cognisant of the virtues of regional integration in promoting pan-African integration, the Abuja Declaration, which was directly derived from the LAP and has been under implementation since 1994, divided the African countries into five regional blocs: North Africa, West Africa, South Africa, East Africa and Central Africa. When the LPA was agreed, it was foreseen that the concrete integration schemes in these regions should spearhead pan-African integration in six phases and over a 34-year period (1994–2007), culminating in the establishment of the AEC in 2027. The AEC should have permitted intra-African free trade, free factor mobility and common currency.

However, in practice, the regionalisation dynamics in Africa, which of course preceded both the LAP and Abuja Declaration, have tended to take rather 'autonomous' courses, resulting in the proliferation of regional integration schemes, usually with configurations cutting across the five 'defined' regions and exhibiting overlapping memberships.

In subsequent developments, articles 3 (especially sub-article (c) on 'accelerate the political and socio-economic integration of the continent', and sub-article (l) on 'co-ordinate and harmonise policies between existing and future RECs for the gradual attainment of the objectives of the Union') of the AU Constitutive Act of 2000 reiterate the role of RECs as building blocs for the AEC. Presumably in view of the realities on the ground, the AU has chosen to pursue a pragmatic approach, and designated eight major trade-driven economic integration blocs as being the key pillars of Africa's integration: *Union du Maghreb Arabe* (UMA), *Communauté des EtatsSahélo-Sahariens* (CEN-SAD),[5] Common Market for Eastern and Southern Africa (COMESA), EAC, ECCAS, Inter-Governmental Authority on Development (IGAD) Economic Community of West African States (ECOWAS) and SADC (cf. Table 5.5).

Besides, the AU recognises several lesser integration schemes: *Communauté Économique des Pays des Grand Lacs* (CEPGL), SACU, Mano River Union (MRU), *Union Économique et Monétaire Oust Africaine* (UEMOA),[6] *Communauté Économique et Monétaire d'Afrique Centrale* (CEMAC) which is an organ of ECCAS, Indian Ocean Commission (IOC) (cf. Table 5.6).

Some reference to measures, which are relevant for industrial development is also contained in other key blueprints of the AU, such as Sirte Declaration of 2009, New Partnership for Africa's Development (NEPAD) of 2001, Accra

Table 5.4 Evolution frameworks driving the pan-African integration agenda

Framework	Stipulations relevant for industrial development
1 Monrovia Declaration of 1979	• Outlines the continent's development approach from 1980 onward • Prioritises the following: • Establishment of a sound industrial base within each country in accordance with each country's resource endowments • Physical integration of the continent through the expansion of a transport and communications network • Development of capabilities to maintain sovereignty over the region's natural resources by the government and peoples of Africa • Establishment of mutually beneficial and equitable relations between Africa and the rest of the international community • Attainment of an increase in the approximately 5% share of intra-African trade in the total trade of Africa • Attainment of self-sufficiency in food • Pursued following objectives: • Establishment of self-sustaining, internally located process of development and economic growth • Achievement of sub-regional and regional collective self-reliance • Development of human resources to ensure their greater participation in the development process • *Establishment of industrialisation patterns that are consistent with the socio-economic environment of each country, and not a simple importation of foreign industrialisation patterns*
2 LPA & Final Act of LPA of April 1980	• Outlines the continent's development approach from 1980 onward • Stresses development of the following: • Priority sectors • Skills and training for participation • Institutions at the national, sub-regional and regional levels • Criticises past approaches to industrialisation in Africa, which had tended to be carbon-copies of foreign patterns of industrialisation • Advocates establishment of sound industrial base in the (African) region

continued

Table 5.4 Continued

Framework	Stipulations relevant for industrial development

3 Treaty Establishing the AEC commonly known as the 'Abuja Treaty' of June 1991	• Focal measures on industry, science and technology, which are contained in Chapter IX, prioritise:
	  • Harmonisation of industrialisation policies
	  • Prepare master plans for each REC
	 • Develop basic industries (food and agro-based industries, building and construction, metallurgical, mechanical, electrical and electronics, chemical and petro-chemical, forestry, energy, textile and leather, transport and communication, biotechnologies)
	 • Promote small-scale industries
	 • Strengthen financing institutions
	 • Strengthen pan-African institutions for promotion of industrialisation (i.e. African Regional Centre for technology, African Regional Centre for Design and Manufacture, African Industrial Development Fund)
	 • Facilitate transfer of industrial technology through training and exchange of experiences
	 • Establish industrial data and information base
	 • Promote specialisation
	 • Harmonise standards
	 • Other measures also relevant for industrial development:
	  • Seeks to take economic integration to a new level as outlined in particularly Chapter IV (RECs), Chapter V (CU and liberalisation of trade)
	  • Measures on education and training (contained in Chapter XII) as well as human resources (contained in Chapter XII) are essential for developing knowledge and skills capacities in African countries needed for industrialisation

4 Sirte Declaration of 9 September 1999	• Declaration is relevant as a general framework for promoting Africa's industrial development
	 • Expresses the resolve by African leaders to:
	  • Establish the AU
	  • Accelerate the implementation of the AEC
	 • Expresses the resolve to strengthen the RECs

5 Constitutive Act of the AU of July 2000	• Reiterates the role of RECs as building blocks for the AEC, and hence:
	  • Acceleration of the political and socio-economic integration of the continent
	  • Co-ordination of policies of RECs

6 NEPAD of July 2001	• The priorities identified for development are essential for developing diverse capacities needed to stir industrial development: infrastructure, human resources, science and technology, agriculture, finance, mining, manufacturing, tourism, services, trade liberalisation, environment, culture

continued

Table 5.4 Continued

Framework	Stipulations relevant for industrial development

7 The Accra Declaration on the creation of AU of 2007	• Reiterates the pursuance of the goal to unify Africa into the United States of Africa, and hence:
	  • Formation of the government of the Union
	  • Rationalisation of RECs
	  • Harmonise activities of RECs
	  • Define/clarify relationship between RECs and the Union

8 AUC 1st Strategic Plan 2004–2007	• Promoting regional integration as one of the main activities of the strategic plan
	• The Strategic Plan's review reveals the following:
	  • 30% of planned actions fully completed within schedule
	  • 48% of planned actions were behind schedule

9 AUC 2nd Strategic Plan 2009–2012	• The Objectives are largely grouped under the pillar 'development, integration, and cooperation' and embrace: promoting sustainable economic development, promoting social and human development, formulating frameworks for sharing statistics and R&D capacities
10. AUC 3rd Strategic Plan 2014–2017	• The strategic concerns and priorities, which directly target industrial development refer to 'developing the Agro-processing and businesses sectors' and are part of the second cluster of priorities • Moreover, the development priorities aspired to by the remaining clusters (peace and security, inclusive economic development, human capacity, institutional capacity, gender mainstreaming, people centred AU) embrace essential measures for industrial development as well

Source: Author. Based on (1) The cited treaties (see also list of references at the end of this chapter), (2) Sekgoma (1994).

Notes
AEC = African Economic Community; AU = African Union; AUC = African Union Commission; LPA = Lagos Plan of Action; NEPAD = New Partnership for Africa's Development; RECs = Regional Economic Communities.

Declaration of 2007 on the creation of the AU, AUC Draft Strategic Plan for 2014–2019, AUC Strategic Plan for 2007 to 2009, AUC Strategic Plan that covered the period 2004–2007 (cf. table 5.4, AUC 2004, 2009, 2013).

Though the first strategic plan did not seem to have a clear indication on industrial development, its priorities (establish an effective and responsible African Union; build consensus around a shared vision and agenda in the continent; promote the emergence of societies based on the principles of the rule of law, good governance and human security; promote regional economic co-operation as a foundation for irreversible integration in the continent; develop integration infrastructure; address the structural causes of poverty and under-development; enhance the dynamism of African culture and creativity) have nevertheless a bearing on this (cf. AUC 2004). The same lack of explicit

Table 5.5 Major regional integration schemes recognised by the AU as being the pillars of the African integration

REC	Description	Current Member States
CEN-SAD	• Biggest integration schemes in terms of membership • This is the Community of Sahel-Saharan States • Initially established on 4 February 1998 by six countries: Burkina Faso, Chad, Libya, Mali, Niger and Sudan	Benin, Burkina Faso, Chad, Central African Republic, Comoros, Côte d'Ivoire, Djibouti, Egypt, Gambia, Ghana, Guinea-Bissau, Kenya, Liberia, Libya, Mali, Morocco, Niger, Nigeria, São Tomé and Príncipe, Senegal, Sierra Leone, Somalia, Sudan, Togo, Tunisia (total: 27)
COMESA	• Large integration scheme with members from Eastern, Southern and North Africa • Founded in 1993 as a successor to the Preferential Trade Area for Eastern and Southern Africa (PTA), which was established in 1981 • Headquarters: Lusaka, Zambia	Burundi, Comoros, Democratic Republic of the Congo, Djibouti, Egypt, Eritrea, Ethiopia, Kenya, Libya, Madagascar, Malawi, Mauritius, Rwanda, Seychelles, Sudan, Swaziland, Uganda, Zambia, Zimbabwe (total: 19)
EAC	• Second iteration of East African integration • Based on a Treaty signed in 1999 • Headquarters: Arusha, Tanzania	Burundi, Kenya, Rwanda, Tanzania, Uganda (total: 5)
ECCAS	• Established in 1983 to replace the 'Customs and Economic Union of Central Africa' established by the Brazzaville Treaty in 1966 • Headquarters: Libreville, Gabon	Angola, Burundi, Cameroon, Central African Republic, Chad Congo (Brazzaville), Democratic Republic of Congo, Equatorial Guinea, Gabon, Rwanda, São Tomé and Príncipe (total: 11)
IGAD	• Formed in 1986 as 'Intergovernmental Authority on Drought and Development' (IGADD); and changed to IGAD in 1996 • Headquarters: Djibouti	Djibouti, Eritrea, Ethiopia, Kenya, Somalia, Sudan and Uganda (total: 7)
ECOWAS	• Treaty to establish the REC was signed in 1975 • Headquarters: Abuja, Nigeria	Benin, Burkina Faso, Cape Verde, Côte d'Ivoire, Gambia, Ghana, Guinea-Bissau, Liberia, Mali, Nigeria, Senegal, Sierra Leone, Togo (total: 13)

continued

Table 5.5 Continued

REC	Description	Current Member States
SADC	• Established in 1992, to replace the Southern African Development Coordination Conference (SADCC), which was formed in Lusaka, Zambia, in 1980 • Headquarters: Gaborone, Botswana	Angola, Botswana, Democratic Republic of Congo, Lesotho, Madagascar, Malawi, Mauritius, Mozambique, Namibia, Seychelles, South Africa, Swaziland, United Republic of Tanzania, Zambia, Zimbabwe (total: 15)
UMA	• Brings together North African Arab countries • Established through the Marrakech Treaty of 1989 • Headquarters: Rabat-Agdal, Kingdom of Morocco	Algeria, Libya, Mauritania, Morocco, and Tunisia (total: 5)

Source: Author. Based on relevant treaties (see also list of references at the end of this chapter).

Notes
CEN-SAD = Communauté des Etats Sahélo-Sahariens; COMESA = The Common Market for Eastern and Southern Africa; EAC = The East African Community; ECCAS = The Economic Community of Central African States IGAD = Inter-Governmental Authority on Development; UMA = Union Maghreb de Arabe; SADC = Southern African Development Community.

reference to industrial development is true also for the next two strategic Plans (AUC 2009, 2013), but notably, they include objectives and priorities whose attainment will create the necessary conditions for industrial development.

5.4 Regional integration and industrialisation in the East African Community

5.4.1 The tides and ebbs of integration in East Africa

As highlighted in subsection 5.2.1, the story of the first iteration of the EAC goes back to its origin in 1894, and ends with its temporary collapse in 1977 (cf. Table 5.2).

However, the collapse of the EAC did not mean the end of interactions among the member states. The negotiations of the distribution of assets of the defunct organisation were conducted and concluded in the period from 1977 to 1983. Moreover, the negotiations produced something very important for the future of the sub-region: rather than burying integration efforts in East Africa, the mediation agreement did in effect set the stage for the second EAC iteration. Hence, this period (i.e. 1977–1983) can rightfully be seen as an overlapping phase between the two iterations: signalling the end of the first, and the beginning of the later.

Efforts to re-establish co-operation were revived in earnest in 1996, when the Secretariat of the Permanent Tripartite Commission for East African

Table 5.6 Minor regional integration schemes recognised by the AU as being the pillars of the African integration

REC	Description	Current Member States
CEMAC	Established in 1994 and became operational in 1999. Founder members were: Cameroon, Central African Republic, Chad, Congo (Brazzaville), Equatorial Guinea and Gabon.	Cameroon, Central African Republic, Chad, Congo (Brazzaville), Equatorial Guinea and Gabon (total: 6)
CEPGL	Established in 1978 by Burundi, Rwanda and Zaire (now DR Congo), following the Agreement of Gisenyi, Rwanda of 20 September 1976	Burundi, Democratic Republic of Congo and Rwanda (total: 3)
IOC	• Created in 1982 at Port-Louis, Mauritius by five Indian ocean island states of the coast of Mainland Africa • Institutionalised the Victoria Agreement of 1984 Seychelles	Comoros, Madagascar, Mauritius, Reunion and Seychelles (total: 5)
MRU	• Initially established in 1973 by Liberia and Sierra Leone	Guinea, Liberia and Sierra Leone (total: 3)
SACU	• Initially established by the 1889 Customs Union Convention between the British Colony of Cape of Good Hope and the Orange Free State Boer Republic • New agreement signed on 29 June 1910, extending membership to (i) Union of South Africa, and (ii) British High Commission Territories (HCTs), i.e. Basutoland (Lesotho), Bechuanaland (Botswana) and Swaziland. South West (i.e. Namibia), while under South Africa's administration was a de facto member, but eventually became a de jure member after attaining its independence in 1990 • SACU Agreement of 11 December 1969 was signed by the sovereign states of Botswana, Lesotho and Swaziland (BLS) and South Africa • Current Agreement was signed in 2002 by Botswana, Lesotho Namibia, South Africa, Swaziland	Botswana, Lesotho Namibia, South Africa, Swaziland (total: 5)
UEMOA/ W·AEMU	• Initially created on 12 May 1962, and then known as *Union Monétaire Ouest Africaine* (UMOA), i.e. West African Monetary Union (WAMU). Founder members were: Côte d'Ivoire, Dahomey (now Bénin), Haute-Volta or Upper Volta (now Burkina Faso), Mali, Mauritanie, Niger and Sénégal • Formally transformed to its current structure in January 1994	Benin, Burkina Faso, Cote d'Ivoire, Guinea-Bissau, Mali, Niger, Senegal, and Togo (total: 8)

Source: Author. Based on relevant treaties (see also list of references at the end of this chapter).

Notes
CEMAC = *Communauté Économique et Monétaire d'Afrique Centrale*; CEPGL = *Communauté Économique des Pays des Grand Lacs*; IOC = The Indian Ocean Commission; MRU = Mano River Union; SACU = Southern African Customs Union; UEMOA/WAMEMU = *Union Économique et Monétaire Oust Africaine/West African Economic and Monetary Union*.

Co-operation was set up at the EAC headquarters in Arusha, Tanzania. In 1997 the East African Heads of States started the process of upgrading the Agreement that set up the Commission into a Treaty. In 1999 they signed the treaty re-establishing the EAC. The objectives of the EAC are to develop policies and programmes aimed at widening and deepening co-operation on political, economic, social and cultural fields, research and technology, defence, security and legal and judicial affairs. Its members are now Kenya, Uganda, Tanzania, Rwanda and Burundi with a population of 135 million and a GDP of over US$95 billion. The EAC has an operating CU, and launched its common market in July 2010. Its roadmap includes a common currency and the creation of a single state. In addition to its secretariat, the EAC has a judiciary and a legislature made of representatives from member states.

5.4.2 Past industrialisation efforts in the East African Community

5.4.2.1 Industrialisation promotion measures and their deficits

Already during its first iteration, the EAC states pursued collaboration in promoting industrialisation. The support measures included: direct government participation in industrial ventures through State-owned Enterprises (SOEs), allocation of specific industries to specific countries, creation of EABD to provide industrial finance, and using trade barriers to protect industries in weaker member countries (EAC 2012; Matambalya 2011).

However, despite the good intentions, the adopted measures had several weak spots:

a *Over-proportional government participation in entrepreneurial activities.* Most notable, little or no efforts were made to develop indigenous and local entrepreneurs, to serve as captains of private-sector driven industrialisation.

b *An attempt at a dirigiste approach at national industrial specialisation.* Accordingly, there was a distributive measure, involving direct allocation of industries to individual member countries. However, the allocation was not respected by the member states – which went ahead to establish industries of their own, supposed to be established in other countries.

c *Limited industrial finance.* The creation EADB to support industrialisation proved to be futile, due to the bank's shortfalls in terms of liquidity and specific instruments to meaningfully finance industrial projects.

d *Suffocation of competition and the benefits associated with it.* Under this arrangement, industries from the weaker economies were protected by imposing tariffs on trade with a member country, with which it had a trade deficit. Hence, instead of promoting competition and reaping the benefits which come with it, there was an attempt to suffocate it. This was surely not the best way to develop competitive industrial ventures in the region.

5.4.2.2   Other caveats

As pointed out in EAC (2012), Matambalya (2011), etc., the primary caveat was that the undertaken industrialisation efforts during this period were characterised by a *lack of holistic agenda – embracing all essential elements – to develop the necessary conditions for industrial transformation.* Imperatively, the EAC countries did not tackle industrial development in a holistic manner.

Thus, besides the weaknesses that were embedded in the adopted 'governance framework', there were no concerted efforts to develop diverse:

a   FiR capacities, which are essential for industrialisation – including diversified sources of funding, and diversified funding instruments. For the interested reader, Chapters 12 and 13 of this book dwell in detail on the pertinent issues.

b   NFIR capacities for industrialisation. Meant here are capacities related to industrial entrepreneurship, industrial knowledge and skills, institutions organisations to promote industrial development, physical infrastructure, and technologies to support sustainable industrialisation. In this case as well, for the interested reader, Chapters 12 and 13 of this book dwell in detail on the pertinent issues.

The results of this approach, which was characterised by lack of comprehensive agendas with complementary and coherent provisions, to promote industrial transformation in the EAC countries, was rather predictable, and it failed to trigger industrial transformation.

The basic challenges were exacerbated by the apparent lack of political commitment, and the existence of social and political instabilities, particularly in Uganda. Overall, towards the end of the first iteration of the EAC, the poisoned relations and mutual mistrust among the member states did not provide the best conditions for cooperation for industrial development.

Also, the international economic relations were not leveraged for the industrialisation of the EAC countries. Consequently, despite the existence of such schemes, as the various co-operation agreements between the Africa, Caribbean and Pacific (ACP) group of nations, and the European Economic Community (EEC) and later the European Union (EU), the integration of the EAC countries in the global economy remained heavily marked by their role as suppliers of agricultural and mineral raw materials to the rest of the world, especially the more advanced economies.

5.4.3   East Africa's industrial performance: emerging conclusions

The performances of the EAC industrial sectors have been reminiscent of the performances of African countries in general, as discussed in detail in Chapter 4 of this book. Table 5.7 shows the ranks of the Competitive Industrial Performance (CIP) Index occupied by the EAC countries in 2010, from a global sample of 135 countries.

Table 5.7 Ranks of the CIP Index occupied by the EAC countries in 2010

CIP ranking	Country	CIP Index
102	Kenya	0.0100
106	Tanzania	0.0085
120	Uganda	0.0040
129	Rwanda	0.0022
132	Burundi	0.0006
By comparison		
1	Global highest: *Japan*	0.5409
	Global average	0.0846
42	African highest: *South Africa*	0.0722
	African average	0.0135
133	Global lowest: *Iraq, Gambia, Eritrea*	0.0000

Source: Based on UNIDO (2013).

Notes
CIP Index = Comparative Industrial Performance Index.

Notably, all EAC countries lie far below the global average and even the African average (cf. Chapter 4 of this book for a more detailed account of the CIP Index and ranking of African and comparator countries).

5.4.4 Using industrialisation to propel the second iteration of East African integration

Economic integration is an important target in the integration process that is pursued by the EAC. In this connection, the interdependence and interlocking of the 'real economies' (i.e. investments, production, trade, and labour markets) provide reliable measures of the strength of regional economic integration. Moreover, the fact that international economic relations are driven by international trade, while international trade is, in turn, dominated by manufactured goods, underlines the role of industrialisation in propelling the integration of the 'real economies'.

Consequently, the EAC Partner States recognise the essentiality of industrialisation as a development strategy. But they continue to display a high proportion of primary commodity exports, mainly low-skilled labour-intensive manufacturing based on imported technologies, minor economic growth rates, high levels of unemployment, and only low levels of purchasing power.

Cognisant of these interfaces between industrialisation on the one hand, and economic growth and development, on the other side, the EAC Partner States have formulated their sentiments about industrialisation in several of their direction-giving documents, including:

a   *The Treaty Establishing the East African Community.*
b   *The East African Community Common Market Protocol.*
c   *The East African Community Development Strategy 2011/2012–2015/2016.*

d   *The East African Community Industrialization Policy: Opening New Opportunities for Growth and Expansion of Cross-border Manufacturing and
Upgrading of Small and Medium Enterprises (SMEs).*

e   *East African Community Industrialization Strategy 2012–2032: Structural
Transformation of the Manufacturing Sector Through Higher Value Addi-
tion and Product Diversification Based on Comparative and Competitive
Advantages of the Region.*

Apart from expressing the resolve, these blueprints outline the concrete interventions needed for the development and meaningful integration of the EAC into
the global industrial economy.

5.4.4.1 Industrialisation in the Treaty establishing the East African Community

Article 1(2) of the Treaty establishing the EAC stipulates strengthening intra-
regional industrial relations (EAC 2012: i–ii). Thereupon, Article 79 is dedicated
to industrial development. Thus, the Partner States shall take such steps in the
field of industrial development to promote self-sustaining and balanced industrial growth, improve the competitiveness of the industrial sectors and encourage
the development of indigenous entrepreneurs (EAC 2012: 55).

To achieve the ambition for industrial development, the Treaty specifies
further in Article 80 the strategy and priority areas for promoting industrialisation. It calls upon the Partner States to establish a regional industrial development strategy (cf. EAC 2012: 55).

In terms of priorities, the same Article (i.e. 80) urges the Partner States to
promote intra-community industrial linkages, facilitate the development of specific
types of industries (small- and medium-scale industries, basic capital and intermediate goods industries, food and agro-industries), rationalise investments and the
full use of established industries so as to promote efficiency in production, promote
research and technological capabilities (through industrial research and development – R&D – transfer, acquisition, adaptation and development of modern technology, training, management and consultancy services through the establishment of
joint industrial institutions and other infrastructural facilities), harmonise and rationalise investment incentives, disseminate and exchange industrial and technological
information, avoid double taxation, and take such other measures for the purposes
of Article 79 of this Treaty as the Council may determine (cf. EAC 2012: 55–56).

5.4.4.2 East African Community Common Market Protocol

Several Articles of the East African Community Common Market Protocol have
a bearing on the industrial development of the region, including Article 5, Article
44 and Article 45.

Article 5(3)(l) on the 'Scope of Co-operation in the Common Market' underlines
the agreement of the Partner States to promote industrial development for the attainment of sustainable growth and development in the Community (EAC 2009: 8–9).

Article 44 articulates 'Co-operation in Industrial Development' (cf. EAC 2009: 44–45). Through it, the EAC countries resolve to co-operate in activities related to the production of goods and services, so as to attain sustainable growth and development. Thus, they agree to adopt common principles to achieve the following:

> Promote linkages among industries and other economic sectors; Promote value addition and product diversification to improve resource utilisation; Promote industrial research and development, transfer, acquisitions, adaptation and development of modern technology; Promote sustainable and balanced industrialisation in the Community to cater for the least industrialised Partner States; Facilitate the development of micro, small and medium industries and promote indigenous entrepreneurs; Promote investment and employment opportunities in the Community; Promote knowledge based industries; Promote industrial productivity and competitiveness of industries at national, Community and international levels; Promote sustainable industrial development that ensures environmental protection, management and efficient resource utilisation; Disseminate and exchange industrial and technological information.

Furthermore, the article vests powers with the Council of Ministers to issue directives and regulations on various issues, so as to facilitate industrial co-operation, including on: implementation of the Industrial Development Strategy, promotion of technologies and infrastructure, improvement of quality and technical regulatory infrastructure to ensure compliance of industrial products to standards and technical regulations, establishment of physical infrastructure for industrial development, establishment of a regional mechanism for developing human capacity, support for regional *fora* for Public-Private Partnership and Civil Society dialogue, support regional industrial productive base (including for capital, intermediate goods, tools and implements), other measures that may be necessary (cf. EAC 2009: 45–46).

Article 45 on 'Co-operation in Agriculture and Food Security' seeks to, among other things, promote agro processing and value addition to agricultural products (cf. Article 45[2e]). It also endeavours to establish and promote the production and availability of farm inputs and implements in sufficient quantities in the Partner States (cf. Article 45[3m]), which can only be achieved if there is industrial transformation.

5.4.4.2 East African Community Development Strategy 2011/2012–2015/2016

The broad priority areas in the next decade (2011–2020) identified in this strategy include improving global competitiveness for faster and sustainable economic growth and achievement of the status of a newly industrialised region (cf. EAC 2011: 15).

This ambitious strategy identifies several areas of focus: legal and administrative framework, infrastructure, energy, macroeconomic environment, health, education and training (primary level, higher level), financial markets, technology and innovation, economic efficiency (in the areas of production and distribution, international trade (through the creation of the COMESA-EAC-SADC tripartite FTA) and the identification of new international markets (cf. EAC 2011: 15).

In relation to industrial entrepreneurship, the strategy recognises the need to support the development of Micro, Small and Medium Enterprises (MSMEs), which it argues 'has the potential of addressing the development needs of the region such as poverty reduction, technological innovation, economic linkages and reduction of disparities in regional development if well mainstreamed into the formal economy (EAC 2011: 38).

Imperatively, apart from explicit reference to the need to address the FiR capacity gaps, this blueprint does also envision the tackling – albeit partially – of most NFiR capacity gaps.

5.4.4.3 East African Community Industrialisation Policy

The Vision of the East African Community Industrialisation Policy is 'a globally competitive environment-friendly and sustainable industrial sector, capable of significantly improving the living standards of East Africa by 2032' (EAC 2012: 10).

The policy is guided by nine principles. These include enhancing equitable industrialisation in the region, strengthening and exploiting policy synergies between industrial policy and other sectoral policy instruments, promoting strategic dialogues between the private and public sectors, strengthening industry linkages between large and MSMEs, promoting targeted industry value chains with widespread linkages and economic benefits extending across the region, promoting industrialisation on the basis of comparative advantage, and enhancing skills and knowledge for industrialisation, and market-led approach to industrialisation. Another important principle is ensuring that the regional industrial policy institutional framework for implementation provides for well-defined and predictable roles of Partner States and EAC institutions, with a clear institutional decision-making framework within the region (cf. EAC 2012: 8).

The policy *selects* six priority sectors, where it purports there are regional comparative advantage, on the basis of factor endowment. They include agro-processing, iron ore and other mineral processing, petrochemicals and gas processing, fertilisers and agro-chemicals, pharmaceuticals and energy and bio-fuels. The policy intends to channel investments into these sectors. Investors in these sectors will be registered as 'strategic regional investors' and benefit from incentives. The attractiveness of the sector, in connection with growth and market share, was another criterion that was used to select the winners (EAC 2012: 9).

Categorisation as 'strategic regional investor' is also tied to meeting other conditions: foster complementarities or enhance collaborative production in the region, scope of investments that require pooling of resources to ensure economies of scale, contribution to linkages (both backwards and forward) in the value chain with a regional dimension, contribution to employment generation, presence in at least two EAC countries (EAC 2012: 9).

As outlined in EAC (2012: 11–12), the planned policy interventions seek to achieve five major development targets:

a   Diversification of the manufacturing base. This should follow the selected priority sectors. The process should be guided and aided by investments and value addition action plans, PPP, industry promotion award schemes. An important undertaking shall involve establishing a centre for the development of strategic industries/enterprises, to manage the industrial transformation scheme.
b   Strengthening institutional capabilities for industrial policy design and management. This should be done at both national and regional levels.
c   Strengthening R&D, technology and innovation capabilities.
d   Expand trade in manufactured products. It sets two thresholds. First, ratio of intra-regional manufactured exports to total manufactured imports should be at least 25 per cent by 2032. Second, the ratio of manufactured exports to total merchandise exports should be at least 60 per cent by 2032.
e   Transforming MSMEs into viable and sustainable business entities. They should contribute at least 50 per cent of manufacturing GDP.

5.4.4.4 East African Community Industrialisation Strategy 2012–2032

The East African Community Industrialisation Strategy dwells in detail on the industrialisation theme in the Partner States. To achieve the ambition for industrial development, the Strategy identifies six priority sectors, i.e. Iron ore and other mineral processing, Fertilisers and agro-chemicals, Pharmaceuticals, Petrochemicals and gas processing, Energy and Bio-fuels.

Furthermore, the Strategy identifies eight major intervention measures that it deems as being necessary in order to effectively implement the EAC industrialisation policy. These include: sector-specific master/action plans for the development of strategic value chains, schemes for investment in strategic regional industries, strengthening the investment environment to encourage value addition, enhancing conformity to regional and international standards – of the product (manufacturing) quality, and specification; enhancing of industrial policy management, formulation, implementation and monitoring at national and regional levels; development of Public Private Partnership (PPP) to ensure collaboration in the establishment of strategic regional industries; developing the capacity of industrial data generation, management and dissemination; increasing demand for locally manufactured goods through regional branding and other strategies and increasing regional exports through Regional Free Zones (RFZ), Special Economic Zones (SEZ) and other measures (cf. EAC 2012: i–ii).

5.5 Regional integration and industrialisation in the Economic Community for West African States

5.5.1 Evolution of the Economic Community for West African States

Although the ECOWAS was not officially established until 1975, there were several preceding milestones. In this regard, the idea to establish a co-operation arrangement for West African states goes back to President William Tubman of Liberia, who made a proposal in that regard in 1964. Subsequently, a first agreement among West African States was signed by Côte d'Ivoire, Guinea, Liberia and Sierra Leone in February 1965, though it did not result in co-operation in practice.

In April 1972, the Nigerian military leader of the time General Yakubu Gowon and his Togolose counterpart, General Gnassingbé Eyadéma re-launched the idea of West African regionalisation in April 1972. Apart from the drawing-up of proposals, consultations involving 12 other countries from the sub-region were conducted in July and August 1973, in order to solicit support for the initiative.

Several meetings of potential member states were held in different countries in the sub-region, to examine the draft treaty: in Lomé, Togo in December 1973, in Accra Ghana in January 1974, in Monrovia, Liberia in January 1975. Eventually, a treaty setting up the ECOWAS, also known as the Lagos Treaty, was signed in Lagos on 28 May 1975 by 15 countries. The founder states were Benin, Côte d'Ivoire, The Gambia, Ghana, Guinea, Guinea-Bissau, Liberia, Mali, Mauritania, Niger, Nigeria, Upper Volta (now Burkina Faso), Senegal, Sierra Leone and Togo.

The mission of ECOWAS was stipulated as being to promote economic integration in all fields of economic activity, particularly industry, transport, telecommunications, energy, agriculture, natural resources, commerce, monetary and financial questions, and social and cultural matters. The ultimate goal was to establish an economic and monetary union.

In 1977, Cape Verde acceded to ECOWAS, becoming its sixteenth member.

Some of the notable subsequent developments include:

a   The signing of a non-aggression protocol in 1990, building on two earlier agreements of 1978 and 1981.
b   The signing of a Protocol on Mutual Defence Assistance in 1981 that provided for the creation of an Allied Armed Force of the Community.
c   The signing of a revised ECOWAS treaty on 24 July 1993. The revisions – intended to accelerate integration – established a West African Parliament, an Economic and Social Council and an ECOWAS Court of Justice, to replace the existing Tribunal.

In December 1999, Mauritania withdrew from ECOWAS. Therefore, as of 2012, the block had 15 members, a population of about 270 million and an estimated GDP of US$400 billion.

5.5.2 *Overview of the industrial performance of the Economic Community of West African States*

The performances of the industrial sectors of the ECOWAS countries appear to be generally in line with the performances of African countries in general, as discussed in detail in Chapter 4 of this book. Table 5.8 shows the ranks of the CIP Index occupied by the five EAC countries that could be ranked by UNIDO in 2010. Data is from a global sample of 135 countries. For the remaining ten ECOWAS countries, relevant data and information were not available.

Notably, all five countries lie far below the global average (which is 0.0846). Also, from the sample of five, only Côte d'Ivoire and Nigeria have CIP indices, which are above the African average (which is 0.0135). In this case as well, for the interested reader, Chapter 4 of this book gives a more detailed account of the CIP Index and ranking of African and comparator countries.

5.5.2 *Using industrialisation to propel West African integration*

There have been obvious efforts by the ECOWAS countries to harness industrialisation as a development strategy. In this connection, ECOWAS, as a regional bloc, has articulated its sentiments about industrialisation-driven development in several of its blueprints, including:

a   The Treaty Establishing the ECOWAS.
b   Revised Treaty of the ECOWAS (1993).
c   The West African Common Industrial Policy (WACIP).

In this case as well, apart from expressing the resolve to pursue an industrial development path, these blueprints outline the concrete interventions needed for

Table 5.8 Ranks of the CIP Index occupied by the ECOWAS countries in 2010

CIP ranking	Country	CIP Index
89	Côte d'Ivoire	0.0166
95	Nigeria	0.0143
101	Senegal	0.0100
118	Ghana	0.0043
124	Cape Verde	0.0032
133	The Gambia	0.0000
By comparison		
1	Global highest: *Japan*	0.5409
	Global average	0.0846
42	African highest: *South Africa*	0.0722
	African average	0.0135
133	Global lowest: *Iraq, Gambia, Eritrea*	0.0000

Source: Based on UNIDO (2013).

Notes
CIP Index = Comparative Industrial Performance Index.

the development and meaningful integration of the ECOWAS countries in the global economy. The proposed measures take into account the diverse circumstances that impact internal development and shape international economic relations between ECOWAS member states and the rest of the world, such as Africa Growth Opportunity Act (AGOA), NEPAD, WTO Agreements, Millennium Development Goals (MDGs), etc. (cf. ECOWAS 2010: 37–38).

5.5.3.1 Industrialisation in the treaty establishing the West African Economic Community

ECOWAS was established through the 'Multilateral Treaty of the Economic Community of West African States', which was concluded at Lagos on 28 May 1975. Promoting co-operation in industrial activities is explicitly mentioned in Article 2 as one of the aims of the Treaty.

Thereupon, Articles 28–32, which are dedicated to industrial development specify concrete measures through which industrial transformation should be achieved. These measures include:

a   *Exchange of information on major industrial projects.* This was specified to cover information on industrial projects' feasibility studies, industrial projects' reports, industrial foreign businesses operating in the countries, industrial development experiences, industrial research and information. Other specified issues included conducting joint industrial studies, and jointly financing research and transfer of technology (TOT), and jointly developing new products whose production use materials common in some or all countries in the bloc (cf. Article 29).

b   *Harmonisation of industrial incentives and industrial development plans.* The harmonisation of policies should create similar conducive conditions across the region, in support of industrial development. Also, member countries agree to exchange industrial plans, so as to avoid what the Treaty terms 'unhealthy competition' (cf. Article 30).

c   *Personnel exchange, training and joint ventures.* Thus, apart from exchange of experts at all levels and in different fields, the countries agree to undertake joint industrial projects. Experts may also be trained in the technical training institutions within the bloc (cf. Article 31).

d   *Remedial measures.* The issues at stake here are accelerating industrial development, ensuring equitable industrial development within the region and reducing the gap in industrial development to the rest of the world (cf. Article 32).

5.5.3.2 Industrialisation in the 'Revised Treaty of the Economic Community of West African States'

The objective of the 'Revised Treaty of the Economic Community of West African States' signed in Cotonou in 1993 is to pursue regional integration, with the intention of establishing an Economic Union (EU) (cf. sub-article e 3[1], sub-article 3[2] [d] and sub-articles 3[2] [e] to 3[2] [j]). In this connection, it stipulates the promotion of integration programmes, projects and activities in industry, alongside those related to human resources, education, energy, money and finance, science and technology – all of which are critical ingredients of an industrial development regime. Other areas in which projects and activities are specified are agriculture and natural resources, transport and communications, trade, taxation, economic reform policies, information, culture, services, health, tourism and legal matters (cf. sub-article 3[2] [a]). It also embraces harmonising and co-ordinating policies for the protection of the environment (cf. sub-article 3[2] [b]), and supporting the establishment of joint production enterprises (cf. sub-article 3[2] [c]).

Subsequently, Article 26 articulates explicitly the bloc's industrialisation agenda. Among other things, it underlines the resolve to co-operate in industry, and thereby:

a   Identifies several priority industries: food and agro-based industries, building and construction industries, metallurgical industries, mechanical industries, electrical industries, electronics industries, computer industries, pharmaceutical industries, chemical industries, petrochemical industries, forestry industries, energy industries, textile and leather industries, transport and communications industries, bio-technology industries and tourist and cultural industries (cf. sub-article 3[a]).
b   Seeks also to: strengthen or establish private and public multinational industrial projects, promote small and medium scale industries (SMSIs), promote intermediate industries to increase the local component of industrial output in the bloc, prepare a regional master industrialisation plan to guide the establishment of industries, encourage the establishment of specialised financing institutions for multinational industrial projects, facilitate development of multinational enterprises, encourage participation of the region's entrepreneurs in the regional industrialisation process, promote the sale and consumption of strategic industrial products manufactured in the region, promote regional technical co-operation and the exchange of experience in industrial technology and implement technical training programmes, establish regional data and a statistical information base to support industrial development at the regional and continental levels, promote (on the basis of natural resource endowments) industrial specialisation and adopt common standards and appropriate quality control systems (cf. sub-article 3[b] to 3[l]).

5.5.3.2 *West African Common Industrial Policy*

WACIP's vision statement is 'to maintain a solid industrial structure, which is globally competitive, environment-friendly and capable of significantly improving the living standards of the people by 2030'. It underscores the resolve of the members of ECOWAS to 'collectively becoming an important player in the

globalization process in the framework of sustainable industrial development'
(cf. ECOWAS 2010: 37–38).

As specified in section 4 of Part II (cf. ECOWAS 2010: 38), in order to achieve this ambition, WACIP pursues the specific objectives of progressively:

a   Diversifying and broadening the region's industrial production base by raising the local raw material processing from the current rates of 15 per cent to 20 per cent, to an average of 30 per cent by 2030. This should be facilitated by upgrading existing industrial capacities, and developing new ones.
b   Increasing the manufacturing industry's share of regional GDP from current averages of 6 per cent to 7 per cent, to an average of 20 per cent by 2030.
c   Increasing intra-ECOWAS trade from the current level of less than 12 per cent, to a target of 40 per cent by 2030. In this regard, manufactured goods are targeted to constitute 50 per cent of intra-regional trade.
d   Increasing the volume of exports of goods manufactured in West Africa to the global market, from the current level of 0.1 per cent to 1 per cent by 2030. The development of skills, industrial competitiveness and quality infrastructure (standardisation, accreditation and certification), particularly in the areas of information, communication and transport are identified as being important propellers to facilitate the achievement of this goal.

The same section explicitly identifies the intervention measures, which can be summarised into: private sector development (PSD) in order to make it more competitive, development of industrial production capacities, development of infrastructure, development of support services, facilitate international exchange of experiences of the private sector among member countries of the bloc, implement investment competition rules, balance inter-country economic development, establish viable industrial financing systems and mobile resources for industrial upgrading from diverse sources, prompt implementation of the Common External Tariff (CET) that is already being implemented by some of the member states (ECOWAS 2010: 39).

5.6 Africa's regional integration and industrialisation: conclusions and way forward

5.6.1 Conclusions

Theory suggests that regional integration can play a role in stimulating industrialisation. This is because it makes the member countries of a bloc more attractive for industrial investments – especially for manufacturing investments – due to 'large market' considerations. However, for this to happen the circumstances must be right, also in terms of other factors that define a location's quality. Consistent with the analytical philosophy of this book, these other factors include the FiR capacities and NFiR capacities in the country aspiring to industrialise.

Using the EAC and ECOWAS as case studies, this chapter has examined and related industrialisation and regionalisation efforts in Africa from a historical perspective. It has highlighted the evolution of the regional integration phenomenon in Africa. Also, it has discussed implicit and explicit measures to support industrialisation embedded in the regionalisation schemes, highlighting their purported strengths and caveats.

Thus, the broad conclusions are summarised in the subsequent subsections.

5.6.1.1 Significance of integration schemes for industrialisation

Regional integration initiatives, undertaken both during and after the colonial period, were relevant for promoting industrial transformation. However, because the colonial territories were supposed to serve as peripheries of the colonial centres, industrialisation was *de jure* and de facto suppressed. To the extent that the colonial rulers found industrialisation necessary, its development was limited scope-wise (only some basic industrial activities, modelled upon Import Substitution Industrialisation – ISI – promoted through high tariffs), and in terms of spatial distribution (limited to a few selected key seats of power). Also, because the measures in this category were characterised by lack of holistic agendas, they had little chances of triggering meaningful industrialisation.

The integration schemes proliferated in the post-colonial era. They also contained some ample and elaborate provisions to promote industrialisation. However, it is also clear that the African countries were not the masters of their economic development agenda. Due to poor performance of the economies, and the deficits in terms of FiR, matters became increasingly dictated or at least influenced by bilateral donors and multilateral donors. Consequently, the industrial development agenda remained largely symbolic, and could not be implemented as planned. Instead, there was a clear shift *from country-initiated schemes* towards a plethora of *externally initiated and resourced schemes*. Examples of these schemes that had a great bearing for Africa's industrialisation, because they addressed one or the other capacity gaps, include: Implementation Strategy of the Action Plan for the Accelerated Industrial Development for Africa (AIDA), Alliance for Industrialisation of Africa (AIA), African Productive Capacity Initiative (APCI), Cairo Agenda of Action (CAA), Industrial Development Decade for Africa (IDDA) I and II, Millennium Development Goals (MDGs), Structural Adjustment Programmes (SAPs) dictated by the Bretton Woods Institutions (BWI), United Nations Programme for the African Economic Recovery and Development (UN-PAAERD), United Nations Transport and Communications Decade for Africa (UNTACDA) I and II and African (Accelerated) Agribusiness and Agro-industries Development Initiative (3ADI). The schemes, which are introduced in Chapter 1, are discussed in detail in Chapter 6 of this book.

5.6.1.2 Caveats of industrialisation provisions of the most recent integration schemes

The most recent provisions on industrialisation, in both the EAC and ECOWAS, are very comprehensive and elaborate. In the cases of both RECs, the documents are of an improved quality, and there are obvious attempts to address most of the gaps that should be tackled, to achieve industrial transformation in African countries. However, they too are not without caveats:

a   The most obvious caveats of the EAC industrialisation agenda include a *narrow conceptual base* (i.e. they correctly promote industrialisation on the basis of comparative advantage, but remain largely silent on competitive advantage).
    Also, the agenda lacks concrete action plans to promote *Large Scale Industrial Enterprises* (LSIEs) as well as *Small and Medium Scale Industrial Enterprises* (SMSIEs). Furthermore, there are no concrete action plans for *mineral beneficiation* and for the development of *agribusiness and agro-industries*. Also, its financing strategy is incomplete – it does not exhaust the possible sources of industrial finance.
b   ECOWAS's relevant industrial promotion provisions appear to be comprehensive, and generally the quality of the documents are vividly better, compared to those of the EAC. However, given the poor performance of the countries, it is clear that it has not been possible to translate the 'correct rhetoric' into actual industrial development actions.
c   Lack of ambition. For instance, it is hard to see how WACIP's target of increasing value adding to locally produced raw materials from the current levels of 15–20 per cent, to an average of 30 per cent by 2030, would make any country 'industrialised'. This is a clear example of benchmarking problems through which very modest targets are set, the achievement of which will not bring about the desired development results.

5.6.1.3 Performance of the industrial economies

In terms of results, the performances of the industrial sectors of these two RECs (i.e. EAC and ECOWAS) have been reminiscent of the performances of African countries in general (cf. Chapter 4 of this book). In this connection, the overall verdict can be derived from where Africa stands today in the global industrial economy. As conspicuously demonstrated by the analysis of the two RECs, some 50 years after most of the countries regained (at least their political) independence, they belong to the least industrialised – with none categorised by the United Nations Industrial Development Organization (UNIDO) as being industrialised. The continent's potential to produce diversified and value added manufactured goods remains largely untapped.

The implications about the developmental effect of the industrialisation agenda cannot be missed. Seemingly, the various frameworks (policies, strategies, treaties, action plans, etc.) guiding regional integration have not helped

Africa to industrialise. Altogether, the following generalisations hold – at least in part – for all member countries of the two RECs:

a   The immense potential of the agriculture and industrial sectors, as sources of agricultural and mineral raw materials have not been leveraged for industrialisation (cf. ECOSOC, UNECA, AU 2013; OAU 1980).
b   Industrialisation is still at a very early stage of development (UNIDO 2013).
c   The manufacturing base is very narrow. Literally, all countries produce just a handful of industrial goods, of which only a few can trade competitively in international markets (cf. ECOSOC, UNECA, AU 2013; UNIDO 2013).

5.6.2 Improving Africa's industrial performance: which way forward?

At the moment, things appear to be rather good, and the narrative, especially about Africa's economic growth, is positive and optimistic. As noted by ECOSOC, UNECA, AU (2013):

Since the early 1990s, Africa has been experiencing robust growth rates.... It is worth noting that six of the world's ten fastest-growing economies (Democratic Republic of Congo, Ethiopia, Ghana, Mozambique, Tanzania, and Zambia) are in Africa, recording at least 7 per cent growth rate. The optimism from around the globe has led some commentators to predict that the average African economy will outpace its Asian counterpart in the next five years. The respected Economist magazine, which dubbed Africa a decade ago as the *hopeless continent* is currently highlighting its economic prospects, calling Africa the *hopeful continent*.

However, we also know that this impressive performance is not exclusively driven by the right sources of growth. Apart from macroeconomic policy reforms, it has been attributable to, among other things, discoveries and exploitation of oil and ores, surge in commodity demand, commodity price booms, inflows of Official Development Assistance (ODA) reduced debt burdens, inflow of Foreign Direct Investments (FDI) to buy strategic resources usually in the extractive industry (cf. ECOSOC, UNECA, AU 2013) and the Service Sector.

But, for the growth that we witness now to be sustainable, African countries need to get the sources of growth right. They need industrial transformation, in tandem with the transformation of the agricultural and mineral sectors, as the bases of a sustainable industrial sector.

Therefore, African economies need to develop diverse industrial capacities – and hence capacities to add value to their large reservoir of natural and agricultural resources.

Also, while both market size and locational qualities (of which diverse FiR and NFiR capacities play a key role) are necessary conditions for sustainable transformation, taken in isolation none presents sufficient conditions for the same industrial development. Therefore measures to deepen intra-regional market integration should be adopted. This means African RECs and countries should move faster to realise a single African market.

Moreover, as pointed out in Matambalya (2011), in view of the experiences of the EAC and ECOWAS economies, the following should be seriously considered in the architecture of the industrial development agenda of African RECs:

a   Shift from *activist* and *specific* industrial policy to a careful mixture of both *activist* and *specific* and *neutral* policies. This means a hybrid agenda that recognises the role of the various forms of government intervention, and private sector.
b   The capacity of African RECs and their individual member countries to achieve industrial development largely depends on the ability to mobilise and deploy diverse FiR and NFiR capacities. Thus, it is crucial to focus on creating diverse NFiR capacities (entrepreneurship, knowledge and skills, institutions, physical infrastructure, technology base), and FiR capacities (financial institutions and financing instruments).
c   A mandatory strategic, selective and responsible involvement of the government in the development of the real industrial economy. Hence, governments should participate, through equity, in industrial ventures, particularly those involving large capital outlays. This is necessary if the region's endowments are to be leveraged for industrialisation.
d   Setting thresholds for indigenous and local entrepreneurial participation in industrial investments involving the extraction of major resources, such as mining. Furthermore, this should ensure mineral beneficiation.
e   Political commitment of the member states of African RECs to achieving industrial development.
f   Negotiating conducive forms of interactions between member countries of African RECs and other countries in the global industrial economy. International economic partnerships – bilateral, regional and multilateral – should be beneficent to African countries.

Finally, it is worthwhile noting that there have evidently been many attempts to find an answer to Africa's great developmental question through industrialisation. To this end, some good blueprints have been developed again and again. However, the main limitation appears to be that the rhetoric contained in them does not translate into concrete action plans for industrialisation. To set Africa on an industrial development trajectory, this caveat must be overcome.

Notes

1 A good example here is the Customs Union (CU) between the European Union (EU) and Israel.
2 A good example in this case is the evolution of the relationship between the European Economic Community (EEC) and later European Union (EU) and African Caribbean

and Pacific (ACP) group of nations through several arrangements (year signed in brackets): 'Regime of Associations' of the Treaty of Rome (1957), Youndé I (1963) and II (169) Conventions, Lomé I (1975), II (1979), III (1984), and to IV (1989) Conventions; Cotonou Agreement (2000), and Interim Economic Partnership Agreements (EPAs) initialled by African groups from 2007 onward.

3 Older CUs include, (i) CU in Spain and Portugal (1845–1860), and (ii) The German *Zollvrein* (i.e. German CU), which existed from 1834 to 1871 and linked almost all German States (cf. Henderson 1981).

4 The ECU was the predecessor to the Customs Union of Central African States, which later tuned into the Economic Commission for Central African States (ECCAS).

5 Community of Sahel-Saharan States.

6 In English: West African Economic and Monetary Union (WAEMU).

References

AU (2001). *The New Partnership for Africa's Development*. African Union. October.

AUC (2004). *Strategic Plan of the Commission of the African Union. Volume 2: 2004–2007 Strategic Framework of the Commission of the African Union*. African Union Commission. May.

AUC (2009). *Strategic Plan 2009–2012*. African Union Commission. Addis Ababa. 19 May.

AUC (2013). *Third Draft Strategic Plan 2014–2017*. African Union Commission. Addis Ababa. 13 May.

Checchini, P., Catinat, M. and Jacquemin, A. (1990). *Benefits of a Single Market*. Wildwood House, Aldershot, Hants.

Cornett, A. (1999). *Regional Integration and Regional Development?: Concepts and Empirical Relevance*. Paper presented at the 38th Congress of the European Regional Integration, Dublin.

DeRosa, D. (1998). *Regional Integration Arrangements: Static Economic Theory, Quantitative Findings, and Policy Guidelines*. Background Paper for World Bank Policy Research Report.

EAC (2009). *Protocol on the Establishment of the East African Community Common Market*. East African Community. Arusha.

EAC (2011). *EAC Development Strategy (2011/12–2015/16): Deepening and Accelerating Integration – One People, One Destiny*. August.

EAC (2012). *The East African Industrialisation Policy in Brief: Opening Opportunities for Growth and Expansion of Cross Border Manufacturing and Upgrading Small and Medium Enterprises*. East African Community. Arusha. August.

ECOSOC, UNECA, AU (2013). *Industrialization for an Emerging Africa*. Aide Memoire of Meeting of the Committee of Experts of the Sixth Joint Annual Meetings of the ECA Conference of African Ministers of Finance, Planning and Economic Development and AU Conference of Ministers of Economy and Finance. United Nations Economic and Social Council, Economic Commission For Africa, and African Union. Abidjan. 21–24 March.

ECOWAS (2010). *West African Common Industrial Policy*. Economic Community of West African States. July.

Ernits, R. (2003). Location as the reason for the problems of old industrialised settlements: The case of Estonia. *European Journal of Spatial Development*. No. 4. February.

Feinstein, C. (2005). *An Economic History of South Africa: Conquest, Discrimination, and Development*. Cambridge University Press. Cambridge.

Gareth, A. (2010). *African Economic Development and Colonial Legacies*. International Development Policy Series. The Graduate Institute. Geneva.

Harris, J. (1980). Market size, industrialization, and regional integration. *Social and Economic Studies*. Vol. 29, No. 4. Special Issues in Honour of Sir William Arthur Lewis 1979 Nobel Laureate (December 1980), pp. 76–84.

Henderson, W. (1981). *The German Zollverein and the European Economic Community*. In: *Zeitschrift für die gesamte Staatswissenschaft*/Journal of Institutional and Theoretical Economics. Bd. 137, H. 3, Economic Reconstruction in Europe: The Reintegration of Western Germany: A Symposium. September, pp. 491–507.

Kilby, P. (1975). Manufacturing in Colonial Africa. In Gan, H. and Duignan, P. (eds) *Colonialism in Africa 1870–1960, Vol. 4, The Economics of Colonialism 1870–1960*. Cambridge University Press. Cambridge, pp. 470–520.

Matambalya, F. (2011). *Lessons from Earlier Industrialization Policy Initiatives in Africa: Experiences of Industrial Policy Management in the EAC*. Presentation at the Conference 'High-level Policy Dialogue Conference on EAC Industrialisation Policy and Strategy', held at Ole Sereni Hotel, Nairobi, 2–4 May. East African Community and *Gesellschaft für Internationale Zusammenarbeit*. May.

OAU (1980). *Lagos Plan of Action for the Economic Development of Africa 1980–2000*. Organisation of African Unity. Addis Ababa.

Sekgoma, G. (1994). The Lagos Plan of Action and some aspects of development in Sierra Leone. *Pula: Botswana Journal of Development Studies*. Vol. 8. No. 2.

UNECA (2004). *Assessing Regional Integration in Africa*. United Nations Economic Commission for Africa. Addis Ababa.

UNIDO (2013). *Competitive Industrial Performance Report 2012/2013*. United Nations Industrial Development Organization. Vienna.

Viner, J. (1950). *The Customs Union Issues*. Carnegie Endowment for International Peace. New York.

Websites

ECOWAS: History. Available at: http://globaledge.msu.edu/trade-blocs/ecowas/history.

www.ngrguardiannews.com/national-news/82161-ecowas-seeks-support-for-industrialisation-policy.

6 Pan-African and multilateral schemes and Africa's industrialisation

Synthesis of substance and legacy

Francis A.S.T. Matambalya

6.1 Antecedents

This chapter delves into the many pan-African and multilateral schemes intended to set Africa on an industrial transformation trajectory. The departure point is that, cognisant of the essence of industrialisation, literally all governments in post-colonial Africa and their international development partners have prioritised industrial development, and initiated measures to realise this goal. Most of the industrialisation schemes undertaken in the immediate post-colonial period were nationally conceived.[1]

However, partly in tandem with efforts undertaken at national levels, complementary schemes were conceived and carried out at sub-regional levels (cf. Chapter 5 of this book),[2] and within the framework of pan-African economic governance. Though the Organisation of African Unity (OAU) and later the African Union (AU) were the main custodians of these schemes, their architecture and implementation involved also different United Nations (UN) institutions, such as the United Nations Industrial Development Organization (UNIDO), United Nations Economic Commission for Africa (UNECA), International Trade Centre (ITC), etc.

Furthermore, African countries have been eligible for different multilateral schemes seeking to promote industrial development. While some of these schemes were specifically designed for Africa, others targeted all developing countries with similar industrialisation needs.

Table 6.1 presents a flowchart of various schemes. It implies a proliferation of schemes, which were also characterised by significant overlaps.[3]

6.2 Pan-African economic governance and industrialisation

The contemporary evolution of pan-African economic governance initiatives can be traced to the 1980 Lagos Plan of Action for the Development of Africa and the 1991 Abuja Treaty that established the African Economic Community (AEC). The treaty envisaged Regional Economic Communities (RECs) as the building blocks for the AEC. It called upon member states to strengthen existing RECs and provided timeframes for creating new ones where they did not exist.

Table 6.1 Evolution of the schemes for the industrialisation of African countries from the late 1970s onward

Scheme	Late 1970s to 1990														1991 to 2000										Beyond 2000	
	77	78	79	80	81	82	83	84	85	86	87	88	89	90	91	92	93	94	95	96	97	98	99	2000	Early[a]	Later[b]
1 UNTACDA I	█	█	█	█	█	█	█	█	█	█	█	█	█													
2 IDDA I				█	█	█	█	█	█	█	█	█	█	█	█	█	█	█	█	█	█	█	█	█	█	
3 UN-PAAERD										█	█	█	█	█												
4 UNTACDA II												█	█	█	█	█	█	█	█	█	█	█	█	█	█	
5 SAP				█	█	█	█	█	█	█	█	█	█	█	█	█	█	█	█	█	█	█	█			
6 UNNADAF															█	█	█	█	█	█	█	█	█	█		
7 IDDA II																	█	█	█	█	█	█	█	█	█	
8 CAA																			█	█	█	█	█	█	█	
9 AIA																							█	█	█	
10 MDGs																							█	█	█	
11 APCI																									█	
12 AIDA																									█	█
13 3ADI																									█	█

Sources: Author. Based on different sources.

Notes

a from first half of first decade onward, b from second half of first decade onward. AIA = Alliance for Industrialisation of Africa; AIDA = Accelerated Industrial Development of Africa; APCI = African Productive Capacity Initiative; CAA = Cairo Agenda of Action; IDDA = Industrial Development Decade for Africa; MDGs = Millennium Development Goals; PAAERD = Programme of Action for the African Economic Recovery and Development; SAP = Structural Adjustment Programme; UN = United Nations; UNTACDA = United Nations Transport and Communications Decade in Africa

Moreover, the African Union has designated eight RECs[4] as the base for Africa's economic integration, while recognising another six[5] as also being important (cf. Chapter 5 of this book).

In connection to industrialisation, the schemes under the domination of pan-Africanism can be divided into two distinct phases. The first phase includes those schemes that were launched between the late 1970s and the late 1980s, thus coinciding with the second and third post-colonial decades. The second phase comprises programmes initiated from the early 1990s onward, and therefore largely from the fourth post-colonial decade onward.

6.2.1 Schemes launched during the second and third post-colonial decades

Considering that most African countries became independent in the early 1960s, the period in question is between the early 1970s and early 1990s. This was a time of major reforms across the African continent. Four major schemes were initiated during this time, including UNTACDA I (1977–1988), IDDA I (1980–2000), UNTACDA II (1988–2000). Notably, while their implementation period partly overlapped, all were concluded by 2000.

6.2.1.1 First United Nations Transport and Communications Decade in Africa

Considering the importance of the transport and communications sector for Africa's development endeavours, UNECA Conference of Ministers adopted in March 1977 a resolution requesting the United Nations General Assembly (UNGA) to proclaim a United Nations Transport and Communications Decade in Africa (UNTACDA). The intention of the proclamation was to focus attention on the special needs of transport and communications in Africa.

Consequently, the resolution was endorsed by the Economic and Social Council (ECOSOC), and the first United Nations Transport and Communications Decade in Africa (abbreviated as UNTACDA I) was officially proclaimed by UNGA through its resolution 32/160 of 19 December 1977. UNTACDA I was to cover the period 1978–1988.

In spite of UNTACDA I, several constraints continued to exist and African countries continued to be plagued by a poor state of transport networks and low transport network connectivity. This manifested the wide gap between planned targets and the level of achievement. Obvious challenges and constraints include: inappropriate national policies (or rather inappropriate 'governance frameworks') to guide the planned efforts, non-implementation or limited implementation of planned activities to support industrial development (including those in international agreements), inadequate institutional capacity, inappropriate technological solutions, and inadequate human resources capacity. Consequently, Africa continued to have the least developed rolling stock among the major regions of the world.

6.2.1.2 First industrial development decade for Africa

From the concepts and objectives of the Lagos Plan of Action emerged the idea of a decade specifically devoted to translate the goals of the Lagos Plan of Action into industrial programmes and projects. In this connection, the *Industrial Development Decade for Africa* (IDDA) was proclaimed by the United Nations General Assembly and the 83rd plenary meeting of 5 December 1980. The assembly also called upon UNIDO and UNECA to cooperate closely with the OAU, to formulate proposals to implement the programme for IDDA and to monitor its progress.

Subsequently, proposals for an IDDA I, 1980–1990 were adopted at the Sixth Conference of African Ministers of Industry, held at Addis Ababa, Ethiopia in November 1981. As more programmes evolved, the arrangement later became popular under the name First Industrial Development Decade for Africa (IDDA I). It aimed to use industrialisation as a means of attaining Africa's self-reliance and self-sustainment. Therefore, IDDA was to translate LAP into industrial development programmes and industrial development projects.

6.2.1.3 Continuation of IDDA I and SAP

In reality, the implementation of IDDA I did not appear to deliver the expected results, and the programme's implementation timeline was extended beyond 1990, i.e. to 2000. One remarkable 'coincidence' is that IDDA I ran concurrently with the newly created World Bank's development instrument, the Structural Adjustments Programme (SAP), funded by structural adjustment loans. SAP prescribed to African countries macro-economic reforms, market and price deregulation, and trade liberalisation.

One of the obvious caveats of IDDA I was that it was rooted in a top-down decision model, with the key players being OAU, UNECA, and United Nations Industrial Development Organization (UNIDO). Thus, it crucially lacked an interactive approach in management. Implicitly, decisions made by OAU, UNECA, and UNIDO were expected to filter down to sub-regional (REC levels) and eventually to country levels (cf. Figure 6.1).

The Bujumbura Ministerial Conference of 1986 recommended evaluation of IDDA I, subsequent to which an appraisal was carried out in 1988. Several conclusions were reached: the success of initiative was presumably prevented by among other things:

a   The disastrous economic performance circumstances of the 1980s (which were manifested by: over borrowing, vagaries of weather, institutional deficiencies, desolate or absence of physical infrastructure, and apparently also wrong policy stance).

b   A lack of an implementation strategy. This meant that there was neither a co-ordination mechanism, nor a mechanism for monitoring progress.

The SAP, on teh other hand, ushered in the end of Africa's Policy Space, and caused long-term damage to the continent's cream of economic emancipation

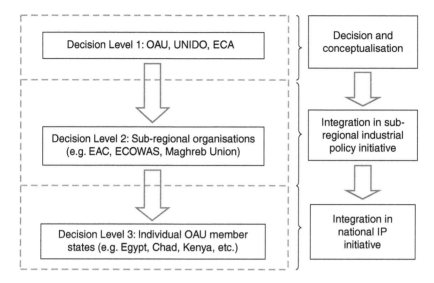

Figure 6.1 Decision flows in a centralised decion model *à la* IDDA I.

Notes
ECA = (United Nations) Economic Commission for Africa; ECOWAS = Economic Community of West African States; EAC = East African Community; IDDA = Industrial Development Decade for Africa; OAU = Organisatiuon of African Unity; UNIDO = United Nations Industrial Development Organization.

and freedom. Sadly, SAP did not guarantee the creation of sustainable capacities for Africa's 'organic' development.

6.2.1.4 Second United Nations Transport and Communications Decade in Africa

The evaluation of the implementation of UNTACDA I, which was undertaken in 1988, revealed major inadequacies of the transport and communications systems in Africa and their inabilities to promote economic growth and development, in spite of the efforts made by African Governments and donors. These findings prompted the UNECA Conference of Ministers in 1988 to request UNGA to proclaim a second UNTACDA. Accordingly, by its resolution 43/179 of 20 December 1988, UNGA proclaimed UNTACDA II, to cover the period 1991–2000.

After a two-year period (i.e. from 1989 to 1991), during which the partners identified and elaborated the main objectives of UNTACDA II, and which were subsequently adopted by the Conference of African Ministers of Transport, Communications and Planning in February 1991 in Abuja, Nigeria, the implementation of UNTACDA II started in 1991.

The goals of UNTACDA II were to establish an efficient integrated transport and communications system as a basis for the physical integration of Africa, so as to facilitate traffic movement, foster trade, and enable the achievement of self-sustained economic development as envisaged in the Abuja Treaty establishing AEC.

Some of the main ways in which UNTACDA II differed from UNTACDA I were that:

a   A bottom-up approach was used in the design of the programme (i.e. global objectives, strategies, and mechanisms), thereby making its African ownership more vivid.
b   A better management structure, which included National Co-ordinating Committees (NCCs), Sub-regional Working Groups, Sub-sectoral Working Groups, a Resource Mobilization Committee (RMC) that after the mid-term review was renamed the Advisory Committee for Programme Promotion (ACPP), Inter-Agency Co-ordinating Committee (IACC), and the specification of the lead agency.
c   Several evaluations were built in, i.e. it was decided to evaluate it every three years, starting in 1994, so that corrective action could be taken before it was too late.

6.2.2 Schemes launched during the fourth and fifth post-colonial decades

In this case, the period in question is between the early 1990s to the first decade of the 2000s. This period involved further reforms, which were undertaken largely in response to the subdued developmental impact of the schemes launched earlier. Significant among the new schemes coinciding with this phase are IDDA II (1993 onward), CAA (1995 onward), AIA (1996 onward), New Partnership for Africa's Development (NEPAD) from 2001 onward, implementation strategy of the Action Plan for the Accelerated Industrial Development of Africa (AIDA) (2008 onward), and 3ADI (2009 onwards). Though nominally, these initiatives are still running, in fact most of them are dormant or have never been seriously implemented.

6.2.2.1 Second industrial development decade for Africa

The second Industrial Development Decade for Africa (IDDA II) was proclaimed by the Harare Ministerial on 29th June 1989, and its implementation was to run from 1993 to 2002.

The IDDA II was developed in the context of several weaknesses related to IDDA I and SAP. The most cited ones include: limited awareness about IDDA I by stakeholders, lack of implementation strategy, underdevelopment of entrepreneurship and enterprise development, and ostensibly poorly managed privatisation programmes, attribution of de-industrialisation to DDA I, poor/mixed results from SAP, Africa's continued dependence on external financing, continued human resources underdevelopment in the continent, limitations of the continent's sub-regional institutions (underlined by inadequate co-ordination, consultations, co-operation; as well as resource deficiencies).

The design of IDDA II took into account several considerations: decentralisation, country-ownership of programmes, anchoring in regional integration, bottom-up decision model, redefinition of the role of the state, rationalising/refocusing the use of resources to achieve greater impact, involvement of development partners (UNIDO, donors), equitable distribution of projects among member states.

IDDA II sought to progressively achieve the African Common Market, and eventually the African Economic Union (AEU). Its components included: national programming, integrated sub-regional programmes, and integrated regional programmes.

In terms of UNIDO's management structure for IDDA II, the co-ordination unit for Sub-Saharan Africa (SSA) was integrated in the Africa Bureau, while the Arab Africa countries were co-ordinated by the Arab Countries Bureau.

IDDA II followed an integrated approach, which embraced actions for the optimisation of sectoral interlinkages, improvement of public enterprise performance, building entrepreneurship and entrepreneurial base, mainstreaming informal sector, mainstreaming Small Scale Enterprises (SSE), market orientation, industrial culture, regional co-operation and integration, and environmental sensitivity. Figure 6.2 depicts IDDA II's action-oriented integrated approach.

6.2.2.2 Cairo Agenda of Action

The CAA was adopted in 1995. It sought to mobilise domestic and international resources, and deploy them to achieve: governance, peace, stability

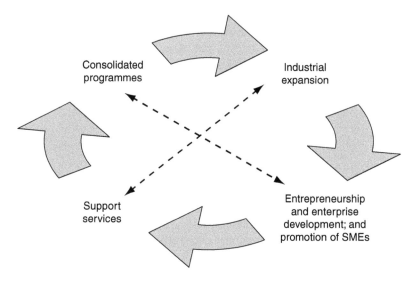

Figure 6.2 Elements of an action-oriented programme *à la* IDDA II.

Notes
IDDA = Industrial Development Decade for Africa; SMEs = Small and Medium Scale Enterprises.

and development, food security, Human Resource Development (HRD) and Capacity Building (CB), and regional economic co-operation and integration.

Concerning industrial development, it focused on achieving: structural change and transformation, increasing incomes and employment, and diversifying exports.

6.2.2.3 Alliance for Industrialisation of Africa

Initiated in 1996 by the then OAU, with support of UNIDO in co-operation with UNECA, AIA aimed at revitalising the industrial development of the member states of the OAU. Generally, it aimed at boosting the implementation of IDDA II in light of new challenges emerging from: conclusion of the Uruguay round, and the increased scope and intensity of globalisation. Specifically, it sought to provide a mechanism for African leaders to define appropriate industrial development strategies, and to mobilise political will and resources to their achievement.

6.2.2.4 New Partnership for Africa's Development

NEPAD adopted by African Leaders in 2001 identified economic transformation through industrialisation as a critical vehicle for growth and poverty reduction in the region.[6] Hence, Trade, Industry, Market Access, and Private sector development are some of the nine priority sectors in the AU/NEPAD African Action Plan 2010–2015.

Though the ideas, which are advocated in its sectoral priorities, appear not to be always logically clustered, and do not always follow a coherent sequence, generally NEPAD is a monumental initiative, which if fully implemented will see Africa go a long way towards achieving industrial transformation. This is because it identifies several capacity gaps that must be addressed in order to put African countries on a sustainable development path.

Also scattered within the document are several measures that are relevant for developing a conducive governance framework[7] to guide the economic transformation of African countries.

A NEPAD ON THE ESSENTIAL CAPACITIES FOR SUSTAINABLE
DEVELOPMENT

In line with the industrial development philosophy propagated in this book (cf. Chapter 13), Table 6.2 attempts to logically cluster the priority sectors identified for development by NEPAD into measures relevant for the development of Financial Resource (FiR) capacities, and measures relevant for the development of Non-Financial Resource (NFiR) capacities.

Notably, the proposed measures to address FiR capacities underline the need to diverse the sources of resources for development finance. However, the proposed measures have two gaps. First, they fall short of explaining the needs to redress the underdevelopment of financial institutions in Africa.

Table 6.2 Logical clustering of NEPAD's sectoral priorities into measures intended to develop FiR and NFiR capacities

	Challenge	Priority measures
Measures to develop FiR capacities	Sources of financial resources	Mobilise domestic resources, debt relief, ODA, private capital flows
Measures to develop NFiR capacities	Infrastructure capacities	Bridge gaps in ICTs, energy, transport, water and sanitation
	Human resources capacities	Brain gain,[1] education, health
	Technological capacities	Science and technology platforms

Source: Author. Based on AU (2001).

Notes
1 This is achieved through facilitating brain circulation, and thereby reversing brain drain into brain gain.
ODA = Official Development Assistance; FiR = Financial Resources; NFiR = Non-Financial Resources.

Second, they overlook the need to develop financial instruments, which are essential to finance large scale development projects, of the nature required to transform Africa.

The measures to develop NFiR capacities are a lot more comprehensive: identifying priorities in infrastructure, human resources, and technology. Actions related to another important NFiR capacity, i.e. industrial entrepreneurship, are presented under the sub-heading 'resources'.

Nevertheless, in this case as well, there are shortfalls. A notable omission related to NFiR capacities refers to the need to develop diverse institutions (i.e. organisations), both public and private and across all sectors, to advocate and support the process of economic transformation.

B NEPAD ON THE GOVERNANCE FRAMEWORK FOR SUSTAINABLE DEVELOPMENT

NEPAD is also conscious of the influence of the internal and external forces of a *governance framework* (cf. also Chapters 4, 5, 11, 12, 13, and 14) for sustainable development. Explicit reference to issues relevant for a conducive governance framework in the proposed programme of action includes the need for the promotion of African exports, as well as in the removal of Non-Tariff Barriers (NTBs). Hence, among other things, improving customs procedures, increasing intra-regional trade through promoting cross-border interaction among firms, negotiating measures and agreements to facilitate access to world market by African products, trade liberalisation through regional trade agreements, are seen as necessary conditions for encouraging African exports. Likewise, the improvement of Africa's access to foreign markets is deemed necessary for encouraging participation in the international trading system (cf. AU 2001: 55–58).

6.2.2.5 African Productive Capacity Initiative

The African Productive Capacity Initiative (APCI) was launched by the AU in July 2004, as NEPAD's sustainable industrial development strategy. It aimed at promoting manufacturing value-added in African countries. The initiatives approach included the following:

a   Build an African common vision of productive capacity based on the value chain approach.
b   Highlight sectoral priorities as part of specific segments of the value chain based on comparative advantage.
c   Harmonise industrial policies/strategies at national/regional levels based on co-operation/collaboration.
d   Facilitate implementation of the African Peer Review Mechanism (APRM) on industrial performance/competencies based on benchmarking.
e   Suggest sub-regional programmes for productive capacity upgrading backed by a financial facility African Productive Capacity Facilities (APCF).

However, in view of Africa's massive needs, it proved to be a very limited scope and focus. AIDA was developed partly in response to this need.

6.2.2.6 African Union's implementation strategy of the action plan for the accelerated industrial development of Africa

The African Union's Implementation Strategy of the Action Plan for the Accelerated Industrial Development of Africa (AIDA) is a comprehensive document, which intends to put African countries on a sustainable industrial development trajectory. It is, presumably, the best developed and most ambitious document intended to guide Africa's industrialisation available to date.

In order to fully grasp the strategy, it is important to revisit four key documents: *Strategy for the implementation of the plan of action for accelerated industrial development of Africa* (cf. AU 2008), *Summary of the strategy for the implementation of the action plan for the accelerated industrial development of Africa* (cf. AU and UNIDO 2010a), *Financing and Resource Mobilisation Strategy (FRMS)* appended to the strategy as Annex A (cf. AU and UNIDO 2010b), and *Monitoring and Evaluation (M&E) Framework* appended to the strategy as Annex A (cf. AU and UNIDO 2010b).

A MAIN DOCUMENT

The main document – that is, the strategy itself – was developed (with UNIDO support) at the extra-ordinary Conference of African Ministers of Industry (CAMI), held in Midrand (South Africa) in September 2007. It was subsequently presented to, considered, and endorsed by the 10th Session of the Heads of States and Governments (HoS/G summit) of the African Union, which was held in Addis Ababa in January 2008 (see AU 2008).

The strategy stresses the essence of industrialisation for economic transformation, and:

a   Acknowledges Africa's industrial underdevelopment as a development challenge.
b   Reflects on ways to overcome the constraints against industrialisation.
c   Underlines the new confidence emanating from enhanced governance (and presumably, the dynamism in political commitment).
d   Lists 54 projects, which should be implemented in order to realise the ambition of AIDA. In addition to grouping them in seven clusters (industrial policy and institutional directions; upgrading production and trade capacities; promoting infrastructure and energy development for industrial processes; industrial technical skills for Africa's development; industrial innovation systems, R&D, and technical development; financing and resource mobilisation; and sustainable development) and 20 programmes, it also categorises them into 26 immediate term (IT) projects, 19 short-term (ST) projects, and nine long-term (LT) projects. It also presents the general contours of 53 of the 54 projects.

B THE ANNEXES

The Annexes to the strategy were developed from 2009 to 2010, also with UNIDO support. The FRMS presents a logframe matrix for the financing and resource mobilisation for the implementation of the plan of action for AIDA, a mapping of the resource requirements and gaps in relation to the strategy for the implementation of the plan of action for AIDA, and budget estimates for the implementation of the 53 (of the 54) projects, which are fully described in the document.

The M&E Framework developed for the implementation strategy of the action plan for AIDA is consistent with the Results-Based Management (RBM) style. It describes a results-based system for monitoring and evaluating the progress of the programmes and projects included in the strategy. For each project, four types of performance measurement indicators are developed: input indicators, output indicators, outcome indicators, and impact indicators.

C THE SUMMARY

The *Summary of the strategy for the implementation of the action plan for the accelerated industrial development of Africa* synthesises both the main document (i.e. the strategy), and the Annexes (i.e. FRMS, and M&E Framework). Imperatively, this synthesis is intended to introduce to the stakeholders or any other interested reader to the 'Strategy for the implementation of the action plan for the accelerated industrial development of Africa', inclusive of its annexes.

6.2.2.7 Agribusiness and Agro-Industries Development Initiative

The African Agribusiness and Agro-Industries Development Initiative (3ADI) is an initiative that has been developed by several multilateral development institutions, in collaboration with the African Union. Apart from FAO, the other leading agencies supporting the initiative are International Fund for Agricultural Development (IFAD) and the UNIDO.

Generally, the 3ADI intends to develop competitive, sustainable, and inclusive agro-industries and agribusinesses in Africa, as a pathway to increased economic growth and food security. The initiative is designed to increase private sector investment into the agriculture sector in African countries, through the mobilisation and deployment of resources for agribusiness and agro-industrial development. The intention is to harness the diverse sources of resources: domestic, regional, and international financial systems (cf. AU *et al.* 2010).

Concretely, the 3ADI aims at accelerating the development of the agribusiness and agro-industries sectors that ensure value-addition to Africa's agricultural products; so that by the year 2020, the agriculture sectors in African countries, as well as Least Developed Countries (LDCs), are made up of highly productive and profitable agricultural value chains.

The 3ADI is in line with the *Sirte Declaration on Investing in Agriculture for Economic Growth and Food Security*, wherein African HoS/G explicitly acknowledge the need for proactive measures and interventions to increase investments in agriculture and the continued improvement of sector policies for accelerated economic growth (cf. AU *et al.* 2010).

6.3 Multilateral system and Africa's industrialisation

Africa has engaged with the multilateral system in its efforts to achieve industrialisation. The SAPs implemented in almost every African countries were prescribed by and designed with assistance of the BWIs, namely the International Monetary Fund (IMF) and World Bank. Such schemes were deemed as being indispensable in creating the necessary conditions for evolvement of free market economies in African countries, by removing 'excess' government controls and promoting market competition as part of the neo-liberal agenda followed by the BWIs.

Several other economic development schemes designed specifically for Africa or for developing countries are also relevant for industrial transformation of African countries.

6.3.1 Structural Adjustment Programmes

The Structural Adjustment Programmes (SAPs) ran largely from 1980 to 1999. Their aim was to liberalise the economies that were deemed as being excessively controlled. The instruments that were prescribed and used to achieve this contentious goal included: removal of monetary controls, exchange rate reforms/adjustments, elimination of subsidies, liberalisation of commodity marketing, development of private sector, privatisation, and de-regulations of labour relations.

The proponents of SAP saw in it instruments for addressing the debt crisis. Invariably, it was foreseen as a means for furthering the goals of IDDA I, under the changed circumstances.

6.3.2 Multilateral pledges to spur industrialisation in African countries

Apart from country, sub-regional, and pan-African undertakings, there has been international co-operation within the multilateral framework, which could be leveraged for the industrialisation of developing countries including those from Africa. The three most notable of such initiatives are: New Delhi Declaration on Industrialization of Developing Countries, Lima Declaration and Plan of Action on Industrial Development and Cooperation, Millennium Development Goals (MDGs).

6.3.2.1 New Delhi Declaration and Plan of Action on Industrialisation of Developing Countries

The New Delhi Declaration and Plan of Action on Industrialisation of Developing Countries was a product of the Third General Conference of UNIDO, which was held in New Delhi, India from 21st January to 8th February 1980. According to the proposal presented at the Conference, the activities of Transnational Corporations (TNCs) could be channelled in directions compatible with the industrial development needs of the host developing countries. Concretely, it was anticipated that TNCs can help developing countries in the development of international norms and guidelines, as well as through research and technical co-operation. It was also realised that a code of conduct was required to guide the behaviour of TNCs on the one hand, and the treatment of TNCs by the host countries, on the other hand (cf. UNIDO 1979: 29).

Therefore, commensurate with the proposal presented at the Conference, the main thrust of the declaration was the resolve to channel the activities of TNCs in directions compatible with the industrial development needs of developing countries.

6.3.2.2 Lima Declaration and Plan of Action on Industrial Development and Cooperation

The Lima Declaration and Plan of Action on Industrial Development and Cooperation was a product of the Second General Conference of UNIDO, which was held in Lima, Peru, from 12th to 26th March 1975. In view of the urgent needs of the developing countries, the declaration expressed

firm intention to promote industrial development through concerted measures at the national, sub-regional, regional, interregional and international
levels with a view to modernizing the economies of the developing countries, and in particular those of the least developed countries, and eliminating all forms of foreign political domination and socio-economic
exploitation wherever they might exist.

(UNIDO 1975: 4)

The declaration was militated by the depressing realities on the ground then:
though

the developing countries constitute 70 per cent of the world population and
generate less than 7 per cent of industrial production ... the gap between the
developed and developing countries has been widened owing, inter alia, to
the persistence of obstacles in the way of the establishment of a new international economic order based on equity and justice

(UNIDO 1975: 3)

The declaration sought to create a new international economic order through
several measures:

a   Establishment of a system of consultations at UNIDO and other appropriate
    international bodies between developed and developing countries.
b   Policy reforms, particularly by developed countries, to support diversified
    export portfolio of developing countries.
c   Seek to raise the share of the developing countries in total world industrial
    production, to the maximum possible, with a minimum threshold of 25 per
    cent by the year 2000, while also ensuring that industrial growth is evenly
    distributed among the developing countries.
d   Adoption by developing countries, measures (including nationalisation)
    which give them sovereignty over natural resources (both terrestrial and
    marine), and the full utilisation for development of these resources, as well
    as human (including women) and material potential at their disposal (both
    individually as well as with the frameworks of economic co-operation).
e   Raising the general cultural standards of the people, coupled with the devel-
    opment of a qualified work force in developing countries.
f   Full implementation of the principles set out in the Charter of the Economic
    Rights and Duties of States (which include the duties and rights to eliminate
    colonialism, apartheid, racial discrimination, neo-colonialism, occupation
    and all forms of foreign aggression, and domination and the economic and
    social consequences thereof, as a prerequisite for development).
g   Giving special attention to least developed countries, which should enjoy a
    net transfer of resources from the developed countries (and capable develop-
    ing countries) in the form of technical and financial resources as well as
    capital goods, to enable the least developed countries in conformity with the
    policies and plans for development, to accelerate their industrialisation.

h   Avoiding wasteful consumption, particularly by developed countries, considering the needs to conserve non-renewable resources.

6.3.2.3 *United Nations system-wide development programmes for Africa*

Two UN system-wide programmes are worth mentioning here. They include the United Nations Program of Action for the African Economic Recovery and Development (UN-PAAERD), and the United Nations New Agenda for the Development of Africa (UN-NADAF).

UN-PAAERD (1986–1990) was designed as a UN system-wide plan of action, and adopted by UNGA at its 8th plenary meeting, held on 1st June 1986. Among its many measures, those which are specifically relevant for industrial development included: rehabilitation of agro-related industries, raising the level of agricultural investments, modernising agriculture (through agricultural research, and increased use of agro chemicals, mechanisation, and modern farm and processing machinery), betterment of infrastructure (transport and communication, marketing), removal of trade barriers, development of human resources, reform of agricultural and other policies.

UN-NADAF, another UN system-wide development programme for Africa, was adopted through resolution 46/151 by the UNGA held on 18th December 1991. It reiterated support for Africa's economic recovery and development efforts, and urged UN member states to integrate the programme's priorities in their mandates and allocate sufficient funds to this end.

Generally tailored to fit all, it has been argued that UN-NADAF did not address the specific requirements of countries. For instance, because of its inward-oriented development strategy reminiscent of ISI, it was opposed to Mauritius' externally oriented economic policies that were more in line with EOI efforts (cf. Ratsimbaharison 2003: 145).

The overall critical evaluation by Ratsimbaharison (2003) of these programmes is instructive of the realities on the ground:

> The United Nations failed to rally the international community, failed to coordinate disparate development efforts, failed to charge a single specific entity with the responsibility of administering its programs, and failed to learn adequately from the failure of its first program in developing its successor. Hopefully, students of international relations can learn from this scathing account of UN General Assembly failures, even if the assembly itself could not.
>
> (available at: http://muse.jhu.edu/journals/at/summary/v052/
> 52.2schafer.html)

Among the shortfalls pointed out are: the way these programmes were designed (by African nations without adequate input from the wider body of nations, while these were meant to be international efforts), their adoption by the

UN without a formal voting (made them look like they were being imposed by African countries on other UN member states), and there was no institutional responsibility of administering them. Consequently, the UN failed to mobilise (especially financial) resources required to finance their implementation. This was catastrophic for the programmes, considering that the financial requirements for measures associated with human resources development alone under UN-PAAERD were US$7 billion (cf. UN 1986).

Therefore, we come to the conclusion that the process (i.e. the UN's programmes formulation modalities) matters, and influences the capacity to achieve the specified goals (cf. http://muse.jhu.edu/journals/at/summary/v052/52.2schafer.html).

6.3.2.4 Millennium Development Goals

Structural transformation, especially the growth of manufacturing, is one of the prerequisites for sustainable wealth generation and poverty reduction. Thus, the MDGs can be achieved through economic growth arising from structural changes in the African countries.

The MDGs were adopted by the UN in 2000 and address dimensions that are global in scope and significance and country specific in application. They stem from the September 2000 Millennium Declaration signed by the leaders of 189 UN member states. They were subsequently reaffirmed in 2002 at the Monterrey International Conference on Financing for Development, and the Johannesburg Summit on Sustainable Development.

The eight MDGs include: eradication of poverty and hunger, achievement of Universal Primary Education (UPE), promotion of gender equality and empowerment of women, reduction of child mortality, improvement of maternal health, combat HIV/Aids, malaria, and other diseases, ensure environmental sustainability, and develop global partnership for development.

The achievement of each one of these goals can contribute, to different degrees, to accumulating the necessary capacities for industrialisation. For instance, within the context of the MDGs, international partnerships for development, such as through aid for trade, are deemed as a potential that can be harnessed to promote industrial transformation in African and other developing countries. Conversely, the degree of a country's industrial development plays a role in the achievement of each of the specified goals. For instance, a country whose industrial economy is more advanced is also likely to have resources needed to improve its literacy rate.

The challenge surrounding the MDGs is that, for many African countries, they look more like a wish list, which cannot be achieved with the anticipated time frame, i.e. the year 2015. In addition, they contain no specific measures intended to promote industrial transformation. Moreover, achieving many of them will not change Africa's status of being the continent with the poorest and least developed people.

6.4 Conclusions and way forward

6.4.1 Conclusions

Industrialisation initiatives running parallel to the many schemes designed since the 1970s have led to many success stories, particularly in South East Asia (SEA). In contrast, despite a multitude of industrialisation initiatives, to date, the prevailing situation is that the level of development of industrial productive capacities is extremely low across Africa. Though no comprehensive assessment for the various industrialisation schemes has ever been carried out, some useful clues crystallise from the analysis in this chapter:

a   *Proliferation and disconnections.* Over the last ca. five decades, there has been a proliferation of industrialisation schemes. The various schemes have tended to overlap, with no clear mechanism to relate them to each other. The situation means also that there is no clear focus of efforts and resources to promote industrialisation in African countries. The situation is exacerbated by the poor inter-institutional linkages at the levels of intervention: national, regional, pan-African, and multilateral.

b   *General nature of schemes.* True, the malaise facing the African economies is very similar in general. However, in detail they tend to differ from country to country. In a few cases, even the general challenges differ in some countries, for instance between the best performing developing countries like Botswana and Mauritius, and the rest of the developing countries as well as African LDCs. The generic nature of the industrial development measures fail to capture these diversities.

c   *Anchoring in 'fragmented' and 'deficitary' governance framework.* The framework emphasises largely policy, and does not clearly articulate the roles of the other direction-giving frameworks (such as strategies, laws and regulations, international protocols, etc.), and the inter-relationships amongst the various frameworks.

d   *Half-done things.* Though industrialisation is a process that needs comprehensive, concerted, and sustained action programme, the implementation time frame for each scheme was significantly limited. In nominal terms, the average lifetime of the 12 schemes over ca. five decades is four years. In real terms, it was presumably shorter, as some of the schemes, like the APCI, were hardly implemented. Also, there was an immediate shift to 3ADI, even before the AIDA was implemented. Overall, this means that a lot of resources – time, human capital, financial, etc. – are wasted on designing schemes that are either only partially implemented or even not implemented at all. This casts doubt on the prospects for success in industrialising African countries under these circumstances.

e   *Resource deficiencies and decoupling from 'organic' industrialisation.* The prospects for the success of the schemes have also been hampered by failure to mobilise and deploy sufficient amounts of Financial Resources

(FiR) and Non-Financial Resources (NFiR) to implement any specific programme. The proliferation of schemes means also that the little available resources are further spread thin, thereby becoming ineffectual. This further means that there is a *lack of link of schemes to 'organic' industrialisation* – manifested by (i) failure to comprehensively address the question of 'local' capacity requirements, and (ii) failure to articulate local industrial development (LID) through entrepreneurship and enterprise development.

f   *Absence of results-based Monitoring and Evaluation (M&E).* Lack of an implementation follow-up mechanism, e.g. a Monitoring and Evaluation (M&E) framework is a serious shortcoming. The implicit lack of a management instrument led to either partial and haphazard implementation of the initiatives or non-implementation of the initiatives (as many were literally forgotten immediately after being pronounced), etc.

g   *Poor performance of industrial sectors in African countries.* A wide gap still exists between planned industrialisation targets and the level of achievement. Among the bottom 12 least industrialised countries, as measured by UNDO's Competitive Industrial Performance (CIP) Index, ten come from Africa (cf. Chapter 4 of this book, and UNIDO 2013).

In short, the multitude of schemers did not help African countries to develop critical masses of industrial productive capacities. Subsequent to the absence of such capacities, the little achievement in terms of economic growth and development that is observed in most African economies tends to be largely driven by consumption rather than by investments.

6.4.1.1 Commitment by international partners

It is highly questionable whether international partners, such as TNCs, could be committed to Africa's industrial transformation. Hence issues like promoting mutually beneficial engagement between TNCs and developing countries, or promoting resource sovereignty in developing countries, appear to be based more on wishes than on realpolitik.

6.4.2 Way forward

In view of the issues revealed in the analysis in this chapter, the following measures should be undertaken in order to increase the prospects for industrial development in African countries:

a   Industrial development plans should, essentially, be tailor-made for countries. In this regard, a national drive to industrialise should be a product of concerted action, and be based on comprehensive, integrated, and sustained measures.

b Countries are responsible for their own industrialisation. African countries must come of age, and exercise sovereignty over the management of their industrial development efforts. In this connection, sub-regional, regional, and multilateral measures to support industrialisation in African countries must be complementary to, instead of being *in lieu* of country-tailored industrialisation agendas.

c As part of its broad industrialisation agenda, each African country must have a clear strategy for mobilising and prudently deploying sufficient amounts of FiR and NFiR to achieve this goal. These, alongside a conducive governance framework, proper leveraging of international partnerships (through regional integration, and other forms of international economic partnerships), and proper leveraging of multilateral co-operation, are essential ingredients for industrial development (see Chapter 13 of this book for detailed analysis of this point).

d As part of its broad industrialisation agenda, each African country must devise and use a results-based M&E Framework to assess and manage its industrialisation trajectory.

Notes

1 These industrial development schemes during the early post-colonial period, which have also been mentioned in Chapter 1 (cf. Figure 1.3), are beyond the planned scope of this volume, and will not be discussed further.

2 The sub-regional schemes, whose discussion is beyond the scope of this chapter, are discussed in detail in Chapter 5 of this book.

3 In practice, while some of the initiatives were not effectively implemented, other were only partially implemented, while others were not implemented at all.

4 These include: *Union du Maghreb Arabe* (UMA), Community of Sahel-Saharan States (CEN-SAD), Common Market for Eastern and Southern Africa (COMESA), East African Community (EAC), Economic Community of Central African States (ECCAS), Inter-Governmental Authority on Development (IGAD), Economic Community of West African States (ECOWAS), and Southern African Development Community (SADC).

5 These include: *Communauté Économique des Pays des Grand Lacs* (CEPGL), Southern African Customs Union (SACU), Mano River Union (MRU), West African Economic and Monetary Union (UEMOA), Central African Economic and Monetary Community (CEMAC), Indian Ocean Commission (IOC).

6 NEPAD emerged through the blending of ideas, which were contained in three different initiatives: (i) Millennium Partnership for Africa's Recovery Programme (MAP) launched by the leaders of South Africa, Algeria, and Nigeria; (ii) OMEGA Plan by Senegal's President Abdoulaye Wade; and (iii) Compact for African Recovery (CAR) prepared by the United Nations Economic Commission for Africa (UNECA). The three initiatives were merged in July 2001 by the OAU/AU Summit and named as 'New African Initiative'. Later, the name of the hybrid initiative was changed to NEPAD.

7 In the understanding in this book, a the typical elements of governance frameworks at the national level, which are referred to here include: broad development philosophy (usually expressed in terms of ideological stance), development visions (usually expressed as national development vision), strategies, policies, and laws and regulations (cf. Chapter 13 of this book for a detailed discussion of the concept).

References

AU (2001). *The New Partnership for Africa's Development.* African Union. October.

AU (2008). *Strategy for the Implementation of the Plan of Action for Accelerated Industrial Development of Africa.* Report of the Conference of African Ministers of Industry (CAMI) 18th Ordinary Session, Durban, 24–28 October.

AU and UNIDO (2010a). *Introduction To and Summary of the Strategy for the Implementation of the Action Plan for the Accelerated Industrial Development of Africa.* Background material for the Stakeholders' Workshop on the implementation of the action plan for the accelerated industrial development of Africa, Addis Ababa, March 2010. African Union and United Nations Industrial Development Organization. Vienna. February.

AU and UNIDO (2010b). *Financing and Resource Mobilisation Strategy and Monitoring and Evaluation Framework for the Implementation Strategy of the AU Action Plan for the Accelerated Industrial Development of Africa.* Background Paper. African Union and United Nations Industrial Development Organization. Vienna. March. Figure 4.

AU, UNIDO, FAO and IFAD (2010). African Agribusiness and Agro-industries Development Initiative. 3ADI. African Union, United Nations Industrial Development Organization, Food and Agriculture Organization of the United Nations, International Fund for Agricultural Development. Vienna.

Matambalya, F. (2008). *Analysis of Industrial Strategies and Policies in Africa.* Unpublished Teaching Notes. IDEP/UNIDO short-term course on industrial policy analysis in Africa. Dakar, Senegal. April–May.

OAU, UNECA, and UN (1997). *Industrial Development Decade for Africa (IDDA) II.* Report of the Mid-Term Programme Evaluation. Organization of African Unity, United Nations Economic Commission for Africa, United Nations. 21 April.

Ratsimbaharison, A. (2003). *The Failure of the United Nations Development Programs for Africa.* Lanham, MD: University Press of America.

UN (1980). *Resolution Adopted by the General Assembly 35/66. Industrial Development Co-operation: A Third General Conference of the United Nations Industrial Development Organization.* United Nations. 5 December.

UN (1986). *United Nations Programme of Action for African Economic Recovery and Development 1986–1990.* United Nations General Assembly. 1 June.

UN (1993). *United Nations New Agenda for the Development of Africa in the 1990s.* United Nations. 23 December.

UNECOSOC and UNECA (2009). *A Report on Transport: Summary.* Report for the Sixth Session of the Committee on Food Security and Sustainable Development Regional Implementation Meeting for the Eighteenth Session of the Conference on Sustainable Development, 27–30 October 2009, Addis Ababa, Ethiopia. United Nations Economic and Social Council and Economic Commission for Africa. 29 September. Addis Ababa.

UNIDO (1975). *Lima Declaration and Plan of Action on Industrial Development and Cooperation.* Second General Conference of UNIDO. United Nations Industrial Development Organization. Lima, Peru. March.

UNIDO (1979). *Third General Conference of UNIDO.* Report. United Nations Industrial Development Organization. New Delhi. 6 December.

UNIDO (2004). *The Role of Industrial Development in the Achievement of the Millennium Development Goals.* United Nations Industrial Development Organisation. Vienna. June.

UNIDO (2005). *Capability Building for Catching-up: Historical, Empirical and Policy Dimensions.* Industrial Development Report 2005. Vienna.

UNIDO (2009). *Breaking-in and Moving up: New Industrial Challenges for the Bottom Billion and Middle Income Countries.* Industrial Development Report 2009. Vienna.

UNIDO (2013). *Competitive Industrial Performance Report 2012/2013.* United Nations Industrial Development Organization. Vienna.

UNIDO and CAMI (2005). *Progress Report on the Implementation of the African Productive Capacity Initiative.* Report presented at the 3rd CAMI. United Nations Industrial Development Organization and Conference of African Ministers of Industry. Harare. January.

Websites

e-International Relations, available at: www.e-ir.info/2011/07/19/%E2%80%98another-false-dawn-for-africa-%E2%80%99-discuss-this-assessment-of-nepad/).

United Nations Transport and Communications Decade in Africa (available at: www.africa.upenn.edu/ECA/ECAmin_trnsprt.html.

http://muse.jhu.edu/journals/at/summary/v052/52.2schafer.html).

Part III

Country case studies of integration of industrialisation in the national development agenda

7 Integration of the industrialisation agenda in the national development strategy

Lessons from the Federal Republic of Ethiopia

Kibre Moges Belete

7.1 Contextualising the need for industrial transformation

The urgency for a strategy to guide Ethiopia's industrial transformation as a means for overall economic development is underlined by the characteristics of the country's economy. As may be deduced in the following subsections, a good impression of the status quo is given by the country's macroeconomic structure, dominance of subsistence agriculture, and the infancy and unbalanced nature of the manufacturing sector. Further evidences are given in the overall infrastructural deficits, and inherent challenges of industrialising a traditional agricultural economy,

7.1.1 Macroeconomic structure

The prime objective of industrialisation is to bring about structural change – a change from backward/traditional techniques of producing goods and services to a knowledge based industrial production system. Thus any treatise of an industrialisation strategy inevitably needs to investigate the structure of the relevant economy.

The Ethiopian economy is still deeply traditional. Not only production and service activities in agriculture are traditional, but even non-agricultural sectors, such as manufacturing, trade, etc., are characterised by activities involving large unskilled labour and animal power. A study on the private sector economic activities in 2007 revealed that for a ten-year average, 1995/96–2004/05, traditional economic activities account for about 60 per cent of the national income (Teshome and Belete, 2007).[1] Table 7.1 portrays the structure of the economy at an aggregate level. Over the five-year period, agriculture, which is entirely dependent on weather conditions, unskilled labour and animal draught power, accounts, on average, for nearly half (48.4 per cent) of the gross domestic product (GDP).[2] On the other hand, manufacturing, which involves largely partially automated activities, has a share of less than 5 per cent. The relative shares of other modern sectors, such as finance, construction, power, etc., are respectively quite small.

Table 7.1 Sectoral shares in GDP, employment and export (per cent)

Economic sectors	GDP (2005/06–2009/10)	Employment (2005)	Export (2005/06–2009/10)
Agriculture & Allied Activities	48.4	80.2	83.2
Mining & Quarrying	0.5	0.3	8.7
Manufacturing	4.0	4.9	8.1
LMSI	*2.7*	*0.4*	*7.5*
SSI	*0.4*	*0.3*	*0.6*
Cottage industries	*0.9*	*4.1*	*–*
Electricity & Water	1.4	0.1	0
Construction	5.1	1.4	0
Trade	13.8	5.2	0
Transport & Communication	4.5	0.5	0
Financial Intermediaries	1.8	0.1	0
Education	2.6	0.9	0
Health and Social Work	0.7	0.2	0
Public Administration and Defence	3.5	1.2	0
Real Estate and Business	8.6	0.2	0
Other Services*	5.1	4.8	0
Total	100.0	100.0	100.0

Source: EEA Database, May 2011; CSA, 2010a, 2010b.

Notes

* Other services include hotels and restaurants, private household activities, extra territorial organisations and bodies, other social, cultural, personal and household activities.

The contribution of economic sectors to the overall employment level of the country reveals the same story. Traditional agriculture alone accounts for about 82 per cent of the total employment, whereas manufacturing accounts for less than 5 per cent.[3] Note also that the bulk of employment in manufacturing is due to traditional cottage industries (4.1 per cent). The share of large- and medium-scale industries (LMSI) as well as small-scale industries is insignificant – 0.4 and 0.3 per cent respectively. This is typical of a least developed economy.

Agriculture is also the main source of foreign currency earning.[4] Similar to all other least developed economies, Ethiopia's exports are dominated by primary agricultural commodities, such as coffee, pulses, oilseeds, etc. Such commodities account for over 83 per cent of total export. Mining, which is largely a single commodity phenomenon – gold – has a share of 8.7 per cent of total export. Manufacturing holds the balance – 8.1 per cent.

Trade, which has the second largest share in GDP (13.8 per cent), is not due to external trade. Ethiopia's total external trade is quite minuscule. During the same period, import and export together makes only 7.7 per cent of GDP. The relatively high share of trade is due to domestic trade in which a large proportion of the population across the country is engaged in small and micro level trade activities.

Moreover, for decades, the country has been increasingly recording both internal and external imbalances. For instance, over the past five-year period, 2006/07–2010/11, revenues financed only two-thirds of expenditures, hence relying on external grants and deficit financing (inflationary money creation) for the balance. Similarly, the country's external trade gap is nearly three times its export earning, hence dependent on transfers (mainly loans and grants) from the rest of the world. For the same period, import cover of international reserve holding was, on average, only for 1.7 months (IMF, 2009).

By all accounts, therefore, the overall structure of the Ethiopian economy reveals the state of a least industrialised economy, largely dominated by traditional activities.

7.1.2 Dominance of subsistence agriculture

Commercial farming in Ethiopia is not widespread. Following a regime change in the early 1990s, the few large-scale state farms that were initiated in the 1980s have been discouraged, and some dismantled and replaced by pieces of individual peasant farms. A study in 2001/02 estimated large and medium-sized state and commercial farms cover only 3.2 per cent of total agricultural land and 2.4 per cent of total output (EEA, 2007).[5] Moreover, due to restricted property rights on land, the most critical means of production, the opportunity for creating large commercial farms is highly limited.[6] Large-size land is acquired only from the state through leasehold. As a result, crop farming is dominated by fragmented and small-size peasant farm plots scattered across the country. Table 7.2 depicts the details.

Though the average national land holding for peasant farms is about 1.15 ha per farmer (or farm household), more than half of the farmers (57.4 per cent) hold on average about 0.59 hectare only, and account for nearly a quarter (23 per cent) of the total farm land (Table 7.2). Another 26 per cent of the farmers hold, on average 1.42 hectare per farmer. This implies that over 83 per cent of the smallholders manage to survive with less than a hectare (0.71 ha) per farmer. What is not shown in the table, however, is the number of pieces of farm plots a farmer manages, irrespective of the total plot size. Most of the farmers have more than one plot, disjointly located at different places, making application of mechanised farms and irrigation less feasible. Farm plots are fragmented and often covered with different types of essential crops for household consumption. Hence, application of economies of scale is quite remote.

Table 7.2 Size of peasant farm plots and land holding (2007/08)

Plot size	Proportion of farm land (%)	Average land holding (ha)	Proportion of smallholders (%)
Up to 1 ha	22.8	0.59	57.4
1.01–2 ha	32.1	1.42	26.0
2.01–5 ha	37.5	2.85	15.1
5.01–10 ha	6.6	6.3	1.2
Over 10 ha	1.0	14.06	0.3

Source: EEA, 2009.

Also, even when application of irrigation is feasible, such a land holding structure suggests the challenge for expanding an irrigation system. A tract of land sized hundreds of hectares may be owned by hundreds of farmers. To bring many fragmented lands under a single management system and create a large-scale irrigated farm is, therefore, practically challenging as convergence of interest of too many farmers is difficult if not impossible to arrive at. As a result, irrigation in peasant farms is insignificant. In 2008/09, only 1.4 per cent (164,370 ha) of total cropped land was irrigated (EEA, 2009).[7] Therefore, peasant farms are entirely dependent on rainfall; irrespective of the size of land whether there would be a reasonable harvest in any season is not known *a priori*.

Moreover, the fact that agriculture depends on weather conditions further impacts on the application of modern technical inputs, particularly fertiliser. Disregarding the knowhow of farming techniques, some argue that application of modern technical inputs is scale neutral. However, application of expensive modern technical inputs involves high risk, as farmers have to be sure of the weather conditions. Only 20 per cent of the farmers, largely in regions where adequate and timely rainfall is somewhat reliable, apply fertiliser. Similarly, only 15 per cent of the total cultivated land is fertilised (EEA, 2009). And even when it is applied, the rate of fertilisation is largely low – less than 50 per cent of the recommended rate – in order to minimise the risk of crop loss. This limits the level of productivity. In 2008/09, when weather conditions were quite ideal for production, the average productivity level for cereals, which accounts for 90 per cent of agricultural output, was only 16.5 quintals per hectare (EEA, 2009). For cereals, productivity in Asia today is as high as 40 quintals per hectare.

So what we have is an economy dominated by subsistence agriculture, which at the same time is not only the source of food and employment for about 80 per cent of the population, but also the source of foreign exchange earnings (Table 7.1). Extensive exploitation of natural resources with traditional means has been going on for generations without adequate environmental concern. Further aggravated by fast increasing population pressure, agriculture is now being subjected to extensive environmental degradation – soil erosion, deforestation and frequent drought. The traditional approach of maintaining the minimum per capita food requirement for the fast increasing population through cropping additional marginal land, therefore, may not be sustained in the face of declining soil productivity, irrespective of the extent of fertilisation. The seemingly favourable weather conditions and promising growth in agriculture, and the economy at large in the last few years may not continue, after all the same situation, considerable growth, had been observed throughout the 1960s up until the second half of the 1970s, but was not sustained further.

Over the decades, productivity of land has been declining; food prices have been increasing; drought recurring; and poverty deepening. Incidence of poverty is as high as 45.4 per cent in rural areas. For long, agriculture has been underfunded. Therefore, recovery strategies that exclude change in production structure could hardly bring about sustained productivity growth.

7.1.3 *Infant and structurally unbalanced manufacturing sector*

7.1.3.1 *Size structure of firms and scale economies*

Manufacturing in the country is partly an off-shoot of agricultural activities. Major manufacturing enterprises were established for processing agricultural commodities such as cotton, hides and skins, cereals, sugar cane, fruits and vegetables, etc., for the domestic market.

The manufacturing sector is still dwarf. As underlined earlier, manufacturing industries in general have a limited role in the national economy – be it for employment, production or export (Table 7.1). In 2009/10 there were about 2,172 large- and medium-scale (LMSM) and 43,338 small-scale (SSM) industries employing a total of only 185,000 and 139,000 workers respectively (CSA, 2010a, 2011).[8] This implies, on average, employment capacity of 69 and three workers per firm respectively. Manufacturing enterprises of all grades: large, medium and small, together account for an employment share of only 0.7 per cent of the total work force in the country. Even including traditional workers in cottage manufacturing, current employment capacity is less than 5 per cent (Table 7.3). Hence, both small-scale industries, as well as those regarded as large and medium scale are in effect quite small size.

Similarly, the contribution of manufacturing industries in the total national income is quite insignificant. The same table shows that, LMS industries account for only 2.7 per cent of GDP, and small-scale industries for an insignificant 0.5 per cent. Another way of showing this is that manufacturing industries altogether turn out goods worth only US\$40 per capita per year, leaving a large gap to be met through imports.

Manufacturing industries are heavily dependent on imports for intermediate inputs, while their capacity to export is highly limited. In 2009/10, the sector exported only 2.8 per cent of its total value of production (CSA, 2011). This is equivalent to about 8 per cent of total export of the country (Table 7.1). Except for leather, Ethiopian manufactured goods are less competitive in international markets.

Table 7.3 Size of firms by employment grouping (2008/09)

Employment grouping (no. of workers)	Percentage shares in		
	No. of enterprises	Labour force	Value added share
Less than 26	53.5	6.5	**2.8**
26 to 50	15.2	4.8	**3.2**
51 to 100	11.1	7.5	**6.1**
101 to 200	6.7	7.9	**8.0**
201 to 500	7.8	19.0	**20.4**
501 to 1,000	4.0	23.8	**31.2**
Above 1,000	1.6	30.6	**28.2**

Source: CSA, 2010a.

It is obvious that, among other factors, low unit cost of production is substantially influenced by firm size. International competition tends to put limitations to the minimum size of firms, thereby the minimum unit cost of production, to be internationally competitive. Given other factors, the larger the size of firms, the lower the costs of production, and hence the better the status of competitiveness.[9] Another significant advantage of large firms is the capability to internalise all costs and externalities thereby reducing external dependency and increasing the resilience against adverse impacts of external factors.

As shown in Table 7.3, most firms (53.5 per cent) employ between ten and 25 workers only; and another 15 per cent, between 26 and 50. However, these two groups of firms, together, account for only 11 per cent of the labour force, and 6 per cent of the value added. Even by the standard of low income countries these are small firms proper.

On the other end of the scale, few large size firms, each employing more than 500 workers, account for only 5.6 per cent of total firms. However, they have dominant employment and value-added shares – 54 and 60 per cent, respectively. The largest group, employing over 1,000 workers, is dominant in the sugar, textile and cement industries.

What can be inferred from this section is that, even disregarding the total number of firms, which is very small for a country with relatively large population size – over 80 million – most industries are composed of largely micro and small-scale firms. Given their current minuscule size, the overwhelming majority of firms may not be able to exploit scale economies and reduce their unit cost significantly.

A INPUT STRUCTURE

Inputs to manufacturing industries involve raw materials and intermediates. In a mature industrial economy the largest proportion of the latter is accessed from within the manufacturing sector itself. This is not the case in Ethiopian manufacturing. As noted above, most industries are consciously established to exploit internally available raw materials, the natural resource advantage. Hence, raw material inputs are directly accessed from the domestic market. For intermediate inputs, however, the sector is heavily dependent on imports. For all industries, the values of imported intermediate goods account for over half of total inputs.

The proportion of imported inputs to total is also an indicator of the degree of external dependency. Table 7.4 indicates this proportion for the five-year period 2005/06–2009/10. Most industries, established to exploit domestic raw materials, including food and beverages, textiles, leather, wood and furniture, cement and non-metallic products, require limited intermediate inputs, on average, less than 50 per cent of total inputs, while the rest, such as engineering, chemical, rubber and plastic, paper and paper products, depend on imports for 80–99 per cent of their inputs.

Irrespective of the extent of dependency, the lack of any improvement over time is perhaps more concerning. Over the five-year period, import dependency

Table 7.4 Input structure by industrial group (per cent) (2005/06–2009/10)

Industrial group	2005/06	2006/07	2007/08	2008/09	2009/10	Average
Food and beverages	20.6	23.8	27.9	31.1	24.8	**25.6**
Leather	21.0	21.6	23.6	26.1	34.4	**25.3**
Non-metallic products	9.5	19.2	19.8	18.6	58.1	**25.0**
Textiles	40.9	41.5	29.6	46.1	37.0	**39.0**
Wearing apparel	31.2	52.7	37.3	34.9	50.3	**41.3**
Wood and furniture	36.1	47.1	33.4	40.5	29.8	**37.4**
Paper, p. products and printing	78.9	71.7	81.5	73.7	59.5	**73.1**
Chemical and chemical products	83.1	78.5	87.1	79.9	70.5	**79.8**
Rubber and plastic products	91.8	95.4	77.2	95.0	92.3	**90.3**
Basic iron and steel	67.2	98.9	99.8	80.4	79.1	**85.1**
Fabricated metal products	92.6	87.5	80.2	86.6	84.6	**86.3**
Machinery and equipment	99.7	96.2	97.7	94.8	85.1	**94.7**
Motor vehicles: parts, accessories	94.7	85.0	97.1	93.6	98.5	**93.8**
All industries	50.1	58.3	53.6	52.6	51.0	**53.1**

Source: CSA, 2011.

has not diminished in any of the industrial groups (Table 7.4), implying the lack of policy direction towards expanding competitive import replacing intermediate goods industries. In fact the policy focus is still on consumption goods industries.

B PRODUCTION STRUCTURE

As early as in the 1920s, manufacturing in Ethiopia kicked off with simple processing industries based on reliable and easily exploitable agricultural resources, such as sugar cane, cotton, hides and skins, etc. Availability of raw materials and the domestic market were important criteria to decide on the type of industries to establish. Figure 7.1 portrays the relative production share of large- and medium-scale industries.

For decades, food and beverages processing industries, such as grain mills, sugar, malt and malt liquors, soft drinks, etc., remain dominant in manufacturing activities, though their relative share seems to have declined in recent years. Hence, between the first and second half of the last decade, the production share of this industrial group fell, on average, by 10 percentage points. But, with a share of about one-third of total production, it still remains, by far, the most dominant activity in manufacturing.

During the decade, particularly in the second half, the high priority accorded to infrastructure: roads, power and housing, led to the fast expansion of construction industries, both metallic and non-metallic, such as structural metals, cement, cement products, etc. During 2004/05–2008/09, these groups of industries together account for about 20 per cent of total manufacturing output.

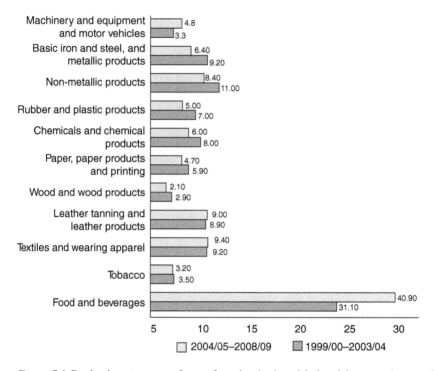

Figure 7.1 Production structure of manufacturing by broad industrial groups (per cent) (1999/2000–2003/04 and 2004/05–2008/09) (source: Author. Based on CSA, 2005, 2010a.

Industries of high importance for industrialisation, including machinery and equipment, industrial chemical, electrical and electronics, etc., have little significance.

Manufacturing in the country, therefore, is largely composed of consumption goods industries. Capital goods industries, on the other hand, are literally insignificant, accounting for only 12 per cent of total output. So are intermediate goods industries.

C SECTORAL LINKAGES

A related aspect of the input structure of manufacturing is its linkages with the rest of the economy, particularly agriculture. Of the total inputs required for manufacturing industries, 33.7 per cent is acquired from agriculture, 1.7 per cent from mining and 12 per cent from within manufacturing (Table 7.5). The remaining half of its input demand, 52.6 per cent, is imported. While nearly all raw other materials demand is supplied within the domestic economy, mainly from agriculture, the bulk of intermediate inputs demand is met from the rest of the world.

Table 7.5 Proportion of inputs to agriculture and manufacturing by source (per cent) (2008/09)

Supplying sector	Input to agriculture	Input to manufacturing
Agriculture	65.2	33.7
Manufacturing	1.4	12.0
Mining	0	1.7
ROW (export)	33.3	52.6
Total	100	100

Source: SCA, 2010; EEA database; Table 7.1.

Manufacturing itself produces a small proportion of own inputs – 12 per cent of total or 17.7 per cent of intermediates. This indicates the structural imbalance within the sector. The structural problem is not limited to its incapacity to meet own inputs demand. Its contribution to agriculture's input demand is also insignificant, just 1.4 per cent. For its modern technical inputs, such as fertiliser, pesticides, insecticides, etc., agriculture entirely depends on imports.

The manufacturing industry in the country has, therefore, serious internal structural problem. Most of the industries are consumption based agro-processing industries, hence, cannot meet the intermediate goods (let alone capital goods) demand of the sector. From the point of view of sectoral linkages, therefore, the manufacturing sector is structurally less integrated. While its backward linkage with agriculture demand for raw material inputs is relatively strong, its forward linkage, supply of inputs to agriculture, is literally non-existent. As it stands now, the sector is so structurally weak that neither it supports the growth of other sectors, particularly agriculture, in supplying inputs, nor does it satisfy own intermediates demand to any meaningful extent.

D MARKET STRUCTURE

As hinted above, most manufacturing industries were primarily established to meet local market demand. Currently only a handful of industrial groups, including leather tanning, clothing and footwear, sugar and sugar confectionery, and fruits and vegetables, are regularly exporting, while some others are attempting to find markets, meanwhile shipping out small bundles occasionally.

The only export oriented industry that supplies about two-thirds of its production to external markets is leather tanning. Over the five-year period 2005/06 to 2009/10, on average, 60.1 per cent of its production had been exported annually (Table 7.6). Its local market is largely the footwear industry, which is also attempting to get a foothold in international markets. Currently about 16 per cent of its production is destined for international markets. Also clothing, and fruits and vegetables processing industries are increasingly making efforts to exploit international markets, currently exporting just over 12 per cent of their respective output.

All other industries are largely at the experimental stage, searching for entry into the international markets, currently supplying small bundles. Considering

Table 7.6 Share of export in total sales by industrial group (per cent) (2005/06–2009/10)

Industrial group	Export value as a proportion of total sales (per cent)					
	2005/06	2006/07	2007/08	2008/09	2009/10	Average
Leather tanning & dressing	77.7	51.2	54.4	68.8	48.2	**60.1**
Sugar and sugar confectionery	14.4	10.2	9.7	10.2	0.5	**9.0**
Fruits and vegetables	15.5	12.4	11.5	11.9	13.2	**12.9**
Textiles	10.8	11.9	14.1	12.4	12.9	**12.4**
Footwear	5.0	13.5	25.5	20.6	16.3	**16.2**
Wearing apparel	1.1	17.0	26.1	8.4	12.9	**13.1**
Other exporting industries	0.4	1.3	0.5	0.4	1.1	**0.7**
All exporting industries	11.4	11.7	6.1	4.1	3.0	**7.3**

Source: Based on CSA, 2011.

the performance of all manufacturing industries, over the years, they have been able to export, on average, only less than 10 per cent of their total output. This is equivalent to only 8 per cent of the total country's export (Table 7.1). In general, manufacturing in Ethiopia is only partially integrated into the external markets – strongly for its inputs but loosely for its output.

E TECHNOLOGICAL CAPABILITY

Technical capability refers to the skill, technical knowledge and organisational coherence that enable productive enterprises to utilise machinery and equipment, as well as technical information efficiently. As such, it involves the technology embodied in physical equipment, the educational qualification of employees, the skills and learning acquired by employees through training and experience, the entrepreneurial and managerial skills, and the degree of interactions and informa- tion flow between industries and firms. These elements constitute the determi- nants of technological development. In the case of most developing countries, including Ethiopia, technological capability is also influenced by various other factors, including the appropriateness of imported and deployed technologies to the countries' endowments of labour/skill, the capability of fully assimilating or internalising the technologies, and hence ability to use them at best practices, ability of upgrading the technologies, extent of diffusion of knowledge within a country, etc.

   Though many factors determine the degree of industrialisation of a country, technological capability is, perhaps, the single most dominant factor. The status of technology can be shown using various factors such as investment rates, educational status and technical knowledge of employees, entrepreneurial and managerial skill, degree of automation of plants, quality control, maintenance capability, etc. Some of these issues are addressed below to show the state of technology in Ethiopian manufacturing industries.

F CAPITAL STOCK

Developing technological capability requires adequate and continuous investment not only on machinery and equipment and related assets, but also on
information, research and development, labour education and technical
know-how, etc. Total capital stock for the entire manufacturing industry in
2008/09, the highest recorded ever, was only about one billion dollars.[10] The corresponding capital stock per labour was about US$6,600, which is quite small.
Similarly, capital per unit of manufacturing firm was about US$456,000. This is
primarily a reflection of the size of manufacturing firms, which are largely small
scale.

Overall, as depicted in Figure 7.2, while total capital has been rising, the comparable capital stock per labour remains stagnant, while capital stock per firm is
on a consistent decline – meaning the average firm is becoming ever smaller.

Apart from the low level of investment, hence capital stock, its distribution
by industrial groups reveals a highly skewed pattern. As shown in Table 7.7, in
the five-year period, food and beverages industries alone account, on average,
for 36.4 per cent of the capital stock. Moreover, four industrial groups alone:
food and beverages, textiles, leather tanning and non-metallic minerals, account
for nearly 70 per cent of total capital stock. These are largely consumption goods
industries. On the other hand, capital goods industries that create wide and significant externalities by introducing new embodied hardware technologies to the
economy, on average, account for less than 10 per cent. In light of the critical
role of the latter for technological capability building, the existing structure
shows weak technological capacity. The past investment pattern was not favouring technological advancement.

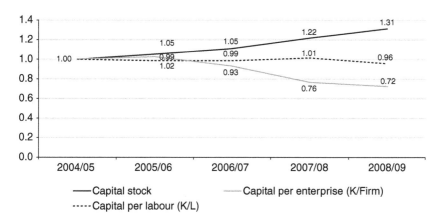

Figure 7.2 Index of evolution of capital stock and investment, selected years
(2004/05 = 100) (source: Author. Based on data from CSA, 2006, 2010a and
National Bank of Ethiopia (available at: www.nbe.gov.et/annualbulletin/)).

Notes
Computations based on replacement and/or expansion in thousands of US dollars.

Table 7.7 Share in capital stock by industrial group (per cent) (2005/06–2009/10)

Industrial group	2005/06	2006/07	2007/08	2008/09	2009/10	Average
Food and beverages	38.4	33.7	42.4	36.9	30.3	**36.4**
Tobacco	1.7	2.1	1.7	1.5	0.9	**1.7**
Textiles and wearing apparel	10.7	12.0	7.5	12.1	14.8	**11.4**
Leather tanning and dressing	7.0	8.0	7.1	6.0	5.4	**6.7**
Wood and w. products	2.1	2.0	2.6	4.1	3.9	**2.9**
Paper, p. products and printing	3.5	3.8	3.8	3.1	5.0	**3.8**
Chemical and chemical products	5.7	5.8	5.4	5.5	5.2	**5.6**
Rubber and plastic products	6.9	7.3	8.1	8.1	5.4	**7.2**
Non-metallic mineral products	12.9	13.5	13.0	15.6	15.0	**14.1**
Basic iron and steel	5.6	4.2	2.4	2.4	3.7	**3.7**
Fabricated metal products	3.9	3.4	4.4	3.5	7.4	**4.5**
Machinery and equipment	0.2	0.1	0.3	0.1	0.7	**0.3**
Motor vehicles	1.4	4.0	1.4	1.1	1.7	**1.7**

Source: CSA, 2011.

Similarly, intermediate goods producing industries are relatively under-capitalised. In fact, pivotal industries, with strong industrial linkages and instrumental for inducing industrial expansion as well as creating an internally vibrant and less dependent manufacturing sector, such as industrial chemicals, fertiliser, electrical and electronics, etc., do not yet exist in the country.

G AGE STRUCTURE OF FIRMS

It is obvious that latest generation machinery and equipment is relatively high-tech oriented, and hence technically more efficient or more productive than earlier ones. The age structure of firms, therefore, reflects the degree of hardware complexity and efficiency and, in turn, the competitive status of firms.

A survey on manufacturing industries in Ethiopia examined the age structure of firms (EEA, 2005). Firms were asked about the 'year of establishment' of plants, and if they were new at purchase. Some 52 per cent of the total manufacturing firms were in operation for not longer than ten years. Another 19 per cent were between 11 and 20 years, while the remaining 29 per cent, over 20 (Table 7.8).

It is of course difficult to draw a border line for the number of years in which a given hardware remains technically efficient and competitive, as progress in technology is continuous and dynamic. In today's technological dynamism, even a period of 5–10 years may be long for one generation machinery to remain technologically competitive. However, based on general experience, depreciation of plants, particularly in developing countries, lasts for, at least, 10–15 years, though hardware may not remain efficient throughout the whole period. In light of this general framework, about 50 per cent of manufacturing firms in Ethiopia may have difficulty in being technically productive and competing with new

Table 7.8 Age structure of firms (2005)

Number of years	No. of firms	Share (%)
<5	181	21
6–10	267	31
11–15	124	14
16–20	50	5
21–30	93	11
>30	142	18

Source: Adapted from EEA, 2005, Table 2.6, p. 33.

generation firms. Moreover, as discussed above, replacement investment on machinery and equipment is very small. In this context, nearly half of the manufacturing firms are nevertheless obsolete.

In addition, as experience indicates, developing countries often purchase second hand or older generation machinery and equipment. If so, the above age structure, which is based on years of establishment of firms, may not provide the whole story about the relative technological status of machinery and equipment in manufacturing. To gauge this, firms were also asked whether plants were new at establishment/purchase: 54 per cent claimed that they were new, while 32 per cent confirmed that they were second hand. The remaining 14 per cent do not know the status of their firms at purchase. This suggests that, at least, one-third of the plants, which have been operational for the last 10–15 years, might actually be technically more obsolete than expected.

H PRODUCTION ENGINEERING

A direct reflection of the technological level of hardware is the degree of automation. Today's production engineering is fully automated, largely robotic, and computer driven and controlled. The role of labour is being reduced to educated and high skill demanding operational activities and supervision, supported by precision tools and equipment. In developing countries, however, this may not be largely the case.

In Ethiopia, the same survey on manufacturing industries confirmed that 10 per cent of the firms are fully automated, while the vast majority (90 per cent) are automated for only 50 per cent of their activities, the remaining being manually operated (EEA, 2005). This is the sort of technology identified for its labour-intensiveness, where very difficult tasks are power driven and the remaining manually performed. Therefore, Ethiopian manufacturing firms are, to a great extent, partially automated.

I EDUCATIONAL STATUS OF THE WORKFORCE

Today, even the most labour-intensive and the simplest production process, such as, for instance, garment industries, leather tanning, etc., requires skilled labour capable of understanding and internalising the process, as well as utilising machinery and equipment of recent generation at best practices. This further leads to making changes in the production process thereby improving product quality and productivity. This is precisely the process of building up technological capability. But, such a process primarily requires a good background, not only of basic education but also technical knowledge. Hence, the level and type of education that labour acquires is an important determinant of technological capability building.

Table 7.9 shows the educational status of the workforce. Considering general qualifications first, 10 per cent of the workforce is illiterate; 45 per cent is at elementary school level (grades 1 to 8), and hence can only write and read; and another 35 per cent is at high school level (grades 9 to 12), but with no skill at all. The remaining 7 and 2.5 per cent are diploma and degree holders, respectively. Astonishingly, over 90 per cent of the workforce has no skill at all, at least upon joining the firms. Neither does there exist any system of on-job training industry-wide. Of the entire workforce, less than 1 per cent is said to have received short-term training. Thus, whatever skill the labour force has, it is acquired only through experience.

From the point of view of technological capability building in manufacturing, the technical knowledge of production workers is a key factor. In this regard, only 12 per cent of the total workforce (or 19 per cent of production workers) is engaged in technical activities. The remaining 80 per cent of the productive force has no technical knowledge at all. Even among the technical workers only 2 per cent of them have diploma and above. Thus, nearly all technical workers have acquired their skill only through long experience on the job.

Moreover, one of the major determinants of competitiveness is product quality. In this connection, only 2.8 per cent of the workforce is engaged in quality control activities. Internal quality standard control is little known in manufacturing. The public quality and standard control organisation does not seem to have the capacity to cover all firms/goods. Forty per cent of the enterprises responded that they have never been visited by any external

Table 7.9 Levels of education of manufacturing workforce (2005)

Level of education	Proportion of work force category				
	Total labour	Technical staff	Quality control	Semi-skilled	Unskilled
Illiterate	10.1	0.9	0.0	2.4	5.4
1 to 8 (grade)	45.0	3.4	0.3	12.0	20.0
9 to 12 (grade)	35.4	5.2	1.8	11.4	6.1
Diploma	7.2	1.9	0.4	1.2	0.0
Degree	2.4	0.4	0.2	0.0	0.0
Total	100	11.8	2.8	27.0	31.5

Source: EEA, 2005.

quality/standard control agent, government or otherwise. Only a few manufacturing firms have ISO 9000 or 14000 (EEA, 2005).

What can be summarised from this section is that the key determinants of productivity in manufacturing industries, such as investment, degree of automation of plants, age structure of firms, educational status of workers, sources to acquire technical information, etc., indicate that favourable conditions for industrial development are not yet in place, and grossly lacking. Some of the factors are external to firms/industries, demanding the government to deliver them.

7.1.4 Infrastructure deficit

Provision of adequate infrastructure, both social and economic, helps determine a country's success in diversifying production, expanding trade, coping with population growth, reducing poverty or improving environmental conditions. Infrastructure capacity needs to be in place ahead of time to respond to effective demand from production and service sectors, thereby raising productivities and lowering costs. Infrastructure provision has to grow step by step with economic output.

As infrastructure largely involves public goods, such as roads, rails, power, telecommunications, major dams and channel works for irrigation and drainage, education, piped water supply, etc., and as all these incur substantial investment costs, governments, particularly in developing countries, have leading roles in the provision and maintenance of infrastructure.

Because of the burden of infrastructure provision on the budget, however, developing countries understandably face a wide infrastructure deficit. Ethiopia, a least developed traditional economy, with a large rural population (70 million) sparsely settled across 1.14 million square kilometres of land, faces a huge challenge with providing basic infrastructure. Despite the recent conspicuous effort of the public sector in upgrading and expanding infrastructure provision, particularly in roads and power, the state of infrastructure in the country is still one of the least developed and falls much short of demand.

7.1.4.1 Surface and air transport

With respect to surface transport, reasonable road corridors join major administrative towns to the capital – Addis Ababa. Though in poor condition, Ethiopia also has road links with its neighbours: Kenya, Eritrea, Sudan and Somalia. However, the general road density in the country is very low, less than half of the average for low income countries (Table 7.10).

Rural road accessibility, in particular, is very poor. Only about 10 per cent of the rural population is within two kilometres from all-weather road. Rural population access to all-weather roads requires *"tripling the length of the classified road network, a much higher level of effort than would be involved in most neighbouring countries"* (Foster and Morella, 2011). Rails are little known in Ethiopia. There is only a single and outdated rail corridor running from the centre to Djibouti. Even this is not currently functional.

Table 7.10 Infrastructure status in Ethiopia (2008)

Infrastructure	Ethiopia	LIC
Paved road density (km² of arable land)	35.8	86.6
Unpaved road density (km² of arable land)	121.5	504.7
Rural accessibility (% of rural pop within 2 km from all-season road)	10.3	21.7
Installed power generation capacity (MW per million people)	9.8	24.4
Power consumption (KWh/capita)	33.6	99.5
Access to electricity (% of population)	12.0	15.4
Urban access to electricity (% of population)	86.0	71.0
Rural access to electricity (% population)	2.0	12.0

Source: Adapted from Foster and Morella, 2011, Tables 2 and 5.

Notes
LIC = Low Income Countries.
Arable land refers to land that could be settled around, hence with economic potential.

Ethiopia has one of the leading airlines in Africa which has developed competitive international networks. However, its domestic services are quite limited, as are flight schedules. Overall, extending air services to towns of business and economic importance remain challenging. On-going efforts involve the construction of airports in all regional administrative capitals.

7.1.4.2 Energy

Ethiopia is endowed with vast energy potential from different sources, including hydropower, geothermal, wind, solar, woody biomass, natural gas and coal. However, biomass (i.e. traditional sources) such as wood, charcoal, etc., accounts for 89 per cent of energy consumption. Petroleum fuels and electric power account for the remaining 7.6 and 1.1 per cent. The largest proportion of electric power supply, about 40 per cent, is consumed by industries, while the balance is consumed by households (33 per cent) and the service sector (26 per cent) (EEA, 2009).

Despite the least contribution to overall consumption and employment, Ethiopia has considerable hydropower potential. It is even said that it has the potential to be one of the major power exporters in Africa, only next to the Democratic Republic of the Congo, though the challenge of resourcing long-term finance to exploit available potential remains a major bottle neck. Today, Ethiopia has one of the least developed power systems even by Sub-Saharan standards. Installed generation capacity is only about ten megawatts per a million population, which is much less than half of the average for low-income countries (Table 7.10). Consumption per capita, 33.6 KWh, is only one-third of the corresponding level for low-income countries. Given the size of the population and the relatively large and scattered settlement pattern of the population, the challenge of rural electrification is daunting. Only 2 per cent of the rural population, against 12 per cent for low-income countries average, has access to electricity. Electric power rationing is still practiced even in the capital city – Addis Ababa. Given the essential role of power for development, Ethiopia has a long way to go before it reasonably meets the domestic demand, and avoids the adverse impact of power constraint on the economy.

7.1.4.3 Irrigation

Apart from power generation, water resource management is critical for irrigation. For the last four decades, Ethiopia has been frequently affected by droughts, thereby keeping productivities in agriculture very low. It is estimated that unfavourable weather condition reduces growth, on average, by one percentage point annually (Foster and Morella). Currently only about 3 per cent, or 290,000 hectares, of the total cultivated area is said to be irrigated. But this accounts for less than 10 per cent of total irrigable land in the country. It should be underlined that irrespective of the cost burden, however, it is an insurmountable challenge to think of transforming agriculture, and the economy without irrigation. To rely on the currently fast changing natural weather condition for the longer-term development is a self-defeating strategy.

7.1.4.4 ICT Coverage

ICT coverage is important for the competitiveness of an economy. The provision of ICT services is currently the monopoly of the state, while the coverage is the lowest in Africa. Barely 9.9 per cent of the population, compared with 48.2 per cent for the low-income countries average, is covered by GSM signals (Table 7.11). Mobile phone subscribers are only 1.6 per 100 people, against 15.1 for low-income countries, while internet subscribers are very insignificant. Similarly, internet bandwidth in Ethiopia, which is about 0.3 mega-bites per second per capita, is too low compared with low-income countries average. However, though rural coverage is still disproportionately low, fixed line services in Ethiopia fairly compares with that of low-income countries.

Despite the low cost of ICT services for internal calls, coverage is comparatively low, all because of the policy environment which does not allow private investment, except on joint venture with the government, in ICT operation.

Table 7.11 Comparative ICT coverage in Ethiopia and LICs

Detail	Ethiopia	LICs
GSM coverage (% of population)	9.9	48.2
Mobile phone (subscribers/100 people)	1.6	15.1
Fixed line phones (subscribers/100 people)	1.0	0.8
Internet bandwidth (mega-bites/second/capita)	0.3	5.8
Internet (subscribers/100 people)	0.0	0.1

Source: Adapted from Minges *et al.* in Foster and Morella, 2011, Table 6.

Notes
LIC = Low Income Countries.

7.1.5 Implicit challenges of industrialising a traditional agricultural economy

Economic history demonstrates that industrialisation is the only proven mechanism/approach to break out of poverty sustainably. All advanced and newly industrialising economies today pursued this same path to bring about socio-economic development. To date there is no precedence otherwise. The challenging issue, however, is how best to industrialise. What is the reliable and speedy option of industrialisation for today's low-income (poor) economies given existing socio-economic backwardness and fast changing international economic order?

In the early models of economic development, since agriculture has been considered primarily as a reservoir of low labour productivity, much emphasis has been put on the need for industrial development, mainly manufacturing, with little or no attention paid to the former (Lewis, 1954; Ranis and Fei, 1961). Agriculture being characterised with surplus labour, capital was thought to be the only factor constraining industrial development (Mellor, 1986). Moreover, while earlier industrial establishments were primarily meant to meet domestic markets demand, little thought was given for agriculture as potentially the major market. The idea was that 'supply creates its own demand', i.e. wages in the modern sectors, industry and services, would create additional demand to clear the industrial goods market. Hence, even within the domestic market, the importance of agriculture was little appreciated. Post-colonial Africa's approach to development was a typical case of such industrialisation strategy (Badiane, 1999).

Moreover, particularly in an economy where the bulk of the population depends on agriculture, an industrialisation strategy which mainly focuses on industrial sector expansion implies an attempt to absorb scores of millions of agricultural workers through industrial wage labour. Even assuming that investment dynamics in the modern private sector, encouraged by globalisation, would accelerate international (bilateral and multilateral) capital flows, it is difficult to create employment for a large stock of agricultural population within a foreseeable time period. In most developing countries, particularly least developed ones, the manufacturing sector employs less than 5 per cent of the population. A study on related issue notes that

> for countries with an initial agricultural share of 80% and a labour force growth rate of 3%, it would take 142 years to reach this turning point, the structural transformation turning point, even with rapid growth of 4% of non-farm employment
>
> (Gabre Medhin and Johnston, 1999)

This suggests that such a strategy of industrial development is at best a trickling down approach. Moreover, irrespective of capital and market constraints, it would be quite a tall task to maintain social stability in any developing country for such a long period, particularly in a situation where agriculture itself is on the decline and failing to feed the very population depending on it for survival.

In practice this model failed to deliver the desired result. Africa still remains least industrialised. Not only lack of adequate capital, but also lack of effective domestic demand and least competitiveness in international markets remain major constraints (Badiane, 1999). For Ethiopia too, the relevance of this model is quite remote. As explained in the previous sections, the Ethiopian economy is characterised by subsistence agriculture, on which the bulk of the population depends for its livelihood and a manufacturing sector heavily dominated by small-scale and micro firms. As a result of which the country largely depends on imports for food deficits and manufactured goods. How then could Ethiopia industrialise? Is it through expanding manufacturing industries, or via agricultural development (based on natural comparative advantage), or focusing on trade (either import substitution or export promotion), or a combination of these? Heavily constrained by critical factors of industrialisation, such as capital, market, skilled labour and hard currency, and also with the bulk of the population depending on agriculture for its livelihood, the initial phase of industrialisation needs to focus mainly on agricultural recovery. Such recovery in agriculture helps raise the supply of food, thereby stabilising prices; generate additional foreign exchange necessary to finance the initial transformation process; increase agricultural incomes, thereby creating demand for manufactured inputs and consumer goods, further stimulating production in non-agricultural sectors; and contribute to financial deepening through more saving and public tax revenue.

Growth acceleration in agriculture, at the initial phase, then becomes a crucial element of the industrialisation process. However, agriculture can neither absorb the surplus labour, nor transform by itself to a highly productive activity without significant input from manufacturing. It should be recognised that even the most labour-intensive production technique, despite improvement in productivity levels, could hardly absorb the growing labour force in agriculture (Mellor, 1986). Agriculture does not create multiple division of labour within itself to accommodate a large labour force. Moreover, substantial increase in productivity calls for structural change in production, which implies introducing medium- and large-scale farms, increase use of technical inputs and labour-saving machinery and equipment, use of irrigation, etc., all largely supplied by the industrial sector. Thus an essential measure at the first phase of the industrialisation process is to create an interface with the manufacturing sector, i.e. identifying and promoting manufacturing industries having direct and close linkages (input-output linkages) with agriculture. These industries then serve as strategic industries not only to reinforce the development of agriculture, but also drive growth within the manufacturing sector.

Thus in a country like Ethiopia, industrialisation needs to be a process whereby a predominantly agrarian economy is transformed into a diversified and productive economy dominated by manufacturing and services (Gabre Medhin and Johnston, 1999). But at the initial phase of the process, industrialisation, nevertheless, implies industrialising agriculture. Growth in agriculture alone, however, would not be sufficient to solve deep rooted poverty problems. Agriculture does not create sufficient wealth. Thus, apart from its essential short- to medium-term role noted in the preceding paragraphs, its pivotal role is to induce growth in non-agricultural sectors through both forward and backward (demand and supply) linkages with the rest of the economy. What this means is that the fundamental problem of industrialisation in a subsistence economy is the transition from large agricultural bases, often unproductive ones, to, first of all, more productive agricultural bases, and next to expanding the manufacturing sector, i.e. an integrated agricultural and industrial development (Romer, 1991).

7.2 Industrialisation strategy in a historical context: lessons from success stories

The industrialisation strategies of some East Asian countries, particularly strategies focusing on industrial and trade sectors, have been studied by many authors (Amsden, 1989; Wade, 1990; Lall, 1996). The interest here is on priority settings and complementarities between economic sectors at the initial stage of the industrialisation process. The question is: did these newly industrialisers delay agricultural productivity growth in favour of industrial sectors' development? The following sub-sections offer useful explanations.

7.2.1 Investment in agriculture

This sub-section highlights agriculture at an early phase of industrialisation, using today's industrialising Asian economies. This sub-section relies heavily on 'African Development: Lessons from Asia' (Winrock International, 1991).

7.2.1.1 Chinese Taipei

The experience of Chinese Taipei (popularly known as Taiwan) is said to have much relevance to Africa as its development model first focused on agriculture and then integrated it with industry successfully. Taiwan emphasised small-scale industry by integrating it into the agricultural development framework, and then to the export economy. Moreover, it is also said that its experience confirms key lessons from earlier experience in Japan (Gabre Medhin and Johnston, 1999).

First, agricultural output was increased within the framework of existing small-scale farming system. Labour-intensive technological innovations and involved divisible inputs, especially the improved seed-fertiliser combinations, spread widely. These innovations enabled significant increases in total factor productivity within the agricultural sector. As such innovations were to some extent scale neutral, small-scale farm units too adopted them incrementally. A large and growing percentage of the farm population significantly benefited from the increases in farm productivity and output. This formed the basis for the ensuing Green Revolution.

The first boom in Taiwan was in agriculture, mainly rice and sugar, which was then diversified to new crops: mushrooms and asparagus. This was largely followed by processing, before the big industrialisation drive in textiles kicked off. But this was done under a policy framework which encouraged broad rural activities, including non-agricultural activities, particularly small- and medium-scale enterprises.

Triggered by the rising agricultural income, hence rural consumption demand, the rural non-farm economy expanded considerably.

> The pull for the expansion of rural industrialisation came from broad-based rural demand, resulting from increased farm cash incomes as agricultural productivity and commercialization rose. In both Taiwan and Japan, rural industrialization was based on the widespread emergence of small- and medium scale enterprises, with an average of eight employees. These SMEs played a key role, not only in fostering the structural transformation, but also in providing the basis for the industrial strength of Taiwan and Japan in years to come
>
> (Gabre Medhin and Johnston, 1999, p. 5)

As agricultural production and rural incomes grew rapidly in the 1960s, small and medium enterprises also mushroomed rapidly in this period. The faster the growth in agriculture, the faster the decline in its size, i.e. in production, employment and foreign currency earning.

Heavy investment in agriculture was later followed by land reforms. The government-owned and other lands were distributed to tillers. So a fairly equal distribution of assets prevailed. This was a policy to maintain incentives in agriculture while at the same time moving resources from agriculture into other sectors.

In the 1960s agriculture was growing quite fast that nearly 30 per cent of the total savings of the Taiwanese society was from agriculture. By the 1960s not only farm cash receipts steeply increased, but the increase in the off-farm income of farm households was even greater.

> By 1966 over one-third of the total income of farm families was coming from non-agricultural sources, and that share was rising rapidly because of structural transformation and especially the mushrooming of small and medium enterprises in Taiwan's rural non-farm economy.
>
> (Gabre Medhin and Johnston, 1999, p. 40)

7.2.1.2 China

China's growth surge today is based on agriculture. It is said that China has pushed against its available arable land base for a millennium; and any time when there were bad crops, millions of people died. But China's breakthrough came with the rise in agricultural productivity. 'Once technology came along after WWII to permit agricultural productivity to rise, they jumped on it and that was their salvation. Then discovering exports and all of that has been the second round of salvation' (Timmer, 1991).

7.2.1.3 Sample ASEAN countries

The development path taken by three ASEAN countries – Indonesia, Malaysia and Thailand – give useful insights. The three countries invested intensively and deliberately in their natural resource bases which were largely agricultural. They followed their comparative advantage. Malaysia invested in rubber and palm oil and exported them, which was crucial for its further development; Thailand emphasised rice and some other food crops as well but became successful in exporting rice, which carried its development for a long time and enabled it to further diversify; Indonesia too followed the same approach. Indonesia is not only an oil exporter; it also exports a range of agricultural commodities including cocoa, tea, coffee, palm oil and rubber. Indonesia invested heavily in agriculture (Romer, 1991).

In general, therefore, governments in these countries invested heavily to increase productivity in agriculture through support for rural infrastructure, research and extension, fertiliser subsidies and price support systems. Rapidly increasing agricultural productivity helped establish the basis for industrialisation, through lower food costs and exports. Malaysia and Thailand first developed their export agriculture; Indonesia used its oil resource and agriculture. In all these economies exports were the leading sectors of the economies.

In general, the East Asian economies, other than Thailand, but including Japan after the Second World War, had serious problems of food shortages and perceived insecurity at the household level. These countries overcame such serious problems by raising agricultural productivity and further introducing land reform. It was recognised that unless agricultural productivity increases sustainably in food crops specially, but also in export crops, economic reform would run into all kinds of constraints that will make difficult the sustained release of resources from agriculture into the industrial and service sectors. Long-term leadership stability did not take place until there was a sense that the issue of food security was no longer a daily concern. Hence, solving agricultural problems, particularly that of small farmers, including marketing problems, indeed came first (Timmer, 1991).

East Asian industrialisers also invested heavily in infrastructure. Because of a long history of investment in rural roads, irrigation and research on technical inputs, such as fertiliser and improved seeds, Asian agriculture became easily integrated into the national economy. It is also said that in all Asian countries colonised by the Japanese, the latter put a lot of infrastructure into the rural areas, including irrigation, roads, electric power lines, etc., that are important preconditions for development. And they did so for their own reasons – adequate and cheap food supply (Ranis, 1991).

An important lesson emerging from the experience of Asian industrialisers, therefore, is that the structural transformation of a predominantly agrarian economy cannot be achieved without sustained and substantial increase in agricultural productivity. Substantial and sustainable growth of agriculture and the rural economy is of critical importance not only as a source of savings, but also as a source of cheap food that keeps wage rates low during industrialisation. Also, promoting the structural linkage between agriculture and industry is a pivotal strategic issue. Finally, infrastructure is simply a precondition for industrialisation.

7.3 Fundamentals of industrial development strategy of Ethiopia

7.3.1 Main strategic orientations

A careful dissection of Ethiopia's industrialisation strategy reveals that it is actually based on a blend of several strategic orientations. In this regard, at least six considerations characterise the industrialisation strategy: Agricultural Development Led Industrialisation (ADLI), labour-intensive production mode, export-led industrialisation, private sector-led industrialisation, developmental state capitalism and Foreign Direct Investments (FDI) for industrialisation.

7.3.1.1 Agricultural development-led industrialisation

ADLI is basically a sectoral programme meant to increase agricultural productivities substantially, thereby enhancing the food security status of the country. The idea is that in the Ethiopian context where, on the one hand, the overwhelming population relies on agriculture for its livelihood, and on the other, agricultural activities are still largely traditional, this sector has to recover and guarantee food security first, thereby reducing poverty, if the industrial development programme is to be successful.[11]

But how does this lead to industrial development? Primarily, the strategy aspires to increase agricultural productivity significantly. Then through the income effect, demand for non-agricultural consumption goods and inputs would increase. Obviously, demand for services is also expected to increase. A rise in agricultural productivity also implies increased output of agricultural raw materials feeding manufacturing industries and export, thereby increasing the scope of foreign currency earning. Triggered by substantial demand, manufacturing industries will further expand to meet the required demand, thereby reinforcing growth in agriculture.

ADLI involves some strong assumptions. It assumes existence of strong backward and forward linkages of agriculture and supply responsiveness to demand in both industry and agriculture. While studies argue for the prevalence of quite a strong (elastic) backward linkage of agriculture, its forward linkage is relatively weak.[12] Moreover, on the supply side, the responsiveness of industry to growth in agriculture is quite limited, after all demand (market) is only one of the many aspects influencing supply. Given this weak supply response and poor performance of agriculture, the success of ADLI cannot be guaranteed a priori (Adelman and Vogel, 1992; Gabre Medhin and Johnston, 1999). Hence, the challenge is not only increasing the supply of agriculture, which is indeed critical, but also the supply responsiveness of manufacturing, particularly given its current structural problem and extremely weak technological status.[13]

7.3.1.2 Labour-intensive production mode

The strategy contends that resource allocation needs to be in line with the relatively abundant resources in the country. Ethiopia's competitive edge today is its cheap labour, not capital or technology. Hence, at this initial stage of the industrialisation process, the strategy should focus on labour-intensive (or capital-saving) industries. As most industries having close linkages with agriculture, such as agro-processing industries, are labour-intensive, such industries meet the requirements of the industrialisation strategy. The strategy concluded that based on 'countries' development experiences and fundamentals of economic science, there is no alternative for faster development and efficient resource allocation except pursuing a labour-intensive mode of development' (Ministry of Information, 2002, p. 31). But it also acknowledges that as labour in Ethiopia is unskilled, and hence less productive, focus on upgrading its skill, hence increasing productivity levels, should be part of the strategy.

However, the intention here is not a clear-cut choice of labour-intensive industrialisation over capital-intensive industrialisation. Instead, it indicates in broad terms the sort of industries that the government would like to promote at this stage of development, through incentives or forms of government's support. Otherwise, the government recognises the importance of both labour- and capital-intensive dimensions of an integrated industrialisation strategy.

However, preference for a labour-intensive approach, particularly in export-oriented industries, may be debatable as the possibility of becoming internationally competitive is quite limited given the poor skill of Ethiopian labour. Also, investors may not opt for a labour-intensive approach as technology, which is the major determinant of productivity, is largely embodied with capital rather than labour. Moreover, as demonstrated over 2006–09, inflation inevitably raises wages thereby further weakening the competitive status of industries in international markets. The government hardly controls food or other prices and regulates markets to maintain living standards.

As noted in the background to the strategy, agro-processing industries are most labour-intensive, but least productive of all industrial groups in the sector. Currently, to overcome this shortcoming the government is extensively updating the hardware of textile, leather and other agro-processing industries under its control. What this means is that further new investments in such industries would inevitably shift towards relatively more capital-intensive rather than labour-intensive approach. A typical example in this regard is Hong Kong, where, in the 1980s, 35 per cent of the labour force was made redundant due to lack of competitiveness of the industries. Enterprises of older generation technology, employing labour-intensive mode of production, were no more competitive and had to be replaced by new advanced technologies, employing highly skilled labour. Earlier technology enterprises were relocated to remote areas of China, producing goods for local consumption. Hence, in practice labour-intensive industrial development today may not be quite relevant, particularly in tradable industries. Competitiveness today involves not only price but also product quality, shape, variety, precision, etc., which are better addressed by new generation technologies. Cheap labour alone could not make industries competitive; nor is cheap labour the prime factor.

So the strategy of labour-intensive industrialisation, on the grounds that cheap but unskilled labour is, relatively, the most abundant resource of the country, may not lead to competitiveness and faster industrialisation. Competitiveness and labour-intensiveness are not necessarily complementary. Technologically leading industries, such as knowledge-based engineering industries, though not labour intensive, are critical for industrialisation. Such industries, therefore, need to be rewarded, at least equally, as labour-intensive ones. In fact, in the longer term, larger employment would be generated by investing in technology-intensive, rather than on the phasing-out labour-intensive industries.

7.3.1.3 Export-led industrialisation

According to this, while agricultural development determines the pace and direction of industrial sector development, the exporting sub-sector takes the lead and determines the pace and direction of industries within the sector. Exporting industries take a leading role because firms' overall efficiency can only be reliably asserted if they are capable of exporting. For tradable goods industries, management efficiency, labour skill, technological capability, marketing technique, cost and quality competitiveness, etc., can all be gauged by firms' capacity to export. In today's globalised world, industrial development depends on its competitiveness. As noted above, the economy requires large foreign exchange to import intermediates, particularly capital goods. Such large foreign currency earning cannot be secured by exporting agricultural raw materials only. Exporting manufactured goods should be the objective of industrialisation and that in the near future. That is why exporting industries are said to be leading industries.

But there are some important issues that need to be addressed in this context. While the strategy of actively exploiting international markets is commendable at all times, particularly during the early phase of industrialisation, focusing on exporting alone as the central strategy may not be a sound approach. This is so because exporting could not be the only criteria for measuring efficiency. There are enterprises producing non-tradable goods that are more efficient than some exporting ones. Such industries have high productivity, large capacity to generate employment, ability to turn out quality products, greater linkages within manufacturing, etc. Primarily, industrialisation is not about exporting or amassing foreign exchange; it is about generating greater division of labour to absorb large employment at higher productivity level. Therefore, focus should also be given to such non-exporting but efficient enterprises.

There is also an important issue left out in this connection. It is difficult to comprehend export-promotion without import-replacement. One of the basic objectives of an export drive is to expand import-replacing industries. Today, Ethiopia is heavily dependent on imports, not only for capital and intermediate goods, but also for critical consumption goods. For instance, enterprises producing industrial chemicals are the ones having the largest linkages within the sector. Industrial chemicals account for about 50 per cent of the foreign exchange need for the manufacturing sector. Thus promoting such industries would save substantial foreign exchange. Strategic and efficient import-replacing industries, therefore, should also be the focus of any series industrialisation strategy.

Moreover, the strategy sounds quite ambitious. Export capability demands highly productive and marketing efficiency, hence competitiveness. But this is largely a derivative of industrialisation. Industrialisation leads to international competitiveness and in turn to substantial export capability of manufactured goods. Large export capability of manufactures, at an early phase of industrialisation, can hardly be realised in today's competitive world. Hence, there is a one-way causation: industrial development results in high export capacity of manufactures. Ethiopia today has the least exporting capacity of both manufactures and agricultural commodities. So, while export of industrial goods has to be encouraged, industrialisation through substantial export, at such initial stage of industrialisation, could be frustrating. Thus, it might be worth moderating the strategy.

7.3.1.4 Private sector-led industrialisation

Ethiopia has gone through a socialist mode of economic management for a decade-and-a half, before the current government came to power at the opening of the 1990s. The modern private sector had been entirely marginalised during the former regime. With a change in economic policy regime, which reintroduced a market based economic management, the modern private sector has been reintroduced back into the economy.[14]

However, the strategy differentiates between two groups of private sector capitalists: developmental and rent-seeking ones. While the former are those who make additional wealth through production and service activities, the latter refers to those tagged as not only uncompetitive, but also those seeking wealth through corruption and subsidies (protection, exemption, etc.). Therefore, the strategy involves measures that encourage the former, i.e. developmental capitalists (the government claims itself to be a developmental state) and discouraging rent-seeking capitalists.[15]

7.3.1.5 Developmental state capitalism

The role of the state is very strong in Ethiopia's capitalist transformation. Apart from the necessary role of a state to provide public goods, state intervention in a developing market economy draws its justification from market failure to address technology, information and co-ordination externalities. At an early phase of industrialisation, creating and developing markets and conscious and calculated intervention to accelerate economic growth, also calls for the state to act (Amsden, 1989).

The strategy claims for the existence of objective realities in Ethiopia that call for intervention, including not only extensive market failure and the need for a faster development, but also the existence of an entrenched dependent business class (rent-seeking capitalists) that the state has to disable/paralyse and weak developmental entrepreneurs that need to be supported. Accordingly, the strategy argues for the state to provide strong and able leading role for successful industrial development.

The strategy also recognises the need for careful selection of areas, adequate financial resources and implementation capacity of the state for successful intervention. It also argues that intervention should be a short-term measure until market forces and the private sector gain strength and capacity to guide the economy.

The strategy document, however, does not go far enough to specify areas of market failure, and measures and instruments of intervention even in a broader context. Obviously, in many areas, including rural finance, information access to economic opportunities, acquisition of technology, access to infrastructure, etc., markets are either fragmented/immature or not existing at all. However, if market failure is said to exist, then this requires explicitly identifying the markets, addressing how and what sort of intervention to employ, what instruments to use, etc. If rent-seeking economic activity is said to prevail, then it requires specifying the system that leads to such activity. If individual business agents are the problems, then it is a matter of drawing appropriate regulation and implementing effectively. Targeting individual business elites, rather than improving the system would not be a solution. What needs to be addressed is whether the current system of political and economic governance effectively deters rent-seeking activities.

Currently, the state's intervention in the economy is pervasive. As it regards land as a source of rent-seeking activities, land is state owned. It owns commercial banks; has a monopoly on telecommunications for its attractive revenue;[16] controls large-scale manufacturing industries, etc. It grants land to activities and individual entrepreneurs that it believes to be developmental. For instance, lavish lease rights are granted to investors in floriculture; large tracts of land are sold on lease to foreign investors in agriculture at reasonably low prices; it lends to investors on the basis of strategic political criteria (Altenburg, 2010); it intervenes in distribution systems, to cut out middle men regarded as having abused oligopolistic market power and prohibits hoarding, etc. Despite minor differences, such measures are largely remnants of the socialist regime

It is also imperative that in a market economy, the role of the state needs to be complementary to that of the private sector. In formulating policies and strategies, sectoral or national, an essential measure of the government is to build evidence based, participatory and transparent institutional learning processes.

Information regarding the business environment is easily accessible to the private sector but not so for the public. Hence, industrial policy making should be a strategic collaboration between the private and public sectors with the aim of uncovering, where the most significant obstacles to restructuring lie, what type of intervention would be effective to remove them, what implementation strategy is preferable, etc. However, the existing strategy and policy-making process is entirely the domain of the state, exclusive of the private sector. Decisions are taken in a non-transparent and discretionary manner and implementation is largely carried out forcefully. 'Moreover, especially the relationships between government, ruling party, state-owned enterprises and endowment-owned enterprises are quite opaque' (Altenburg, 2010, p. 21).

Also the private sector can hardly organise itself on business defined criteria to guard its interest. The private sector is required to organise in line with the political, i.e. ethnic based, administrative structure. Independent policy think tanks are not invited to bring in their expertise on industrial development strategies and policies while being drafted.

7.3.1.6   Foreign direct investments for industrialisation

On the one hand, in an LDC like Ethiopia, most entrepreneurs have limited capital, weak technological knowhow, poor market networking and less efficient administrative and organisational capacity. On the other hand, these are the strong assets of foreign investors. Hence, there is a realisation in Ethiopia that, in order to be successful, the country's industrialisation strategy must be able to attract considerable FDI.

However, the strategy also notes that foreign investment does also involve some disadvantages to host economies, of which capital mobility, hence early withdrawal of capital, is the most serious one. This has strong strategic implications: first, foreign capital is not likely to be the central player in the industrialisation process, which is a long-term phenomenon; second, key sectors that have extensive growth linkages to the overall economy need to be carefully scrutinised whether they have to be opened up for foreign investment. For instance, foreign investment is not allowed in economic areas such as small-scale and micro enterprises, import (except LPG, bitumen), export (of coffee, hides and skins, pulses and oilseeds, etc., if not own production), financial institutions, telecommunications (except on joint venture), retail and wholesale trade (except petroleum and own locally produced products), etc. (MFA, 2005).

Other disadvantages, of strategic concern include keeping important activities such as R&D, market networking techniques, etc., as secrets, thereby denying host economies the opportunity to acquire expertise. In such cases, the strategy is to consciously deal with investors to make sure that the latter provides local industrialists/counterparts access to such expertise.

The strategy also emphasises the importance of appreciating foreign investment in its broader context. Foreign investors are not only those with large capital but also those with management knowhow, marketing expertise, etc., who would like entry to host markets with limited capital. There is a need to attract such investors under joint ventures.

Irrespective of the pros and cons of foreign investment, however, the strategy accords due importance to foreign investment and calls for measures to create conducive environment such as providing legal protection, political stability, hardworking and skilled labour force, efficient judicial system, adequate infrastructure, efficient administrative structure, etc.

An issue of concern that is often raised by foreign investors is the discriminatory investment policy, particularly barriers to telecommunications, financial institutions and foreign trade, i.e. economic activities involving lucrative business activities. Ethiopia is one of the least FDI recipient countries. As such, it would have been more useful to take a moderate approach than openly declare closed investment areas, which may likely create deterrence to all categories of investors. Rather than closing the doors, entry could have been made on the basis of varying terms and conditions referring to individual/specific investors, thereby accommodating the government's concern. Conditions could be made to vary either by sector, enterprise, origin, etc., thereby addressing the weaknesses of individual and specific investors.

7.3.2 Policy frameworks

In connection with what may be characterised as policy frameworks, Ethiopia's industrialisation strategy is predicated on the need to create a conducive environment through a stable macroeconomic framework, conducive financial system, reliable infrastructure and education and training.

7.3.2.1 Stable macroeconomic environment

The significance of a microeconomic stability for growth is not contestable. It is a necessary, though not a sufficient, condition for industrial development. The issue, however, is how it is best addressed, and whether it produces the desired result. For macroeconomic stability, the strategy acknowledges the need to maintain low inflation, low interest rate variability and realistic exchange rate of the domestic currency.

To this end, the central bank directly sets the minimum deposit rate while leaving the lending rate to be determined by the market. To date, foreign exchange transaction is directly controlled by the state. Until very recently, it has been rationed through an auction system, though now made to be accessed through banks for import-export activities at a rate fixed by the central bank. Ethiopia has a tightly managed exchange rate, described by the government as a managed float (classified by IMF as a de facto crawl-like arrangement) with no predetermined path for the exchange rate. The domestic currency (the Birr) has been significantly devalued repeatedly in the last two decades and continuously made to depreciate against the dollar and other major hard currencies. Since the current government took power in the early 1990s, the domestic currency depreciated over eight-fold. Foreign exchange transaction is still not privatised. The strategy argues that privatising foreign exchange would cause significant macroeconomic destabilisation.

Ethiopia knows no serious inflationary pressure throughout its history. In a traditional economy, this is no surprise. Only when serious drought occurs do prices of agricultural products rise notably, thereby inducing general price increases. Only recently, since 2007, did serious inflation, in the order of 40–60 per cent, cause economic destabilisation (IMF, 2008).

Despite dedicated effort, however, it has never been easy for the government to maintain macroeconomic stability in practice. Real interest rate has been negative throughout the period. Irrespective of continuous deep devaluation, the exchange rate remains unstable. For most of the years, foreign reserve holding remained as low as 1.2 to two months of import cover. Moreover, maintaining a balanced budget as one of the key criteria for macroeconomic stability has never been met throughout the period. Ethiopia depends on foreign aid for about one-third of the total annual expenditure. Without a balanced budget, inflation inevitably creeps in, thereby retarding productive investment. Inflation today is the most serious concern in the country.

7.3.2.2 Conducive financial system

Following the nationalisation of private banks in the mid-1970s, Ethiopia's financial sector remained, for long, very weak. Still there are no financial establishments such as venture capital companies, stock markets, leasing companies, etc. Even today, only commercial banks, insurance companies and micro-finance institutions operate at rudimentary levels. An important policy measure of the current government has been to open the financial sector for domestic private investment. Today, there are nearly 20 banks and insurance companies, as well as a number of micro-finance institutions. Three of the banks and an insurance company are owned by the state. The state-owned Commercial Bank of Ethiopia is the most dominant of all banks, particularly in deposits and capital shares. In today's Ethiopia, therefore, private and state-owned financial institutions operate side-by-side. The strategy acknowledges that successful industrialisation could not be realised without a significant development of the existing infant financial sector.

But the industrialisation strategy has some unique features when it comes to financial institutions, perhaps mirroring some East Asian Model. State-owned financial institutions, irrespective of their dominance, are regarded as key instruments for promoting strategic activities/enterprises – through direct credit, favourable loan rates and grace periods, etc. Hence, unlike other enterprises, state-owned banks and insurance companies remain under the control of the state, and are unlikely to be privatised in the near future.

Similarly, the financial sector is closed for foreign investment. Three points are raised as an argument. First, the central bank (i.e. the National Bank of Ethiopia) is said to be weak in controlling the complex system of operation of foreign banks. Second, as the foreign exchange regime is still under the control of the government, this policy would not be effectively implemented if foreign banks are allowed to operate. Lastly, infant private commercial banks could not stand the competitive pressure from foreign banks, and as such, the economy could fall under the control of the latter. The strategy argues that under such conditions, opening the financial sector for foreign investment could destabilise the financial system and the economy at large.

With regard to financial policies, the implications of state ownership and ban on foreign entry are far reaching. If state-owned banks are to be used as promotional instruments, then they may be forced to operate outside business principles. Moreover, the central bank could not have effective power to impose its directives on state-owned banks and insurance companies. State-owned banks are led by a Board of Directors, whose members, particularly chairpersons, include senior Ministers. Such a system may introduce a lack of transparency. Under such circumstances, state- and endowment-owned firms, as well as firms owned by renowned business leaders, may secure an unfair advantage over private business at large.

Similarly, keeping at bay foreign investment in the financial sector, in turn, may create a strong deterrence to foreign investment in all other sectors. As foreign investment in the financial sector induces FDI in other sectors, banning it could have an adverse impact on investment outside the financial sector. There are rich experiences of other countries on handling foreign investment in the financial sector, so as to moderate its adverse impact, while at the same time capitalising on its benefits. A number of different measures, including restricting location of operation, defining a capital ceiling, identifying the currency of operation, and also adopting very close control by the central bank could be employed to limit the possible abuse of regulations and directives by foreign investors (Teshome and Belete, 2007). The argument that 'central bank's weak capacity to make effective supervision would leave foreign banks unchecked to abuse financial regulations' is not a sound argument, as this is a short-term phenomenon. Updating the skill of the already well-established and experienced staff of the central bank should not take more than a few years. Moreover, Ethiopia's demand for financial resources is still untapped. The demand-supply gap is quite wide. Even if foreign banks become dominant in some lucrative sectors, such as in external trade, there remain wide sectors demanding financial services. Moreover, infant industries do learn. Foreign banks would not remain dominant for too long. Hence, keeping at bay foreign investment for too long may not be quite advantageous.

In fact, many argue that Ethiopia's accession to the WTO may remain stalled for a long time, because of its reluctance to allow foreign investment in the financial sector, among others. It is now nearly a decade since Ethiopia submitted its membership application, though limited progress has been made to date.

7.3.2.3 Reliable infrastructure

The strategy accords high priority to infrastructure provision, due to not only the country's poor infrastructure capacity, which is one of the least in Africa, but also for its importance as a precondition for both agricultural and industrial development. The emphasis is on roads, rails, telecommunications and electric power.

Road transport is the main mode of transportation in Ethiopia. However, in light of the country's mountainous landscape, coupled with the scattered settlement pattern of the population, road construction requires large capital, thereby limiting the extent of provision of a country-wide road network. Thus, the strategy recognises the need to construct standard roads linking urban towns in the country and extensive but lower grade feeder and rural roads. For this, the strategy is to establish a road-fund and use a labour-intensive approach to construct, particularly, low-cost rural roads. Accordingly, considerable construction works have been undertaken across the country since the turn of the century.

Railway: Ethiopia has only a single and outdated rail line running from Djibouti to Addis Ababa, the capital. Perhaps the difficult terrain might have contributed to the under-provision of rail services in the country. Aware of this fact, the strategy envisages construction of a rail-road relay system, where large road transport networks converge at rail-stations feeding trains and vice versa, thereby creating an efficient surface transport network, minimising the cost burden. According to the strategy, the Ethiopia–Djibouti railway would be contracted out to a private operator under a long-term concession.

Based on Ethiopia's long and successful experience in running an internationally acclaimed airline service, expanding domestic air routes, i.e. linking all administrative capitals and resource rich towns together, is seen as a strategically viable and important infrastructure network. Accordingly, over the decade, airports in major towns have been upgraded to an international standard and new ones built in nearly all regional administrative towns. Still, however, more work is required to link other towns of business importance.

Furthermore, as noted earlier, access to modern telecommunication facilities (mobile, internet, etc.) in Ethiopia is appalling. Unlike many developing countries, however, the strategy of redressing this backwardness is not necessarily private investment, though the policy allows public-private joint venture. In fact, to maximise profit, private companies are said to prefer focusing on urban centres that relatively have high population concentration, but not sparsely populated rural areas. This indicates market failure. Moreover, it is not consistent with ADLI. The strategy, therefore, is to keep telecommunications under government monopoly and use the proceeds secured from high concentration urban centres to expand services to rural areas. Also, as one of the major problems of the public sector in such high tech business is the lack of management knowhow, the government sub-contracted telecom management to a foreign company.

The joint venture, however, has its own implication. To dictate its plan, the government wants to hold a majority share. But this deters private investors. As noted earlier, keeping such a lucrative business closed for foreign private investment may have further indirect repercussions. One of the strong demands of WTO members for accession is to revoke such monopoly power.

Despite the fact that Ethiopia is considered to be one of the water-towers in the region, current hydro-electric power generation, for a population of over 82 million, is under one thousand megawatts (EEA, 2009). Electric power is rationed even in the capital city let alone in other parts of the country. Industries close down for days weekly. The strategy acknowledges the acute shortage of power and calls for significant expansion of hydroelectric power supply as a pre-requisite for industrial development.

Accordingly, construction of hydro-electric power dams have been under way for the last decade or so. The recently launched mega hydroelectric dam project on the Blue Nile basin, capable of generating over 5,200 megawatt, is one of the initiatives to address the power supply shortage. The government is planning to mobilise financial resources internally through different means, including float-ing government bonds. The strategy argues that it is even possible to export power to neighbouring countries, such as Sudan, Djibouti, Egypt, etc. If success-ful, this might as well improve regional stability.

To overcome capital and technical constraints, private investment is allowed in power generation and distribution, only keeping national grid transmission lines installation under government control, though there is still no promising response from the former.

Large construction projects, such as roads, hydroelectric dams, etc., are largely financed from internal sources — money creation and forced contribution by the public at large. This, however, might have been the major factor for the recently surging inflationary pressure, which is still not under control.[17] With the on-going rate of infrastructure expansion and mode of financing, it is likely that macroeconomic destabilisation will continue further.

Another shortcoming related to construction works is the tendency to priori-tise non-economic criteria as opposed to economic ones. In light of acute capital constraint, on the one hand, and the large capital that infrastructure construction demands, on the other, it is logical, at least at this early stage, to focus provision of infrastructure in areas of high economic/resource potential. Currently large capital is wasted in building roads and international airports in regions of less economic importance, but for the sake of what might be regarded as economics of affection.

7.3.2.4 Education and training

Another focus area of the strategy is education and training. It argues that a skilled, disciplined and hardworking labour force is required to increase produc-tivity, maintain industrial peace and attract substantial foreign investment. Cur-rently, the Ethiopian labour force, in general, does not meet such qualifications essential for industrial development.

The strategy advocates for extensive expansion of Technical and Vocational Education and Training (TVET) along with academic disciplines. To this end, compulsory high school education is made to wind up at grade ten after which students join either a preparatory school for higher education or TVET. Those with relatively better grade points in high school join the former for further studies in natural science, engineering, social science, etc. Currently, natural science and engineering colleges account for a significant proportion of graduates with a first degree. The remaining, after studying for less than two years or so in TVET, join the work force. Depending on one's own ability, however, better performers in TVET can also join colleges for further education.

The strategy also acknowledges the need for accelerated expansion of higher education. Accordingly, since the turn of the century, two or more new public colleges become operational yearly. Private sector education is also expanding fast. Currently there are over 25 universities and a number of colleges.

The strategy also calls for co-ordinating technical and vocational education and training with the industrial sectors' manpower demand, i.e. number of workers and type of skill. It also demands introducing an apprenticeship programme for TVET fresh graduates, for instance, such as the German model. The strategy also requires for a change in the objective and orientation of the educational system in general towards producing workers aspiring to establish own enterprises rather than longing only for employment. To this end, it argues for the need to teach entrepreneurship as a subject in higher education and training institutions.

What is also important for industrialisation is the strengthening and/or expansion of specialised institutions, directly meant to enhance the skill of the industrial workforce. Such institutions include leather and leather products, textile and apparel, sugar, dairy and meat, horticulture, etc. Similarly, productivity improving demonstration centres, established earlier for supporting micro and small enterprises are decentralised to all regional administrative capitals. Such centres are now regarded as essential institutions for accelerating the industrialisation process.

Great significance is accorded to education, technical and vocational training, and specialised productivity enhancing institutions. These measures are very much in line with the strategy of some of the fast industrialising East Asian countries such as S. Korea and Taiwan. The focus on science and engineering and technical education in general is highly commendable. However, the quality/ standard of education is unbelievably deteriorating at all levels. Nearly all universities, with the exception of few earlier established ones, don't have text books/libraries, qualified lecturers and other essential facilities. The current education system is not actually producing a qualified and skilled workforce at any level, but only an easily trainable workforce at all levels. It should be understood that human resource development is all about quality of education and skill, not just about quantity.

7.3.2.5 *Administrative structure and judicial system*

The strategy also emphasises the need for establishing an efficient and development supporting administrative structure and judicial system. In practice, however, the judicial system is neither independent nor efficient. Both the administrative and judicial systems are naked political instruments serving the interest of the regime in power (Teshome and Belete, 2007).

7.3.3 Sub-sectoral prioritisation and incentive schemes

The strategy contends that creating a conducive environment alone is not a sufficient condition for industrialisation. The measures suggested earlier benefit all industries. The strategy argues that no country, including in East Asia, has run successful industrialisation only by creating conducive environment. Rapid and sustainable industrial development needs further identifying of strategic industries and providing direct support.

The strategy identifies five industrial groups as priority areas for promotion, including textiles and wearing apparel; meat, leather and leather products; agro-processing industries; construction; and small and micro enterprises. Each of these industrial groups satisfies either one or more of the underlying principles stated earlier for industrialisation.

7.3.3.1 Textiles and wearing apparel

This industrial group largely adopts a labour-intensive production technique. It also has close linkages with agriculture for raw material inputs, such as cotton. Moreover, there is a wide international market for textiles and clothing, hence the opportunity to export. It also meets all the underlying principles for industrial development.

As all other industrial groups, this too is characterised by a low productivity level. Thus the immediate move is to improve its productivity significantly and sustainably. The first move is to establish a Co-ordinating Body (or Forum), constituting of all stakeholders involved directly or indirectly in textiles and wearing apparel activities, to co-ordinate measures to develop industries engaged in such activities. This body is tasked with studying specific problems and constraints limiting the growth of the sub-sector, find possible solutions, plan and guide implementation programmes. Government is to play a central role in the Co-ordinating Body. The Co-ordinating Body will also be actively engaged in searching out and inviting investors, particularly quality product producing and marketing companies, looking for foreign market access, supporting entrepreneurs interested to invest in supporting industries such as packaging, industrial chemicals.

Once a tangible development plan is in place and implementation under way, government will initially provide general support in manpower training, marketing, land provision, etc., for all industries engaged in textiles and wearing apparel. Also, tariff protection for a fixed period of time, until enterprises gain some experience, could be provided. For those enterprises capable of penetrating external markets, further incentives would follow, including availing export finance at favourable interest rate, access to investment loans on a priority basis from development banks, etc. This is on top of other incentives common for all exporters such as duty drawback, VAT exemption on imports, etc.

As a first move, the strategy is considering picking state-owned textiles and wearing apparel enterprises for direct support to raise productivities and accelerate export. Also, the government is to continue strengthening already established institutions, such as the Textiles Institute, Export market information service centre, etc.

7.3.3.2 Meat, leather and leather products

This industrial group not only satisfies all the underlying principles stated earlier, but also exports a consistently significant volume of leather and leather products. The same strategy used for the textiles and wearing apparel sub-sector applies here too: it will have its own Co-ordinating Body and similar incentives would be granted. In this case too, the government will strengthen specialised institutions and relevant supporting organisations, such as the Leather Institutes, Livestock and Livestock Products Marketing Authority, etc. The major challenge in this industrial group is meeting the Sanitary and Phyto-Sanitary requirements.

7.3.3.3 Agro-processing industries

This is a broad sub-sector involving different industrial groups in the manufacturing sector. However, all agro-processing industrial groups depend on agriculture for raw materials, hence have close linkages. Moreover, most agro-processing industries are labour-intensive, and also have the prospect to join export markets. Similar to textiles and leather, corresponding Co-ordinating Bodies, for similar groups of agro-processing industries, would be established to study and further develop the respective industrial groups. Agro-processing industries are also eligible for similar incentives noted above for textiles and leather.

7.3.3.4 Construction industries

The construction industry, as such, is neither export oriented, nor closely linked to agriculture. However, it is labour intensive and has a critical role in every investment and sector of the economy. Its backward linkages involve a number of other industrial activities, including cement, metal, woodwork, glass, electrical materials, etc. As such, it is identified as one of the priority areas. Similar to the industrial groups noted above, the strategy is to establish a Co-ordinating Body to study the sub-sector, galvanise necessary supports and move to implementation.

7.3.3.5 Small and micro companies

SMEs are not only labour intensive but also largely agriculture based for raw materials. But they are not export-oriented, at least, not at this stage. High employment capacity is the relative merit of SMEs. These characteristics make SMEs a priority area for government support.

SMEs too have to establish Co-ordinating Forums to lead their development. Except for direct financial support, because of their large number, SMEs qualify for other supports including training, consultancy service, market provision, land provision at low lease rate, tax exemption, etc. The strategy also encourages municipalities to create low-cost industry villages for SMEs. The government will also strengthen the already existing SMEs Supporting and Co-ordinating Centre. A related strategic support is to link SMEs to government development projects. The government gives priority to SMEs to undertake certain development projects, such as construction of buildings, production of cement, wood and metal works, etc. The government can as well help SMEs in securing sub-contracts from medium and large-scale companies.

SMEs, however, are too many, and are scattered across the country, operating largely in the informal sector, hence quite challenging to organise and provide support for. Moreover, the strategy focuses not just on SMEs engaged in manufacturing, but in all economic sectors. Practically, even for countries with adequate financial and other resources, it is not easy to organise and support all SMEs operating across economic sectors meaningfully. In Ethiopia, while it is possible to support better organised small and micro companies, with training, and perhaps access to land, it would be quite a burden to think of addressing the problem of SMEs in general.

7.4 Summary of observations

Some important issues arise, particularly in connection with the selection of industries and the incentive structure. The strategy seems to capitalise on existing natural resource based industries, having static comparative advantage, which is commendable. Given that entrepreneurs in the country have quite rich experience in dealing with such agricultural resource based industries, such as textiles, leather, etc.; and that there are relatively reliable and less expensive raw material supply; and also that such industries do not involve complex operation, and not demand highly skilled labour, it is beneficial to focus more on such industries, particularly at the initial phase of the industrialisation process. However, industrialisation is not only about industries of static comparative advantage; it is largely about creating and developing industries of dynamic comparative advantage. The strategy entirely excludes technologically leading industries of great dynamic comparative advantage, such as engineering industries – chemical, electrical and mechanical industries. Excluding industries of dynamic comparative advantage creates a serious shortcoming.

With respect to incentives, the eligibility criteria for support are restrictive. Exporting is the only criterion for rewarding enterprises. Non-exporting enterprises that are highly productive and engaged in innovative activities such as introducing new products and technology, etc., are not considered worth the incentive. Also, the strategy exclusively emphasises exporting industries, while giving little attention to competitive import-replacing and non-tradable industries. Even industries supplying critical inputs to prioritised industries, such as chemical industries, are not given due attention. This approach may not be advantageous. In fact, such input-supplying industries may as well have a critical role for the initial development of textiles and leather industries. Today, chemicals account for half of the foreign exchange required to import intermediate inputs for the manufacturing sector. Even in countries where export promotion has been a central strategy, the overarching objective has been domestic industrial development. As such, the practice has been using export-promotion and import-substitution as complementary strategies, but not discriminating competitive import-replacing industries. A foreign exchange saving industry is as important as an exporting one. Such an idea, however, does not seem to have much room in the strategy, thereby introducing some inconsistency.

Moreover, incentives for exporting enterprises, such as subsidised credit, land grant, etc., are blanket subsidies, i.e. their magnitude, time limit, etc., are not known. Though said to be performance based, the extent is not known. Hence, there is no mechanism for cost-benefit analysis of such interventions. Unless a further implementation strategy is in place for addressing such issues, blanket incentives may not deliver the desired outcome.

Some of the justifications for promotional measures may be questionable. The strategy argues that 'intervention is justified because arguably these sectors would not have emerged spontaneously without public support' (Ministry of Information, 2002, p. 222). As noted earlier, textiles and leather industries have been operating for over half-a-century. Now there is a relatively large number of firms in each industry, as the private sector joined the rank. The leather tanning industry has been exporting for decades.[18] So, apart from certain interventions, such as upgrading machinery and equipment of state-owned firms, market information, and the like, additional incentives, such as provision of subsidised credit, subsidised land, tariff protection, etc., are less justifiable.

Thus, the central objective of providing additional incentives seems to keep firms exporting and improve from experience. In fact state-owned industries are encouraged to export for the sake of foreign exchange earnings, even at prices below the cost of production.

7.5 Conclusion and the way forward

Development needs vision, i.e. sustainable and integrated national growth strategy. Though incomplete and unpolished, Ethiopia has one – 'The Industrial Development Strategy of Ethiopia'. The strategy attempts to integrate agriculture with industry, providing more focus on the former at the initial stage of the industrial processes. Also, the strategy relies heavily on internal resources, including for financial needs. As such, the strategy basically has the right setting and framework. However, apart from comments noted in the different sections above, it lacks completeness, and needs to address a number of issues, the major of which include the following.

The manufacturing sector is not only small in size, but is also haunted with serious structural problems. It is a sector constituting largely small-size consumption goods producing firms, grossly lacking intermediate and capital goods industries. The strategy, as a long-term phenomenon, fails to address this structural problem of the sector. In fact, the strategy never mentions anything about structural problems of the manufacturing sector.

As noted earlier, lack of technological capability is the major weakness of the manufacturing sector. Studies have shown that the same labour-intensive industries identified for promotion are at the same time the ones having the lowest productivity levels in manufacturing. Despite this, however, the strategy never discusses the issue of improving technological capability. Technology diffusion within manufacturing, access to technologically leading industries, local or abroad, choice of technology in manufacturing investment, are not addressed.

Probably, a distinguishing feature of an industrial policy is the institutional setting – close collaboration between the public and private sectors. This is so because the capacity of any least developed, or even a developing country, to access all required information to design and implement an industrial policy country wide is limited. Identifying constraints and opportunities, i.e. identifying location where externalities arise, making effective interventions, sharing implementation responsibilities, evaluating results, etc., inevitably calls for close private sector involvement. In Ethiopia such a public-private forum is largely a token. It is true that SOEs are represented by an agency, reporting to the council of ministers; similarly, endowments are looked after by high ranking party members and have close hearing to top ranking government officials; certain leading business individuals are said to have direct access to top ranking policy makers. But apart from ad hoc and irregular meetings between the Ethiopian Chambers of Commerce and the Ministry of Trade and Industry, whenever the latter wishes to, there has never been any formal public-private dialogue forum, to conduct any economic development programme.

Also, it is not stated how to implement the strategy in light of the multilateral (WTO) trade laws and regional trade and economic integration agreements. It is now almost a decade since the country has submitted its application for WTO membership. Ethiopia is also contemplating to sign the Economic Partnership Agreement (EPA) with the EU. Come WTO membership and EPA, so will the obligations. For instance, it would be a challenging task, particularly in the longer term, to keep and use high tariffs and subsidies for protection and promotion. It is also a tall task to keep entry barriers to key economic sectors, such as banks and insurance companies for long without repercussions. Such measures are not consistent with the ambition of attracting substantial foreign investment. Hence, there is a need to come up with an implementation strategy, consistent with forthcoming major regional and multilateral agreements.

Private property, particularly related to land, which is the major means of production, is a critical issue in industrial development. For the last three decades, state ownership of land has been the major constraint of economic development in the country. Hence, there may be a need to improve private property rights in order to accelerate the industrialisation process. State-owned enterprises and assets did exist in many advanced market economies during the periods of industrialisation; but were used as instruments for promoting, not retarding, private sector growth.

Though the strategy advocates the need to rely largely on internal financial resources, the debt burden may pose some limitation for accelerated industrial development. Currently, Ethiopia depends on foreign aid for at least one-third of its budget. But donors may not be much interested in industrial expansion. Thus, the strategy of foreign debt management during industrialisation needs to be addressed.

Domestic competition is not given due importance. The emphasis of the strategy is to 'join hands together and compete in international markets'. While the latter is appreciable, healthy internal competition is instrumental to create efficient and productive enterprises. Internal competition would be a spring board for further competition in international markets.

Some Asian large economies, such as China, India and Pakistan have been growing as fast as some East Asian countries, despite the fact that they relied less on export-led growth strategy, except very recently. The fact that they have large internal markets makes exporting less desperate than some East Asian small economies. Hence such economies are models on their own. They did well by focusing largely on internal markets, i.e. promoting investment, liberalising and allowing competition to infuse their markets. Moreover, apart from population pressure, which is quite a factor, what are even more important are the sources of growth: how it is generated and sustained. Ethiopia too has a population large enough to allow economies of scale. Hence, experiences of those countries are noteworthy.

The issue of governance is also critical. What kind of governance is preferable for running a successful industrialisation programme? Successful industrial development requires the state to be accepted by the people at large. Stability is a crucial factor for long-term industrial development. Stability does not mean staying in power for a long time. Stability implies legitimacy and acceptability by the public at large. With a state that is not acceptable, it would be a tall task to implement any successful economic reform programme. If acceptable, and once some economic progress is attained on a sustainable basis, further democratisation could be easier and inevitable.

The other issue, related to governance, is the economy of affection. While different tribal/ethnic groupings exist in most countries worldwide, the way differences are managed varies significantly. In countries where mature democracy has not taken root, including Ethiopia, political favours tend to guide economic policies. In clientilistic regimes, favours move the economy. Speedy economic transformation, however, requires cleaning the tendency of strong tribal tinge. Governments with any tribal tinge lack legitimacy, thereby facing difficulty in implementing any viable development policy.

Notes

1 Traditional implies any activity operated manually using unskilled labour and/or animal power.
2 Annual average GDP for the period is about US$23,467 million.
3 Total employment refers to the working age population of rural dwellers in agriculture plus actual employment in other sectors.
4 Average annual export for the period was US$1,856.
5 Average size of large- and medium-scale farms was about 320 hectares.
6 For the last three decades, land in Ethiopia has been state owned. There is no free market for land.
7 It should, however, be recognised that, apart from the structure of land holding, physical conditions, i.e. lack of water surplus and flat terrain, etc., limits the extent of irrigable land, though there is still much potential for further application of irrigation. Some studies noting the problems involved in expanding irrigation in the Sub-Saharan region, concludes that irrigation may not be the main source of food production (Rosegrant and Perez, 1997).
8 Power driven manufacturing industries employing ten or more workers are classified as large and medium scale (LMS) while those employing less than ten workers using power driven machines are grouped under small scale industries (SSMI). Those using largely self-employed manual labour are grouped under cottage industries (CI).
9 This, however, does not imply that small firms are inefficient.
10 Financial figures need to be taken cautiously. Not all firms use a standard and acceptable system of accounting. These figures have never been systematically checked by external bodies, apart from firms' owners/managers who provide the report.
11 Ethiopia has also other, largely overlapping, programmes to address poverty – most notably the Sustainable Development and Poverty Reduction Programme (SDPRP) and the Plan for Accelerated and Sustained Development to End Poverty (PASDEP).
12 One of the shortcomings of ADLI is its exclusion of the external sector – import and export. Relaxing this closed model, lack of elastic demand for agricultural goods may not be a constraint for agricultural growth, assuming existence of adequate export demand to fill the gap (see Badiane, 1999).
13 What this implies is that the strategy should envisage positive intervention to address the structural weakness limiting the supply response of the industrial sector.
14 This, however, did not result in a significant rolling back of the state. Government has taken only measured steps towards privatisation, keeping large firms in manufacturing, finance, communications and critical assets such as land under its control.
15 It should, however, be noted that in economics and business rent-seeking refers to

> the extraction of uncompensated value from others without making any contribution to productivity. Rents may be obtained by controlling land and other pre-existing resources; by establishing a position in imperfect markets that allows a firm to set prices above the equilibrium without losing profits to competitors; or by lobbying for government regulations that reduce competition in favor of the incumbent, not because of individual corrupt public officers, or government's official subsidies.
>
> (Altenburg, 2010)

The essence of the strategy might lead to counter-productive measures, as targeting entrepreneurs with adequate capital and long business experience.
16 It is argued that substantial profit from telecom services in towns could be used to roll out the service to rural areas to address government's obligation of universal service provision.
17 While the idea and determination to finance elephant projects internally is insightful, and at times the only means when aid is deliberately made inaccessible for politically

228 *K.M. Belete*

motivated reasons, its implementation with respect to speed, magnitude, timing, etc., has to be cautiously considered so as to mitigate its adverse impact on the public at large.
18 Similarly, the cut-flower industry kicked off without any government support and has been competitive in the international market and profitable for the last 6–7 years. There are over 80 enterprises operating. As such, granting land at low-cost and subsidising air freight charges is less meaningful. Moreover, the Ethiopian Airline operates competitively at international level, implying that its service charge could not be much higher than international prices.

References

Adelman, I. and S. Vogel (1992). The Relevance of ADLI for Sub-Saharan Africa, in *Industrialization Based on Agricultural Development: African Development Perspective Yearbook 1990/91*, H. Bass *et al.* (eds), Bremen, Germany, Research Group on African Development Perspectives.
Altenberg, T. (2010). *Industrial Policy in Africa*, German Development Institute Discussion Paper 2010, Bonn.
Amsden, A. (1989). *Asia's Next Giant: South Korea and Late Industrialization*, New York, Oxford University Press.
Badiane, O. (1999). *Agricultural Recovery and Structural Transformation in African Countries*, Paper prepared for the Fourth Workshop on Structural Transformation in Africa, Nairobi, 27–30 July 1999.
Belete, K.M. (2011). *Principles and Agreements of the WTO: Membership Benefits and Obligations*. Training manual to the business community in Ethiopia, August, Addis Ababa, EEA.
Central Statistical Agency (2005). *Report on Large and Medium Scale Manufacturing and Electricity Industry Survey 2003/04*. Addis Ababa.
Central Statistical Agency (2006). *Report on Large and Medium Scale Manufacturing and Electricity Industry Survey 2004/05*. Addis Ababa.
Central Statistical Agency (2010a). *Report on Large and Medium Scale Manufacturing and Electricity Industry Survey 2008/09*. Addis Ababa.
Central Statistical Agency (2010b). *Report on Small Scale Manufacturing Industries Survey 2008/09*. Addis Ababa.
Central Statistical Agency (2011). *Report on Large and Medium Scale Manufacturing and Electricity Industry Survey 2009/10*. Addis Ababa.
Ethiopian Economic Association (2005). *Report on the Ethiopian Economy*, Vol. IV, 2004/05, December, Addis Ababa.
Ethiopian Economic Association (2007). *Report on the Ethiopian Economy*, Vol. V, 2005/06, March, Addis Ababa.
Ethiopian Economic Association (2008). *Report on the Ethiopian Economy*, Vol. VI, 2006/07, September, Addis Ababa.
Ethiopian Economic Association (2009). *Report on the Ethiopian Economy*, Vol. VII, 2007/08, December, Addis Ababa.
Ethiopian Economic Association (2011). *Ethiopian Economic Association Database*. Addis Ababa.
Foster, V. and E. Morella (2011). *Ethiopia's Infrastructure*. WPS5595, Washington DC, World Bank.
Gabre Medhin, E. and B. Johnston (1999). *Accelerating Africa's Structural Transformation:*

Lessons from East Asia, Paper presented at the workshop on Agricultural Transformation in Africa, Nairobi, 27–30 July.

International Monetary Fund (2008). *The Federal Democratic Republic of Ethiopia: Selected Issues*. Country Report No. 08/259, July.

International Monetary Fund (2009). *The Federal Democratic Republic of Ethiopia: Request for a 14-Month Arrangement under the Exogenous Shocks Facility*, Country Report No. 09/296, September.

Lall, S. (1996). *Learning from the Asian Tigers: Studies in Technology and Industrial Policy*, New York and London, Macmillan & St. Martin's Press.

Lewis, W.A. (1954). *Economic Development with Unlimited Supplies*. The Manchester School, Vol. 2, Manchester, University of Manchester.

Mellor, J.W. (1986). Agriculture on the Road to Industrialization, in *Development Strategies Reconsidered*. J.P. Lewis and V. Kallab (eds), *ODC Policy Perspective* 5: 67–90.

Ministry of Foreign Affairs (2005). *Policy Handbook*, Vol. I, January, Addis Ababa.

Ministry of Information (2002). *Industrial Development Strategy of Ethiopia*, Amharic version, August, Addis Ababa.

Ranis, G. (1991). Taiwan as a Classic Model of Asian Development Success, in *African Development: Lessons from Asia*, USA, Winrock International Institute for Agricultural Development.

Ranis, G. and J.H. Fei (1961). A Theory of Economic Development. *American Economic Review*, vol. LI, No. 4.

Romer, M. (1991). What Are the Key Lessons from Asian Development Success Stories, in *African Development: Lessons from Asia*, USA, Winrock International Institute for Agricultural Development.

Rosegrant, W. and N. Perez (1997). *Water Resource Development in Africa: A Review and Synthesis of Issues, Potentials, and Strategies for the Future*. EPTD Discussion Paper No. 28, September, IFPRI.

Teshome, T. and K.M. Belete (2007). *On the Road to Private Sector Led Economic Growth: Creating and Building Institutions in Ethiopia*. Study sponsored by Addis Ababa Chambers of Commerce and Financed by the Swedish International Development Agency. EEA, April, Addis Ababa.

Timmer, P. (1991). What Are the Key Lessons from Asian Development Success Stories, in *African Development: Lessons from Asia*, USA, Winrock International Institute for Agricultural Development.

Wade, R. (1990). Governing the Market: Economic Theory and the Role of Government in *East Asian Industrialization*, Princeton, Princeton University Press.

Winrock International Institute (1991). *African Development: Lessons from Asia*, USA, Winrock International Institute for Agricultural Development.

World Bank. (2004). *Ethiopia: Country Report, 2004*, Washington DC, World Bank.

8 Integration of the industrialisation agenda in the national development strategy

Lessons from Namibia

Henning Melber

8.1 Introduction

In 1884 the German empire proclaimed most of the territory that belongs to today's Namibia as its first colonial possession and named it accordingly 'German South West Africa'.

After Germany lost World War I, the Treaty of Versailles transferred authority over the country as a C-mandate to the British Crown, which in turn delegated the administrative responsibility to the Union of South Africa. This mandate was abused as a de facto annexation. The neighbouring territory of South West Africa was subsequently administered like a fifth province. In fact, South Africa refused to comply with the reporting obligation it had entered under the trusteeship agreement with the League of Nations. The administration of South West Africa (i.e. present day Namibia) by South Africa as a de facto Province continued after World War II, while the United Nations (UN) system had replaced the League of Nations. In essence, South West Africa became a 'trust betrayed'.

Namibia became during the late 1960s the programmatic new name for the country, symbolising the aspirations of the colonised majority for self-determination and sovereignty. But it required the collapse of the Soviet regime and the end of the Cold War period, until finally as part of a global kind of appeasement, the UN was able to implement a transition towards Independence in 1989/90. Based on UN-supervised elections in November 1989 and a Constitution drafted in December/January 1989/90, the country became a sovereign state with the former liberation movement as legitimate, democratically elected government. Since then South West People's Organisation (SWAPO) transformed into SWAPO Party and retained absolute political power in every parliamentary and presidential election held regularly every five years. With the integration of the only deep-sea port of Walvis Bay, which was occupied as an enclave by South Africa until 28 February 1994, the territorial integrity was finally fully restored.

Thus, the Republic of Namibia was a latecomer in the decolonisation of Africa. Independence was celebrated only on 21 March 1990 after more than a century of colonial rule. The process towards independence involved and took

30 years of organised anti-colonial resistance by SWAPO of Namibia as the internationally recognised liberation movement before the country achieved self-determination.

While South West Africa during the 30 years of the German colonial period remained – in terms of the high costs the maintenance of colonial rule required for military and other policing expenditure as well as infrastructural investment – a fiscal liability for the imperial dreams that came true, the discovery of diamonds along the coastal Namib desert near Lüderitzbucht in 1908 resulted in a booming rush. The mineral wealth of the country (including copper, gold, zinc and other precious metals and stones, to which more recently uranium oxide added considerable value) ever since then made explorations and investments attractive for foreign mining companies. After World War II South Africa also established a vibrant fishing industry mainly in Walvis Bay (and to a lesser extent in Lüderitzbucht) for exploitation of the considerable offshore biomass. Based on mining, fishing, commercial agriculture (originally Karakul pelts, now mainly cattle) and since Independence increasingly also overseas tourism, the country offers attractive opportunities for those seeking to generate profits by means of mainly resource extraction.

8.2 Industrialisation in colonial Namibia and its legacy

Namibia's manufacturing sector was never a meaningful contributing factor to the economy. During the last decades of South African administration it even declined further. In 1960 it accounted for an estimated 9 per cent of GDP, but amounted in the mid-1980s only to some 5 per cent (United Nations Institute for Namibia (UNIN) 1986: 54). Food and beverages were around two-thirds of the total value of processed goods, with fish and meat products as the most important export commodities in the food processing industry. Wood processing (furniture) was another noteworthy locally existing activity.

Based on the absolute structural dependence of Namibia's economy from neighbouring South Africa and the resource extraction in mining, fishing and agriculture with hardly any value-adding activities prior to export of the raw materials, Namibia's secondary sector was at Independence in an obviously chronically and deliberately underdeveloped status. Only some 6,000 people were estimated to be in employment in small and medium enterprises in the industrial sector at the end of the 1980s (Halbach 2000: 28). They were mainly concentrated in the capital Windhoek and a few operations in the coastal town of Swakopmund. Walvis Bay as the deep-sea harbour and second biggest town with the fishing industry and some smaller companies was at Independence in 1990 still held hostage as an enclave by South Africa. Its reintegration into Namibia in 1994 allowed subsequently the establishment of a coastal micro-region along the axis Walvis Bay–Swakopmund, including the mining town of Arandis further inland (Simon and Ekobo 2008). This gateway since then created new – albeit limited and at times (such as in the case of the large-scale uranium exploitation) environmentally rather ambiguous – opportunities.

Bigger economic enterprises operating in the territory remained however almost exclusively under South African or other foreign, often multinational ownership and the companies were only interested in the transfer of profits. With the exception of mainly two family businesses operating on a slightly larger scale[1] hardly any investment was undertaken into strengthening a local industry, which would create employment opportunities. Namibia had the typical characteristics of a so-called underdeveloped economy: it produced (in the primary sector) what it did not consume and consumed (in terms of manufactured goods) what it did not produce.

At Independence, Namibia became a member state of the Southern African Development Community (SADC) and the Southern African Customs Union (SACU). The country's economy remained closely linked to South Africa. The Namibian Dollar (N$) as own local currency but non-convertible outside of Namibia was introduced in 1993, but remains as a logical result of the close economic ties pegged to the South African Rand (ZAR). With an area of over 825,000 square kilometres and a total population estimated in 2012 at around 2.3 million people the country is one of the most sparsely populated in the world. Despite a high influx into towns from the rural areas the urban population is currently estimated at below 40 per cent. Only the capital Windhoek and the harbour town of Walvis Bay are truly bigger cities, while the most densely populated parts of Northern Namibia have with the exception of not more than a handful of towns no urban centres. The country's landscape is characterised largely by desert and semi-desert areas with the Namib along the Atlantic coast in the West and the Kalahari to the East. The natural beauty and the resources contrast with the challenges these factors create for a meaningful economic 'take off'. Even the relative wealth of natural local resources seems alone not a guarantee for sustainable development, which would have an industrial component as an integral part of the country's prospective socio-economic development.

8.3 Blueprints for industrialisation in post-colonial Namibia and their impact

8.3.1 Preliminary efforts by the United Nations

A first concerted effort to draft preliminary recommendations for a post-colonial industrialisation policy was initiated at the United Nations Institute for Namibia (UNIN). Thus, the Institute did, among other things, undertake the following:

a   Since the mid-1970s it trained Namibians in exile for running the administration after Independence and planned for a post-colonial transformation of the society.

b   It drafted a comprehensive multi-sector analysis and identified the challenges for an independent Namibia. Diverse parameters of an industrial development strategy were defined, with their drive stipulated as aiming 'at accelerated economic growth, reducing economic dependence, maximizing the use of the country's available natural resources, creating substantial employment, and promoting equitable distribution of national wealth' (cf. UNIN 1986: 58).

c   The broad recommendations for the industrialisation of Namibia were in complement with the identification of challenges in the process of industrialisation, including among other things: the needs for institutional infrastructure, skills and capabilities, technological facilities and capacities, physical infrastructure and public utilities, and water resource management and the transport system.

8.3.2 Further undertakings after independence

8.3.2.1 Creation of governance institutions and devise of direction-giving frameworks

After the attainment of Independence, many governance institutions had to be established from scratch, and the Namibian state and public administration had to be properly constituted. This included among others the creation of a National Planning Commission (NPC). However, the Commission was never equipped with the autonomy and authority to design and execute responsibly and independently of other line ministries an integrated socio-economic development strategy (cf. Melber 2000: 145 150).

It was indicative for the lack of co-ordination that in 1992 a new direction-giving blueprint was released. A White Paper on Industrial Development was adopted as the first effort by the new government institutions not by the NPC but through the Ministry for Trade and Industry (MTI) to provide a coherent set of measures. The programmatic blueprint designed a five-year policy framework with over 40 recommendations providing guidelines for the period 1992–97.[2] These constituted the basis for the introduction of a range of incentives seeking to promote investment for manufacturing. Furthermore, in a compilation of sectoral development programmes for 1991–93 the main objective defined for industrial development by MTI was 'to assist in the expansion of the manufacturing base ... by encouraging the establishment and promotion of small and medium-scale industries' (Republic of Namibia 1993: 118). Thus, as outlined in the Republic of Namibia (1993: 120), projects were identified in the following range of sectors for further investigation:

a   The food sector: meat slaughtering and processing; dairy products; canning and preserving; and processing of grain and other food products.

b   Textiles, clothing and leather: cotton ginning, spinning, weaving and finishing of textiles; tailoring; carpets; knitted products; rope and cordage; other textile products; footwear and leather products; and furs.

c   Wood, wood products and furniture: saw mill, wood seasoning, furniture, and curios.

d   Paper products, printing and publishing: pulp, paper, paperboard, and their products; printing; publishing; and allied industries.
e   Chemical products: fertilisers, insecticides and pesticides; soaps, detergents, toiletries and pharmaceuticals; inks, glues, polishes, etc.; and plastic products.
f   Non-metallic mineral products: structural clay products including bricks; stone crushing; glass; cement; and associated products.
g   Metals and metal products: non-ferrous metals smelting, purification, etc.; steel smelter; structural metal products; and machinery, equipment and motor parts.
h   Other: jewellery and related products.

8.3.2.2 Overview of selected projects and their legacies

Nominally, the undertakings delineated in subsection 8.3.2.1 sound like a well-planned action programme. It led to the creation of several projects.

However, the implementation of the projects left a lot to be desired. Especially a variety of so-called white elephants (grand plans for over-ambitious new projects bordering on megalomania) entered the headlines of the media after their failure as a result of mainly financial speculations with fraudulent intentions by dubious foreign investors were disclosed during the early to mid 1990s. To cite some examples:

a   A large-scale cotton plantation project with promised foreign investment turned out to be tantamount to sheer fantasy, so did the plans for a sugar plantation and refinery and a tractor scheme, all announced with huge fanfare by the MTI for the Northern Namibian region. At the end those much publicised promises for major investments turned out to be essentially scams seeking to appropriate public funds. Independent Namibia seemed to attract all kind of improper business promises by dubious characters, none of which turned out to be seriously considering an investment.
b   The Namibianisation of the biomass along the Atlantic coast through the allocation of fishing quota only to local residents – a much applauded initiative by the Ministry – intended to be a first step towards establishing a locally owned fishing industry. But the result was mainly an individual privatisation of this resource without subsequent productive investments into a local value-adding economy. The quotas were allocated on the basis of political merits instead of competence of the recipients and in turn mainly sold again to those international fishing companies which had vested interests in the lucrative business. The quota holders hardly ever re-invested the revenue but used the income for private consumption. Soon the fragile ecology suffered from over-fishing, which required to limit quota allocations and total allowable catches to restore the stock, while the continued exploitation of the resources with value-added activities happened either on board of the vessels or further abroad. The fishing sector has since then not created any additional employment (cf. Melber 2003) and remains more often than not ailing.[3]

Besides the cited examples, many of the other identified potential activities listed above by the MTI agenda of 1992/93 were never followed up systematically. Rather, favourable investment environments were, if at all, created for foreign companies, which were able to use the opportunities offered for lucrative businesses in the interest of their shareholders abroad. Not surprisingly, the White Paper showed little effect towards a re-design of the economic value generated. To quote Hansohm (2000: 76) in relation to an overview after the first decade of Independence: 'Within manufacturing exports, there is no sustainable trend towards diversification and deepening. Rather, the relative importance of raw material processing (meat, fish) has increased – from 63 percent (1981) to 76 percent (1997).'

Contrary to practical evidence, the MTI was nonetheless eager to claim progress. As summarised in Republic of Namibia (2000: 139), in a parallel stock taking overview on occasion of celebrating the first decade of Independence:

> The Export Processing Zone Act (Act No. 9 of 1995) established Namibia's EPZ regime to serve as a tax haven for export-oriented manufacturing enterprises in exchange for technology transfer, capital inflow, skills development and job creation. The Policy and Programme for the Development of Small and Medium-Sized Enterprises, approved by Cabinet in 1997, provides the policy framework for the development of this sector as key to the creation of employment and wealth.

The Ministry was keen to stress the achievements since Independence and proudly claimed measurable growth in the manufacturing industry, which more than doubled its contribution to the GDP from barely 5 per cent at Independence to more than 10 per cent in 1995, when a total of 278 manufacturing establishments were registered in the country with a total employment of some 21,000 people, around 4.5 per cent of the economically active workforce (Republic of Namibia 2000: 146).

8.3.2.3 Critical assessment of the blueprints for industrialisation

In retrospect, it is more accurate to argue that, the White Paper of 1992 as a guiding maxim of Namibia's industrialisation aspirations, had much less relevance than suggested, and little to no measurable impact was diagnosed when the policy was reviewed in 1998. The critical assessment concluded that weaknesses in the design and changes in real development necessitated a revision of the industrial policy and that 'the importance of manufacturing output has not been growing in a sustainable way, but rather fluctuates in line with changes in natural resource environment' (Republic of Namibia 1999: 10).

It also observed that the MTI had not followed a clear infant industry protection policy (Republic of Namibia 1999: 27), nor had it followed up on most other suggestions to enhance industrial development by creating a more favourable environment.

In summary, the policy effectiveness was limited by several factors, including lack of knowledge of the White Paper in both the public and the private sector, hardly any links to other policies, no proper assessment of the human and resource capacity of the Ministry, absence of specific sectoral targets, no proper consideration of technology or labour and labour relations as well as the role of non-state actors (Republic of Namibia 1999: xiii).

Also almost a decade into Independence a parallel effort examined the policy for sustainability in Namibia. It concluded that most institutions for sustainable development were in place, while 'their impact on decision making could be improved'. As major challenges it identified the need 'to improve the ability of institutions to support development in Namibia, and to clarify Namibia's vision for sustainable development'. The analysis stressed that 'cooperation between institutions is vital since many development and policy initiatives can only be initiated by government departments' (Blackie and Tarr 1999: 19).

Lack of institutional collaboration, especially on an inter-ministerial level, has ever since Independence been a deficit and marred the formulation and subsequent implementation of a comprehensive, inter-ministerial policy, as these assessments a decade into sovereign Namibia suggested and underlined.

8.3.2.4 Reviewing and rolling over the blueprints for industrialisation

On the basis of the review of the 1992 White Paper the MTI started to prepare a new 'Industrial Policy Beyond 2000', which resulted in draft versions in 1999 and 2003. It repeated large parts of the earlier shopping list of 1993 as quoted above, but: 'A deeper analysis of the real competitive advantages in these subsectors was, however, neither presented nor called for' (Rosendahl 2010: 21). At the end of the day, the document for unknown reasons was never presented to Parliament nor officially adopted. Again, to cite (Rosendahl 2010: 21), 20 years into the Republic of Namibia, a sectorial analysis concluded:

> As a result of this prolonged process of drafting new industrial policies, the 1992 White Paper is formally still valid today. Even MTI, however, has only copies of the 1998 Review of the White Paper available. This illustrates the fact that there is currently a 'policy void' in Namibia when it comes to policies and strategies for private sector development and industrial transformation.

On the Government's side, in contrast with all these sobering conclusions and limiting factors, however, a 'prosperous and industrialized Namibia' became an integral part of the official slogan summarising 'Vision 2030'. Drafted since the turn of the century upon instruction of the country's first Head of State, President Sam Nujoma, and officially released before his retirement, the blueprint continues to serve as the official reference point for Namibia's developmental ambitions. As in stipulated in Republic of Namibia (2004: 16), paragraph 2.1.2. ('Industrialised Nation') summarises the following goal:

As an industrialised country, Namibia's income per capita base had grown to be equivalent to that of the upper income countries, resulting in a change in status from a lower middle income country to a high income country. Manufacturing and the service sector constitute about 80 percent of the country's gross domestic product. The country largely exports processed goods, which account for not less than 70 percent of total exports. This has given rise to a significant reduction in the export of raw material. Namibia has an established network modern infrastructure such as rail, road, telecommunication and port facilities. The country has a critical mass of knowledge workers and the contribution of the small and medium-size enterprises to GDP is not less than 30 percent. Unemployment has been significantly reduced to less than 5 percent of the work force.

Despite such an overtly unrealistic vision, which does not bear any resemblance with a scope for achievement based on a reality check, hardly anyone in Namibian policy dares to cast a doubt on this high-flying manifesto. Though being at best a compilation of wishful thinking seeking to please the utopian fantasies of an elder statesman void of any anchoring in what is realistically possible, 'virtually no actor in Namibia … openly questions the relevance of the objectives stated' (Rosendahl 2010: 18). On the contrary, Vision 2030 remains the official developmental gospel of the government.

As from the end of 2011, the government started new initiatives to draft an industrial policy for Namibia, after this – as shown above – has been a largely dormant issue since the White Paper of 1992. Again the reference point was however Vision 2030 with the declared policy aim that the manufacturing and services sector will make up about 80 per cent of Namibia's GDP by 2030 and that processed goods must account for not less than 70 per cent (Duddy 2011). According to a draft document, small and medium enterprises should contribute a minimum of 30 per cent to GDP. As the Minister of Trade and Industry announced at a national budget review session in early 2012, the industrial development policy was approved by Cabinet and would soon be tabled in the National Assembly (Smit 2012). A local economist affiliated with the Namibian Manufacturers' Association subsequently stressed the need for an Infant Industry Protection (IIP) as a necessary policy tool to enhance Namibia's industrialisation (Roux 2012a, 2012b).[4] To cite Nuyoma (2012), the chief executive officer of the Development Bank of Namibia, while in support of the initiatives, reminded however that much remains to be done:

> Besides the 1992 White Paper on Industrial Development, there is no clear policy driving the country's aspiration to attain industrialisation.… The elements of the 2011 policy are a sound basis … but it is up to the Namibian bodies and enterprises now to take the policy a step further, to address the immediate challenges and build a reality from the blueprint.

The continued ambitions of the blueprint – so far bare of a reality check – were prominently echoed and confirmed by the Namibian Head of State, President

Hifikepunye Pohamba in a speech in mid-2012 when categorically declaring that by 2030: 'The country should be in a position to export processed goods, which should account for not less than 70 percent of total exports' (Republic of Namibia 2012a: 3). Only shortly afterwards Tom Alweendo, Director General of the NPC (and the first Namibian to head as Governor the Bank of Namibia between 2003 and 2010) was the first high-ranking political office bearer courageous and honest enough to indicate doubts. When launching in the presence of President Pohamba the Fourth National Development Plan (NDP4) for 2012/13 to 2016/17 (Republic of Namibia 2012b), he remarked: 'We cannot be too satisfied with our current achievements.' According to him: 'An unrealised vision quickly becomes a nightmare' (both quoted in Duddy 2012a). NDP4 prioritises high and sustained economic growth, job creation and increased income equality as the overarching goals. The basis of the still overtly ambitious plan (which like the three earlier plans risks another failure) is logistics, tourism, manufacturing and agriculture as the pillars. But as a former state secretary in the MTI critically observed, 'to expect the sectors identified in NDP4, as drivers and to obtain the objectives outlines, the State possesses neither the skills nor the capital to realise the set goals by 2017' (Gurirab 2012).

Since then the official industrial policy plan was tabled for ratification in late 2012 before the National Assembly. In his motivation, the Deputy Minister of Trade and Industry pointed out that 'going forward we shall adopt our own Namibian definition of economic development, which shall include, in addition to income based on purchasing power parity, a measure of equity and a reduction in income disparities' (quoted in Heita 2012). As the following section documents, there remains a very long way to go before such a goal is achieved.

8.4 The health of the economy as an indicator of the dividends of post-colonial industrialisation: which lessons can we derive?

8.4.1 Socio-economic characteristics

The monetary income from the natural wealth has turned Namibia in the meantime statistically into a so-called higher middle-income country, though a large part of the population continues to live in poverty. According to the latest National Household Income and Expenditure Review (NHIES) of 2009/10, Namibia's Gini-coefficient, measuring inequality through the discrepancies in the distribution of wealth, declined from 0.701 in 1993/94 to 0.6003 in 2003/04 and dropped insignificantly – or rather stagnated at 0.5971 – for 2009/10 (Namibia Statistics Agency (NSA) 2012: 15 and 19). Other parallel estimates for the Gini-coefficient suggest 0.63 for 2003/04 (Levine et al. 2008: 35).

Their analysis reveals the unequal degree of the consumption patterns with 10 per cent of households with the highest expenditure accounting for more than 50 per cent of total expenditure, contrasted with the 10 per cent of households with the lowest levels of expenditure accounting for just 1 per cent of total expenditure. This means that the wealthiest one-tenth in the country has a consumption level amounting to more than half of the total expenditure. Despite minor deviations this value remains among the highest inequalities in the world. Shifting the focus on the individuals rather than households the picture is even more disturbing, as the wealthier households comprise on average less people than the poorer ones. A numerical breakdown accordingly reveals that 40 per cent of households with the lowest expenditure comprise almost 52 per cent of the population with a total expenditure of 8 per cent. In contrast, 5.6 per cent of the population live in the one-tenth of richest households with 53 per cent of the country's total expenditure (Levine *et al.* 2008: 34).

The NHIES also claims a significant decline in poverty levels from 2003/04 to 2009/10 (NSA 2012: 18), with 19 per cent poor and 10 per cent significantly poor (previously 28 per cent and 14 per cent respectively). However, when measured against the cost of living and the lack of basic social services, as well as other criteria contributing to the Human Development Index, the overall trend is negative. As an UNDP-affiliated economist concluded, 'over time income poverty appears to be decreasing while human poverty is increasing' (Levine 2007: 29).

The Human Development Report for 2011 (based on data for 2010) ranked Namibia at 121 out of 187 countries. Botswana (118) and South Africa (123) held similar ranks.[5] The Gross National Income (GNI) per capita increased by about 82 per cent between 1985 and 2011 and amounted to US$6,206 (2005 PPP$). Its Human Development Index (HDI) of 0.625 was below the average of 0.630 for countries in the medium human development group but above the average of 0.463 for Sub-Saharan African countries. If Namibia's HDI value is discounted for inequality, the HDI falls by 43.5 per cent to 0.353 – much more than for medium HDI countries (23.7 per cent) and Sub-Saharan Africa (34.5 per cent).

The main reason for this discrepancy is the loss due to inequality in income (68.3 per cent, compared with 28.4 per cent for Sub-Saharan Africa and 22.3 per cent for medium HDI countries).The Multidimensional Poverty Index (MPI), introduced in 2010 and based on 2007 data for 2011, suggested that almost half of Namibia's population experiences multiple deprivations. With 0.187 the MPI value is markedly higher than in South Africa (0.057). By all standards, Namibia is 'a rich country with poor people' (Jauch *et al.* 2009).

According to official figures based on a Labour Force Survey of 2008, the unemployment rate has crossed the 50 per cent mark with 51.2 per cent as a wider and 37.6 per cent as a stricter definition respectively (Republic of Namibia 2010). These figures have been contested since then as exaggerated and far too high (Mwinga 2012). They were however largely confirmed by an independent assessment undertaken by a World Bank team in 2012 upon request of the NPC, with only minor downward adjustments to estimations between 45.5 per cent and 48.8 per cent and 30.5 per cent and 34.1 per cent respectively (Ihuhua 2012).

Be as it may and beyond all controversies, the employment situation in Namibia remains without any doubt a serious matter of concern (cf. Eita and

Ashipala 2010; Kanyenze and Lapeyre 2012). This motivated in 2011 a massive targeted capital investment by the government in its annual budget seeking to create over a three-year implementation period more than 100,000 direct and indirect job opportunities (National Planning Commission (NPC) 2011). Starting in the fiscal year 2011/12, the Targeted Intervention Program for Employment and Economic Growth (TIPEEG) focused on agriculture, transport, tourism, housing and sanitation as well as public work programmes. Investment was earmarked to the tune of N\$9.1 billion over three financial years or N\$14.7 billion (including public works programmes) or N\$18.7 billion (also including state owned enterprises investment) respectively (NPC 2011: 6). As could be concluded on occasion of the tabling of the annual budget for 2013/14 on 26 February 2013, the promised results through the exceptional TIPEEG intervention remained clearly behind the expectations, with a claimed number of around 40,000 jobs created during the first two years, namely 27,235 jobs in 2011/12 and 13,885 jobs in 2012/13 respectively (Kuugongelwa-Amadhila 2013: 20).

8.4.2 Conclusion: policy results and failures

The Namibian government officially declares its policy results – based on generous investment incentives for foreign capital, not least through an Export Processing Zone (EPZ) scheme – as a success. An overview after 20 years of Independence proudly claimed that the original dependence on South African imports (about 87 per cent in 1996) through forged trading relations with other countries 'resulted in a gradual reduction in import dependency from South Africa down to 67.85 percent in 2008, representing a 20 percent import diversification' (Republic of Namibia 2000: 226).

Namibia indeed managed to diversify its trade relations, not least through the exchange with the EU market and the rapidly increasing trade relations with China and other emerging economies. But the effects on the economy were so far hardly beneficial for the majority of citizens. The country remains vulnerable to external shocks and has a highly open economy dependent upon outside stakeholders. They remain in business as long as it pays out for them, but do not base their calculations and balances on effects for the local people. These remain to a large extent at the margins of the formal economy or – even worse – are pushed out of it through the foreign companies operating with the sole ultimate interest in profit maximisation. Those under the EPZ regime and many of the foreign mining operations and construction companies (managing to secure big public tenders for undercutting local bidders and hence putting the locally employed in the construction sector at risk being retrenched) are notorious for ignoring minimum wages, workplace security or the demands of organized labour once it implies a reduction of the profit margins (cf. Jauch 2000).

A classical wakeup call had been the Ramatex saga (Jauch 2006; Winterfeldt 2007; Sherbourne 2009: 195–198). Attracted by generous incentives, this Malaysian family owned company made use of the opportunity to produce under the African Growth and Opportunity Act for a limited period of time textiles and apparel for the US-American market in a Windhoek-based factory between 2002 and 2008. At times employing up to 7,000 unqualified local workers (almost exclusively young women) below minimum wages without access to trade union representation in what was declared as factory ground an EPZ, Ramatex generated untaxed profits without any prior investment into the industrial location. The considerable infrastructure necessary, such as water and electricity, a railway line connection and other utilities supply and related logistics, was established at considerable costs covered by the Windhoek municipality or state owned enterprises, while the lease for the industrial site was nominal and symbolic. When the Multi-Fiber Agreement became effective and brought an end to the comparative advantages for the selection of a production site in Namibia, Ramatex closed business almost overnight. What was left behind was large-scale environmental damage, several thousand uncompensated and still unqualified former workers, and a marked financial loss for the Namibian public purse (through government and the Windhoek municipality), which financed the private capital accumulation of a foreign company with several hundred million N$ direct and indirect subsidies without direct benefits for a local economy and its people. As an intimate case study observed:

Enticing as the prospect of export-led industrialisation may seem, the structure within which it is to take place sets narrow limits to its economic implementation, and even narrower ones to its potential for the social progress of the majority of the population.

(Winterfeldt 2007: 89)

Years later negotiations about how best the deserted but in terms of infrastructure fully developed factory site could best be used to limit the damage are still going on (Immanuel 2013).

The Ramatex scandal adds to the at best mixed experiences under the EPZ policy (Sherbourne 2009: 193–195). These were also echoed by a case study into the coastal micro-region, which sobered the expectations that attractive subsidies to lure foreign investment are a panacea for industrial development. Hence, Simon and Ekobo (2008: 69) point out that:

A crucial point to emphasise is that the main employment sectors in this micro-region (namely, fishing, tourism and mining) are highly globalized through patterns of corporate ownership and investment, as well as through strong links to international (market and policy) fluctuations. In this way they may be little affected by – and unresponsive to – local economic initiatives unless there is a strong (local, national and sub-regional) political will to tie them in as economic catalysts, often at considerable direct financial and opportunity cost (in terms of incentives and allowances, and revenues foregone, respectively).

The diversification of economic activities might create the impression that this is by implication mainly to the benefit of the local people. But this is not always the case.[6] As an investigation of regional economic development in Northern Namibia documented, the structural barriers 'such as the size of the Namibian market and unequal competition with South Africa' explain the continued dominance of retailers with a home base in South Africa: 'the footing of powerful actors in the local retail economy who have their supply base in South Africa does not encourage local manufacturing on any scale' (Knutsen 2003: 580). As a local black entrepreneur observed: 'development is coming in, but mostly from the outside. There is growth, but the income is going out again' (Knutsen 2003: 580).

This is just one view from the ground, which adds to the insights that the local environment seems not conducive to an industrialisation of Namibia's economy. To quote (Kadhikwa and Ndalikokule 2007: 30), the constraints diagnosed include:

> High input costs, particularly electricity, transport and harbor charges, the availability of quotas for the fishing industry and low 'throughput' for the meat processing industry, unfair competition from well-established South African companies and a small domestic market which leads to an absence of economy of scale in the manufacturing sector.

But it is not only the lack of material infrastructure and related factors that have to be blamed.[7] Policy matters, and the industrialisation policy of Namibia lacks determination to transform a resource based economy dependent upon external variables into one with domestic priorities. The outcome is a lack of results in line with the declared goals. As concluded by one of the most insightful local economists almost 20 years into Independence: 'Despite all the discussion, the meetings and workshops, the policy documents and the implementation of key initiatives, the performance of Namibia's manufacturing sector has been disappointing' (Sherbourne 2009: 188). This was resonated in one of the latest available economic analyses, which maintained: 'The secondary sector is definitely the problem child of the Namibian economy' (Christiansen 2012: 45).

Meanwhile the compilation of an almost endless series of drafts, reports and recommendations continues almost unabated without a hitherto reliable reference point.[8] So does the self-enrichment of a small segment of Namibian society, namely the new elite (joining the old one) gaining from their access to the control over the country's natural wealth through political offices and positions in the higher civil service. In cohorts with a close network of like-minded, often family and friends, they occupy niches defined under a Black Economic Empowerment (BEE) policy, which allows rent-seeking initiatives mainly in a partnership with foreign interests, thereby siphoning off public funds and assets in terms of natural wealth (Melber 2007).

A particular case in point is next to fishing the mining sector.[9] Such local parasitic beneficiaries, called in popular slang 'fat cats', are a far cry from a new entrepreneurial generation of what could be termed a 'patriotic bourgeoisie' willing to invest profits generated for further productive undertakings, thereby creating employment and further value (cf. Southall and Melber 2009). Where Namibia's economy prospers, it does so with few benefits for a general economic transformation in the interest and for the social wellbeing of ordinary citizens.[10]

Looking into the efforts towards industrialisation more than 20 years after Independence, one has to concur, as pointed out by Christiansen (2012: 51f.), that:

> the country has failed to transform its economy from a producer of raw materials with limited manufacturing of consumer goods to an economy which is based on producing more sophisticated, value-added capital goods and offering high-value services. Instead, the country is still heavily dependent on the mining industry, fishing, meat production and tourism. Development in the manufacturing sector has been particularly slow with hardly any progress towards a more diversified product palette.

This chapter opened with a caveat by warning of a too isolated approach to such a case study. It stressed the need to complement the domestic policy and economy components with a consideration of the external dimensions impacting on the scope and limitations of national economic policy and its effects. Having said that, plans drafted at home do nevertheless – and at times even against all odds – matter. But the best plans are not worth the paper on which they are printed if they are not really tested against realities by being implemented. In the case of Namibia, however, even the plans are not as good as they could and should be.

Notes

1 Most prominently the retail hardware stores, car sales and other import related undertakings, not least in the construction sector by Harold Pupkewitz as well as the food and beverages empire of the Olthaver & List group under Werner List with the South West Breweries as the main asset – after Independence renamed as Namibia Breweries – and with operations also in the dairy industry and hotel business. Both Harold Pupkewitz and Werner List were the old type of entrepreneurs who dominated the local Namibian economy for decades. Werner List died at 80 years of age in 2002, Harold Pupkewitz died at the age of 96 in 2012. Both were the classical tycoons of a foregone era, though on a comparatively modest scale, and at the helm of their family enterprises until the end. Their companies remain among the most influential local operations.

2 It is noteworthy that the original document, drafted by the Ministry for Trade and Industry, is not even any longer available at the Ministry, which had produced the document (Rosendahl 2010: 18, fn. 22).

3 The Minister of Fisheries and Marine Resources Bernhard Esau complained at the end of February 2012 in a speech to the local stakeholders in Walvis Bay about the 'bail out' attitude of the fishing companies, which assumed that the government needed to secure employment by compensating the limited allowed catches and increased costs through higher fishing quota. He maintained that such an attitude defeated the purpose of proper fish management and risked sustainable development. In early 2013 the

Minister also lashed out at the irresponsible behaviour of local recipients of fishing quotas (Hartman 2013).

4 At the beginning of 2013 the government announced that it would end subsidies for the local dairy sector through stopping the eight-year period of trade protection for locally produced UHT milk. Namibia Dairies as a result announced a 50 per cent cut of milk delivery quota, which in turn resulted in the statement by the chairperson of the Dairy Producers Association that this would put 120 people out of work and more than 600,000 litres of locally produced milk out of the market (Shipanga 2013a). At the same time the Cabinet was in the process of finalising negotiations to grant IIP to the local poultry industry (Shipanga 2013b).

5 All figures in this paragraph are from UNDP (2011).

6 The plans by a consortium announced in 2011 to establish the Gecko project, a large-scale industrial park for a phosphate mine, a harbour, sulfuric and phosphoric acid as well as soda ash and bicarbonate plants, a coal fired power station, a desalination plant and possible further heavy industry in parts of the Dorob natural park near Swakopmund might be another gigantic blunder which provoked public confrontation. Vehement protests are raised mainly from those concerned about the ecological impact. But the mega-complex is also in contradiction of the country's constitutional obligation to protect the environment and also diverting from Vision 2030's focus on environmentally friendly economic opportunities and livelihood options (Hartman 2011). The ambitious plans for investment of N\$13 billion into such a chemo-industrial complex in a highly sensitive environment provoked strong resistance by local residents concerned about the damages, and fear of negative impacts also on tourism and fishing. The project requires the original acquisition of 700 ha of the park, a declared natural reserve, for initial developments and has applied to Cabinet in July 2012 accordingly. The plan was to expand the project into a 4,000 ha area within the park as a private public partnership with the government. An original assessment by the NPC reportedly concluded that the project was viable. The decision by Cabinet remained confidential amidst speculations about the future of the plans (Duddy 2012b).

7 Although it needs to be stressed that the most significant bottleneck for any industrialisation plans is currently the shortage of energy supply in the medium term. The public energy utility NamPower announced on 30 March 2012 a critical supply period for electricity during the next years due to power supply problems from South Africa's Eskom and the end of a power purchase agreement with the Zimbabwean power utility Zesa in 2013. A supply deficit of 80 MW was anticipated for the forthcoming winter period, expected to grow to 150 MW by the end of 2013 and to 300 MW by 2015. It was subsequently announced in August 2012 that a coal fired power station with an investment cost of between N\$4 and 7 billion would be fast-tracked, while the potential exploration of the Kudu gas power project off the coast at an estimated investment of N\$9 billion would be shelved.

8 See as one of the latest examples the World Bank sponsored assessment of the potential for microenterprise development, which ends with recommendations for further explorations (Mengistae 2011).

9 Mining remained the most important sector in the economy, contributing in 2010 about 15 per cent of GDP and more than 50 per cent of total export revenue. It is noteworthy that Mines and Energy Minister Isak Katali announced a strategic mineral policy in parliament on 20 April 2011. It transferred control of uranium, copper, gold, zinc and coal to the state-owned Epangelo mining company, including the allocation of exploration and mining licences. The minister admitted that BEE had been exploited in the purchase of exploration licences, which were secured by local BEE front companies on behalf of foreign-owned companies. Such deals had the sole aim of making 'phenomenal amounts' of money for a few to the disadvantage of the state revenue coffers.

10 The finance minister announced at an international investment forum in Windhoek at the end of November 2011 – during which Ohorongo Cement, a subsidiary of the German company Schwenk, received the international investor award 2011 as the continent's most advanced cement producer (which made the biggest single foreign investment in Namibia since Independence) – that foreign direct investment had increased by 34 per cent during the previous year. This contrasted with the constant net outflow of capital, estimated at between N$5 and 8 billion. A law reform was initiated during the same year to the effect that institutional investors (such as insurance companies, unit trusts and pension funds) should keep a minimum of 35 per cent of their total assets in the country.

References

Blackie, R. and Tarr, P. (1999). *Government policies on sustainable development in Namibia*. Windhoek: Directorate of Environmental Affairs/Ministry of Environment and Tourism (Research Discussion Paper No. 28).

Christiansen, T. (2012). Assessing Namibia's performance two decades after independence. Part II: Sectoral analysis. *Journal of Namibian Studies*, No. 11, 29–61.

Duddy, J.-M. (2011). Industrial policy wake-up call. *The Namibian*, 22 November.

Duddy, J.-M. (2012a). Alweendo not satisfied with development alternatives. *The Namibian*, 20 July.

Duddy, J.-M. (2012b). Gecko needs Dorob chunk for industry. *The Namibian*, 31 July.

Eita, J. and Ashipala, J. (2010). Determinants of unemployment in Namibia. *International Journal of Business and Management*, Vol. 5, No. 10, 92–104.

Gurirab, T. (2012). NDP4: Good times and good life. *The Namibian*, 24 July.

Halbach, A. (2000). *Namibia. Wirtschaft, Politik, Gesellschaft nach zehn Jahren Unabhängigkeit*. Windhoek: Namibia Wissenschaftliche Gesellschaft and München: Weltforum.

Hansohm, D. (2000). Industrialisation. In H. Melber (ed.), *Namibia: A decade of Independence 1990–2000*. Windhoek: Namibian Economic Policy Research Unit.

Hartman, A. (2011). Vision Industrial Park versus Vision 2030. *The Namibian*, 16 August.

Hartman, A. (2013). Esau condemns 'sins' of fishing industry. *The Namibian*, 5 March.

Heita, D. (2012). Namibia: MPs to ratify industrial policy. *New Era*, 28 October.

Ihuhua, C. (2012). World Bank confirms 51.2% jobless rate. *Namibian Sun*, 20 March.

Immanuel, S. (2013). Talks on lease of Ramatex building stall. *The Namibian*, 13 March.

Jauch, H. (2000). Export Processing Zones and the quest for sustainable development: A Southern African perspective. *Environment & Urbanization*, Vol. 14, No. 1, 101–113.

Jauch, Herbert (2006). Africa's clothing and textile industry: The case of Ramatex in Namibia, in Herbert Jauch and Rudolf Traub-Merz (eds), *The future of the textile and clothing industry in sub-Saharan Africa*. Bonn: Friedrich-Ebert-Stiftung.

Jauch, H., Edwards, L. and Cupido, B. (2009). *A rich country with poor people. Inequality in Namibia*. Windhoek: Labour Resource and Research Institute.

Kadhikwa, G. and Ndalikokule, V. (2007). *Assessing the potential of the manufacturing sector in Namibia*. Windhoek: Bank of Namibia/Research Department (BoN Occasional Paper OP-1/2007).

Kanyenze, G. and Lapeyre, F. (2012). *Growth, employment and decent work in Namibia: A situation analysis*. Geneva: International Labour Office/Employment Policy Department (Employment Sector/Employment Working Paper No. 81).

Knutsen, H. (2003). Black entrepreneurs, local embeddedness and regional economic development in Northern Namibia. *Journal of Modern African Studies*, Vol. 41, No. 4, 555–586.

Kuugongelwa-Amadhila, S. (2013). *2013/14 budget statement. Growing the economy, optimizing development outcomes. Jointly doing more with less.* Windhoek: Republic of Namibia.

Levine, S. (2007). *Trends in human development and human poverty in Namibia.* Background paper to the Namibia Human Development Report. Windhoek: UNDP.

Levine, S., Roberts, B., May, J., Bhorat, H., Duclos, J-Y., Thorbecke, E. and Araar, A. (2008). *A review of poverty and inequality in Namibia.* Windhoek: Central Bureau of Statistics/National Planning Commission.

Melber, H. (2000). Development and aid. In H. Melber (ed.). *Namibia. A decade of independence, 1990–2000.* Windhoek: Namibian Economic Policy Research Unit.

Melber, H. (2003). Of big fish & small fry: The fishing industry in Namibia, *Review of African Political Economy*, Vol. 30, No. 95, 142–148.

Melber, H. (2007). Poverty, politics, power and privilege: Namibia's black economic elite formation, in H. Melber (ed.), *Transitions in Namibia. Which changes for whom?* Uppsala: Nordic Africa Institute.

Mengistae, T. (2011). *Promoting entrepreneurship in Namibia: Constraints to microenterprise development.* Washington: The World Bank.

Mwinga, M. (2012). *Unemployment in Namibia: Measurement problems, causes & policies.* Windhoek: First Capital Treasury Solutions (First Capital Working Paper Series).

NSA (2012), *Namibia household income & expenditure survey 2009/10. Summary.* Windhoek: Namibia Statistics Agency.

NPC (2011). *Targeted intervention program for employment and economic growth (TIPEEG).* Windhoek: National Planning Commission.

Nuyoma, D. (2012). A blueprint for industrialization. *The Namibian*, 27 June.

Republic of Namibia (1993). *Working for a better Namibia. Sectoral development programmes.* Review of 1991–93 and Plans for the Future. Windhoek: The Office of the Prime Minister.

Republic of Namibia (1999). *Review of the 1992 White Paper on industrial development.* Windhoek: Ministry of Trade and Industry.

Republic of Namibia (2000). *Namibia: A decade of peace, democracy and prosperity 1990–2000.* Windhoek: Office of the Prime Minister.

Republic of Namibia (2004). *Namibia Vision 2030. Policy framework for long-term national development.* Windhoek: Office of the President.

Republic of Namibia (2010). *Namibia labour force survey 2008.* Windhoek: Ministry of Labour and Social Welfare/Directorate of Labour Market Services.

Republic of Namibia (2012a). *Statement by His Excellency Hifikepunye Pohamba, President of the Republic of Namibia on the occasion of the official opening of the Namibia Standards Institution (NSI) Fishery Inspection Centre.* Lüderitz, 1 June.

Republic of Namibia (2012b). *Namibia's Fourth National Development Plan NDP 4, 2012/13 to 2016/17.* Windhoek: National Planning Commission.

Rosendahl, Christina (2010). *Industrial policy in Namibia.* Bonn: Deutsches Institut für Entwicklungspolitik (Discussion Paper 5/2010).

Roux, W. (2012a). Infant industry protection: A policy tool to enhance Namibia's industrialisation. *The Namibian*, 13 April.

Roux, W. (2012b). Part II: Infant industry protection: A policy tool to enhance Namibia's industrialisation. *The Namibian*, 20 April.

Sherbourne, R. (2009). *Guide to the Namibian economy 2009*. Windhoek: Institute for Public Policy Research.

Shipanga, S. (2013a). No more protection for dairy sector. *The Namibian*, 26 February.

Shipanga, S. (2013b). Cabinet moves to protect poultry industry. *The Namibian*, 12 March.

Simon, D. and Ekobo, S. (2008). *Walvis Bay-Swakopmund: Desert micro-region and aspiring regional gateway*. In Fredrik Söderbaum and Ian Taylor (eds), *Afro-regions. The dynamics of cross-border micro-regionalism in Africa*. Uppsala: Nordic Africa Institute.

Smit, N. (2012). Industrial development policy ready. *The Namibian*, 2 March.

Southall, Roger and Melber, Henning (2009). Conclusion. Towards a response, in Roger Southall and Henning Melber (eds), *A new scramble for Africa? Imperialism, investment and development*. Scottsville: University of KwaZulu-Natal Press.

UNDP (2011). *Human development report 2011. Sustainability and equity: A better future for all. Explanatory note on 2011 HDR composite indices. Namibia* (http://hdr-stats.undp.org/images/explanations/NAM.pdf; accessed 5 March 2013).

UNIN (1986). *Perspectives for national reconstruction and development. Abridged version*. Lusaka: United Nations Institute for Namibia.

Winterfeldt, V. (2007). *Liberated economy? The case of Ramatex Textiles Namibia*. In H. Melber (ed.). *Transitions in Namibia. Which changes for whom?* Uppsala. The Nordic Africa Institute.

Part IV

The industrial development agenda in the African–European Union co-operation arrangements

9 Industrial development in Sub-Saharan African–European Union co-operation arrangements

Francis A.S.T. Matambalya

This chapter explores the genesis and evolution of the industrial development agenda in Sub-Saharan Africa (SSA)-European Union (EU) co-operation arrangements. It highlights the emphasis of the co-operation, and probes its instruments, institutional (organisational) arrangements, financial resources and disbursement instruments, etc. (on industrial co-operation) in the ACP-EU co-operation agreements (Convention of Application, Youndé I and II Conventions, Lomé I to IV Convention, and Cotonou Agreement on which is based the Economic Partnership Agreements EPAs). The analysis in this chapter asks and attempts to answer the question, as to whether co-operation has benefiited African countries, by stimulating industrial transformation.

9.1 Genesis

The co-operation between Africa and the European Union (EU) emerged out of a long tradition of contacts between the European powers and the African states. In this regard, the initial contacts between the European powers and Sub-Saharan Africa (SSA) were established largely through exploration, trade and later colonialism.

Eventually and in particular in post-colonial Africa, these relations got new institutional anchors, in the form of a new broad co-operation framework involving the EU on the one hand, and the Africa, Caribbean and Pacific (ACP) group of countries, on the other hand. Therefore, the SSA beneficiary countries of industrial co-operation with the EU invariably refer to the African ACP countries (henceforth, AACP countries). In this chapter, the synonyms SSA and AACP are interchangeably used.

9.2 Industrial co-operation as a theme of EU co-operation with the ACP group of nations

Industrial development has always been part of the agenda for co-operation between the EU and the countries of SSA. This agenda, the goal of which has been to promote economic transformation in SSA, has traditionally been conceived under the broad framework of ACP–EU co-operation.

In this connection, the EU, as the stronger of the two parties, has been having a relatively comprehensive agenda to support industrial development in AACP countries. The agenda has centred around the mobilisation and deployment of Financial Resources (FiR), targeting different beneficiaries in both SSA and the EU, which were regarded as viable vehicles for cementing industrial co-operation between the two groups of countries. Moreover, Non-Financial resources (NFiR) could be provided, largely through various forms of Technical Assistance (TA).

Altogether, the scope of support has been widely defined to embrace: restoring and optimising the use of existing industrial capacities, industrial enterprise development and diversification, promoting co-operation between AACP and EU industrial firms, strengthening Small and Medium Size Enterprises (SMEs), marketing AACP industrial products, providing industrial training, providing industrial information, encouraging legal, fiscal and economic reforms conducive to the development of an enterprise culture, transfer and acquisition of technology, and creation of jobs (EC 1995).

Moreover, the responsibilities for implementing the co-operation have been shared by several institutions. Also, diverse financing instruments were created to deploy the resources. Likewise, different institutions were used as channels for the deployment of such resources.

The diversities of institutions, instruments, sources of resources and types of resources seek to provide a flexible approach, capable of addressing the many needs of the AACP countries.

This chapter revisits and highlights the main issues in SSA–EU industrial co-operation including: institutions involved in promoting industrial co-operation, types of resources dedicated to promote industrial co-operation, industrial co-operation financing instruments, institutional beneficiaries of the industrial co-operation programmes and the channels used to deploy the resources to foster industrial development.

9.3 Evolution and emphasis of industrial co-operation provisions

9.3.1 Core instruments

The industrial co-operation between the EU and its partners from the AACP countries has evolved over time, in line with the evolvement of the partnership arrangements. In particular, provisions on industrial co-operation have been explicitly included in the co-operation since the Lomé I Convention through to the current arrangements that are spawning out of the Cotonou Agreement. An analytical overview of the evolution and emphasis of AACP–EU industrial co-operation is tabulated below. The summary includes the sectoral focus and the specific objectives pursued by the various activities of the co-operation (see Table 9.1).

9.3.1.1 Treaty of Rome

Through the Treaty of Rome, EEC countries undertook to support economic and social development endeavours of the Overseas Countries and Territories (OCTs) associated with the then European colonial powers'. The support was contained in broad-based economic co-operation, through wide-ranging measures, engulfing trade liberalisation, and development of agriculture. The relevant provisions were contained in the Treaty's 'Part Four: Association of the Overseas Countries and Territories', which is divided into articles 131 to 136 (EC 1957: 46–47).

The most significant concessions to the OCTs are promoting investments required for their progressive development (Article 132) and preferential MA (Article 133) (EC 1957: 46–47).

To facilitate investments (which in this context largely meant EEC investments in OCTs), the 'Association Regime' granted non-discriminatory rights of establishment to European firms (EC 1957: 46–47).

9.3.1.2 Instruments in Youndé I Convention

The Youndé I Convention sought to promote the economic and social development of *Association of African States and Madagascar* (AASM)[1], by establishing close economic relations between them and the EECs. Accordingly, article 131 of the Convention stipulates that the

> purpose of this Association shall be to promote the economic and social development of the countries and territories and to establish close economic relations between them and the Community as a whole. The Association shall in the first place permit the furthering of the interests and prosperity of the inhabitants of these countries and territories in such a manner as to lead them to the economic, social- and cultural-development to which they aspire.
>
> (cf. EC 1963: 1)

Considering the disparity in the levels of development between the two parties (i.e. EEC and AASM), and the industrial development philosophy of the time, the Convention allowed the AASM to protect their infant industries, and thus expand their production (cf. EC 1963: 1).

To finance Youndé I, European Development Fund (EDF) 1 was established, with 581 million units of account (cf. EC 1963: 2). However, apart from grants to AASM, the financing of the co-operation arrangements were also going to be channelled through the European Investment Bank (EIB) (including through normal interest rate loans), and special concessional loans (cf. EC 1963: 9).

Further useful measures included those for assistance to AASM to achieve production expansion and diversification (to which 230 million units of accounts were allocated), and to a system to stabilise the prices for agricultural exports – thereby stabilising the revenues (cf. EC 1963: 10–12). These measures had a great bearing on the prospects for industrial transformation of the AASM.

Table 9.1 Evolution of the emphasis of AACP–EU industrial co-operation

| AACP–EU co-operation framework | | Emphasis of industrial co-operation | |
Framework	Time frame	Sectoral focus	Objective/targeted outcome
Treaty of Rome, Part IV 'Association of the OCTs'	1957–1963	• Agriculture • Other sectors	• Trade liberalisation in favour of OCTs • Investments required for the progressive development of the OCTs • Relatively free movement of labour from OCTs to EEC
Youndé I Convention	1963–1969	• Infrastructure projects • Trade • Investments	• Reciprocal trade liberalisation • Promote inflow of private investments • Public sector support in fields like communication, health, welfare, cultural affairs, irrigation, etc.
Youndé II Convention	1969–1975	• Infrastructure projects • Trade • Investments	• EEC trade liberalisation in favour of AASM • Financial support to AASM • TA to AASM
Lomé I Convention	1975–1980	• Industries manufacturing semi-finished products • Industries manufacturing finished products • Industries processing raw materials • Infrastructure supporting industrial development (energy, transport and communication, industrial research, industrial training) • SMEs	• Achievement of development and diversification of industry in AACP countries • Increased AACP–EC industrial relations, including in trade • Increased linkages between industry and other sectors, especially agriculture • Facilitate transfer of (appropriate) technology to AACP countries • Enhanced industrial research capacity of AACP countries • Enhanced industrial skills training for AACP countries • Increased international marketing of industrial products from ACP countries • Increased participation of ACP nationals in industrial undertakings • Increased participation of EU firms in industrial development in AACP countries • Better trained AACP industrial personnel • AACP countries are better connected to firms and institutions in the European community that possess technology and knowhow • Access and acquisition by AACP firms of patent owned by firms in the EC is facilitated • Links between industrial SMEs and LSEs strengthened

Lomé II Convention	1980–1985	• Generally, as in Lomé I
		• Development and stabilisation of mining sector through SYSMIN
			• All objectives specified in Lomé I
			• Modernisation of the mining sector for:
			  • Creating jobs in AACP countries
			  • Generating incomes
			  • Stabilisation of mineral export revenues
			  • Stabilisation of supply of mineral raw materials in the EU countries

Lomé III Convention	1985–1990	• Agricultural sector development • Rural sector development	• Creating jobs • Generating incomes • Achieving production of essential products

Lomé IV Convention	1990–1995	• Agricultural development
		• Rural development
		• Development of other sectors:
		  • Mining
		  • Energy
		  • Infrastructure
		  • Services
		• Private sector
			• Creating jobs
			• Generating incomes
			• Achieving production of essential products
			• Greater inter-sectoral integration
			• Increased manufacturing
			• Increased processing
			• Increased sectoral diversification
			• Maximisation of local value added
			• Increased manufactured exports
			• Sustainable management of natural resources
			• Protection of the environment
			• Increase industrial capacity utilisation
			• Rehabilitation of existing industries
			• Creation of stable environment for FDI in AACP countries
			• Enhanced local private sector, particularly SMEs

Sources: Based on: EC (1969). EC (1963). EC (1977). EC (1996). EC (1995).

Notes

AASM = Association of African States and Madagascar; EEC = European Economic Community; OCTs = Overseas countries and Territories; TA = Technical Assistance; AACP = African ACP countries; ACP = Africa, Caribbean and Pacific group of nations; EU = European Union; SYSMIN = Système Minerais (i.e. a system for stabilising the mineral sectors of the economy); FDI = Foreign Direct Investments; SMEs = Small and Medium-Sized Enterprises.

9.3.1.3 Instruments in Youndé II Convention

Article 1 of Youndé II Convention stipulates that

> The provisions of this Convention have as their object the promotion of co-operation between the Contracting Parties, with a view to furthering the economic and social development of the Associated States by increasing their trade and by putting into effect measures of financial intervention and technical co-operation.
>
> By means of these provisions, the Contracting Parties intend to develop their economic relations, to strengthen the economic structure and economic independence of the Associated States and promote their industrialisation, to encourage African regional co-operation and to contribute to the advancement of international trade.
>
> (EC 1969: 1)

9.3.1.4 Instruments in Lomé I Convention

Already the Lomé I Convention introduced a comprehensive agenda of industrial co-operation. The relevant document 'The ACP – EEC Convention of Lomé: Texts Relating to Industrial Cooperation' is 101 pages long (see EC 1977). Apart from articulating the objectives of co-operation (Articles 26 to 29), Lomé I Convention created the *Committee on Industrial Cooperation* (CIC) through Article 35, Decision No. 1/76, and Decision No. 5/77.

The CIC drew its members from both sides of the partner states. It was established to implement the industrial co-operation by examining issues (e.g. problems identified by the AACP countries and the European Community) for industrial co-operation, and oversee the activities of the CID. The CIC reported to the (joint) Committee of (ACP–EC) Ambassadors. Thus, it performed also other tasks assigned to it by the Committee of Ambassadors (see EC 1977).

Lomé I Convention also created the *Centre for Industrial Development* (CID) in 1977, which was later renamed the Centre for the Development of Industry (CDI). In the framework of the Cotonou Agreement, the CDI was renamed the Centre for the Development of Enterprise (CDE). This Centre is essentially an *Industrial Development Promotion Organisation* (IDPO). Its functions included: gathering and disseminating information about the conditions and opportunities for industrial co-operation, carrying out studies on the possibilities and potential for industrial development of the AACP countries, organising and facilitating contacts of meetings between actors in industrial development in the AACP countries and those from the EC, providing industrial information and support services, identifying opportunities for industrial training and applied research for ACP states (see EC 1977).

STABEX, a special facility encapsulating a programme for stabilisation of agricultural export earnings, served as an important complementary source of revenue. It made available funds to ACP countries that offset losses of export earnings on a wide number of agricultural products; cocoa, coffee, groundnuts, tea and others, as a result of crop failures and price falls. The funds could have been used to diversify the economy, by investing in industrial development.

9.3.1.5 Evolution of instruments in Lomé II Convention

The Lomé II Convention contains also large volumes of '*Texts relating to industrial co-operation*'. They largely continued what has been initiated in the Lomé I Convention. The CID and CIC continued to be strong actors in the endeavour to industrialise the ACP countries.

A very notable development associated with this Convention was the introduction of SYSMIN, as a 'special financing facility', to use the terminology of the Lomé Convention. Unlike the STABEX, SYSMIN was nominally more relevant for the development of industry, as it targeted one of its sub-sectors, i.e. mining. The system was meant to stabilise the mineral sectors of the economy. Funds were provided to keep the sector buoyant even in times of difficulty. The eight minerals that were initially targeted included: alumina, bauxite, cobalt, copper, iron, manganese, phosphates and tin (cf. EC 1996).

It was generally anticipated that the huge revenues that are usually associated with the mineral economy will enable the AACP countries to finance major industrialisation projects, thereby diversifying the economies in a very meaningful way for sustainable development (cf. EC 1996).

Figure 9.1 shows the amount of money that was allocated by SYSMIN under the Lomé II Convention (i.e. ECU 282) and the facility evolved in the subsequent arrangements. The EC and EIB are the key institutions charged, responsible for managing the facility (EC 1996).

9.3.1.6 Evolution of instruments in Lomé III Convention

A new approach to industrial co-operation was already reflected in the provisions of the Lomé III Convention, and was further enhanced in the Lomé IV Convention. The two Conventions scaled up the ambition for industrialisation,

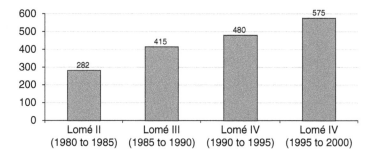

Figure 9.1 Amounts of funds allocated to Lomé II–Lomé IV Conventions.

by articulating the need for greater inter-sectoral integration, increased support for private sector and increased support for diversification.

The Lomé III Convention introduced the idea of linking industrial co-operation to rural and agricultural development, as a means for promoting economic transformation (EC 1995). Accordingly, rural development projects became a focus of funds for EDF 6 (receiving an allocation of ECU7.4 billion) to promote food security and combat desertification and drought. This idea was later scaled up by the Lomé IV Convention (cf. next sub-section).

In a time during which the trend was to scale back commitment to mining, SYSMIN was in contrast scaled up and allocated ECU415 million. Also, soft loans, with only 1 per cent interest rates, a 40-year payback period and a grace period of 10 years were availed (cf. EC 1996).

9.3.1.7 Evolution of instruments in Lomé IV Convention

Lomé IV expanded further the linkage of industrial co-operation to rural and agricultural development. It added two new titles to the industrial co-operation agenda:

a   Title V (industrial development, manufacturing and processing) sought to maximise the production and export of manufactured products. In order to achieve this, it stipulates the co-ordination of sectoral strategies for agricultural and rural development, mining, energy, infrastructure and services (EC 1995).
b   Title VIII (Enterprise Development) sought to promote Foreign Direct Investments (FDI), by creating stable environment in the AACP countries. It also stipulated the need to strengthen the role of the domestic private sector in the industrial economy (EC 1995).

9.3.2 Supplementary instruments

Preferential trade arrangements are seen as important tools that support the industrialisation process. In a global environment, where multilateral trade liberalisation is slow, they are seen as a useful alternative. Therefore, the trade preferences extended by the EU to its AACP partners have been traditionally seen as complements of the core industrial co-operation provisions. Likewise, the regional integration processes in the AACP countries, which benefit from EU support, constitute important complementary instruments for the promotion of industrial development.

9.4 Institutions for promoting industrial co-operation

Concerning the core instruments, several institutions have been given the responsibility for the implementation of industrial co-operation between the EU AACP countries. EU institutions include the EIB – which has been one of the major bodies concerned with promoting investments in AACP countries, and the European Commission. The EIB programming exercise has traditionally served as a guide for prioritising projects.

The CDI, a joint ACP–EU institution is – alongside the EIB – the other major body that has been involved in promoting investments in AACP countries. Its approach has been one of deliberate country and project focus: concentrating on a few countries, as well as on a small number of viable projects. It has also advocated a co-operation approach, which is based on the decentralisation of its activities (EC 1995).

In addition, institutions of various stripes from AACP countries have been involved in the co-operation. They include: Ministries, local financial interme-diaries, local technical intermediaries, technical Business Development Service Providers (BDSP), etc. Examples of local financial intermediaries are Development Banks (DBs), Development Finance Institutions (DFIs). Exam-ples of local technical intermediaries are such Business Development Service Providers (BDSPs), and IDPOs. Some institutions, such as IDPOs, served in dual capacities – both as local financial intermediaries and local technical intermediaries. Also, some IDPOs, like Malawi's Small Enterprise Develop-ment Organisation (SEDOM), were established with financial support from the EU (see EC 1995).

With the exception of activities carried out by the EIB, the framework for country-focused industrial co-operation measures has been provided by five-year National Indicative Programmes (NIP). This is, in essence, a national financing programme that specifies the main sectors to be supported, and outlines the sec-toral policies needed to support the achievement of the aspiration.

9.5 Resources dedicated to promotion of industrial co-operation

The resources to promote AACP–EU industrial co-operation (linked to the core instruments) have largely been made available in the form of FiR. Moreover, there has been also non-direct FiR, which has traditionally been dispensed in the form of TA.

In this connection, the main sources of funding have included the EDF, the SYSMIN, European Community Investment Partners (ECIP) and EIB. Figure 9.2 shows the evolution of EDF allocations from EDF 1 to EDF 8. Notably, the gross amounts grew around 29-fold from the inception of the fund (in the 1958–1968 period) to the 1995–2000 period.

EDF allocated substantial amounts of funds to infrastructure projects. With explicit reference to industry, Table 9.2 gives an impression of how much support from the EU has gone into supporting industry in the AACP countries. It presents overviews of EDF resources dedicated to this purpose (for selected EDFs). Though no breakdown could be obtained to show how much of the resources blocs of countries went to each of the three ACPs, it is gives useful insights.

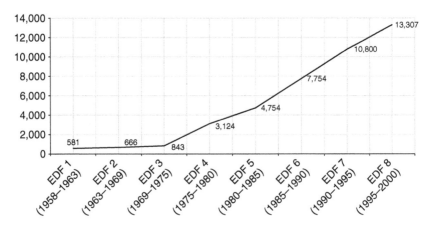

Figure 9.2 Funds allocated to EDF 1–EDF 8 (source: Based on EC (1996)).

Table 9.2 Resources dedicated to industrial development in ACP countries, selected EDFs

EDF	Arrangement/time frame	Number of countries		Dedicated FiR	
		EC	ACP	Amount in €	Percentage of EDF
5	Lomé II/1980 to 1985	9	58	0.77526	18
6	Lomé III/1985 to 1990	10	65	1.709834	13.7

Source: Based on (1) EC (1995), (2) Gavas (2012).

Notes
ACP = Africa, Caribbean and Pacific group of nations; EDF = European Development Fund; FiR = Financial resources.

9.6 Financing instruments

In the long-lasting SSA–EU industrial co-operation several instruments have been designed and tried. These instruments have targeted *different beneficiaries*, using FiR from different EU *sources*, and dispensing such resources through *different financing channels*. Table 9.3 gives an overview of these financing instruments (grants, loans, risk capital, investment capital and technical assistance), with brief descriptions of what they constitute and how they operated (in terms of beneficiaries and funding channels).

As mentioned earlier, all members of the ACP group of nations that have been targeted by successive ACP–EU co-operation arrangements (e.g. Convention of Application of the Treaty of Rome, Youndé Conventions, Lomé Conventions, Cotonou Agreement, etc.) have been eligible to these instruments. The AACP countries constituted the largest bloc in the ACP group of nations.

When South Africa and joined the group, relevant instruments were defined in the financing protocol of the Trade and Cooperation Agreement (TDCA).

Table 9.3 Financing instruments of SSA–EU industrial co-operation

Financing instrument		Beneficiaries	Funding channel
Instrument	Description		
Grant	• These grants were provided to SSA signatories to the Lomé Conventions • Individual contacts between firms in the SSA and EU countries were arranged by CDI • Support given to EU SMEs to internationalise	• SMEs from Africa • SSA local financial intermediaries • SSA local technical intermediaries • SMEs from EU	• EDF • CDI
Loan	• Targeted private sector projects • Major source of funding were EIB own resources • EC also funded investment project studies • Support joint ventures • Support EU financial intermediaries to promote SMEs in SSA countries • Support local (i.e. African) financial intermediaries to promote SMEs in SSA countries • Improve local (African) lending institutions • Provide other forms of technical assistance	• Industrial energy • Mining • Tourism	EIB EC
Risk capital	• Targeted private sector projects • Sources of funding were EDF and EU budget • Support joint ventures • Support EU financial intermediaries to promote SMEs in SSA countries • Support local (i.e. African) financial intermediaries to promote SMEs in SSA countries • Improve local (African) lending institutions • Finance project studies • Provide other forms of technical assistance	• Industrial energy • Mining • Tourism	EIB
Investment capital	• Support direct investments by EU companies in South Africa • Support investments by local South African companies • Support joint ventures between EU and South African companies • Support investments based on licensing agreements between EU and South African companies • Support technical assistance in investment projects	• EU private sector • South Africa's private sector	ECIP

continued

Table 9.3 Continued

Financing instrument		Beneficiaries	Funding channel
Instrument	Description		

Technical assistance	• Seek to promote industrial development in SSA through long-lasting ties of co-operation between SMEs from SSA and the EU
	• Uses three types of 'networks' or 'local antennae' or 'intermediaries' in SSA countries
	
	  • Commercial organsations
	  • Financial organisations
	  • DFIs, etc. in SSA countries to provide technical assistance
	
	• Uses three types of 'networks' or 'local antennae' or 'intermediaries' in the EU countries
	
	  • Commercial organisations
	  • Financial organisations
	  • DFIs, etc., in SSA countries to provide technical assistance
		• SMEs in SSA and EU
		• Commercial organisations in SSA and EU
		• Financial organisations in SSA and EU
		• DFIs in SSA and EU
		• Private sector manufacturing industries in SSA
		• Public sector manufacturing industries in SSA
		• Parastatal manufacturing industries in SSA
			CDI

Source: Based on EC (1995).

Notes
ACP = Africa, Caribbean and Pacific group of nations; CDI = Centre for the Development of Industry; DFIs = Development Finance Institutions; EC = European Commission; ECIP = European Community Investment Partners; EDF = European Development Fund; EIB = European Investment Bank; EU = European Union; SMEs = Small and Medium-Sized Enterprises; SSA = Sub-Saharan Africa.

9.7 Has co-operation between AACP–EU countries been relevant for industrialisation?

By the look of things, it is hard, even for the most optimistic supporter of SSA–EU co-operation arrangements, to argue that co-operation between these groups of countries has been beneficial to Africa in connection with industrial development. Today, most of the least industrialised countries in the world are to be found in this part of Africa. In a situation that suggests a stand-still in industrial transformation, the continent has largely remained at the primary stage of development, dominated by pre-industrial modes of agriculture, production and export of agricultural crops with little value addition and extraction of natural resources like minerals and export of the same with little beneficiation.

As described in one European Commission (EC) report, between 1965 and 1990 – a period that coincides with the Youndé I and II Conventions (1963–1974) and Lomé I to III Conventions (1975–1990), the manufacturing sector's share of Gross Domestic Product (GDP) remained around 10 per cent.

At the same time, in the comparator Asian countries the sector grew by 5 per cent annually, to reach GDP shares of 28 per cent in Asia and 23 per cent in Latin America (see EC 1995: 7).

Africa's industry, to this day, is at an elementary stage of development. It still consists largely of some agricultural processing, and light industries in consumer products (food, beverages, tobacco, textile, garment and leather industries). Despite many African countries enjoying own resource endowments, the manufacturing industry in many of them depends on imported raw materials, intermediate inputs. This is addition to dependence on industrial capital goods and machinery, which in Africa must almost exclusively be imported. Also, intra-industry linkages, as well as linkages between industry and other sectors, are still underdeveloped, essentially making industry an 'enclave economy' in most African countries.

Africa's disappointing industrial performance is attributed to the same old malaise, which can be summed up as productive resources capacity constraints (manifested as structural constraints): inappropriate policies, lack of industrial finance, industrial knowledge and skills gaps, industrial entrepreneurship gaps, industrial technology gaps, gaps in institutional or organisational framework to promote industrialisation, gaps in infrastructure for industrial development. Regardless of the terminology used by different authors, essentially, the same constraints against Africa's industrialisation identified in old and in contemporary literature (see EC 1995, UNIDO 2013, etc.).

Overall, the stagnation of Africa's industrial transformation can be attributed to a lack of a systematic, coherent and sustainable agenda to develop the essential FiR capacities and NFiR capacities, as well as to the confused and constantly shifting governance framework. This has led to insufficient and uncompetitive industrial economic activities along the entire value chain: industrial investments, industrial production and industrial trade.

And notably: decade-long and on-going co-operation with the EU does not seem to have improved the situation, which has in many cases deteriorated, to the extent of seeing some AACP countries setting on the path of de-industrialisation in the worst case scenario, and industrial stagnation in the best case scenario.[2] This is evidenced by the Competitive Industrial Development (CIP) Index of the AACP countries (cf. Chapters 4 and 6 in this book, as well as UNIDO 2013). Presumably, the prevailing international economic order (or at least part of it) prevented AACP–EU co-operation to inspire Africa's industrialisation, and instead reinforced and perpetuated existing lop-sided relations in the global economy: an industrialised EU as the 'centre', and the AACP as the 'periphery'.

A more comprehensive overview of SSA's industrial development performance and gaps vis-à-vis the rest of the world is detailed in Chapter 4 of this book.

9.8 Which are the lessons for the way forward?

Truly, the EU has been hailed as the most important bloc of donor countries. The EDF, its main instrument for delivering development aid to AACP countries and other ACP countries (which now number 78) is the world's largest, and most advanced financial and political contractual framework for North–South co-operation.

However, it is equally true that development aid has historically attracted little resource, leading to such resources being spread really thinly amongst the many ACP countries, as well as amongst the diverse development needs. Other flaws that have been pointed out from time to time include: huge disparities between budgeted and actually disbursed funds, limited relevance of supported projects for sustainable economic transformation, inefficient use of aid resources, dominance of the vested interests of the EEC and now EU at the expense of the genuine development interests of the ACP countries (cf. Maasdorp and Whiteside 1993; ECDPM 1996; Grynberg 1996; Matambalya 1999: 199–223; Gavas 2012).

Oblivious of these deficits, traditionally, African–EU co-operation and the resources tied to the implementation of this partnership, have been surrounded by a lot of rhetoric, rituals and reciprocated congratulations. This state of affairs has continued over decades, even though everybody knows that the arrangements have largely fallen short of delivering the development dividends that they were intended to. The rhetoric has tended to eclipse the reality.

It is high time to become practical: which means moving beyond rhetoric and focusing on real actions. Re-engineering African–EU co-operation to make it deliver industrial development requires a concrete and action-oriented agenda, targeting the elimination of the many flaws.

Note

1 The African parties to this arrangement included: Burundi, Cameroon, Central African Republic, Chad, Congo (Brazzaville), Congo (Kinshasa), Dahomey, Gabon, Ivory Coast, Madagascar, Mali, Mauritania, Niger, Rwanda, Senegal, Somalia, Togo, and Upper Volta.
2 As a technical term, *deindustrialisation* refers to the structural processes of industrial decline through disinvestment, relocation, or both.

References

EC (1957). Treaty of Rome. European Commission.
EC (1963). *The New Convention of Association between the EEC, the African States and Madagascar.* Information Memo P-23/63, July 1963. European Commission. Brussels. July.
EC (1969). *Convention of Association between the European Economic Community and the African and Malagasy States Associated with that Community and Annexed Documents.* Signed in Yaounde on 29 July 1969. European Commission. Brussels.
EC (1977). *The ACP–EEC Convention of Lome: Texts Relating to Industrial Cooperation.* European Commission. Brussels. 31 August.
EC (1995). *Industrial and Economic Co-operation between the European Union and the Developing Countries.* Directorate General for Development. European Commission. Brussels.
EC (1996). *SYSMIN and Mining Development. European Commission. DE 83.* Brussels. January.

ECDPM (1996). *The Future of the EU-ACP Relations Beyond the Lomé IV Convention: Synthesis of Working Group Discussions.* ECDPM Conference. Maastricht. 12–14 June.

Gavas, M. (2012). *Reviewing the Evidence: How Well Does the European Development Fund Perform?* Unpublished Paper. Overseas Development Institute. 31 January. (available at: www.odi.org.uk/sites/odi.org.uk/files/odi-assets/publications-opinion-files/8218.pdf).

Grynberg, R. (1996). *The Pacific ACP States and the End of the Lomé Convention.* Paper presented at a seminar organised by the Friedrich-Ebert-Foundation on 'The Future of Lome'. Maastricht. 12–14 June.

Maasdorp, G. and Whiteside, A. (1993). *Rethinking Economic Cooperation in Southern Africa: Trade and Investment.* Konrad-Adenauer-Stiftung, Johannesburg.

Matambalya, F. (1999). *The Merits and Demerits of EU Policies Towards Associated Developing Countries: An Empirical Analysis of the EU-SADC Trade and Overall Economic Relations within the Framework of the Lomé Convention.* Peter Lang Science Publishers, Bern/Frankfurt/New York/Paris/Vienna, 2nd revised edition.

UNIDO (2013). *Competitive Industrial Performance Report 2012/2013.* United Nations Industrial Development Organization, Vienna.

10 Union du Maghreb Arabe– European Union industrial co-operation

Achievements, limitations, and way forward

Francis A.S.T. Matambalya and Imen Belhadj

10.1 Prelude

'We want to help Algeria build a real industry of automobile and satisfy growing needs of the market'; this was an enthusiastic declaration made by a Chinese diplomat in Algiers in 2009.

(cf. Metaoui 2009)[1]

Although the overall share of global Foreign Direct Investments (FDI) flows from the People's Republic of China (PRC) to the Maghreb countries is still small, the trend is growing. To corroborate this, whereas in 2003, the Maghreb share of pan-African stock of FDI from PRC was just 2.5 per cent, by 2010 it had risen to 8.2 per cent (cf. Pairault 2013a, 2013b).

Visibly, PRC's investment engagement in the member states of the *Union du Maghreb Arabe* (UMA) of North Africa are targeting industrial co-operation. A report issued recently by the African Development Bank (AfDB) argues that PRC's investment has expanded from the energy and mineral sectors in some North African countries, towards providing capital to set up manufacturing and assembly plants in areas as diverse as textiles on the one extreme to and automobiles on the other. This is an encouraging sign for investments in the UMA region (Alden and Aggad-Clerx 2012: 6).

Moreover, the report highlighted the Chinese decision to establish some of its flagship Economic and Trade Co-operation Zones (ETCZs) in the UMA region, linked to meeting both the growing domestic demand in these host countries, and to serving as a platform for access to other markets. Overall, these developments demonstrate a resolve and willingness by the PRC to engage in long-term relations, and to deepen economic co-operation with its North African UMA partners.

The question that needs to be raised here is, why do the UMA countries have to wait for the Far East giant, PRC, to help them build their own industrial productive capacities? The question is even more taunting, considering that these very same UMA countries have been engaged in long-standing economic interactions with countries from a region that is truly an 'industrial pioneer and giant' – Europe and especially the EU with which they have maintained formalised relationships with for decades, if not centuries!

10.2 Objective of the chapter

Like elsewehere in the world, there is an enduring realisation in the UMA countries that industrialisation is vital for economic growth and development. Therefore, the development of the industrial sector has been an important consideration of the development agenda for each member state of UMA, including also in the context of their co-operation with the EU.

The growing reliance of the UMA countries on Chinese engagement in the region to spur industrial development alluded to in the previous paragraphs, highlights the necessity to evaluate the developmental outcomes and impact of the EU–UMA industrial co-operation agenda.

Accordingly, this chapter analyses the industrial development agenda in the co-operation arrangements between the EU and the member countries of UMA. It reviews empirical literature to expose the evolution of institutional platforms for co-operation between the two groups of countries. However, it is worthwhile noting that one Maghreb state, Mauritania, belongs to the African, Caribbean and Pacific (ACP) group of countries. Therefore, its relationship with the EU has evolved differently, namely, under the ACP–EU co-operation agreements, i.e. Convention of application, Youndé I and II Conventions, Lomé I to IV Conventions, and Cotonou Agreement as well as the Economic Partnership Agreement (EPAs) which are expected to spawn from it. Hence, the discussions in this chapter are in many ways not relevant for the country.

For Algeria, Morocco, and Tunisia, the chapter also makes an anecdotal overview of industrial co-operation between the EU and the country in question. Furthermore, the chapter probes the practical impact of the Euro-Med partnership on industrial development in the UMA region, briefly looking at the achievements and the limitations. In addition, using the Competitive Industrial Performance (CIP) Index published by the United Nations Industrial Development Organisation (UNIDO), the chapter places the three Maghreb countries for which data is available (Algeria, Morocco, and Tunisia) in a global comparison in the competitiveness of the industrial sector. On the basis of the analysis, it derives lessons and proposes the way forward vis-à-vis the UMA–EU industrial co-operation agenda.

10.3 Institutionalised platforms for Maghreb-European Union co-operation

The Maghreb and EU are very close regional blocs, which are linked by the Mediterranean Sea. Not only are the two regions linked geographically, but have also very long-standing cultural, political, and social interactions running at least several centuries back. In their evolvement, the complex relationships of the countries belonging to the two blocs have been influenced by bilateral colonial interactions, beginning with the Arab colonisation of parts of Southern Europe, and more recently marked by the colonial legacy of some European countries in UMA countries.

The relationships that we are concerned with in this chapter are those of the post-European colonialism epoch.[2] Following decolonisation, the EU's predecessor, the European Economic Community (EEC) provided a welcome vehicle to develop economic ties between the Community and the newly independent Maghreb states. Thus, several institutional platforms have emerged on both sides of the divide (i.e. Europe and Maghreb), and played different roles in linking the two groups of countries. These platforms pursued broad co-operation aims (cultural, economic, social, political), and the substance of co-operation differed from one initiative to another. However, as a common denominator, they did also offer the institutional platforms for promoting industrial co-operation between the Maghreb countries and their European counterparts, with particular emphasis on the industrial transformation needs of the former. For instance, they all granted some form of preferential Market Access (MA) for industrial goods, which benefitted the UMA countries. Hence, comprehending the relevant co-operation platforms is essential for gauging the past industrial development efforts, as well as the future industrial development prospects of the UMA countries.

The succeeding sub-sections analytically explore these platforms, starting with Maghreb-driven joint schemes to foster their international co-operation with the EU, and followed by EU-led schemes for co-operation with the Maghreb countries.

10.3.1 Maghreb-driven joint schemes to foster international co-operation

In the post-colonial era, the Maghreb states designed several joint schemes, to both guide co-operation amongst them, as well as co-operation with external partners. Some of the initiatives brought together only Maghreb countries, while others involved also Arab countries from outside the Maghreb region. Also, while some of the undertakings were comprehensive and involved forming institutions, others simply created programmes. Furthermore, though economic co-operation was at the centre of the anticipated co-operation, the actual scope tended to transcend the economics of international relations and sought to provide the foundation for co-operation in other areas, particularly but not restricted to cultural, political, and social spheres.

Notable initiatives include: *Conseil Permanent Consultatif du Maghreb* (CPCM) of 1964, UMA of 1997, Agadir Treaty of 2004 that guided the *Agadir Process*, and Greater Arab Free Trade Area (GAFTA) established in 2005. Syntheses of these initiatives are given in the following sub-sections.

10.3.1.1 Conseil Permanent Consultatif du Maghreb

The first initiative, which sought to develop institutionalised links between the Maghreb countries and their European counterparts, was launched five decades ago, through the establishment of CPCM. This co-operation forum was established by the first Conference of Maghreb Economic Ministers, which was held in Tunis in 1964 and attended by four newly independent states – which had been colonies of European powers: Algeria, Libya, Morocco, and Tunisia.

The aim of CPCM was three-fold:

a   To co-ordinate and harmonise the development plans of the four countries.
b   To foster Maghrebi intra-regional trade.
c   To foster and co-ordinate relations between the Maghreb countries and the then EEC (which has now evolved into the EU).

Unfortunately, these plans never came to fruition. Numerous political, economic, and institutional factors led to the dissolution of the CPCM in 1977 (cf. Behr 2010).

10.3.1.2 Union du Maghreb Arabe

UMA was launched in 1989 as a trade-driven Regional Trade Agreement (RTA). The founder member states were Algeria, Libya, Morocco, and Tunisia.

Apart from the quest for economic integration, through deeper trade and broad economic integration, the scheme encompassed political co-operation (e.g. through foreign policy), and co-operation in security matters (e.g. through defence policy).

As one of the key milestones of the trade and broad economic integration, the establishment of a Customs Union (CU) was planned for 1995, to be followed by the creation of a Common Market (CM) by 2000.

However, so far, the countries have faltered in their pursuance of both milestones. Serious political differences have obstructed the integration process.

The integration process in the Maghreb through UMA is still tottering, despite efforts in recent years to revive the co-operation.

10.3.1.3 The Agadir Treaty

The Agadir Agreement was signed on 25 February 2004 in Rabat (Morocco), pursuant to the *Agadir Declaration* which was signed in Agadir (Morocco) by the founder members on 8 May 2004. It came into force in March 2007, bringing together four Arab countries: two from the Maghreb (Morocco, Tunisia), another from North Africa (Egypt), and one from the Middle Eastern Arab peninsula (Jordan).

The Agadir agreement launched a process, the *Agadir Process*, which aims at liberalising trade amongst the member states, by building on existing integration agreements (cf. Behr 2010, and www.bilaterals.org/spip.php?rubrique168).

Membership is open to all Arab countries that are members of the Arab League and the GAFTA. The Agreement itself is also linked to the EU through an Association Agreement (AA),[3] which seeks to facilitate Arab states and EU integration, within the broader EU-Mediterranean co-operation framework. One of the benefits of this link, which is quite important for the industrialisation aspirations of the Maghreb countries, is that the EU allows its Mediterranean partners to cumulate value-added – meaning that it turns a blind eye to where value was added, for the purpose of preferential tariffs (cf. bilaterals.org, available at: www.bilaterals.org/spip.php?rubrique168).

It is important also to note at this juncture that the *Agadir Process* is supported financially by the EU. This is because the EU regards it as an important building block for the Euro-Mediterranean Free Trade Area (EUROMED FTA) through the promotion of sub-regional integration schemes and concrete projects (cf. Behr 2010).

Some authors have attributed the emergence of the *Agadir Process* to the shortfalls of the hub-and-spoke system that resulted from the adoption of the EU's Association Agreements, making it deliver inconsequential benefits to the Arab countries. Imperatively, deeper integration by the Arab countries was seen as the more promising option, and presumably a necessary condition for meaningful partnership between European countries and the Arab counterparts (cf. Chourou 2004; Wippel 2005).

The overall verdict is that the Agreement has not brought the anticipated benefits to the member countries. This has been partly due to the erosion of any potential gains by other existing preferential trade agreements. For instance, barely two weeks after it entered into force, conflicts between the Agadir Agreement and the USA–Morocco FTA emerged – mainly because the USA's MA preferences extended to Morocco only consider value added domestically in that one country (cf. bilaterals.org, available at: www.bilaterals.org/spip. php?rubrique168).

10.3.1.4 Greater Arab Free Trade Area

The GAFTA is a pan-Arab regional integration initiative. The decision to create it was reached in 1997 by 17 of the 22 member states of the Arab League: Bahrain, Egypt, Iraq, Jordan, Kuwait, Lebanon, Libya, Morocco, Oman, Palestine, Qatar, Saudi Arabia, Syria, Sudan, Tunisia, United Arab Emirates, and Yemen. It was formally launched in 2005. It is sometimes referred to as the Pan Arab Free Trade Area (PAFTA).

The significance of GAFTA for industrial development in the Maghreb (and of course other Arab countries) is embodied in the initiative's aim. The FTA namely seeks to liberalise trade in industrial and agricultural products across the region, but excluding services and investment.

The general verdict is that, though GAFTA sends out the right signals, its effects have so far been limited by several circumstances, including restrictive Rules of Origin (RoO), exclusion of Non-Tariff Barriers (NTBs) in the liberalisation scheme, and the absence of a Dispute Settlement Mechanism (DSM) (cf. Behr 2010).

Industrialisation in UMA-EU co-operation 271

10.3.2 EU-driven schemes to foster co-operation with the Maghreb states

Apart from bilateral co-operation through AAs, the UMA states have been linked to the EU through a range of measures which either target only the Mediterranean countries, or target Mediterranean and neighbours of the EU. These other arrangements include: Global Mediterranean Policy (GMP), Renovated Mediterranean Policy (RMP), Euro-Mediterranean Partnership (EMP), Union for the Mediterranean (UfM), and European Neighbourhood Policy (ENP).

10.3.2.1 Bilateral co-operation through Association Agreements

The AAs are treaties between EU and third countries, which create a framework for co-operation between the two parties. Typically, though the initiative has tended to come from the EU,[4] the AAs have been negotiated between the EU and the potential beneficiary country.

Usually, AAs' co-operation areas broadly encapsulate political, trade, social, cultural, and security issues. Their significance for industrialisation arises from the fact that they extend to the beneficiary country, access to the EU market of industrial goods, and in this connection, allow bilateral cumulation of origin status. The cumulation provisions encourage investment co-operation, as the products exported to the EU can be produced by EU firms in collaboration with firms from the beneficiary country. The AAs also contain a financial protocol, which is a development assistance instrument (cf. Matambalya 1999: 104).

Table 10.1 shows the evolution of AAs between the EU and third countries from within Europe, since the inception of this type of arrangement.

Notably, almost all these countries have meanwhile acceded to the EU (e.g. Czech Republic, Cyprus, Hungary, Malta, Poland, Slovak Republic, etc.), while Turkey, which is among the exceptions, has applied for membership.

Also, AAs between the EU and the Maghreb countries are a relatively new trend. To puts things straight, it is important to note the following historical facts:

a   The *Treaty of Rome* (which was signed on 28 February 1957 and came into effect on 1 January 1958), which created the EEC, included two French dependent Maghreb countries under Overseas Countries and Territories (OCTs): Algeria and Mauritania.

b   Both the *Youndé I Convention*[5] and *Youndé II Convention*[6] included Mauritania among the countries of the Association of African States and Madagascar (AASM), linked to the EEC through this particular post-colonial Convention.

c   The *Lomé I Convention*,[7] *Lomé II Convention*,[8] *Lomé III Convention*,[9] and *Lomé IV Convention*[10] which included Mauritania among the African, Caribbean and Pacific (ACP) group of nations, linked these frameworks to the EEC and later to the EU.

d   The *Cotonou Agreement* (which was signed on 23 June 2000) included Mauritania in the ACP group of nations, which are linked to the EU.

Table 10.1 Overview of the varieties of association agreements established between EU and European countries

	Signed	Type of agreement	Current status
Albania	2006	SAA	SIF
Bosnia & Herzegovina	2008	SAA	SIF
Croatia	2001	SAA	SIF
Cyprus	1972	AA	NLIF
Estonia, Lithuania, Latvia	1998	AA	NLIF
Iceland, Norway, Lichtenstein	1992	AA	SIF
Bulgaria, Czech Republic, Romania, Slovakia	1995	AA	NLIF
Slovenia	1999	AA	NLIF
Former Yugoslav Republic of Macedonia	2001	SAA	SIF
Hungary, Poland	1994	AA	NLIF
Montenegro	2007	SAA	SIF
Turkey	1963	AA	SIF

Source: European Union External Association, available at http://eeas.europa.eu/association/.

Notes
AA = Association Agreement; fYRoM = Former Yugoslav Republic of Macedonia; NLIF = No longer in force; SAA = Stabilisation and Association Agreement; SIF = Still in Force.

In the post-colonial period, the EEC had trade-driven co-operation agreements with Tunisia and Morocco in 1969; and co-operation agreements with Algeria. However, these agreements did not have the format of a typical AA.[11] As highlighted in the previous paragraphs, the relations with Mauritania have been based on the regulations of the Youndé I and II Conventions, Lomé Conventions I to IV Conventions, and the Cotonou Agreement.

The CPCM discussed earlier attempted to create a common platform for the Maghreb countries to relate with the EU. Due to its dysfunctionality, and in the aftermath of its eventual collapse, there was a setback of the co-operation efforts between the Maghreb and EEC states at a bloc level. Consequently, with the exception of Mauritania, these relationships took place largely through the bilateral channel, i.e. involving individual Maghreb countries on the one side, and the EU on the other side. From 1976 to 2010, AAs were signed by the EEC on the one side, and individual Maghreb countries on the other (cf. Table 10.2).

10.3.2.2 European Mediterranean schemes and relations to the Maghreb

The architecture of the EU's institutional schemes guiding relationship to the Maghreb countries have largely fallen within the broadly defined frameworks of co-operation between the EU and the entire Mediterranean region.

Hence, since the early 1970s, several Euro-Mediterranean schemes have emerged, of which the most notable include: GMP of 1972, RMP of 1989, EMP of 1995, and the *Barcelona Process*, ENP that was proposed by the EC in 2003

Table 10.2 Overview of the varieties of association agreements established between EU and UMA countries

	Algeria		*Libya*		*Mauritania*	*Morocco*	*Tunisia*
Signed	2002	1976	Not yet signed; negotiations in May 2010	*2002*	March 2008	*1996*	*1995*
Entered into force	September 2005	–	–		–	March 2000	March 1998
Type of agreement	AA	AA	AA		AA AA	AA	AA
Status	SIF	NLIF	–		NLIF SIF	SIF	–

Source: Author. Based on European Union External Association, available at http://eeas.europa.eu/association/.

Notes
AA = Association Agreement; UMA = Union du Maghreb Arabe; EU = European Union; NLIF = No Longer in Force; SIF = Still in Force.

and focused on the EU's links with all the Union's neighbours after the enlargement of 1 May 2004, and UfM of 2008. Their syntheses are presented in the following sub-sections. The last three of these initiatives are also summarised in Table 10.3.

A GLOBAL MEDITERRANEAN POLICY

The GMP was a 1972 unilateral policy initiative of the EEC, planned to benefit its Mediterranean partners. It outlined three policy issues:

a *Enhanced industrial MA.* Its significance for the *Maghrebi* industrial development efforts is that it provided more complete MA of industrialised goods to the EEC. It was hoped to stimulate export-led growth of the Maghrebi economies by allowing them to exploit economies of scale.
b *Industrial financing.* It created separate financial protocols that extended financial aid and loans to Mediterranean countries. Its significance for the Maghrebi in connection with industrialisation is underlined by the fact that the financing was dedicated to such critical issues as transfer of technology (ToT) and development of skills (through worker training).
c *Joint institutional platforms.* Platforms, in the form of co-operation councils and co-operation committees were established to oversee the implementation of the actions arising from the policy. In this way, some EEC-Maghrebi political dialogue became part of the initiative. Explicitly, this involved the grouping of diverse Mediterranean countries (Spain, Greece and Portugal, Arab *Maghreb* countries, and Arab *Machrek* countries) together as one coherent whole, instead of dealing with them bilaterally.

Table 10.3 Overview of the Maghreb–EU co-operation arrangements

	Algeria	Libya	Mauritania	Morocco	Tunisia
EMP	Free trade area planned for 2017 (postponed to 2020[13])	Observer in the Euro-Med Partnership since 1999	'Special guest' at the foreign ministers' meetings	Free trade area planned for 2012	Member of the Euro-Med Free Trade Area for manufactured goods since 1 January 2008
ENP	Under development (2010)	–	–	Action plan adopted on 27 July 2005	Action plan adopted on 4 July 2005
UfM	Full Member	Observer status	Full member	Full member	Full member
AS	–	–	–	Morocco–EU Summit on 7 March 2010.	Attempts to follow the Moroccan Example

Source: Authors. Based on Behr (2010).

Notes

AS = Advanced Status; EMP = Euro-Med Partnership; ENP = European Neighbourhood Policy; UfM = Union for the Mediterranean.

The GMP led to limited achievements. This is partly attributed to the fact that in actual fact, the EEC was, during the period, focused on the Southern enlargement to Greece (which eventually became a member of the bloc in 1981) and Spain and Portugal (which became members of the bloc in 1986) (cf. Behr 2010).

B RENOVATED MEDITERRANEAN POLICY

The GMP was succeeded by the RMP of 1989. However, real concentration on the initiative was also distracted by another seemingly more important mission for the EU, i.e. the extension to Eastern European countries of the former socialist bloc. Therefore, this policy initiative remained also a statement of intentions, and no more.

C EURO-MEDITERRANEAN PARTNERSHIP

The EMP of 1995 ushered in yet another initiative and change of direction. The re-direction of attention to the Mediterranean is usually attributed to sustained effort by Spain in particular, to put the relationship to the region on more solid ground.

EMP is based on and constituting an extension of arrangements, which were originally negotiated bilaterally between the EU and (individual) Southern Mediterranean States. It was adopted by the EU and the member states gathered in Barcelona, and was anticipated to set in motion the so called *Barcelona Process*.

In terms of substance, EMP details a comprehensive framework for political, economic, and social relations between the European Union and ten Mediterranean countries.[13] It focuses on Mediterranean regional integration and establishment of an FTA in the Mediterranean region. Its three main objectives are:

a *Political and security.* Establishment of a common area of peace and stability through the reinforcement of political and security dialogue.
b *Economic and financial.* Construction of a zone of shared prosperity through an economic and financial partnership and a gradual establishment of an FTA. In this realm of the EMP, the EU provides financial and technical assistance to the Euro-Mediterranean partners through various means. Its MEDA programme is the main financial instrument in the Euro-Med partnership, supporting the implementation process of the AAs and the adoption of key social and economic reforms in the Mediterranean countries. The ENPI and European Investment Bank (EIB) are other important funding sources of the EMP (cf. Brunel 2008: 14).
c *Social, cultural and human.* This involves rapprochement between peoples through a social, cultural, and human partnership encouraging exchanges between civil societies.

D UNION FOR THE MEDITERRANEAN

The UfM is seen as the extension of the EMP but with much more pragmatic spirit. The UfM doesn't focus on political, security, or social issues as was the case with the EMP. Its main focus areas are economy, environment, energy, health, migration, and culture. Instead, it promotes economic integration and democratic reform across 16 North African and Middle Eastern neighbours.[14]

The main goals of the scheme are:

a   The de-pollution of the Mediterranean Sea, including coastal and protected marine areas.
b   The establishment of maritime and land highways that connect ports and improve rail connections so as to facilitate movement of people and goods.
c   A joint civil protection programme on prevention, preparation, and response to natural and man-made disasters.
d   A Mediterranean solar energy plan that explores opportunities for developing alternative energy sources in the region.
e   Euro-Mediterranean University, inaugurated in Slovenia in June 2008.
f   Support of small and medium scale enterprises (SMEs) operating in the region, by assessing their needs and providing technical assistance (TA) and access to business finance.

E EUROPEAN NEIGHBOURHOOD POLICY

The ENP was originally conceived with a focus on the EU's Eastern European neighbours. Later, when the EU came to the conclusion that circumstances needed to be so, especially considering the faltering performances of the *Barcelona Process* encapsulated in EMP, and the UfM, it decided to expand it to incorporate its Mediterranean neighbours too.

The intention, however, was not to replace the existing Barcelona framework, but to complement it with additional provisions of bilateral relations, in order to overcome shortfalls associated with the political reform process in the Mediterranean.[15] This is important, since stable political conditions are essential ingredients for industrial transformation and overall economic development. Incentives, including MA, were extended to countries willing to pursue genuine political reforms. Country-specific Action Plans specified benchmarks and rewards that were supposed to address the particular situation in each partner country (cf. Behr 2010).

Bilateralism is a hallmark of the ENP. Imperatively, it signifies a strategy shift – away from promoting sub-regional integration endeavours such as the *Agadir Process*. Circumventing the challenges associated with a 'regional approach' was expected to inculcate new dynamism into Euro-Mediterranean relationships, pre-empting any deadlocks in which single countries and problems blocked the process.

Bilateralism was also meant to increase 'ownership' of the Action Plans and greater responsibility of the implementation process, which could also be measured and compared between countries. Thus, Morocco was granted an 'Advanced Status' (AS) in 2008 – a status that nominally opens the window for intensified bilateral political and trade relations, including the possibility of a summit between the EU and the country in question (in the case of Morocco, this took place in 2010).

General questions continue to linger on the suitability of ENP for the Arab countries including the Maghreb countries, considering that it was conceived for Eastern Europe and the conditions in the two sets of regions differ. Also, there does not appear to be a departure from the mindset of the hub-and-spoke model, which have made other EU models of development co-operation with developing countries lopsided to benefit the former (i.e. the EU itself) with no clear developmental dividends for the latter (i.e. developing countries). The EU's restricted liberalisation of some of its sectors, such as Agriculture, has also meant that the potential benefits to the Arab countries are restricted (cf. Behr 2010).

10.3 Anecdotes of industrial co-operation of the European Union and Maghreb countries

This section highlights the development of the industrial co-operation between the EU and individual member states of the AMU. Depending on the availability of data and information, only Algeria, Morocco, and Tunisia have been analysed. The co-operation period under review coincides with the post-colonial to the present day.

10.3.1 Industrial co-operation between the European Union and Algeria

The Algerian economy faced different kind of crises especially after the oil crisis of 1986, followed by the debt crisis that stifled all initiatives to get out of this crisis. The negotiations between Algeria and the International Financial Institutions (IFI), i.e. World Bank (WB) and International Monetary Fund (IMF) made the country adopt a Structural Adjustment Programme (SAP).

In 2002, Algeria signed the AA with the EU, within the context of EMP. In 2007, the Support Programme of the Partnership Agreement entered into effect. This programme is valued at €40 million, and is intended to provide all kinds of technical support to Algeria, targeting business enterprises and other institutions.

10.3.2 Industrial co-operation between the European Union and Morocco

Co-operation between Morocco and the EU was launched on 31 March 1969, through the signing of a co-operation agreement, followed by another one in 1976. In 1996, Morocco signed the EMP agreement. This agreement has contributed to the country's economic achievements, as in 2007 it became the fifth economic power in Africa, and the second in the UMA region. Morocco became the first beneficiary from the programmes MEDA 1 (1996–1999) and MEDA 2 (2000–2006) destined to the development of the Mediterranean economic apace (Depuy 2009: 236).[16]

Moreover, the projects financed under the Facility for Euro-Mediterranean Investment and Partnership (FEMIP) between October 2002 and December 2006 amounted to €1.04 billion, and made Morocco one of the main beneficiaries in the Mediterranean region of this fund, behind Egypt and Tunisia. The break-down of funded projects revealed the predominance of funding for infrastructure, including energy and transport, which account for 67 per cent of the total funding received by Morocco under FEMIP (Ismail-Idrissi 2011: 6). The ENPI provided Morocco with an amount of €654 million between 2007 and 2010 to support the Moroccan economic development.

After the success of Morocco in gaining deeper co-operation with the EU through its advanced status of co-operation, Tunisia has also expressed interest in strengthening its partnership with the EU. Tunisia is the country that has made the greatest progress in the implementation of the FTA by eliminating all tariffs for industrial products on 1 January 2008. Bilateral negotiations with the EU regarding the progressive opening up of services and the right of establishment were launched in March 2008, and negotiations have also taken place regarding the liberalisation of trade in agricultural products, processed agricultural products, and fishery products.

10.3.3 Industrial co-operation between the European Union and Tunisia

After independence, in the late 1960s, the Tunisian economy has successfully proceeded with its opening up to the external world, especially to its European neighbours. This opening up helped the Tunisian economy to enter the competitive world market. The European aid and support was highly needed at that time, due to lack of own capital and technological capacities to spur industrial investments. Therefore, Tunisia started to build up long-term co-operation with the EU from the 1970s.

In 1995, Tunisia was the first Southern Mediterranean country to sign up an AA with the EU (cf. Table 10.2). Based on this AA, Tunisia has received a financial support of €1.2 billion from 1996 to 2008; 43 per cent of this loan was destined to the economic reforms and the protection of the economic balance, 25 per cent of it was used to develop the human resources and social security, 16 per cent for the private sector and the amelioration of the business environment, 14 per cent for the management of the natural and the environmental resources, and only 2 per cent destined for the good governance and civil society.

In 2008, the FTA agreement entered into effect, which made Tunisia the first UMA country that started to benefit from the EMP agreements behind this FTA. Thus, Tunisian manufactured goods started to benefit from easy access to the big EU markets of over 500 million consumers. Moreover, the EMP has helped in the ToT and the amelioration of the production tools.

The EMP boosted the European investments in the country, which helped in creating job opportunities in Tunisia. According to official statistics, the value of European investments in Tunisia reached 2270 million Tunisian dinars in 2008, which is about 70 per cent of the total of the FDI in the country. In 2008, the number of European companies in Tunisia reached 2,500 among 2,966 foreign companies. These figures reflect the importance of the linkage between the Tunisian economy and the EU, especially if we take into account that about 80 per cent of Tunisian exports are directed to EU countries.

10.3.4 Summary

The statistics cited in subsections 10.3.1–10.3.3 show that the financial support provided by the Euro-Med initiatives to the Maghreb countries are destined to sectors supporting the industrial development such as infrastructure, human capacities development, and institutional reforms.

However, the funding programmes of EMP and UfM did not provide special funds for the reform of the industrial sector or the promotion of technological research in UMA countries.

Also, lack of clear signs of efforts to support development of industrial entrepreneurship and industrial enterprises in UMA countries further casts doubt on the prospects for success.

10.4 Contribution of the Euro-Med Partnership to industrial development in the Maghreb

An *ex ante* assessment of the contribution of the Euro-Med Partnership to the industrial development in the Maghreb should shed some light on the developmental impact of the arrangements. The current section reflects on the achievements and the limitations of the industrial co-operation between Maghreb countries and the EU.

10.4.1 Achievements

Since the 1970s until today, the EU–UMA co-operation has contributed continuously to the economic and industrial development in the Maghreb countries. The EMP helped Maghreb countries to build up their own experiences in the various aspects: carry out essential reforms (economic, structural, and institutional), benefit from transfer of technology, MA, and improvement of quality standards.

The reforms required by the Barcelona Process regarding the economic, institutional, and legal adjustments, helped in some way to create a favourable environment for the foreign capitals to invest in the Maghreb countries, especially in Tunisia and Morocco where the European standards of reform are highly respected.

Considering the reliance of the development of the industrial sector in the Maghreb countries on the investment capitals, and especially the FDI, these reforms have been crucial. Figure 10.1 shows the variation of the FDI net inflows into Maghreb countries, which is related to the political and economic situation in the region, as well as the global financial crisis. However, among experts in Maghreb–EU relations as well as the Maghrebi economic actors, there are many who argue that the EU is not investing sufficiently in the region (Kaush and Youngs 2009: 963).

Co-operation with the EU helps the Maghreb countries to acquire new technologies in different fields: manufacturing, agriculture, extractive industries.

One of the main goals of EMP is to facilitate the access of Maghreb-made products to the European markets. It helps to improve the Maghrebi exportations and get the Maghrebi economies more integrated in the world economy.

The joint programmes of quality standards training and evaluation provided by the European countries have an impact on the quality standards of the Maghrebi products. This helped the Maghreb countries to produce goods with high quality standards, which can compete with other developing countries products.

10.4.2 Limitations

10.4.2.1 Lack of varieties and dependence on the European demand

Since their independence, the industrial co-operation between Maghreb and the EU has helped the Maghreb countries to build up industrial sectors along a very narrow specialisation. For example, in the case of Algeria and Libya, both are energy-rich countries; the industrial sector is much more limited to the energy and

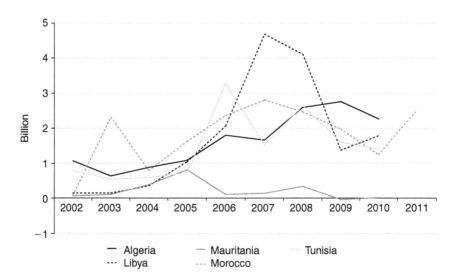

Figure 10.1 Net inflows of FDI in Maghreb countries in US$ (source: World Bank).

hydrocarbons. In the case of Tunisia and Morocco, both are small countries in the Maghreb region and their economic development is mainly based on agriculture, services, and tourism sectors. Despite their limited economic potential, Morocco and Tunisia, in comparison with other Maghreb countries, enjoy a stable political and economic situation, which helps them to attract the attention of foreign investors. Moreover, due to their low production costs including labour costs, their attractive investment environment, and their geographical proximity, the investment markets in Morocco and Tunisia became the preferred destination of the European investors. Therefore, Morocco and Tunisia, with the co-operation of the EU, have expanded their manufacturing production, based on the exploitation of the human capital in both countries. The European investments in the manufacturing sector focus much more on textile/clothing, glass, wood, steel etc.

Overall the Euro-Mediterranean industrial co-operation still focuses on traditional industrial sectors such as textile, raw materials, and tourism as cited in the 'Conclusions of the Conference of the Ministers for Industry of the Union for the Mediterranean' held in Malta on 11 and 12 May 2011. The paper underlined that

> Participants in the conference emphasized the merits of industrial cooperation on both a horizontal and a sectoral level, in such areas as textiles/clothing, space, raw materials and tourism, the latter being a major provider of international investment, employment and foreign exchange and a vector for reconciling peoples and human beings as reiterated at the Euro-Mediterranean Ministerial Conference on Tourism in Fez (April 2008) and Barcelona (May 2010).
>
> ('Conclusions', p. 2)

The same paper mentioned that: 'The participants are expressing their willingness to explore the scope for developing the innovative dimension of industrial cooperation in areas such as biotechnology, value-added manufacturing and advanced services' ('Conclusions', p. 2). This has shown that the patterns of Euro-Med industrial co-operation in general and Euro-Maghreb co-operation seem not to change at least on a short-term view.

A very important point that needs to be mentioned here is that the industrial products, whether in the manufacturing, agriculture, or extractive sectors, are almost similar in the five Maghreb countries, for instance raw materials, agricultural products, textiles, and fishing. This is making the competition very high between the Maghreb countries to get access to the European markets. Moreover, the percentage of their trade with the EU is effectively showing that they were more likely to be competing against each other.

10.4.2.2 Eurocentric and protective policies

Despite all the measures taken by the Maghreb states to fulfil their duties underlined in the AA with the EU, such as economic liberalisation, financial and institutional reforms, the flows of European investments to the Maghreb region were below expectations. Moreover, the Eurocentric nature of the EMP policies and measures are continuously embedding the process of the economic integration, one of the most important objectives declared in the Barcelona Process. On the ground, the borders and barriers between the two shores of the Mediterranean, especially between Maghreb and Europe, were to be preserved for security, political, and economic reasons. The underlined goals of the EMP as for economic integration, the free movement of capitals, persons, and goods was partially reached. The actors in the business sector in the Southern side of the Mediterranean, especially from Maghreb, criticise the protective measures taken by the European partner to control people's circulation from South to North.

In 2005, a fourth chapter on 'Migration, social integration, justice and security' was added to the Barcelona Process. The very rationale of the new UfM is to address issues that have a specifically trans-Mediterranean dimension, such as reducing illegal migration. Migration has been increasingly defined as a security concern.[17] The main reason behind the protective measures taken by the European side on the circulation of people to Europe is the attempt of the EU to control as much as they can the migration flows. This kind of measure is challenging the integrity of the EMP process, as it creates contradiction manifested by economic co-operation and the political division regarding the migration issue.

It is important to underline here that, during recent years, the raising flows of illegal migration is alarming the European side of the potential failure of the Barcelona Process to achieve its declared goals, for instance the economic development and job creations in the Maghreb countries.

10.4.2.3 Slow development of the industrial sector in the Maghreb countries

Figures 10.2 and 10.3 present the development of the percentage share of manufacturing and industry in the GDP of UMA countries from 2002 to 2009. Notably, all the UMA countries except Libya witnessed some regression in the share of manufacturing (cf. Figure 10.2).

However, as demonstrated in Figure 10.3, industry's share of GDP increased slightly between 2002 and 2009 in all UMA countries except Algeria.

The two figures also show the difference of share of GDP for Algeria, Libya, Tunisia, and Morocco. In this case, the energy-rich countries count more on their energy industry, as the share of the GDP is respectively 51.3 per cent and 71.4 per cent for Algeria and Libya in 2009. However, in Tunisia and Morocco the share of manufacturing is higher than industry (16.7 per cent in Tunisia and 16.1 per cent in Morocco).

10.4.2.4 Challenge to intra-Maghreb integration

The Maghreb economic integration is facing numerous political and socio-economic challenges and obstacles such as Algerian-Moroccan relations, the

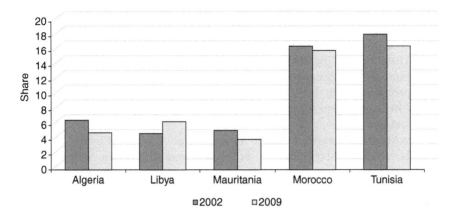

Figure 10.2 Share of manufacturing in GDP (%) (source: European Economic
    Commission).

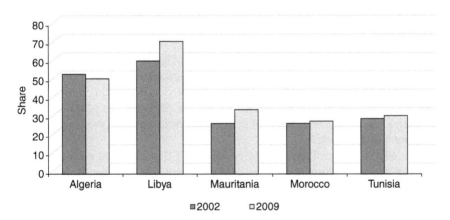

Figure 10.3 Share of industry in GDP (%) (source: European Economic Commission).

Western Sahara issue, Maghreb countries' internal socio-economic conditions,
and security issues. The forms of the Maghreb countries' economies and their
patterns of economic development are very different. Tunisia and Morocco had
more or less liberal economic regimes, with very substantial private sectors in
agriculture, industry, and services. The economy of Algeria is dominated by a
state sector seeking to deal with the difficult social, economic, and political legacies of state-subsidised inefficiency. In Libya the economy was almost wholly in
the hand of the state, with only recently instituted moves to hand such sectors as
retailing back to the private sector, as a mean of compensating for a decade of
state-supervised chaos and shortages.

All in all, the Maghreb economic integration is facing many challenges and
obstacles. Most of these barriers are related to Maghreb countries' internal

weaknesses and result from political, economic, and institutional differences between Maghreb countries themselves. However, the choices made by Maghreb countries regarding their regional integration had also a significant impact on the promotion of the intra-Maghreb economic integration. Maghreb countries chose the EU as the first regional partner rather than to enhance the economic co-operation amongst themselves. Also, they tend to compete against each other in their partnership with the EU, instead of having a co-ordinated approach, which would have only been possible through a functional Maghreb regional integration platform.

The Maghreb integration remain a necessity to be achieved by the Maghreb countries; only the Maghreb countries' commitment to the economic integration of the Maghreb region can boost the process of integration. The EU cannot be blamed for the failure of the integration process in the region, but for the asymmetrical Maghreb–EU interdependence, which make the Maghreb countries adjust their economic plans and reforms according to the EU needs and co-operation orientations rather than the Maghreb economic integration's goals.

10.5 Competitive industrial performance of the Maghreb countries

Table 10.4 compares the CIP index of the three (Algeria, Morocco, and Tunisia) of the five (which includes also Libya and Mauritania) Maghreb countries for which data was available, with a selected benchmark. Data used is from a global sample of 135 countries (cf. UNIDO 2013). The performances of the Maghreb countries are in line with those of African countries, as discussed in detail in Chapter 4 of this book.

Notably, in 2010, all three countries recorded CIP indices that were above the African average (which is 0.0135). However, they lie significantly below the global average (which is 0.0846). Also, they deviate significantly from Africa's

Table 10.4 Ranks of the CIP Index occupied by the Maghreb countries in 2010

CIP ranking	Country	CIP Index
82	Algeria	0.0220
66	Morocco	0.0374
58	Tunisia	0.0476
By comparison		
1	Global highest: *Japan*	0.5409
42	Global average	0.0846
133	African highest: *South Africa*	0.0722
	African average	0.0135
	Global lowest: *Iraq, Gambia, Eritrea*	0.0000

Source: Based on UNIDO (2013).

Notes
CIP Index = Comparative Industrial Performance Index.

best performance by South Africa (which was 0.0722). In this case as well, for the interested reader, Chapter 4 of this book gives a more detailed account of the CIP Index and ranking of African countries, within a broader global comparison.

10.6 Summary of conclusions

The Euro-Med Partnership has been and continues to be a matter of primary concern particularly for the Maghreb countries for which it remains a determining framework for co-operation for development (Aghrout 2000: 2). For the EU, the importance of the partnership seems to be much more limited to some issues of concern, such as security, illegal immigration, and Maghreb immigrants in Europe. The EU might be achieving these goals.

For the Maghreb countries, some of the emerging issues can be summed up in the following points: erosion of coherence between policy and national and regional economic development needs, lopsided dependency, and underachievement in relation to industrialisation.

10.6.1 Erosion of coherence between policy and national and regional economic development needs

It is obvious that one of the possible ways for the Maghreb countries to boost their economic development is to concentrate their efforts on the promotion of their relations with the powerful EU partners. The promotion of this co-operation has certainly an important contribution to the economic development of the Maghreb economies. But at the same time this orientation of the Maghrebi economic policy and foreign co-operation makes Maghreb countries' economic plans lose linkage with the grassroots of the national and intra-regional economic needs.

10.6.2 Lopsided interdependency

In view of the character of links with the EU, the Maghreb countries have tended to look outside much more than inside. They focus on the access of their industrial products to the EU market and neglect the importance of the national and regional market within the Maghreb region itself, as well as in the new emerging one.

Export-oriented industries in different Maghreb countries make their economies heavily dependent on the EU markets in terms of exportation of manufactured goods or in terms of the planning of industrial reforms at the national level. The adjustment of the Maghreb countries' economic development and reform plans according to the initiatives and plans taken by the EU within the framework of EMP, ENP, or UfM is increasing the dependency of the Maghreb countries on the EU economic market.

The global financial crisis, which has exposed the weakness of the old economic powers, like the EU, is an opportunity for the Maghreb countries to review their economic policies both at the national and international levels.

All in all, this stance appears to be oblivious of the ongoing shift in the global economic landscape.

10.6.3 Underachievement in relation to industrialisation

Co-operation with the EU has so far not really helped Maghreb countries to build up their own industry. The industrial sectors built in Maghreb seem to be annexes to the European industries (textile, food, etc.). Overall, the shape of the Maghrebi industrial sector looks like it (one-sidedly) fits much more with the economic needs of the EU itself.

10.7 Way forward

In charting the way forward, the Maghreb countries should bear several considerations in mind. Most importantly, these countries have the potential to expand their own industries and manufacturing production. The region is gifted with key natural and human resources, which it can carefully use to achieve this goal, within the context of a carefully designed and implemented co-operation arrangement with its EU partner. For example, Algeria has the potential and willingness to build up its own automobile industry. This is the case of Tunisia as well, which has succeeded in manufacturing its own mobile phone brand such as Evertek, a trade mark of Cell, which is holding more than 10 per cent of the mobile phone market in Tunisia and is expanding in Morocco, France, and Libya, and planning for future investments in Algeria, Mali, Senegal, and Ivory Coast.

Also, the Maghreb countries should give priority to the intra-regional co-operation plans, and the unification of the decision making regarding the economic co-operation with the EU. This would require that the members of the UMA work as a bloc to deal with their EU counterparty which is itself dealing with the Maghreb countries as one bloc. As long as this goal is not achieved and the Maghreb countries are proceeding singly or competing against each other in their co-operation with the EU, the heavy dependence and the vulnerability of the Maghreb economies may not easily change.

Overall, co-operation with the EU should be harnessed to make the Maghreb countries vividly achieve their development goals.

Notes

1 There is an attempt from the European side to invest in the heavy industries in the Maghreb countries. The Renault-Nissan Tangier automobile factory that opened in Morocco in February 2012 is a case in hand. The EU as a powerful old economic partner of the Maghreb region could take this step earlier, especially with the potentials of the French and German automobile industries, and, in the case of Algeria, could help this big and energy-rich Maghreb country to build its own automobile industry and more.
2 This was done by EEC negotiating bilaterally co-operation agreements with the Maghreb (and other Mediterranean) countries in the early 1960s. These agreements tended to differ considerably in scope and scale, but generally granted some form of

preferential trade access to the industrial goods of partner countries to the common market.

3 The Association Agreement (AA) is a treaty between the European Union (EU) and a non-EU country that creates an embracing framework for co-operation between them. Typically, these agreements normally provide for the progressive liberalisation of trade to various degrees (i.e. Free Trade Area, Customs Union). Other areas frequently covered include the development of political, social, cultural, and security links. In certain cases, they prepare the non-member country for future membership of the European Union (cf. European Union External Action, available at: http://eeas.europa. eu/association/).

4 Legally, the AAs are anchored in the EU's article 217 TFEU (former article 310 and article 238 TEC).

5 It was signed on 20 July 1963 and came into effect on 1 July 1964. It included Mauritania among the 18 countries of the Association of African States and Madagascar (AASM), which were linked to the EEC through this particular post-colonial Convention.

6 It was signed in July 1969 and came into effect on 1 January 1971. It included Mauritania among the 22 countries of the AASM, which were linked to the EEC through this revamped Convention.

7 It was signed on 28 February 1975 and came into effect on 1 April 1976. It included Mauritania among the 46 ACP countries linked to the EEC through this Convention.

8 It was signed in 1979 and came into effect on 1 January 1981. It included Mauritania among the 57 ACP countries linked to the EEC through this Convention.

9 It was signed on 8 December 1984 and became effective on 1 May 1986. It included Mauritania among the 66 ACP countries linked to the EEC through this Convention.

10 It was signed on 15 December 1989 and became effective in 1999. It included Mauritania among the 70 ACP countries linked to the EEC through this Convention.

11 Typically, AAs meet the following criteria: (1) the legal basis for their conclusion is Article 310 (ex 238) TEC; (2) they intend to establish close economic and political co-operation (more than simple co-operation); (3) they create paritary bodies for the management of the co-operation, competent to take decisions that bind the contracting parties; (4) they offer Most Favoured Nation (MFN) treatment; (5) they provide a privileged relationship between the EC and its partner; (6) since 1995 the clause on the respect of human rights and democratic principles is systematically included and constitutes an essential element of the agreement; (7) in a large number of cases, the association agreement replaces a co-operation agreement thereby intensifying the relations between the partners (cf. European Union External Action, available at: http://eeas.europa.eu/association/). However, in detail, they differ from one another (cf. European Union External Action, available at: http://eeas.europa.eu/association/).

12 Algerian News agency, 25 August 2012.

13 The ten Mediterranean countries are: Algeria, Egypt, Israel, Jordan, Lebanon, Morocco, Palestine, Syria, Tunisia, and Turkey.

14 Sixteen Southern Mediterranean, African, and Middle Eastern countries are members of the UfM: Albania, Algeria, Bosnia and Herzegovina, Croatia, Egypt, Israel, Jordan, Lebanon, Mauritania, Monaco, Montenegro, Morocco, the Palestinian Authority, Syria, Tunisia, and Turkey.

15 Thus, ENP was to

> provide greater incentives for political reforms and well-catered development plans ... offer a way around the political deadlock haunting the region and provide for greater 'joint-ownership' ... allow for some much-needed differentiation amongst countries that were at very different stages of their development.
>
> (cf. Behr 2010)

16 The MEDA Regulation is the principal instrument of economic and financial co-operation under the EMP. It was launched in 1996 (MEDA I) and amended in 2000 (MEDA II). It enables the European Union (EU) to provide financial and technical assistance to the countries in the Southern Mediterranean: Algeria, Cyprus, Egypt, Israel, Jordan, Lebanon, Malta, Morocco, the Palestinian Territory, Syria, Tunisia, and Turkey (cf. Europa: Summary of EU Regulation, available at: http://europa.eu/legislation_summaries/external_relations/relations_with_third_countries/mediterranean_partner_countries/r15006_en.htm).

17 Ibid, p. 965.

References

Aghrout, A. (2000). *From Preferential Status to Partnership: The Euro-Maghreb Relationship*. Burlington, VA: Ashgate.

Alden, C. and Aggad-Clerx, F. (2012). *Chinese Investments and Employment Creation in Algeria and Egypt*. Economic Brief. African Development Bank.

Behr, T. (2010). Regional Integration in the Mediterranean: Moving Out of the Deadlock? *Notre Europe*. April.

Brunel C. (2008). Maghreb regional integration. In G. Hufbauer and C. Brunel (eds), *Maghreb Regional and Global Integration: A Dream to be Fulfilled*, Washington: Peterson Institute for International Economics (pp. 7–16).

Chourou, B. (2004). *Arab Regional Integration as a Prerequisite for a Successful Euro-Mediterranean Partnership*. In A. Jünemann (ed.). *Euro-Mediterranean Relations after September 11*. London: Frank Cass.

Dupuy, E. (2009). *Le Maroc et l'Union Europeenne, une relation evidente, exigeante toujours singuliere*. In J.-Y. de Cara, F. Rouvillois, and C. Saint-Prot (eds), *Le Maroc en Marche: le développement politique, social et économique du Maroc*, Paris: CNRS Editions (pp. 234–245).

Ismaili Idrissi, B. (2011). *Analysis of Morocco-European Union Partnership within the Framework of the Advanced Status: Main Features and Challenges*. Committee for Evaluation of Norway's Agreements with the EU, Report No. 21.

Kausch, K. and Youngs, R. (2009). The end of the Euro-Mediterranean vision. *International Affairs*, 85: 963–975.

Matambalya, F. (1999). *The Merits and Demerits of EU Policies Towards Associated Developing Countries*. Frankfurt a.M./Berlin/Bern/New York/Paris/Wien: Peter Lang.

Metaoui, F. (2009). Pekin veut une relation Sino-Algerienne sans visa. *Les Afriques*, 95: 2.

Pairault, T. (2013a). Chinese direct investment in Africa: A state strategy? *Région et développement*, 37.

Pairault, T. (2013b). Economic relations between China and Maghreb countries. In M. Burnay, J.-C. Defraigne, and J. Wouters (eds), *EU–China and the World: Analyzing the Relations with Developing and Emerging Countries*. Cheltenham (UK)/Northampton (USA): Edward Elgar Publishing.

UNIDO (2013). *Competitive Industrial Performance Report 2012/2013*. Vienna: United Nations Industrial Development Organization.

Wippel, S. (2005). *The Agadir Agreement and Open Regionalism*. EuroMeSCo Paper 45, September.

Websites

bilaterals.org, available at: www.bilaterals.org/spip.php?rubrique168. An open publishing website.

Europa: Summary of EU Regulation, available at: http://europa.eu/legislation_summaries/ external_relations/relations_with_third_countries/mediterranean_partner_countries/ r15006_en.htm)

European Union External Action, available at: http://eeas.europa.eu/association/.

Part V

Pathways to industrialisation and economic growth and development of African countries

Digest of stylised facts and considerations for the formulation of the development agenda

11 Pathways to Africa's industrialisation and economic growth and development

A digest of stylised ideas and facts

Francis A.S.T. Matambalya

11.1 Prelude

Industrialisation is widely acknowledged to be a pathway to sustainable economic growth and development. Not only does it drive the generation of knowledge and development of skills – and therefore create the necessary conditions for innovations – but it is also associated with increasing returns to scale (since it is not subjected to fixed supply of essential inputs). It also drives the process of accumulation of capital (as it is capital intensive compared to say agriculture). The other features that make industrialisation foster economic growth and development are: strong backward linkages (e.g. a consumer of inputs from mining and agricultural sectors, etc., as well as a supplier of inputs to those sectors), strong forward linkages (e.g. as a consumer of services from banking, transportation, insurance, etc., as well as a supplier of inputs to those sectors), commanding a big share of international trade (cf. Cornwall 1977; von Tunzelmann 1995; Rowthorn and Ramaswamy 1997; Lall 2005; Collier and Venables 2007; Shen *et al.* 2007; Gault and Zhang 2010; Mokyr 2010; Szirmai 2012; Ciarli *et al.* 2012). For the interested reader, Chapter 2 of this book provides a more detailed account of the pertinent issues.

However, for many African economies, a long way to the achievement of competitive levels of industrial development still lies ahead. Imperatively, determining the appropriate pathways to achieving substantive industrialisation is a prime challenge facing the stakeholders involved in the search of a formula for sustainable economic growth and development in Africa.

The title of this book establishes that international co-operation constitutes a feasible pathway for leveraging the partnership between the European Union (EU) and the African countries, for the industrialisation of the latter. However, achieving this goal requires *getting the determinants of substantive and sustainable industrial development right*. This, in turn, requires answering a key question: which links exist between international co-operation and industrial development? Also, the answers to several other relevant questions would offer precious clues on how to architecture viable industrialisation agendas. Among other things, these questions include:

a   How instructive are the theoretical explications of the industrialisation pro-
     cesses?
b   How is the nature of industrialisation, as an engine for growth, changing?
c   Which lessons can be emulated from the experiences by countries that have
     achieved industrial revolution in the past, or are doing so now?
d   Which lessons can be drawn from the failed cases of industrialisation
     initiatives?

On the whole, it is important to comprehend the determinants of international
disparities in industrial competitiveness from different perspectives. Hence, in a
bid to draw a line between what determines industrialisation success and failure,
the following sections digest the key ideas from theoretical explications, as well
as from the findings of empirical studies on the link between industrialisation
and economic growth and development, industrialisation experiences of countries, and impact of international co-operation on industrial development.[1]

To deliberate on the pathways to Africa's industrialisation and economic
growth and development, this chapter recapitulates the key lessons from theory.
In this case, for a reader interested in a comprehensive review, it is expedient to
revisit Chapter 2 of this book.

Moreover, the chapter recapitulates three stylised facts: economic growth and
development is driven by industrialisation, industrialisation is driven by manufacturing, and therefore manufacturing growth is essential for economic growth
and development. Again, for a reader interested in comprehensive analysis, these
fundamental facts have been inferred to in Chapter 3 of this book.

11.2 Lessons from theoretical postulations about industrialisation and development

Why does Tanzania not export computers to the EU? Why does the EU not
export fresh mangoes to Uganda? Why does Zimbabwe not export smartphones
to Japan? Why does Switzerland export Nescafe to Tanzania, and *also* import
coffee beans from Tanzania? Why do Burundi and Mauritius, both members of
the Common Market for Eastern and Southern African (COMESA), conduct literally no trade with each other at all?

Can economic theory give us clues about the answers to these questions? If
yes, what do we learn from theory? All the posed questions relate to the *patterns
of trade* and the *forces that determine them*. Intuitively, the *patterns of trade* are
determined by the *patterns of production* – generally a country exports what it
produces competitively! And what a country produces and trades has a great
bearing not only on its competitiveness, but equally on its economic growth and
economic development prospects.

Hence, over the centuries, besides trade theories, other theories on growth and
economic development have offered important clues about the significance of
industrialisation. Imperatively, a more comprehensive review should go beyond
trade theories. Commensurate to the discussion in Chapter 2 in this book, this

chapter sums up the lessons and implications for African countries, from a selection of theories. The six families of theories,[2] which are briefly revisited in this chapter, include:

a   *Country-based trade theories;*
b   *Firm-based trade theories;*
c   *Theories of stages of economic development* (i.e. Marxian growth model, Rostow's growth model, and Kaldorian growth model);
d   *Classical theories of growth* (i.e. balanced and unbalanced economic growth and development models, Keynesian classical theory based on Harrod-Domar economic growth and development model);
e   *Neoclassical theories of growth* (based on Swallow-Swan economic growth and development model);
f   Modern economic growth and development theories.

Table 11.1 presents an alternative classification of a selection of theories, which are instructive for understanding the phenomenon and process of industrial development. As with most classifications, this one too is somewhat arbitrary. Also, given the nature of theories, there are inherent overlaps that make their impeccable categorisation impracticable. However, it serves a good purpose of logically grouping the various theories in the main waves of economic thought that have evolved with time.

The simplistic formulation of the many early theories, particularly the models for mathematical estimations (cf. country-based trade theories, Keynesian and neo-classical growth models, etc.) meant that, neither structural change nor industrialisation was explicitly accounted for. Nonetheless, the ideas advanced in these theories gave vital information for understanding the phenomenon of industrial transformation, and the role of structural transformation therein.

11.2.1 Lessons embedded in the country-based trade theories

In the early days of evolution of economic theory, competitiveness was linked to classical theories of trade. Many theories emerging prior to the Second World War are largely country-based (use country as unit of analysis). Two other commonalities join these theories: they were developed by economists, and are useful in analysing inter-industry trade. The key pertinent theories include: *mercantilist theories of trade* (i.e. classical mercantilism or traditional mercantilism, and neo-mercantilism or modern-day mercantilism), *classical trade theories* (i.e. labour theory of value, theory of absolute advantage, theory of comparative advantage), *neo-classical trade theories* (e.g. Heckscher–Ohlin theory).

Between 1500 and 1750 most economists advocated *mercantilism* which promoted the idea of international trade for the purpose of a nation gaining riches by running a trade surplus. Many European countries achieved industrial transformation during this *traditional mercantilist* era. This period was also marked with conquest and predatory exploitation of human and natural resources from

Table 11.1 An alternative classification of instructive theories on industrial development

Sub-category of theories	Sub-sub-category of theories	Examples of key contributors	Derived lessons about drivers of industrialisation
1st wave of theories: The pre-classical economic thought – The mercantilist doctrine			
Traditional mercantilism or classical mercantilism	–	Giovanni Botero (1544–1617) Anotonio Sera (1580–1650) Nicolo Machiavelli (1469–1527)	• *Capital accumulation*, including through: (1) slave trade (as a tradable commodity & source of free labour), (2) super-profits from unpaid or underpaid labour, like in colonies and developing countries • *Cheap agricultural and mineral raw material*, sourced locally and from – especially from colonised countries
2nd wave of theories: Classical economic thought – Classical theories of economic growth and development			
1. Country-based trade theories (also known as: 'endowment-driven', or 'old' or 'traditional' trade theories)	Classical trade theories	Adam Smith's trade-driven model of economic growth (1776)	• *Leverage natural resources* • *Leverage FiR capacities*: (1) mobilisation of capital through savings, (2) investments • *Knowledge & skills capacities*: increased quality and efficiency through division of labour and specialisation • *Leverage institutions*
		David Ricardo: theory of comparative advantage (1817)	• Capital accumulation • Leveraging human resources • Leveraging natural resources
2. Keynesian growth models		Harrod-Domar growth model (1939)	• *Accumulation of capital stock*: driven by (1) savings (endogenous, exogenous), (2) population growth (endogenous, exogenous) • *Investment of the savings* • *Investment-stimulating policies* • *Government investments*

3. Balanced and unbalanced growth theories	Unbalanced growth theories	Hirschmann's unbalanced growth theory (1958) Kaldorian unbalanced growth theory (1966)	• Selective approach to by investing in 'strategic sectors' or sectors with comparative advantage • Self-reinforcing growth through backward and forward linkage effects • Intervention by the State to set the process in motion
	Balanced growth theories	Rosenstein-Rodan's 'balanced growth theory' (1961)	• 'Big-push' through holistic, inclusive approach to investments • Co-ordination of the process by the State

3rd wave of theories: Neo-classical economic thought – Neo-classical theories of economic growth and development

1 Country-based trade theories (also known as: 'endowment-driven', or 'old' or 'traditional' trade theories)	Neo-classical trade theories	Heckscher-Ohlin's factor proportions theory and its derivatives	
2 Growth theories		Solow-Swan growth model (1957)	• Capital accumulation • *Investment of the savings*: Investments: 'big-push' through holistic, inclusive approach to investments • *Labour* • *Technological progress* • *(Co-ordination of the process by the State through)* *Policies that stimulate competitive markets*

4th wave of theories: Theories of the stages of economic growth and development

		Marxian 4-stage model of economic growth	• *FiR capacities*: (1) mobilisation of capital through accumulation, (2) investment of mobilised capital in manufacturing • *Industrial entrepreneurship*: 'Machinofacture' through capitalist mode of production

continued

Table 11.1 Continued

Sub-category of theories	Sub-sub-category of theories	Examples of key contributors	Derived lessons about drivers of industrialisation
		Rostow's 5-stage model of economic growth (1960)	• *FiR capacities*: (1) mobilisation of capital from domestic and foreign sources, (2) investments (of mobilised capital) in the 'right' sectors • Conducive political, social, and institutional framework
		Kaldorian four-stage model of economic growth (1966)	• 'Endogenous growth' through 'learning by doing'

5th wave theories: Modern economic thought and trade theories

Firm-based trade theories	Country similarity theory		
	Product life cycle theory		
	Product differentiation theories		
	Global strategic rivalry theory		
	National competitive advantage theory		

6th wave theories: Modern views on economic growth and development, growth and trade

| Modern theories of economic growth and development | New growth theory | Mankiw *et al.* (1992), Romer (1990 and 1986), Grossman and Helpman (1989), Lucas 1988, etc. | • *FiR capacities*: capital accumulation
• *NFiR capacities*: innovation and technological progress, human resources |

Structural change growth model	Los and Verspagen (2003), Cimoli (1994), Pasinetti (1981), etc.	• *Technological dynamics* • *Demand*
Evolutionary growth models	Ciarli and Lorentz (2010), Ciarli et al. (2010), Saviota and Pyka (2008, and 2004), Dosi et al. (1994), Nelson and Winter (1982), Winters (2007), etc.	• *FiR capacities* (implicit) • *NFiR capacities*: (1) innovation and technological development, (2) labour productivity, (3) entrepreneurial dynamics
Unified growth theory	Galor (2010), Mokyr (2010), Desmeti and Parante (2009), etc.	• *NFiR capacities*: technology, education (for knowledge and skills) • Population growth
Political economy models	Adam and Dercon (2009), Acemoglu and Robinson (2006), North (1991), etc.	• *Governance framework*, i.e. framework that explains the game, e.g. laws and regulations • *Institutions* in the sense of organisations, e.g. political institutions
	Hidalgo and Hausman (2009 and 2008), Hidalgo et al. (2007), Saviti and Franken (2008), Hausman and Rodrik (2003), Funke and Ruhwedel (2001), etc.	• Short-run product focus • Long-run product diversification • Sectoral focus

Source: Author.

the colonies in Africa, Asia, and the 'new' world. For instance, all colonial powers as well as non-colonial European powers benefitted from the slave trade (both as a trade commodity and as a source of free labour) as a vital source of capital accumulation. The colonised countries provided also markets for manufactured goods from colonial powers (cf. Chapter 3).

Imperatively, *traditional mercantilism* is impracticable in today's world. True, the mercantilist notion that sustainable existence of a nation relies on power, while power depended on wealth, is still valid today. However, it is unimaginable that African countries would industrialise and develop by conquering other countries, and (1) using them as sources of de facto trade goods, including slaves, agricultural products, and mineral products, etc., (2) using them as sources of de facto *free* human labour, precious stones, and raw materials, (3) forbidding them to produce certain products (as colonial powers forbade colonies from producing products they could buy from the colonising power, (4) forbidding them from trading with any country other than the colonial power), (5) using them as markets for the manufactured goods, etc.

Moreover, industrialisation is propelled by multiple factors, which are not all ingrained in just having a mercantilist system. Hence, it is likely that mercantilism alone, without complementary measures such as technological change, domestic market integration, etc., would not have brought about industrialisation (cf. Chapter 3 on experiences of countries).

Neither does *neo-mercantilism* appear to be within reach of most African countries. In the open world and liberalised global economy of our time, there is a limit regarding the extent to which a country can effectively promote its own exports (e.g. through production and export subsidies), discourage imports from other countries, subsidise investments by local companies in foreign countries, control capital movements, and exercise currency controls. Many of the measures needed to fully exercise modern day mercantilism would be against the spirit of international economic liberalisation pursued bilaterally, through Regional Economic Agreements (RECs), and multilateral liberalisation. Therefore, even those states that have in our time been noted for their mercantilist stance, such as China, France, Japan, Singapore, etc., did only partially practice mercantilism. These states have largely accepted the market forces (cf. Nester 1991).

Moreover, from the classical and even the neo-classical trade theoretical perspectives,[3] considering the status of the continent's natural resource endowment, it would be rational to expect agricultural and mineral commodities to dominate production and constitute the overwhelming share of the exports of most African countries. Expressed in accordance with the basic construct of the various trade theories, the following scenarios would emerge:

a   Basing on classical theory, and following the *theory of absolute advantage*, a country should (produce and) export those products for which it is more productive than other countries. In return, it should import those products for which other countries are more productive than it is. Imperatively, for

most African counties, agricultural and mineral commodities would dominate production and constitute the overwhelming share of their exports.

The other basic lessons we learn from Adam Smith's classical growth
model (1776) are that capital, which is accumulated through savings, eventually stimulates growth through investments. Smith also recognised the
positive impact of knowledge and skills on the economic, political, and
social welfare of a country, and supported the publicly supported education
system. This is because specialisation increases the quality and efficiency of
labour, thereby impacting economic growth (cf. Table 11.1 in this chapter,
and Chapter 2 of this book).

b   Following the classical theory, ingrained in *David Ricardo's theory of comparative advantage*, agricultural and mineral commodities would dominate
production and constitute the overwhelming share of the exports of most
African countries. This is because the theory recommends that a country
produces and exports those products for which it is *relatively* more productive than other countries, and imports those products for which other countries are *relatively* more productive than it is.

c   Deriving from Heckscher-Ohlin's neo-classical theory, factor endowments
vary among countries. Also, the intensity of resource use differs from the
production of one product to another. Thus, a country will have an
advantage in producing products that intensively use resources (factors of
production) it has in abundance – and this should guide its specialisation in
production and trade. For most African countries, this will almost inevitably
mean specialising in the production and trade of agricultural products as
well as in artisanal mining, since the two factors that they seem to have in
abundance are land and unskilled labour.

A fundamental setback with the postulated and recommended patterns of specialisation – which has conspicuously directed the efforts for economic development
since the emergence of modern African nation states – is that they condemn
African countries to a detrimental position in the global economy. African countries are condemned to specialisation in the production of products, other than
those involving reasonable value adding, a kind of specialisation that will never
make them industrialise. And this is a challenge that even post-colonial African
countries have not been able to rise up to, even to this day.

There are further serious empirical challenges to two stripes of the 'traditional' or 'old' theories (also referred to as 'endowment-driven') of international
trade, i.e. classical and neo-classical theories. As may be deduced from the brief
explanations in the previous paragraphs, according to these theories, the flow of
goods between countries is determined by different manifestations of *comparative advantage* (i.e. differences in opportunity costs of production):
comparative advantage can arise because of (i) productivity differences (cf.
David Ricardo's or simply 'Ricardian' comparative advantage), (ii) a combination of cross-industry differences in factor intensity and cross-country differences in factor abundance (cf. 'Heckscher-Ohlin' comparative advantage). A key

implication of these theories is 'inter-industry trade': that is, countries will specialise in production and export according to industries or sectors. One sector will export, while another sector will import. In this constellation, there is no room for inter-industry trade of the kind usually seen between countries at the same level of development. This is a major caveat, since a large share of international trade is of 'intra-industry' nature: it takes place within industries and between relatively similar trading partners (cf. Grubel and Lloyd 1975).

11.2.2 Lessons embedded in firm-based trade theories

However, we also know that trade theory does recognise strategic competitive advantages, in which a country's trade pattern is not simply determined by which natural endowments it has. Rather, what matters is a combination of factors, in which besides natural resource endowment, acquired capacities (e.g. entrepreneurial capacities, infrastructural capacities, organisational or institutional capacities, and technological skills), as well as access to global factor and product markets play a significant role. As we know, this is the line taken by modern trade theories, as well as international investment theories.

Thus, inspired by the growing importance of international businesses, and the apparent deficiencies of country-based theories, the modern trade analysis theories, which are largely firm-based theories, emerged after the Second World War. This family of theories is attributed to business economists, and provides an explanation of intra-industry trade. Unlike country-based theories, they use several additional factors to explain trade flows: quality, technology, brand names, etc. Key theories in the group include: country similarity theory, product life cycle (PLC) theory, product differentiation theories, scale economies theories, global strategic rivalry (GSR) theory, and Porter's national competitive advantage theory.

Notably, according to the firm-based trade theories, a blend of factors leads firms to 'specialise' in distinct horizontal product varieties, impelling 'intra-industry' trade. These factors include, among other things, consumer preferences, economies of scale, economies of scope, PLC, technological differences. Imperatively, in contrast to the traditional trade theories, where the welfare gains arise from the *differences in opportunity costs of production across industries* and countries, in these 'new trade theories', such gains accrue from *multiple factors* that trade makes available to producers and consumers.

11.2.3 Lessons embedded in theories of 'stages of economic development'

The line of argument taken by the *theories of 'stages of economic development'* is that development comes stagewise. Although the theories' different proponents differ about how many stages there are, there is a general consensus that industrialisation is one of the critical stages that a country must achieve, so as to set on a path to critical levels of growth and development (cf. Marx 1848; Rostow 1960; Kaldor 1966, etc.).

Karl Marx (1848) identifies four stages of growth: (1) pure labour economy producing subsistence goods; (2) early capitalism based on handicraft technologies; (3) emergence of manufacture based on merchants and initial accumulation of capital; (4) modern industry ('machinofacture') based on the capitalist mode of production (cf. Chapter 2 of this book).

The Marxian analysis of economic growth and development leads to the conlcusion that, in order to industrialise, African countries must develop their *Financial Resources (FiR) capacities* through the mobilisation of capital, and the deployment of such capital by investing them in manufacturing, thereby building their capital stock. Moreover, *capitalist industrial entrepreneurship* is an essential factor in fostering modern industry.

According to Walt Rostow (1960), all countries pass through five stages of economic growth and development: (1) traditional society; (2) preconditions for take-off; (3) take-off; (4) drive to maturity; (5) the age of mass consumption. In this model, there exist three explicit pre-conditions for a country to take off and set on a sustainable economic growth and development path: achieve an investment threshold of at least 10 per cent of national income (in which case both domestic and foreign savings can be leveraged to provide investment, and thereby to increase capital stock), adopt a strategy of 'leading' manufacturing sector or sectors, and have in place a conducive framework (political, social, and institutional) to support the growth of the modern sector (cf. also Chapter 2 of this book).

Like Karl Marx (1848), Kaldor (1966) suggests the existence of four stages of economic growth and development: (1) emergence of a domestic consumer goods industry which substitutes for imported consumer goods; (2) development of domestic production of consumer goods, thereby providing the basis for positive net exports; (3) emergence of a domestic capital goods industry substitutes import of capital goods; (4) domestic production of capital good provides a basis for the exports of capital goods (cf. Chapter 2 of this book).

According to the pattern proposed in Kaldor's stages of economic growth model (1966), African countries will have to first develop a consumer goods industry to serve both import substitution and export goals, and then develop a capital goods industry for the same purpose.

A common denominator of the theories of stages of growth is that investments are needed, not only to develop productive infrastructures, but also in equipment and machinery, etc., needed for the production of consumer goods and capital goods. Expressed otherwise (depending on the preferred approach) mobilising and investing capital – in both *infrastructures* and *Social Overhead Capital (SOC)*,[4] as well as in *Direct Production Activities (DPAs)*[5] – to develop the *right sectors* or *strategic sectors* is a crucial link in this notion. Eventually, the leading sectors pull the other sectors through the *linkage effects*, i.e. backward and forward linkages (cf. Rostow 1960; Kaldor 1966; von Tunzelmann 1995; Argyrous 1996).

The overall conclusion is that the consolidation of domestic capacities to produce consumer and capital goods are necessry conditions for substituting imports, as well as for developing own export sectors.

11.2.4 Lessons embedded in 'balanced and unbalanced growth and development' theories

The theories of balanced and unbalanced economic growth and development are based on the existence of of non-linearity effects[6] in a country's industrial transformation process. Implicitly, the patterns of investments, production, and growth are not automatically determined. Instead, they rely on the sectoral concentration of investments, which in turn determines what is produced.

Therefore, the existence of non-linearity effects in growth necessitate interventions, in order to evade the trap of 'non-development'. Hence:

a   The quintessence of the theory is the assertion that the narrowness of markets and the limited market opportunities associated with them, constitute the main obstacles to economic growth and development.[7] Due to the low level of demand for 'modern' goods, there is no incentive for private investment in modern manufacturing sectors. Therefore, the scope for intervention is obvious. This market configuration dictates that only a bundle of complementary investments[8] realised at the same time has the chance of creating mutual demand. Consequently, the theory prioritises investments in sectors with high relations amongst supply, purchasing power, and demand. Government co-ordination and planning is needed, in order to ensure balanced growth (cf. Chapter 2).

Succinctly, the balanced growth theory underlines a 'big push' approach. Presumably, inchmeal investments will not create enough momentum to stir self-propelled and sustainable economic growth and development. It explicitly argues that there is a minimum threshold in terms of resources that must be committed to the process, to make it stand any chance of success. Accordingly, African countries need to mobilise and deploy critical masses of investments, so as to set on a sustainable *economic growth and development trajectory*. This is because ' "launching" a country into self-sustaining growth is a little like getting an airplane off the ground. There is a critical ground speed which must be passed before the craft can become airborne' (cf. Rosenstein-Rodan 1961). From these theories the essentiality of sound development finance for African countries is underlined.

b   When there is unbalanced growth, it becomes essential to identify the sectors that have strong backward and forward linkages, and can be competitive in the short term. The theory stresses the significance of basic and large scale industries in the process of economic growth and development. This in turn encourages the growth of consumer-goods industries, as well as the establishment of ancillaries, thereby generating all-round rises in employment and income. Also, unbalanced growth exerts pressures in the system, calling for new inventions and innovations (Hirschman 1958; Kaldor 1966, 1975). Though industrialisation is considered to lead to growth, state intervention[9] to set this process in motion is needed (cf. Chapter 2 of this book).

In a nutshell, consistent with the theory of unbalanced growth, African countries would be advised to designate and invest in *strategic sectors*, rather than in all sectors simultaneously. This is due to further assumptions that *other sectors* would automatically develop themselves through *forward and backward 'linkages effects'*.

11.2.5 Lessons embedded in Keynesian growth theory

The Keynesian growth model or *Harrod–Domar growth model*, is accredited to Harrod (1939) and Domar (1946). Popularly known as the Harrod–Domar model, it portrays growth as a function of the accumulation of investible capital, which in turn is determined by such exogenous variables as saving rate, population growth, etc. The investments implicitly embrace both investments in infrastructures, and investments (in capital-intensive) production sectors. Also essential are: government policies to stimulate necessary capital investment, and public investment to redress decreasing rate of investment (cf. Chapter 2 of this book).

In this constellation, growth in African countries would be possible, even in the case of limited FiR capacities due to low saving rates, as it can be propelled by 'exogenous increase' in savings (leading to exogenous increase in the accumulation of capital).

11.2.6 Lessons embedded in neoclassical growth theories

Several scholars have contributed to the neoclassical growth theory, which also sought to shed light on the phenomenon of growth (cf. Swan 1956; Solow 1957, etc.). As described in Chapter 2 of this book, in addition to capital as the source of growth, the Solow (1957) model added labour, and technology progress. Also relevant are those policies that stimulate the existence of competitive markets, rather than investments per se.

For African countries, this means that accumulation of capital stock, though a necessary condition for growth, will not be sufficient but need to be complemented by the development of technological capacities, as well as the knowledge and skills of labour. Also, governments should create and sustain the necessary conditions for the existence of competitive markets.

11.2.7 Lessons embedded in modern views on economic growth and development

The *modern views on economic growth and development* which can also be referred to as *modern economic growth and development theories* are divided further into two groups. The first group comprises *modern growth theories*, i.e. New Growth Theory (NGT), structural change growth model, evolutionary growth models, and unified growth theory, and political economy models.

The second group embraces views emerging from the *contemporary theoretical debate of international trade and growth*, which have been advanced by several leading scholars like Funke and Ruhwedel (2001); Hidalgo *et al.* (2007);

Saviotii and Frenken (2008); Hidalgo and Hausman (2008, 2009); Grauwe *et al.* (2010); Fuchs *et al.* (2011), von Hagen and Gabriela (2011), Felipe *et al.* (2012). In Chapter 2 of this book, Ciarli and di Maio give a useful account of the pertinent issues and lessons.

11.2.8 General verdict on lessons embedded in various theories

The postulations associated with each of the theories discussed in sub-sections 11.2.1 and 11.2.7 contribute to better comprehension of the determinants of production and trade patterns. This in turn leads to better understanding of the factors behind competitive positioning of countries in the global economy, taking into account the role that the industrial sector plays in this connection.

Imperatively, in the architecture of Africa's industrialisation strategy, it is, at long last, time to heed the renowned fact: to advance beyond primordial and rather rudimentary thinking about what is needed to propel economic transformation. The evolution of the various theories and their practical applications suggest what countries need to do, so as to efficiently manage the industrial development process. *As a general verdict, we can hypothesise the following linkages*:

a   While the theoretical narrations on industrial development are generally true, no one theory is self-sufficient in explaining the process. In reality, while each theory gives useful hints about how countries become competitive in investments, production, and trade, no single theory can exhaustively explain the pertinent factors. Invariably, each is incomplete if taken in isolation. However, taken together, the various theories comprehensively complement each other, giving a broad picture of the factors that are accountable for the industrial development disparities between countries.

b   The validity of each argument is not static, so that what was valid in the world of David Ricardo may not necessarily be valid in today's world. Therefore, each theory has got to be interpreted in the context of time and other constraining factors, which determine its validity in a given cultural and socio-economic constituency.

11.3 Stylised facts about the determinants of industrialisation from country reviews

Which general lessons can we derive from the past and recent success stories of industrialisation by countries, and use in designing a strategy for leveraging Africa–EU partnership for industrial transformation? Several key observations can be distilled from the anatomies of industrial transformation of nations. In this connection, the narrations in the previous sub-sections (cf. Chapter 3 of this book) link successful industrialisation to a number of characteristics stemming from the industrialising country's economic history. Accordingly, countries succeeded in their industrialisation endeavours because they provided a *regime of conducive factors* for not only investing in industrial production, but also systematically increasing industrial productivity. The regime blended the following factors:

a   Conducive policies and other frameworks (e.g. strategies, laws and regulations, programmes, etc.) of an integrated governance system for stimulating industrialisation.
b   Domestic market integration, through creation of centralised unitary nation states.
c   Flexible, and in particular, pragmatic use of ideology to stimulate industrialisation.
d   Building of critical masses of essential physical infrastructure.
e   Presence of active public and private sector institutions advocating industrialisation.
f   Development of dynamic and diversified industrial entrepreneurship.
g   Systematic accumulation of industrial knowledge and skills.
h   Accumulation of savings and deployment of financial resources into industrialisation.
i   Existence of a favourable cultural milieu.
j   Harnessing the catalytic effects of international economic co-operation at various levels (i.e. bilateral co-operation, regional integration, multilateral co-operation) embracing various aspects, such as investments, trade, capacity development.
k   Focusing the development of vital capacities for industrialisation at the country level.

These factors (or drivers of the industrialisation process) can be seen as the *fundamentals of sustainable economic transformation and growth*. Throughout history, they have played and continue to play key roles, although their actual blending may have differed from one country to another, taking into account its particularities. Their net joint effects are the creation of favourable climate for industrial activities across the entire value chain: from the development of domestic saving potentials (which is essential for the mobilisation of FiR capacities), to the mobilisation of resources from external sources (for investment into industrial development), to the deployment (i.e. actual investments) of those resources, to the pattern and dynamics of industrial production, to the pattern and dynamics of industrial trade.

Chapter 3 of this book gives detailed narrations about the pertinent factors.

11.3.1 Essentiality of conducive framework to guide the process of industrialisation

The governance framework no doubt influences the growth of economic activity and relative economic position. In the context of the analysis in this book, the *governance framework* (cf. also references to this technical term in Chapters 4,

5, 6, 11, 13, and 14) is defined broadly, so that it goes beyond the *policy frame-work* and embraces diverse 'public instruments':

a   *Long-term development vision* from which policy instruments are drawn;
b   *Policies* needed to translate the long-term development vision into action;
c   *Strategies* needed to guide the implementation of policies;
d   *Laws and regulations* to implement policies – that are also essential for the implementation of policies:
e   *Appropriate ideological framework, i.e. (a) to (d)* should happen within the context of a supportive *ideological framework*, which outlines the broad development philosophy and from the long-term development vision and policies are derived.

Therefore, a common defining aspect of early industrialisers, follower industrialisers, and newly industrialising countries has been the ability to design and implement governance frameworks that stimulate high rates of investment in industrial productive capacities, as has been demonstrated in different studies (Singh 1995; Akyuz and Gore 1996; Naughton 2010).

In many developing countries, the supportive governance frameworks have included provisions on the organisation of economic production activities, e.g. through the establishment of (different stripes of) Export Processing Zones (EPZ) in such countries as China, South Korea, Mexico, and Mauritius, etc.

Also, country capacities (at sectoral and macroeconomic levels) are crucial for investment, production, and for international trade competitiveness; of the firms in that country as well as for the country as a whole. Insights related to this fact are expressed and implied in the many country-focused theories of international trade, as well as international trade theories. Such factors as financial resource capacities, infrastructural capacities, knowledge and skills capacities, organisational (or institutional) capacities, physical infrastructural capacities, and technological capacities provide the right business environment in which enterprise can flourish and develop competitive advantages to invest, produce, and trade. In this case as well, the development and sustenance of these capacities are essential, and need heavy and sustained investments.

Another useful feature of the governance framework has been policies propagating economic openness through RECs and multilateral liberalisation, and bilateral arrangements; thereby prompting inward globalisation of industry. This globalisation manifests itself through great degrees of influence held by outside actors in domestic economic development processes. In successful cases of industrialisation, the inward globalisation of industry has been mutually beneficial.

The inward globalisation experienced in the context of the *Japanese-led flying-geese model* (cf. also subsection 11.5.2.1), *EU-led upgrading of industry through integration process* (cf. subsection 11.5.2.2), *Chinese-led bamboo capitalism* (cf. subsection 11.5.2.3), *US support in the industrialisation of South Korea* (cf. subsection 11.5.2.4), present cases of mutually beneficial openness. In contrast, the inward globalisation of industry experienced by the African countries in the context of their association with their EU partners present a case of openness that has systematically benefited one member at the expense of the other (cf. subsection 11.5.1). The main caveat is that it has perpetuated a hierarchical structural complementarity in which the underdeveloped African countries continue to be suppliers of largely agricultural and mineral raw materials to the industrialised EU economies.

11.3.2 Ideology and content of industrialisation strategy: an ideology mix

Consistent with evolution in theory, the strategies pursued by different countries towards industrialisation have been categorised into:

a   Market-driven industrialisation strategy, on the one extreme.
b   State-driven industrialisation strategy, on the other extreme.
c   In between the two extremes are the various stripes of *structuralist industrialisation strategies*, whose common denominator is that they blend elements of market-driven and state-driven strategies (though of course, to various extents). The structuralist industrialisation strategy is essentially state-led industrialisation. Its hallmark is a greater involvement of the government in the industrialisation process, beyond just the provision of conducive environment. In addition to providing a viable governance framework, the state becomes an active and one of the most significant actors in the mobilisation and deployment of (diverse) resources (financial and otherwise) to support the industrialisation process. The essentiality of the government's involvement in the creation of capital stock is in line with observations from empirical studies that non-military public capital stock does indeed improve the productivity of the economy (Aschauer 1988).

Those countries, which are now developed, as well as those countries that are still categorised as developing, have initiated and pursued industrialisation efforts, regardless of the dominant ideology. In actual fact, measured by the role and nature of the state in the process, all the pioneers of industrialisation from the capitalist west (United Kingdom, Germany, France, etc.) to the socialist economies (Russia, etc.) used this approach to realise their ambitions for industrialisation. More recently, in Korea and Singapore, which are seen as models of modern industrial development, the state played a key role in the industrialisation strategy.

Though the performance discrepancy might be a function of government intervention and therefore has an ideological connotation, none of the successful industrialisation strategies has been purely market-driven or purely state-driven, but has as a matter of necessity been a combination of both, and therefore essentially a hybrid.

Yet, the question regarding which issues to emphasise is a question of economic management practices. Apart from mirroring the capacity differences (intellectual and otherwise) among the governments of the individual economies, it determines their performances.

11.3.3 Centrality of infrastructural capacities in the industrialisation process

As part of the investment-driven industrialisation process, countries systematically developed their infrastructural capacities (often, ahead of demand and therefore risking overcapacity). Hence, they built transport infrastructure (e.g. airports, harbours, railways, roads, etc.), energy infrastructure (e.g. generation of electricity), telecommunication infrastructure, etc. The development of infrastructural capacities has been extremely essential in reducing the business transaction costs. For instance, better telecommunications infrastructure reduces the costs of communication and information gathering, thus facilitating business activities.

From an ideological point of view, this interventionist approach in infrastructural capacity development would appear to breach the laws of market-driven allocation of resources, and may lead (at least in the short-term) to over-capacity. However, the actions of governments in the real world have been quite pragmatic and – regardless of their ideological stance – they have intervened to develop and sustain critical masses of infrastructural capacities. The role of the governments is essential, considering the absolute essentiality of infrastructure for industrialisation, the 'public good' character of major infrastructures, and the lack of incentive and inability of the private sector to efficiently and timely provide them.

11.3.4 Essentiality of anchoring sustainable capacities at national level

There is no evidence that any country has managed to develop industrially without developing the essential productive capacities at the national level. Implicitly, though a country may benefit by leveraging capacities beyond the national level (e.g. regional co-operation programmes, inter-regional co-operation programmes, multilateral support programmes), those capacities cannot be *in lieu* of capacities at the national level. Therefore, the primary focus in the development of FiR and Non-Financial Resources (NFiR) capacities must be at the level of individual countries.

11.3.5 Leveraging investment partnerships with more advanced countries

The path to industrialisation, particularly in follower economies, clearly appears to have also benefitted from the existence of investments relations between the less advanced economies and more advanced economies. However, in order for such investments to bear the desired fruits, they must be mutually beneficial, i.e. to benefit the investors as well as the host country.

A special manifestation of mutually beneficial partnership between less and more advanced countries is encapsulated in the *flying geese model* (Akamatsu 1962; Kwan 2002). The model is based on the extension of economic dynamism first from Japan to the Asian Newly Industrialising Economies (NIEs), and then to Association of South East Asian Nations (ASEAN) countries, and eventually to China. Thus, industrialisation is driven by the following:

a   Countries specialise in the export of products in which they enjoy a comparative advantage commensurate with their levels of development.
b   The less developed countries engage in the upgrading of their industrial structures by augmenting their endowment of capital and technology.
c   Foreign Direct Investment (FDI) flows from the more advanced countries to the less developed ones, in the form of relocation of industries.

The contribution of the Japanese-led East Asian economic transformation (of an entire region) did partly leverage the benefits of regional integration.

The other two cases of mutual investment partnerships, though of probably less magnitude, refer to the investment relationships between the USA and its two cold war allies, i.e. South Korea and Chinese Taipei (i.e. Taiwan).

In this connection, the leveraging of mutually beneficial investment partnerships between a less advanced and a more advanced country is made possible through dynamic interplays of their economic relations. Concretely, the less advanced (catching-up) economy benefits from mutual interaction with a more advanced (leading) economy. The benefits are realised through inter-national investments, and international trade; with spin-offs in the form of transfer of knowledge and skills, as well as technology (Xing 2007).

11.3.6 Leveraging aid from more advanced countries for industrial development

The path to industrialisation, particularly in follower economies, clearly appears to have also benefitted from aid. Hence, apart from industrial FDI, countries like Chinese Taipei and South Korea did benefit from aid – which was used for the creation of industrial productive capacities. For instance, from 1952 to 1962, on average around 69 per cent of Korean imports were financed through US aid. Overall, between 1952 and 1980, USAID and its predecessor agency provided US$ 18.7 billion (at constant 2009 prices and exchange rates) to Korea (cf. www.usaid/locations/asia).

11.3.7 Political leadership

Political leadership is an essential dimension of any successful industrialisation strategy. This is because the political leaders are the ones who stay at the top of a system that mobilises and deploys diverse resources for development. They oversee the design and implementation of an effective integrated governance framework, as well as the programmes for the development of FiR capacities and NFiR capacities. Hence, whether in Europe, in America, in Asia, or in Africa, resolute political leadership has been behind every successful industrial transformation episode. This is true of the UK, Japan, USA, South Korea and all other cases.

One of the most cited exemplary roles of political leadership behind an economic transformation success story is South Korea. As in the case of any country, state intervention was necessary to stimulate South Korea's industrial transformation, and overall economic growth and development. Moreover, the country's capacity gaps (both in terms of FiR and NFiR) conferred on the state a great responsibility in ensuring that industrialisation through learning was successful, and that development was sustainable. The country's leader from 1961 to 1979, Park Chung-Hee, is credited to have had a strong political resolve and commitment to create a thriving South Korean state, and to have set in motion a process that has since then been unremittingly carried forward by his successors (cf. Evans *et al.* 1985; Heywood 2013).

In contrast, the overall picture is conspicuously grim in African countries. Historical and contemporary developments show that often Africa's development aspirations are betrayed by a lack of visionary, committed, and resolute political leadership for the achievement of specific objectives. Leadership with a purpose usually ceases once leaders take up office.

11.3.8 Inevitability of institutions

To set on successful industrialisation trajectories, countries from all corners of the world have benefittted from the establishment of appropriate country-specific institutions. Implicitly, in order to achieve the industrialisation aspirations, African countries need, among other things, institutions that will enable them to support the industrial development process by addressing organisational-related macroeconomic and microeconomic impediments to investments in diverse capacities.

11.3.9 Inevitability of knowledge and skills capacities

Expertise in the form of knowledge and skills capacities is essential for the process of industrial transformation. Tasks in industrial production jobs need knowledgable and skilled labour. Also, a country's knowledge and skills capacities enhance the prospects for innovation.

Moreover, these capacities are essential for *industrialisation by learning*. On the technological and knowledge frontier, innovators develop and market new technology. However, the experiences of late comer industrialisation show that industrialisation is achieved through learning. Literally in every country, in the initial stages of the process of systematic industrial transformation, firms leverage existing technologies and knowledge to propel *industrialisation by learning*. This means that a country's firms develop competitiveness on the basis of borrowed or imitated technology. The technology is first made operational and later optimised (cf. Amsden 1989; Heywood 2013).

Legal means of accessing foreign technology include technical assistance (TA), licensing arrangements with technology owners, etc. Many countries have benefitted and continue to benefit from these types of arrangements. In the case of South Korea, for instance, foreign licences resulted in greater economic returns. In addition, restrictions of market entry by multinational organisations helped to make industrial transformation organic.

Like other latecomers, industrialisation latecomers face challenges of scale, scope, financial resources, non-financial resources, skills, entrepreneurial capacities, support organisations (institutions), etc. Depending on how the industrialisation process is managed, industrialisation by learning enables them to circumvent some or even all of these barriers. Among the merits attributed to *industrialisation by learning* are: borrowing technology, borrowing expertise (i.e. knowledge and skills). This way, they avoid invention costs, which are sunk costs (cf. also So 1990; Heywood 2013).

11.3.10 Dynamic entrepreneurship

Entrepreneurial capacities are essential for integration in the global industrial economy, from investments, to production, to international trade. This fact is expressed and implied in the many firm-based theories of international trade, as well as international investment theories. Invariably, economic transformation will not commence in earnest unless enterprises in a country, in their role as the key drivers of economic development, have capacities that make them viable actors in the international investment, production, and trading systems. The development and sustenance of these capacities, which is essential, needs heavy and sustained investments.

Essential industrial entrepreneurship traits include: industrial business start-ups, population of industrial enterprises, sizes of industrial enterprises, sub-sectoral distribution of industrial investments and enterprises, value chain positioning of industrial enterprises, etc.

11.3.11 Stimulating effect of regional integration

Regional integration is associated with direct economic benefits, as well as indirect economic benefits (or non-economic benefits). The former category of benefits is divided into static gains, dynamic gains, and some derivative gains. The latter group of gains is associated with the way the bloc created by countries in an integration scheme can be used to pursue diverse other goals.

11.3.11.1 Direct economic benefits

The Customs Union (CU) theory stands at the centre of the debate of the direct economic benefits, attributed to trade-driven regional integration. This is due to the fact that the first attempts to scholarly explain the economic utility of trade-driven regional integration evolved through CU theory, whose seed was planted by Swiss-American Economist Jacob Viner in the 1950s (cf. Viner 1950). Since then, the original classic CU theory by Viner has been refined to account for *intra-industry trade* (IIT), *economy of scale*, *market size*, and *Non-Tariff Barriers (NTBs)*.

The observed rapid rates of economic growth and development of the member states of the European Economic Community (EEC), and the European Free

Trade Association (EFTA) in the 1960s appeared to corroborate the theoretical postulations that indeed, regional integration positively impacted on the level and growth of economic activity, and thereby on economic development (cf. Brada and Mendez 1995, 1998).

In the current understanding, the gains associated with regional integration can be divided into at least three groups. The two basic groups of gains are those associated with *static effects of integration*, and *dynamic effects of integration*. Besides, there are *derivative gains associated with policy discipline* (i.e. anchoring-in or locking-in policy reforms) and *upwards convergence* of the less advanced members of the economic bloc (to catch up with the more advanced members of the bloc). These following subsections give further elaborations of these gains.

A STATIC GAINS

Building on a set of simple assumptions, in what is referred to as the *orthodox customs theory*, Jacob Viner mainly explained the static effects of regional integration.[10] These are the welfare gains, which result from a one-time reallocation of resources like land, labour, and capital. The static effects depend on the relative trade size, *Trade Creation* (TC) and *Trade Diversion* (TD).

TC occurs when, following tariff reduction in the Regional Trade Agreement (RTA) (which leads to reduction of prices), intra-RTA imports displace less efficient domestic production. TC is stimulated by price and cost advantages of larger markets. In the basic formulation, it can algebraically be computed as:

$$TC = \left(E_m * M^{TP} \right) * \left(\frac{T_1 - T_2}{T_0} \right). \tag{1}$$

In the estimation of *TC*; M^{TP}, E_m, and $\left(\frac{T_1 - T_0}{T_0} \right)$ denote the current volume of imports from current commercial partners (given domestic price P and tariff T), elasticity of import demand (i.e. a percentage change in the demand for imports, when the price of the imports on the domestic market increase by a small percentage), and the change in tariff (given the pre- and post-liberalisation rates of T_0 and T_1) respectively.[11]

Moreover, Viner (1950) contrasted these static gains through TC with static losses attributed to TD. TD may happen in the case of a member state switching consumption of lower cost products imported from outside the RTA to higher costs produced within the region (which can trade, because they face lower tariffs after integration). It can be algebraically estimated using the following basic equation:

$$TDD = \frac{\left(M * M^O * \left(\frac{\delta RP}{RP} * E_s \right) \right)}{M^{TP} + M^O + M^{TP} * \left(\frac{\delta RP}{RP} * E_s \right)}. \tag{2}$$

In the estimation, M^{TP} is as specified in equation 1. E_s, M^O, RP, and δRP denote elasticity of substitution between imports from a partner economy and the rest of the world, imports before liberalisation, relative price, change in relative price. TD is generally welfare reducing, although this may not always be the case. The higher the E_s, the higher the *TD*. The loss from TD is due to the reduction in government revenue as imports from outside the RTA (facing higher tariffs) are replaced by imports from within the region (facing lower or no tariffs) (see Radelet 1997).

Accordingly the net effects of the two dynamics imply net welfare effects and are given by

Net Welfare Effects $= TC - TD$. (3)

Subsequently, the original classic customs union theory by Viner was refined to account for IIT, *economy of scale, market size*, and NTBs.

There is at least an indirect link between TC and industrialisation, as the additional trade revenues can be invested in various capacities that are essential for industrial development.

B DYNAMIC EFFECTS OF INTEGRATION

The dynamic gains of integration stem from the impact that RTAs have on productive capacities, and thereby on the output of a given economy or economic bloc. Several studies give useful hints on how this happens (cf. Balasa 1961; Robson 1987; Langhammer and Hiemenz 1990; de la Torre and Kelly 1992; Radelet 1997; Matambalya 2011). Among other things, integration:

a Stimulates shifts in investments that enhance productive capacities, and thereby expand production. Usually, investments are both increased and more efficiently allocated. The overall gains are often manifested by net increases in economic activity in the region.
b Because the integration process unifies the market for products (i.e. goods and services), and for factors of production (i.e. capital and labour), it encourages a process of *equalisation of factor prices*[12] *and factor returns*, due to free movement of factors of production. This makes the cost of factors of production cheaper.

Overall, because of their associations with investments in the creation of essential productive capacities. which in turn are crucial for the exploitation of the opportunities of enlarged markets, the dynamic effects of regional integration are extremely important for a country's industrial transformation endeavours. The challenge is in ensuring that the new investments actually create and/or enhance the relevant capacities.

The estimation of dynamic effects of regional integration is a more challenging and still evolving field. In practice, different theoretical models have been developed and used.

These models are quite useful. However, it is also reasonable to stress the need for an all-inclusive estimation of the dynamic effects of integration. Such estimation would need to capture and explain the impact of integration on the development of the entire range of FiR capacities: development of banks and Non-Bank Financial Institutions (NBFIs) mobilisation of financial resources from diverse sources, creation of financial instruments appropriate for different financing needs, etc. Also, it will require capturing and explaining the impact of integration on diverse NFiR capacities: entrepreneurial capacities, knowledge and skills capacities, institutional (organisational) capacities, physical infrastructural capacities, and technological capacities.

C DERIVATIVE GAINS OF POLICY DISCIPLINE AND UPWARDS CONVERGENCE

Successful integration schemes, particularly in the case of the EU and to a lesser extent the case of North American Free Trade Area (NAFTA), reveals that apart from the conventional *static gains* and *dynamic gains*, the economic benefits of integration include *lock-in effects*: policy discipline amongst the members of the RTA provides a stable investment environment, and improves the prospects for long-term capital formation, production, and economic growth.

Likewise, there are gains in terms of upward convergence. Imperatively, the relatively less advanced amongst the participating economies will tend to benefit through convergence towards higher levels of output and higher rates of economic growth, which can be harnessed to improve the economic welfare of individuals and institutions.

D NET DIRECT ECONOMIC EFFECTS OF INTEGRATION

In combination, the static and dynamic effects are directly associated with the following:

a   They stimulate the convergence of the growth rates of the member economies towards higher per capita incomes.

b   To the extent that they build local productive capacities, they enable the countries participating in the scheme to integrate more competitively in the global economy.

c   To the extent that they advocate local economic development, they enable the countries to integrate more meaningfully in the global economy.

11.3.11.2 Non-economic benefits or 'indirect' economic benefits

Literature recognises other gains, which though of a non-economic nature, can have indirect economic benefits. Thus, regional integration can be leveraged for regional dialogue, which may help to pursue common political governance, peace, security, and foreign policy objectives. In the same context, members of a regional bloc can harness regional integration for broader international negotiations, in which context their leverage increases compared to negotiations involving single states (cf. Pomfreat and Toren 1980; Langhammer and Hiemenz 1990; Winters 2007).

11.4 Stylised facts about the role of manufacturing in industrialisation-led economic growth and development

Which general lessons can we derive concerning industrialisation as the driver of economic growth and development, and use in designing a strategy for leveraging Africa–EU partnership for industrial transformation? As in the case of anatomies of the industrial transformation of countries, several lessons crystallise from the findings of the empirical studies of the linkages between industrialisation and economic growth and development.

11.4.1 Relationship between aggregate growth and industrial growth

One of the primary evidences arising from the summarised empirical studies is that in the real world situation, aggregate growth is, logically, related to the rate of expansion of the sector with the most favourable growth characteristics. In this context, the industrial economic activities seem to play a special role, particularly through manufacturing. There seems to be a close association across countries between the level of per capita income and the degree of industrialisation, and there also seems to be a close association across countries between the growth of Gross Domestic Product (GDP) and the growth of manufacturing industry. At all epochs of history, the countries with the highest economic growth rates were simultaneously those where the share of industry in GDP was rising most rapidly: this is true of the UK as the leader of the industrial revolution, the early followers (Germany, other European countries), the late followers (Japan, Korea), the countries that in the current nomenclature are referred to as 'newly industrialising countries' (NICs) or emerging economies or even BRICS (Brazil, Russia, India, China, and South Africa).

It is hard to argue convincingly that these associations between manufacturing activity and economic growth and development are accidental. Instead, there is a credible case here where manufacturing industry is indeed the engine of growth and development. Important theoretical contributions are contained in many ground-breaking arguments: Nicholas Kaldor (1966, 1967, 1981), Albert Hirschman (1958). Also countless empirical studies corroborate the offered theoretical arguments (see Kuznets 1973; Chenery *et al.* 1986; Targetti and Thirlwall 1989, etc.).

Overall, it is hard to comprehend the economic transformation process without taking a sectoral approach that distinguishes between increasing returns activities on the one hand (which are associated with industry) and diminishing returns activities. Hence, (as also further evidenced in the analysis of the relationship between industrial development and economic development in Chapter 4) there appears to be no serious challenge to the three famous laws by Kaldor that:

a   The faster the growth of manufacturing, the faster the rate of economic growth of the overall system.
b   There exists a strong positive causal relation between the rate of growth of manufacturing output and the rate of growth of manufacturing productivity.
c   Aggregate productivity is positively associated with the growth of employment in the manufacturing sector.

This may appear to be contrary to the neoclassical approach to economic growth, and its offspring 'new' growth theory, which are not only very supply-oriented, treating factor supplies as exogenously given, but are also very aggregative. They treat all sectors of the economy as if they are alike. They do not explicitly pick out any one sector as more important than another.

11.4.2 Transformation can be realised through different industrial activity patterns

A conspicuous lesson from the experiences of developing countries is that industrial transformation can be triggered by different industrial activity patterns. Table 11.2 highlights the key activities driving industrial transformation in a cross-section of developing countries. Hence, both broad diversification (as in the case of China) and prioritisation (as in the case of Chile, Malaysia, and Mauritius) deliver the goods.

However, as pointed out by the United Nations (UN) in its report *Industrial Development for the 21st Century: Sustainable Development Perspectives* (UN 2007), diversification is a key correlate of economic development, and invariably economic development requires diversification, not specialisation. This is supported by empirical observations that poor countries produce a relatively narrow range of goods, while richer countries are engaged in a broad range of economic activities (including a broad range of industrial activities). Thus, though a viable

Table 11.2 Main activities driving industrial transformation in selected countries

Country	Sub-sectors driving industrial transformation
Chile	Natural resource-driven industrialisation, based on agro-industrial clusters
China	Broadly diversified industrialisation
Malaysia	• Electrical equipment • Electronic equipment
Mauritius	• Clothing and textiles • Tourism

Source: Based on UN (2007).

strategy may be based on product prioritisation initially, it will need to provide for systematic diversification of industrial production activities to cover more sectors and products over time.

11.5 Lessons on the links between international co-operation and industrial development

The tasks involved in developing capacities that are needed for an industrial take-off pose formidable challenges for countries that have weak FiR and NFiR capacities. However, international partnerships provide tools for dealing with these challenges.

The resolution adopted by the General Assembly 35/66 adopted by 'The Third General Conference of the United Nations Industrial Development Organisation' (cf. UN 1980), brings to the point the essence of industrial co-operation in development. It, among other things:

a   Stipulates the redeployment of industrial capacities in the context of international industrial co-operation. Hence, the deployment of resources and technology transfers should help to establish and strengthen the productive capacities of developing countries with a view to stimulating their economies. The process should take into account the potential of developing countries to develop their national resources in conformity with the overall national objectives and priorities and the need to increase their share in world industrial production.

b   Emphasises the need to facilitate the restructuring of world industrial production:

- Supporting increased industrial production in developing countries;
- Extending special and differential treatment to developing countries, where feasible and appropriate, in the context of a general effort to liberalise world trade;
- Liberalising trade to increased market access.

c   Urges the international community to consider concrete measures for restructuring world industrial production. The restructuring exercise should seek to establish a more effective international division of labour which would, among other things:

- Facilitate the redeployment of industry;
- Expand and strengthen the industrial capacities of developing countries;
- Promote the domestic industrial processing of the natural resources of developing countries.

But to which extent have these pleads and pledges been heeded? What have been the practicalities and results of international co-operation for industrial development? A survey of the legacies of selected (key) international economic initiatives should shed light.

11.5.1 Legacy of African–EU co-operation arrangements: lack of coherence between trade and economic growth and development?

The analyses carried out elsewhere in this book provide sound bases for under-standing the legacy of the industrial developmental impact of African–EU co-operation arrangements. In this connection, Chapters 9 and 10 outline the industrial co-operation provisions applicable for the African countries in the African, Caribbean, and Pacific group of countries (AACP) associated with the EU, and Maghreb countries respectively. Moreover, useful insights of the indus-trial performance of African countries are provided in Chapter 4.

In making a judgement about the legacy of African–EU co-operation arrange-ments, at least two issues must be considered:

a   The departure point is that industrial development has always been part of the agenda for co-operation between the EU and their African partners from Sub-Saharan Africa (SSA) (cf. Chapter 9) as well as the Maghreb (cf. Chapter 10). The ostensible goals of the co-operation have been to promote economic growth and development through industrial transformation.

For the SSA countries, traditionally, the industrial co-operation agenda formed part of the broad framework of co-operation between the EU on the one hand, and the Africa, Caribbean, and Pacific (ACP) group of countries, on the other hand (cf. Chapter 9 of this book for a detailed overview). Parallel but different arrangements existed for the Arab Maghreb countries of North Africa (cf. Chapter 10 of this book for a detailed overview).

b   The developmental impact of any development co-operation regime must be judged against the actual successes on the ground.

Now, in spite of the many decades of co-operation, the SSA countries and their sister states from the Arab Maghreb belong to the least industrialised countries in world (cf. Chapter 4 for detailed overviews). The asymmetrical nature of the Afri-can–EU partnership created de facto lopsided dependence of the former to the latter. Invariably, unlike the Japan-inspired East Asian industrialisation through the 'flying-geese' model, the avidly detailed support programmes of the EU have not been able to deliver the expected development results in both African regions.

Altogether, considering that both trade and the broader development agenda (necessarily embracing industrialisation) have been pillars of subsequent Afri-can–EU co-operation arrangements, this suggests that coherence lacked between the two. Ideally, this coherence could only be provided through the industrial co-operation programmes. This is because a well designed and vigorously imple-mented industrial co-operation regime would have ensured that the African countries develop productive capacities, which are essential to enable them to exploit the Market Access (MA) provisions provided by the trade regime.

11.5.2 Legacy of other international economic co-operation initiatives

It is equally important to digest the legacy of the industrial developmental impact of other international economic co-operation arrangements. Though this subject has not been addressed by a separate chapter in this book, we can draw important conclusions from some facts at hand. Five examples are worth examining here: the Japan-led 'flying-geese' industrialisation model, upgrading industry in Europe through EU integration process, the China-centred 'bamboo capitalism' industrialisation model, implications of USA–South Korea co-operation for the latter's industrialisation, and the emerging lessons from the evolving China–Africa co-operation on the latter's industrialisation.

11.5.2.1 Japan-led East Asian industrialisation through the 'flying-geese' model

As a prelude to understanding its role in the political economy of East Asia's industrial relations, it is crucial to know that Japan was the only country in the region that industrialised much earlier. Besides, the country emulated the European model of imperialism, which led it to conquer and colonise its East Asian neighbours.

The 'flying-geese' model of regional economic integration is attributed to the Japanese economist, Kaname Akamatsu (1935, 1937, 1962). It was later elaborated and expanded notably by Kojima (1960, 1970, 1995). Accordingly the 'flying-geese' model predicates the lead role of the developed country in promoting and spreading industrialisation to the less developed countries through their economic integration. As characterised by Hiley (1999: 81):

> the economic growth of the developing countries is explained through mutual interaction between developing and developed countries based on leadership and emulation. The paradigm presupposes dynamic changes in economic relations among advanced (leading) and developing (catching-up) countries.... The basic idea of the paradigm is that a developing country, in an open market context, industrialises and goes through industrial upgrading, step by step, by capitalising on the learning opportunities made available through its external relations with the more advanced world.

The first experimentation with the flying-geese model occurred during Japan's colonisation of its East Asian neighbours. The Chinese revolution of 1949 and Japan's defeat in the Second World War put an end to this experiment. Nevertheless, there is an important lesson to learn from the experience. In what marks a major distinction from European colonisation of, for instance Africa, Japan as an imperial power, located modern heavy and light industries in its colonies: steel, chemicals, hydroelectric facilities, railways, roads, rice mills, textile factories, smelters, oil refineries, shipyards in Korea, and some heavy industries in Manchuria where even today China's heavy industry still is located (Xing 2007).

Concerning its practical application after the Second World War, the model implies that the East Asian countries are flying together, in tiers of countries signifying the different stages of economic development achieved. Japan as the leading goose led the second tier of relatively less developed countries which, in their turn, are followed by the third tier comprising the least developed countries (Xing 2007).

Apparently, the process allows for countries at the higher levels of the ladder to pass over their technologies and industries at the lower levels (Xing 2007). A direct consequence of this phenomenon is that the region has serially produced new significant players in the global economy, as more and more countries advance their industrial competitiveness. Thus:

a   In the first wave, the leading goose, Japan, modernised its economy after the *Meiji* Revolution during the second half of the nineteenth century.
b   The second wave involved four NIEs, which came to be known as the 'four tigers': Hong Kong, Singapore, South Korea, and Taiwan.
c   The third wave embraced ASEAN countries: Indonesia, Malaysia, Thailand, Philippines.
d   The fourth wave of industrialisation involves largely China.
e   The fifth wave includes yet another group of ASEAN countries, the late industrialisers: Vietnam, Lao People's Democratic Republic (PDR), Myanmar, etc.

The realisation of the flying-geese model relied also on access to the rest of the world, as markets, and as suppliers of raw material. Moreover, as members of the western economic bloc, these 'geese' enjoyed the benefits from the US-led global capitalist system (Xing 2007).

Otherwise, the concrete factors, which within the framework of the flying-geese model have enabled East Asian economies to set on the industrialisation path can be summed up as follows:

a   Economic openness.
b   Strong government guidance of the private economy. Invariably, the East Asian model generally accepts government's role in industrialisation and widely practices industrial policy, alongside state industrial entrepreneurship.
c   *Regional division of labour (both horizontal and vertical).* The vertical division of labour follows a pattern in which the advanced economies are the host countries for technologies and high-tech industries, whereas the less developed economies are the suppliers of cheap labour and resources. The horizontal division of labour underlines the prospects for shedding effects from the advanced economies to less advanced economies, in the form of FDIs, (partial and gradual) transfer of technology, and international subcontracting (Xing 2007).
d   *Regional value chains.* Many products go through processing in a number of countries.
e   Solidarity and mutual assistance.

f   *Prudent wage policy.* This has largely been realised by comparatively low
    wages.
g   *Good education and training.*
h   *High saving rates.*
i   *Technology transfer.*
j   *International subcontracting.*
k   *Shifting comparative advantage.* Accordingly, economies at the higher
    levels of the ladder gradually move some of their industries or industrial
    sectors to countries at the lower ladder because of changing comparative
    advantage over time.
l   *Substantial and growing intra-regional FDI.* A salient feature of the
    region's FDI is that most of it comes from the region itself.
m   *Substantial and growing intra-regional trade.* For instance, as indicated in
    Figure 11.1, when the averages of the years 1995–2012 are taken, the level
    of intra-regional exports in Eastern Asia (30.5 per cent) was third, surpassed
    by only the intra-regional exports in developed European countries (70.7 per
    cent), and intra-regional exports in the developed American countries (36.9
    per cent). This compares very favourably with Africa, where the highest
    ratio was scored by Eastern Africa (13.3 per cent).

The Asian 'flying-geese' model provides further proof of the mobility of
manufacturing, and the manifestation of this phenomenon (mobility of manufacturing) in the twenty-first century.

All in all, these lessons provide many clues about the driving factors, and the
resultant patterns underlying East Asia's economic transformation, which can be
emulated by Africa countries, as they seek to leverage international economic
partnership for industrialisation.

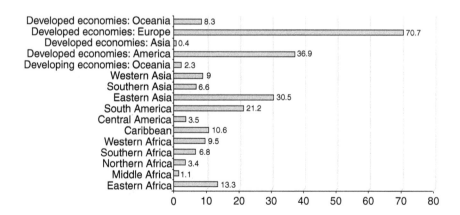

Figure 11.1 Intra-regional exports as percentage of total exports, averages of 1995–2012
(source: Author. Based on UNCTDstat available at: http://unctadstat.unctad.
org/TableViewer/tableView.aspx)).

11.5.2.2 Upgrading industry in Europe through European Union integration process

Empirical reports also show that new, formerly less advanced EU members, such as Spain, Portugal, Ireland, and more lately Czech Republic, Poland, Hungary, etc., benefited from intra-EU international partnership (cf. EC 2007). The bottom line is that intra-EU international co-operation immensely improved the locational qualities of the new entrants to the block and set them on rapid industrial development trajectories, in a process of *equalisation of industrial development*. The benefits emanated from conducive industrial development governance framework, through appropriate block-wide and national policies. The policies encouraged complementary undertakings of the public sector (e.g., through the EU's cohesion and structural funds) and private sectors (largely through investments), which in turn positively impacted the industrial competitiveness of new members.

Concretely, some of the tangible rewards of EU membership included, among other things:

a   Greater industrial policy discipline.
b   Attraction of both private sector and public sector industrial FDI.
c   Benefitting from selective and horizontal aid programmes, which support innovation, infrastructure development and upgrading, industrial education and training, industrial skills development, product upgrading (also partly through new investments), etc.
d   Making access to skilled labour force easier, through industrial labour market reforms in favour of greater industrial labour mobility.
e   Making access to technologies easier, mainly through FDI, etc.

11.5.2.3 China-centred 'bamboo capitalism' model of industrial development

A CONSOLIDATION OF CHINA'S POSITION AS A GLOBAL ECONOMIC CENTRE OF GRAVITY

China's continuous economic significance is manifested by its role in both inward and outward economic globalisation, and globalisation of industry. In this connection, China's impact on growth goes beyond South Asia, and is truly global.

Inward globalisation is demonstrated by, for instance, the consistently good performance in terms of FDI inflows, despite the geopolitical turbulences following the end of the Cold War. China's liberalisation of the economic space has attracted a large amount of foreign investment in labour-intensive and capital- and technology-intensive industries. For instance, Hong Kong has almost moved its entire manufacturing industries to Mainland China while continuing to act as a financial and service centre. Taiwan and Mainland China have developed similar highly symbiotic economic relations in recent years. Due to these shifts, the regional growth pattern and convergence structure has also changed.

Outward globalisation, on the other hand, is manifested by China's increasing role as a foreign investor of choice in all parts of the world. This Chinese alternative source of capital has created a real competition for resources, for instance, in the resource-rich African countries, giving them a new lifeline. China has also become a major exporter of various manufactured goods, overtaking Germany and Japan and surpassing also the USA. When total exports are taken, in 2012, the exports of China, USA, Germany, and Japan were US$2.057 billion, US$1.564 billion, US$1.460 billion, and US$0.774 billion respectively (cf. www.mapsofworld.com/world-top-ten/world-top-ten-exporting-countries-map.html).

B PARADIGM CHANGE: SHIFT FROM VERTICAL INTEGRATION MODEL TO HORIZONTAL INTEGRATION MODEL

China has effectively challenged Japan's position as the central 'locomotive' of propelling the growth of South East Asia. Commensurate with the country's rise, since the 1990s in particular, there has been a paradigm shift away from the Japan-led *'flying-geese' model of vertical economic integration*[13] to the *Chinese bamboo capitalism-led new horizontal model of regional economic integration*. This new model is based on parallel development.

In the context of bamboo capitalism FDI flows in the region have created a pattern of 'parallel development' for the countries of the region in many ways. It has generated diverse and vibrant networks of *local enterprises and industries*. It has also decomposed and extended the supply chains geographically, thus contributing to spatial dispersion of development in which all countries benefit equitably. Overall, capital and trade are horizontally networked (cf. Cheow 2004: 3–4). Imperatively, there is more meaningful and widespread integration of the Asian economies in the regional and global economies.

C CHINESE DIASPORA PROPELLING BOTH INWARD AND OUTWARD GLOBALISATION

The role of Chinese Diaspora networks (i.e. ethnic Chinese networks) has been significant in regional economic integration.

They are major source FDI inflows to China, thus contributing to economic growth. Overseas Chinese networks and the Chinese provinces with special status, such as Hong Kong and Taiwan, are major sources of investments in Mainland China. They blend their capital, technology, diverse entrepreneurial skills, international business exposure, with the Mainland China locational advantages, such as cheap land and abundant supply of low-priced disciplined labour. Chinese Diaspora are also major and sometimes prime sources of capital and entrepreneurship of most of the South East Asian countries (cf. Peng 2000).

The Diaspora Chinese also provide important external market links for goods and services produced in China, in which case they also leverage the international exposure and knowledge of foreign markets with South East Asia and beyond (cf. Peng 2000).

Overall, the Chinese bamboo capitalism model, the main planks of which are horizontal networks for parallel development, contains key ingredients for re-engineering Africa's international partnerships, including the joint Africa–EU industrial development agenda.

11.5.2.4 USA–South Korea co-operation as a model for industrialisation

Thanks to government-led industrialisation efforts, South Korea has experienced rapid and sustained economic growth since the 1960s. By 2005, South Korea's GDP per capita had increased more than 12-fold to more than US$13,000 (Chen and Suh 2007: 5).

A direct comparison with the average Gross Domestic Product (GDP) per capita for Sub-Saharan Africa (SSA), as well as the GDP per capita of an African country at a higher level of development in 1960 (i.e. South Africa) is depicted in Figure 11.2.

Notably, in 1960 South Korea's (GDP) per capita (at constant 2000 US$) was just US$1,153.7, compared to the average for SSA of US$416.1, and South Africa's US$2,203.7. By 2011, South Korea's GDP per capita had increased more than 14 times to US$16,684.2. The comparable figures for SSA and South Africa were US$639.5 or equivalent to a 1.5-fold increase, and US$3,825.1 or a 1.7-fold increase respectively (see Knoemabeta Knowledge Platform; available at: knoema.com/mhrzolg#World).

It is generally agreed that international economic co-operation did play a role in South Korea's phenomenal industrial transformation performance. In this

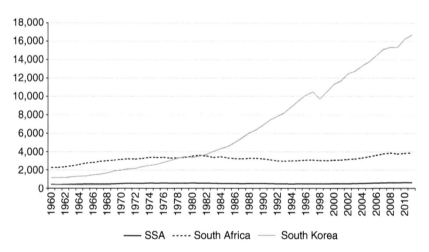

Figure 11.2 Evolution of GDP per capita (at constant 2000 US$) from 1960 to 2010: comparisons of the Africa average, South Africa, and South Korea (source: Knoema (accessed in 2013). GDP Statistics from the World Bank.Knoema[beta] Knowledge Platform. Available at: knoema.com/mhrzolg#World).

Notes
GDP = Gross Domestic Product; SSA = Sub-Saharan Africa.

regard, in view of the extent of the USA's political and economic influence in the Korean peninsula after the Second World War, it would be insincere to discuss South Korea's industrialisation without considering this fact.

11.5.2.5 Industrialisation impact of China's approach to investment co-operation with African countries

Though the China–Africa International Economic Co-operation programme is too young to be comprehensively and conclusively assessed, it is already emerging as a clearly different and far more effective form of international economic co-operation in terms of promoting industrial development in Africa. Contrary to some scepticism, initial reflections suggest that, other than being an obstacle, China's industrial development is in fact an asset for the industrialisation in other developing countries. Some of the salient features of the Chinese model, which differentiate it from the previous, western-dominated models, include the following:

a   Chinese investments are not designed as 'zero sum games', where the foreign investor essentially 'takes it all'. Instead, they encourage substantial capital participation by indigenous and local investors from both the private and public sectors.

b   Chinese investments seek to contribute towards the re-organisation and enhancement of the modes of production in the host countries. The creation of a fully functional Export Processing Zone (EPZ) in Bagamoyo, Tanzania, is a case in hand.

c   It is hard to dispute the fact that the massive investments by Chinese enterprises, for instance, bridge the FiR capacities which most African countries have been facing for decades. They provide essential FiR, which in turn contribute towards the development and/or enhancement of domestic productive capacities in recipient countries. Chinese investments contribute towards very substantial improvement of infrastructural capacities in Africa. The Bagamoyo Sea Port, being built by the Chinese in Tanzania, will be one of the biggest container ports in the world.

11.6 Conclusions and way forward

11.6.1 Conclusions

From the discussions in the preceding sections, it is clear that what countries need to do, in order to efficiently manage the industrial development process, is rather obvious. A viable industrial development regime is a central requirement for each country. Moreover, for such a regime to achieve the ambitious industrial development goals of African countries, it should fulfil a number of characteristics as follows:

a   It should arise out of an amalgamation of ideas from different theories, and different practical experiences. But beyond that, it should be action-oriented.

b   It should not pre-empt the role of the state. Instead, it should recognise and harness (i) the role of an efficient and strong government to guide the private sector, and (ii) the complementary role of states and markets in driving industrialisation.

       This implies further that there should be effective public-private partnership (PPP) in developing the various FiR and NFiR capacities needed to drive industrialisation.

c   It should take into account the particularities of a given economy. Being country-focused means a strong country ownership. Thus, the entire agenda should be tailored to each country's realities. It should also contain a comprehensive menu of measures to choose from, based on international comparison of concrete measures and best practices. This presumes the availability of sufficient policy space for African countries, even if it has got to be within the confines of the rule-based international economic system.

d   Within the context of co-operation between African countries and their EU partners, as well as other international partners, there should be platforms for dialogue and exchange of knowledge and skills with experts from advanced countries. This means also constant efforts to develop knowledge and skills through concrete projects and programmes.

e   Cognisant of the dynamism of the development process, it should be dynamic. Thus, the developmental impact of the various actions must be regularly monitored and evaluated.

11.6.2 Way forward

Development planners and managers in Africa must advance beyond a primordial simplistic mindset of planning the industrialisation process. They should recognise the complex nature of the economic growth and development process, which is affected by many interlinked factors.

    A measure of the merit of international development partnerships, as they exist for instance between the African countries and the EU, go beyond the architecture and effective execution of measures perceived to be essential for prompting and sustaining economic transformation process. The validity of any development co-operation regime must be judged against the actual successes on the ground, in terms of the achieved developmental impact.

Notes

1 The reason behind is that the re-engineering of the African–EU partnership should be part of broad-based efforts to harness international partnerships to develop the capacities needed to propel Africa's industrialisation. Therefore, it is important to digest the lessons from the role of international economic co-operation arrangements on industrial transformation.

2 As hinted in Chapter 2 of this book, these theories can also be differently clustered as into three groups as follows:

    a *Theories of stages of economic growth and development;*

b *Classical theories of economic growth and development* (i.e. classical theories of international trade, balanced and unbalanced growth theories, and Keynesian ad neo-classical growth models);

c *Modern views* (divided further into two groups):

    i *Modern growth theories* including new growth theory, structural change growth model, evolutionary growth models, and unified growth theory, and political economy models;

    ii *Contemporary theoretical debate of international trade and growth.*

3 From the big family of *'endowment-driven' trade theories*, also referred to as the *'old' trade theories* or *'traditional' trade theories* (cf. also Chapter 4), two clusters of theories (i.e. classical and neo-classical theories) also provide an explanation about how international trade influences relative factor rewards (and thereby, income distribution among factors): specialisation across industries that differ in factor intensity changes the relative demand for the various factors of production.

4 In the context of this theory, *Social Overhead Capital* (SOC) comprises those basic devices without which primary, secondary, and tertiary activities cannot function. Investments in SOC include expenditure on roads, irrigation works, energy or power, transport and communications, etc. The investment in these capacities for production creates more economies and this is called divergent series of investment. Typically, such investments are undertaken by *Public agencies* (cf. Hirschman 1958; Rostow 1960).

5 In line with this theory, *Direct Productive Activities* (DPA) are those activities which are a consequence of some investment, add to the flow of final goods and services. It is called convergent series of investment because these projects appropriate more economies than they have created. These series of investments are undertaken by private entrepreneurs. Thus investment in agriculture or industry would be deemed as that belonging to DPA (cf. Hirschman 1958; Rostow 1960).

6 'Non-linearity' refers to

> a situation where the relationship between variables is not simply static or directly proportional to the input, but instead is dynamic and variable. In a factory, for example, the per unit cost may decrease instead of staying constant as the output level rises (due to economies of scale), and may start to rise after the optimum output level is reached (due to diseconomies of scale)
> (cf. www.businessdictionary.com/definition/nonlinearity.html#ixzz2lHgryB00)

This means that in economic estimations, with non-linearity, the effect of the independent variable (IV) X on the dependent variable (DV) Y depends on the level or value of X. For instance, increasing X from 10 to 11 will not produce the same amount of increase in Expected value of Y; E(Y); as increasing X from 20 to 21. Put another way, the effect on Y of a 1 unit increase in X does depends on the value or level of X. This, in effect, means that X somehow interacts with itself. The interaction may be multiplicative, or logarithmic (in which case the estimator will have need to take logarithms of variables), etc.

7 Development is conceived as the *expansion of the market* and an *increase of production (in industrial and other sectors)*. Neither *structural hindrances* nor *market dependencies* are taken into account in the contemplations.

8 Emphasis is placed on capital investment, not on the ways and means of achieving capital formation. It is assumed that, in a traditional society, there is ability and willingness for rational investment decisions along the requirements of the theory. As this will most likely be limited to small sectors of the society, it is not unlikely that simplistic interpretation of the theory will lead to super-imposing a modern sector on the traditional economy, leading to *economic dualism* experienced in many African countries.

9 The term 'state' as used in this context refers to 'a set of organisations, including the administrative and legislative order, with the authority to make and implement

binding rules over all people and all action in a particular territory, using force if necessary' (cf. Evans *et al.* 1985).

10 The basic assumptions in Viner's formulation are:

   i Perfect competition in the product and factor markets.
   ii Perfect intra-country factor mobility, and imperfect inter-country factor mobility.
   iii Full employment and foreign trade equilibrium.
   iv Perfectly price-elastic supply in the world market.
   v Constant tariffs.

   Notably, Viner ignored transportation costs, as well as economies and/or diseconomies of scale. He assumed two integrating countries (which discriminate the rest of the world through the creation of a CU) and used a partial equilibrium model to estimate the impact on trade.

11 Generally, the more advanced the integrating economies, the greater the prospects for exploiting the opportunities of integration. This is attributed to several reasons. First, in contrast to developed economies, which usually seek deeper integration, developing countries have tended to go for narrow integration. The deeper the degree of integration, the higher the percentage of intra-regional trade in total trade. Second, while the degree of trade creation depends on the degree of diversification of the member economies of a trading bloc, developed economies tend to be more diversified. Third, while the benefits of integration depend on the degree of production and trade complementarities and intra-industry trade, developed economies exhibit higher degrees of both.

12 The integration of factor markets causes region-wise convergences of wages/salaries, and the cost of capital. Firms in the factor-deficient member state can source the factor inputs more cheaply from other members of the bloc, which in turn stimulates their ability to produce and trade.

13 To recap once more, this model is based on through investment, transfer, or technology (ToT), and supply of manufactured parts which was based on a hierarchical market exchange and a clear regional division of labour and production activities.

References

Akamatsu, K. (1935). Waga kuni yomo kogyohin no boueki suse (The Trend of Japan's Trade in Woolen Goods). *Shogyo Keizai Ronso* (*Journal of Nagoya Higher Commercial Sc*), 13: 129–212.

Akamatsu, K. (1962). A historical pattern of economic growth in developing countries. *Journal of Developing Economies*, 1(1): 3–25, March–August.

Akyüz, Y. and Gore, C. (1996). The investment–profits nexus in East Asian industrialization. *World Development*, 24(3): 461–470.

Amsden, A. (1989). Industrializing through learning. In *Asia's Next Giant: South Korea and Late Industrialization*. Oxford: Oxford University Press, pp. 1–23.

Argyrous, G. (1996). Cumulative causation and industrial evolution: Kaldor's four stages of industrialization as an evolutionary model. *Journal of Economic Issues* 30(1): 97–119.

Aschauer, D. (1988). Is public expenditure productive?. *Journal of Monetary Economics*, 23: 177–200.

Balasa, B. (1961). *The Theory Of Economic Integration*. Vol. I & II. Homewood: Irwin.

Brada, J. and Mendez, J. (1985). Soviet subsidization of Eastern Europe: The primacy of economics over politics? *Journal of Comparative Economics*, 9(1), March: 80–92.

Brada, J. and Mendez, J. (1998). *An estimate of the dynamic effects of regional economic integration: how effective is the CMEA?: An international comparison.* Commissioned Study's Report to National Council for Soviet and East European Research. Yale University. February.

Chen, D. and Suh, J. (2007). Introduction. In D. Chen and J. Suh (eds), *Korea as a Knowledge Economy: Evolutionary Process and Lessons Learned.* Washington, DC: Korea Development Institute and World Bank Institute; The International Bank for Reconstruction and Development /The World Bank.

Chenery, H., Robinson, S., and Syrquin, M. (1986). *Industrialization and Growth.* New York: Oxford University Press.

Cheow, Eric Teo Chu (2004). China as the center of Asian economic integration. The Jamestown Foundation, *China Brief* 4(15): 3–4.

Ciarli, T., V. Meliciani, and M. Savona (2012). Knowledge dynamics, structural change and the geography of business services. *Journal of Economic Surveys*, 26(3): 445–467.

Collier, P. and Venables, A.J. (2007). Rethinking trade preferences: How Africa can diversify its exports. *World Economy*, 30(8): 1326–1345.

Cornwall, J. (1977). *Modern Capitalism: Its Growth and Transformation.* New York: St. Martin's Press.

de la Torre, A. and Kelly, M. (1992). *Regional trade arrangements.* Occasional Paper No. 93. Washington DC: International Monetary Fund.

Domar, E. (1946). Capital expansion, rate of growth and employment. *Econometrica*, 14(2), April: 137–147.

EC (2007). *Changes in Industrial Competitiveness as a Factor of Integration: Identifying Challenges of the Enlarged Single European Market.* Brussels: European Commission.

Evans, P., Rueschemeyer, D., and Skocpol, T. (1985). On the road towards a more adequate understanding of the role of the state. In P. Evans, D. Rueschemeyer, and T. Skocpol (Eds), *Bringing the State Back In.* Cambridge, England: Cambridge University Press, pp. 16–17.

Felipe, J., Kumar, U., Abdon, A., and Bacate, M. (2012). Product complexity and economic development. *Structural Change and Economic Dynamics*, 23: 36–68.

Fuchs, D., Kalfagianni, A., Clapp, J., and Busch, L. (2011). Introduction to symposium on private agrifood governance: Values, shortcomings and strategies. *Agriculture and Human Values*, 28: 335–344.

Funke, M. and Ruhwedel, R. (2001). Product variety and economic growth: Empirical evidence for the OECD countries. *IMF Staff Papers* 48(2): 225–242.

Gault, F. and Zhang, G. (2010). The role of innovation in the area of development. In E. Kraemer-Mbula and W. Wamae (Eds), *Innovation and the Development Agenda.* Paris: OECD/IDRC.

Grauwe, P. D., Houssay, R., and Piccillo, G. (2010). *China Africa relationship: good for both parts?* Working Paper mimeo, CES, University of Leuven.

Grubel, H., and Lloyd, P. (1975). *Intra-industry Trade: The Theory and Measurement of International Trade in Differentiated Products.* New York: Wiley

Harrod, R. (1939). *The Economic Journal*, 49(193). Blackwell Publishing for the Royal Economic Society. March.

Heywood, L-M. (2013). Why did South Korea grow rich, 1960–1985? *E-international Relations.* 16 March.

Hidalgo, C. and Hausmann, R. (2008). A network view of economic development. *Developing Alternatives*, 12(1): 5–10.

Hidalgo, C. and Hausmann, R. (2009). The building blocks of economic complexity. *Proceedings of the National Academy of Sciences*, 106(26): 10570–10575.

Hidalgo, C., Klinger, B., Abarabási, L., and Hausmann, R. (2007). The product space conditions the development of nations. *Science*, 317(5837): 482–487.

Hiley, M. (1999). Industrial restructuring in ASEAN and the role of Japanese foreign direct investment. *European Business Review*, 99(2): 80–90.

Hirschman, A. (1958). *The Strategy of Economic Development*. New Haven: Yale University Press.

Kaldor, N. (1966). *Causes of the Slow Rate of Economic Growth in the United Kingdom*. Cambridge: Cambridge University Press.

Kaldor, N. (1967). *Strategic Factors in Economic Development*. Ithaca: Cornell University.

Kaldor, N. (1975). Economic growth and the Verdoorn law: A comment on Mr. Rowthorn's article. *Economic Journal*, 85(340): 891–896.

Kaldor, N. (1981). The role of increasing returns, technical progress and cumulative causation in the theory of international trade. *Economie Appliquée*, 24(4): 593–617.

Knoema (accessed in 2013). *GDP Statistics from the World Bank*. Knoemabeta Knowledge Platform. Available at: knoema.com/mhrzolg#World.

Kojima, K. (1960). Capital accumulation and the course of industrialisation, with special reference to Japan. *The Economic Journal*, LXX: 757–768.

Kojima, K. (1970). Towards a theory of agreed specialization: The economics of integration. In W.A. Eltis, M.F.G. Scott, and J.N. Wolfe (eds), *Induction, Growth and Trade, Essays in Honours of Sir Roy Harrod*, Oxford: Clarendon Press.

Kojima, K. (1995). Dynamics of Japanese investment in East Asia. *Hitotsubashi Journal of Economics*, 36: 93–124.

Kuznets, S. (1973). Modern economic growth: Findings and reflections. *The American Economic Review*, 63(3): 247–258.

Kwan, C. (2002). *the rise of China and Asia's flying-geese pattern of economic development: An empirical analysis based on us import statistics*. NRI Papers 52, 1 August.

Lall, S. (2005). *Is African industry competing?* QEH working papers, Queen Elizabeth House, University of Oxford.

Langhammer, R. and Hiemenz, U. (1990). Regional integration among developing countries: Opportunities, obstacles and options. *Kieler Studien*, No. 232.

Marx, K. (1848). The Communist Manifesto. In K. Marx and F. Engels, *Selected Works*, Volume 1. Moscow. February.

Matambalya, F. (2011). Lessons from earlier industrialization policy initiatives in Africa: Experiences of industrial policy management in the EAC. Presentation at the Conference 'High-level Policy Dialogue Conference on EAC Industrialisation Policy and Strategy', held at Ole Sereni Hotel, Nairobi, 2–4 May. East African Community and Gesellschaft für Internationale Zusammenarbeit.

Mokyr, J. (2010). The contribution of economic history to the study of innovation and technical change: 1750–1914. In B.H. Hall and N. Rosenberg (eds), *Handbook of The Economics of Innovation, Vol. 1*, Amsterdam: North-Holland, pp. 11–50.

Naughton, B. (2010). China's distinctive system: Can it be a model for others?, *Journal of Contemporary China*, 19(65), June: 437–460.

Nester, W. (1991). Japanese neomercantilism toward Sub-Saharan Africa. *Africa Today: The Changing Global Balance: Outlook for Africa*, 38(3), (3rd Qtr): 31–51.

Peng, D. (2000). Ethnic Chinese business networks and the Asia-Pacific economic integration. *African and Asian Studies*, 35(2): 229–250.

Pomfret, T. and Toren, B. (1980). Israel and the European common market: An appraisal of the 1975 free trade agreement. *Kieler Studien*, No. 161.

Radelet, S. (1997). *Regional integration and cooperation in Sub-Saharan Africa: Are formal trade agreements the right strategy?* Development Discussion Papers. Harvard Development Discussion Paper No. 59.

Ricardo, D. (1817). *Principles of Political Economy and Taxation*. London: John Murray.

Robson, P. (1987). *The Economics of International Integration*. Third Edition. Boston: Allen and Unwin.

Rosenstein-Rodan, P. (1943). Problems of industrialization of eastern and south-eastern Europe. *Economic Journal*, 53(209), June–September: 202–211.

Rosenstein-Rodan, P. (1961). Notes on the theory of the big push. In H. Ellis and H. Wallich (eds), *Economic Development for Latin America*. London: Macmillan.

Rostow, W. W. (1960). *The Stages of Economic Growth: A Non Communist Manifesto*. Cambridge: Cambridge University Press.

Rowthorn, B. and Ramaswamy, R. (1997). *Deindustrialization: Causes and implications*. IMF Working Papers 97/42, International Monetary Fund.

Saviotti, P. and Frenken, K. (2008). Export variety and the economic performance of countries. *Journal of Evolutionary Economics*, 18: 201–218.

Shen, J., Dunn, D., and Shen, Y. (2007). Challenges facing US manufacturing and strategies. *Journal of Industrial Technology*, 23(2): 2–10.

Singh, A. (1995). *How did East Asia grow so fast? Slow progress towards an analytical consensus*. UNCTAD/OSG/DP/97. No. 97. February.

So, A. (1990). *Social Change and Development. Modernization, Dependency, and World-System Theories*, UK: SAGE Publications Ltd.

Solow, R. (1957). Technical change and the aggregate production function. *The Review of Economics and Statistics*, 39(3): 312–320.

Swan, T. W. (1956). Economic growth and capital accumulation. *Economic Record*, 32: 334–361.

Szirmai, A. (2012). Industrialisation as an engine of growth in developing countries, 1950–2005. *Structural Change and Economic Dynamics*, 23(4): 406–420.

Targetti, F. and Thirlwall, A. (eds). (1989). *Further Essays on Economic Theory and Policy*. London: Duckworth.

UN (1980). *Resolution adopted by the General Assembly 35/66. Industrial development co-operation*. United Nations. New York. 5 December.

UN (2007). *Industrial Development for the 21st Century: Sustainable Development Perspectives*. Department for Economic and Social Affairs. New York.

Vasyechko, O. (2012). A review of FDI theories: An application for transition economies. *International Research Journal of Finance and Economics*. ISSN 1450–2887 Issue 89.

Viner, J. (1950). *The Customs Union Issues*. New York: Carnegie Endowment for International Peace.

von Hagen, O. and Gabriela, A. (2011). The impacts of private standards on producers in developing countries. *Literature Review Series on the Impacts of Private Standards Part II*, Geneva: ITC.

von Tunzelmann, G.N. (1995). *Technology and Industrial Progress: The Foundations of Economic Growth*. Aldershot: Edward Elgar.

Winters, A. (2007). *International Economics*. 4th edition. London and New York: Routledge.

Xing, L. (2007). *East Asian Regional Integration: From Japan-led 'Flying-geese' to China-centred 'Bamboo Capitalism'*. CCIS Research Series. Working Paper No. 3. Centre for Comparative International Studies. Arlborg University.

12 Pathways to industrialisation in Africa

Key considerations and elements of a hybrid strategy

Francis A.S.T. Matambalya

This chapter reiterates the essentiality of industrialisation as a pathway to development. It summarises the key associations between industrialisation and development postulated by theory. It also revisits the practical manifestations of industrialisation as a pathway to economic growth and development, and assesses the contribution of alternative international economic partnership models towards the achievement of this goal. The analysis helps to expose viable options to be emulated by African countries, in leveraging EU partnership for industrialisation. Therefore, the chapter ultimately recommends the essential considerations – what should be the de facto *leitmotif* for the architecture of a feasible strategy to leverage African–EU development co-operation for the industrialisation of the SSA economies and African Maghreb countries.

12.1 Reaffirmed essentiality of industrialisation for development

Industry is essential – and like other regions of the world, Africa needs it for sustainable economic growth and development. This is underscored by lessons from more advanced parts of the world. For instance, in the European Union (EU), one out of four jobs in the private sector is in the manufacturing industry, and at least another one out of four is in associated services that depend on industry as a supplier or as a client. Eighty per cent of all private sector research and development efforts are undertaken in industry – it is a driver of innovation and a provider of solutions to the challenges our societies are confronted with (cf. EC 2010).

For African countries, the merits of industrialisation underline the need:

a   To have well-developed industrial sub-sectors. The economic activities of the various sub-sectors should be properly diversified, and cover the various stages of the value chain (from investments to production, to trade).
b   To be able to harness the spin-offs of industrialisation, in terms of economies of intra-industry and inter-industry linkages, economies of scale, and economies of scope. These abilities should also cover the entire value chain.

c   To be able to leverage industrialisation for the overall health and sustainability of their economies. This would be manifested by high industrial productivity and competitiveness in the international context, creation of enough and quality jobs, etc. (cf. EC 2010).

However, in order to achieve industrialisation, certain basic conditions must be met: existence of diverse types of productive capacities, ability to harness and leverage a country's own natural resources for industrial development, pragmatism to refrain from ideologising and politicising the industrialisation agenda, existence of a functional economic framework in support of investment-led growth, and having in place a feasible country-focused industrialisation agenda. The following sections highlight further the essence of these preconditions.

12.2 Productive capacities: a *sine qua non* for industrialisation

By now, it should be clear to everyone that, though many African countries are rich in natural resources, this fact alone is not going to make them industrialise and achieve critical levels of sustainable economic growth and development. To do so, they need to develop the acquired resource capacities, which will enable them to both (i) meaningfully exploit their resource potential (and stop the 'resource curse') and, (ii) access resources on global resource markets; to produce goods and services competitively along the entire value chain.

These acquired capacities are essentially the productive capacities on which the competitiveness of nations are based. They constitute not only Financial Resources (FiR) capacities, but also diverse Non-Financial Resources (NFiR) capacities. The gaps in terms of these resources manifest the structural constraints against industrial and overall economic transformation observed in African and many other developing economies (EC 1995).

Africa's FiR capacity gaps are evidenced by many factors. They include: underdevelopment of domestic financial markets, lacking capacities to capitalise on and effectively use resources from diverse internal and external sources (AU and UNIDO 2010).

The NFiR capacity gaps include institutional gaps, manifested by lack of strong institutions or organisations to provide support services needed to backstop the process of industrialisation. Also, there are shortages of essential *industrial knowledge and skills*, due to the underdevelopment of human capital. Likewise, critical masses of *technological capacities*, which are needed to catalyse sustainable development, are lacking. An equally serious gap relates to infrastructural capacities to support competitive industrial production (UNIDO 2010).

A *governance framework* (cf. also Chapters 4, 5, 6, 11, 13, and 14) that eases factor accumulation, and therefore stimulates the development of the productive sectors, is essential for industrial and overall economic transformation of a country. Given the content of productive capacity development (entrepreneurial capacities, knowledge and skills capacities, institutional or organisational capacities, physical infrastructural capacities, and technological capacities), it embodies the necessary conditions for improving productivity, and thereby for systematically bridging the productivity gap between a given economic entity (e.g. an African country) and its competitors (e.g. countries from essentially other parts of the world, which are generally more competitive than African countries).

12.3 Ability to meaningfully leverage natural resource wealth for industrialisation

Unique natural resource bases provide most African countries with important levers to achieve industrialisation. In the international economic system that has dominated the world for the past five centuries – particularly Africa's position therein – these assets have, by and large, been of little use for African countries. The *system of management of the international resource economy* has allowed unobstructed access to Africa's resources by its international 'partners', without providing for meaningful returns in terms of Local Economic Development (LED). The end result has been that, while Africa's partners have used agricultural mineral and human resources from the continent to propel their industrial development, this resource utilisation practices have left African countries with multiple scars: depleted ecosystems, depleted natural resources, exhausted soils, etc. – and all that in the midst of frustrated development dreams and widespread poverty.

The portrayed situation must change. African countries can and must harness their resource potential for their own development. However, in order to achieve this they must put into action the realisation that commodities and commodity booms cannot provide solutions for their development aspirations. Instead, they should stop being primarily suppliers of cheap labour, and agricultural and mineral raw materials to other countries, and instead leverage their resource wealth for their own industrialisation. There is one and only one meaningful mode to success: African countries are compelled to seriously engage in the diversification of economic production activities by climbing the value chain ladder. Also, they must develop and safeguard the economic human rights of their people. Both own development efforts, and development efforts within the frameworks of international partnerships must be geared towards achieving this goal.

In this context, African countries should not be deterred by discouraging terminologies, such as *'Resource Curse'*,[1] *'Dutch Disease'*,[2] or the challenges facing them as late industrialising countries. A viable industrial transformation agenda must factor-in all these potential constraints. African countries must meaningfully exploit their agricultural and mineral resources, so as to increase the economic efficiency of their utilisation in domestic manufacturing.

In a bid to leverage the natural resource endowment for industrialisation, industrialisation initiatives must be properly linked to agricultural transformation and rural development efforts. Also, efforts must be geared towards enabling African countries to more meaningfully exploit their mineral wealth, through beneficiation and by developing more complete mineral-based industrial value chains.

The development of own domestic capacities for agribusiness and agro-industries, as well as for mineral beneficiation in African countries has many benefits. They include extracting more value from agricultural and mineral resources that in turn increase a country's wealth, fostering to structural trans-formation (improvement of the structure) of the economy by moving to higher stages of the value chain, creating more and better paying jobs, avoiding expo-sure to commodity price fluctuations, increasing downstream manufacturing and thus changing the composition of a country's exports and imports, etc. (http://africaoil.ning.com/profiles/blogs/madini-africa-brings-about-investment-in-african-mineral).

12.4 A Practical agenda based on broad-based measures to support industrialisation

Efforts to achieve industrial development in Africa have been compromised by a lack of a practical industrialisation agenda, which is free of ideological and polit-ical sentiments. In the same context, like nowhere else, there has been a deliber-ate confusion about the role of the state in the process of industrialisation as well as in the process of economic development as a whole. A viable agenda for transforming Africa industrially must rectify these two caveats.

12.4.1 Avoiding the theoretical fallacy

One of the frustrating lessons about the debate on industrialisation is the polari-sations resulting from the fact that in some occasions, there has been a tendency to reduce the phenomenon to two major competing theoretical frameworks: import-substituting industrialisation (ISI) and export-orientated industrialisation (EOI).[3] The quintessential verdict of such analysis has been that the liberal route under EOI (which is expected to deliver sustainable success) is superior over ISI (which has generally not been able to deliver success, beyond the early stages).

Conspicuously, this interpretation (which paints a black and white picture by, rather mechanistically, on the one hand equating *laissez faire* and EOI with outward-orientation, and on the other hand equating government intervention and ISI with inward-orientation) is, logically, an extreme oversimplification of reality and amounts to a serious conceptual fallacy. It wrongly creates the impression that EOI and ISI are mutually exclusive approaches, and that one strategy is superior over the other in all circumstances.

However, in a real world situation, export-orientation and import substitution are not mutually exclusive phenomena, but would tend to mutually reinforce each other, just like the private sector and the government are essential comple-ments (Moreira 1996).

Also, these two strategies (i.e. EOI and ISI) have empirically delivered dif-ferent results in different circumstances. For instance, as noted by Zepeda *et al.*

(2009), widespread adoption of EOI since the mid-1980s produced mixed results: with some countries (notably, in Latin America) achieving sustained rapid growth, and others (especially in Africa) experiencing low growth rates. Besides, even the Latin American countries which achieved sustained growth had to endure the apparent disconnect between export growth and broad-based economic growth.

Thus, the architecture of a practical industrial development agenda should refrain from rigid theoretical assumptions, and focus on the real issues of the industrialisation process. It should identify measures which deliver results – regardless of whether they concur with EIO or ISI.

Indeed, in pursuing their ambitions for industrialisation, countries have followed various strategies, which seem to blend arguments from different theories. Although the classification of such strategies is not an easy task, as there is no universal formula for doing this – in an attempt to understand the dynamics of industrialisation in developing countries – different authors have come up with alternative ideas about the classification of practical industrialisation efforts (van Dijk and Marcussen 1990, etc.).

Van Dijk and Marcussen (1990) categorises the industrialisation strategies adopted by developing countries into: *EOI strategy, ISI strategy, project import industrialisation strategy*, and *industrialisation strategy under scarce resources*. Table 12.1 summarises these strategies.

Moreover, basing on the comparison of the experiences of developing countries, van Dijk and Marcussen (1990: 1–5) made several useful observations and conclusions:

a   They underline the limitation of this kind of classification, pointing out also that many countries pursue a hybrid strategy, containing some elements of more than one strategy.
b   They conclude that successful industrialisation is a product of a combination of internationalisation of capital, and local accumulation of capital, and a committed involvement of the government.[4]
c   The prospects for industrialisation in developing countries are also influenced by the health of the world economy: worsening in cases of negative trends in the world economy (e.g. recession) and improving with the improvement of the world economy.
d   By sucking resources out of developing countries, the debt crisis and Structural Adjustment Programmes (SAP) also limit their prospects for fast industrialisation.
e   Being latecomers, and the prospects of having to catch up with countries that are not statistic weighs heavily on most developing countries.

The overarching lessons that we derive from the analyses by van Dijk and Marcussen (1990, ibid.) is that the right *industrialisation strategy* is essentially a *hybrid strategy*, which addresses the various development needs of the country concerned. Imperatively, the strategy should, explicitly be adjusted to the

Table 12.1 Typology of industrialisation in the third world

Strategy	Description
1 Export-oriented industrialisation	• Seeks to achieve the manufacturing and exporting finished and semi-finished products • Requires that country pursue liberal trade policies,[1] by opening own markets, while simultaneously getting access to foreign markets • Common policy measures include: trade liberalisation, foreign currency liberalisation, government support for exporting sectors • Strategy largely pursued by NICs
2 Import substitution industrialisation	• Seeks to reduce country's foreign dependency and advocates replacing imports through domestic production • Industrialisation oriented towards producing capital and consumption goods for the home market, as well as neighbouring regional markets • This was the major strategy of choice for LAC
3 Project import industrialisation	• Fast process of industrialisation based on import of turn-key factories • Requires that country has enough FiR capacities (i.e. financing institutions with sufficient liquidity, and the right types of financial instruments) • Requires also that country has the essential NFiR capacities (industrial entrepreneurship skills, industrial knowledge and skills, institutions/organisations to support an industrial economy, physical infrastructure, technological capacities) • Strategy pursued by countries possessing natural resources of 'strategic' nature, such as fossil fuel
4 Industrialisation strategy under scarce resources	• Sporadic, gradual process of import-substitution • Industrialisation dominated by the state • Strategy pursued by the majority of third world countries, particularly those in Africa, given their resource profile

Source: Based on van Dijk and Marcusssen (1990: 1–2).

Notes
1 The theoretical presumptions are that trade openness shifts goods to sectors in which the economy has a comparative advantage, increasing efficiency.
FiR = Financial Resources; LAC = Latin American countries; NFiR = Non-Financial Resources; NIC = Newly Industrialising Country.

particularities of the country vis-à-vis the existing productive capacity gaps that need to be addressed, and development goals that need to be achieved. It should accordingly pick the relevant provisions from each of the main strategies, and blend them into hybrid strategy tailored to the country's needs – which means that a viable hybrid strategy for county A may not be identical to the one for country B.

12.4.2 Freeing the industrialisation agenda from ideological and political sentiments: avoiding the fallacy of the restricted role of the state

Lessons from practice underline the necessity of the industrialisation agenda to reckon the strategic role of the state. It is important to bear in mind the fact that 'only the private sector is flexible, disciplined, and has the capacity to respond to the innovation needs of industry' (as argued by, *inter alia*, McCarthy 2003) is a fallacy, despite being advocated for persistently. It is a fallacy, because, in reality, no country has achieved industrialisation without the state playing a central role. In all cases of successful industrialisation, the state has served as a guiding hand to the private sector, as well as an 'entrepreneur of choice' in given circumstances. To bring it to the point:

> ...if we look around the world, those countries that have grown or are growing through innovation-led growth are countries where the state did not limit itself to just solving 'market failures' but actually developed strategic missions, and was active in directing public investment in particular areas with scale and scope, changing the technological and market landscape in the process. And ironically one of the governments that have been most active on this front is the US government, which is usually depicted in the media (and by politicians) as being more 'market oriented'. From putting a man on the moon, to developing what later became the Internet, the US government, through a host of different public agencies, provided direct financing not only of basic research but also applied research and even early stage public venture capital (indeed Apple received $500,000 directly from public funds). In each case it provided funding for the most high risk/uncertain investments, while the private sector sat waiting behind.
>
> (Mazzucato 2013)

The desirability of the dual role of the government is given further credibility by the exploits of the Chinese 'bamboo capitalism' model which strategically blend state and market – and in which private industrial enterprises, including foreign enterprises, operate harmoniously and successfully alongside public industrial enterprises (Xing 2007).

Therefore, it is not correct for the government to withdraw from entrepreneurial industrial activities on a wholesale basis, as this has happened as part of structural adjustments programmes.

The overall verdict here should be that, the role of the state must be defined to go beyond just 'unleashing' the private sector from its constraints by fixing 'market failures' (investing in 'public goods' like infrastructure or basic research). Though a heavily state-centric industrialisation agenda may be detrimental, *a judicious role of the state is absolutely necessary*. Indeed, in a well-conceived industrialisation agenda – as is the case for a country's overall development agenda – markets and states are essential complements. Therefore, the issue is not about wholesale rolling back the role of the state, but making the state – in its diverse capacities – a more effective agent for industrial transformation (cf. Rodrik 2001; Mazzucato 2013).

Imperatively, the architecture of a practical industrial development agenda should also refrain from ideologising and politicising the process. Indeed, in this case as well, in pursuing aspirations to industrialise, countries have followed various strategies, which have cut across ideological boundaries (van Dijk and Marcussen 1990; Rodrik 2001; Xing 2007; Mazzucato 2013, etc.).

12.5 Harnessing international partnerships for industrialisation

The promotion of industrial transformation in a given country is largely the work of the domestic development agenda. It therefore underlies the responsibilities of local economic actors from both the public and private sectors.

However, no economy operates in isolation, without influences from the rest of the world. Through the interconnections that characterise the global economic system, forces from the international environment do actually influence the process and outcomes of development of FiR capacities and NFiR capacities in a country, and thereby impact its industrial transformation.

In practice, due to their limited economic power, the impact of forces running from the international economic environment can even tend to have an over-proportional developmental impact in the case of developing countries, such as those in Africa. This means that appropriately harnessing the forces that emanate from the global economic system is absolutely essential in safeguarding the industrial transformation of a given developing country.

12.5.1 Harnessing regional integration for industrialisation

The lessons from the industrialisation through regional integration experiences of East Asia suggest that African countries can make regional integration schemes work for industrial transformation (Xing 2007). Apart from political will and resolute political leadership, the preconditions for this include readiness for genuine solidarity amongst the co-operating countries.

Chapter 11 of this book delineates in some detail how the East Asian countries have leveraged both the Japanese-inspired *'flying geese' development model* and the Chinese-inspired *'bamboo capitalism' development model* (cf. Xing 2007) to promote phenomenal industrial transformation processes in East Asia.

12.5.2 Re-engineering Africa–EU partnership

As discussed in detail in Chapters 9 and 10, the African countries of the African, Caribbean and Pacific (ACP) group of countries (henceforth the AACP countries), and the African Maghreb countries, have long-standing relations with the EU, which embrace industrial co-operation.

The rationale to re-engineer AACP–EU co-operation is deeply embedded in the limitations of the past ACP–EU co-operation arrangements. Another important factor that underlines the need for revolutionising the co-operation is the profound changes in the international system since the end of the cold war as manifested by, *inter alia*, shifts in the global economic landscape.

The predominant country-focus of the African Maghreb–EU industrial co-operation arrangements means that the EU's support measures are more likely to have a greater impact in the development of the diverse FiR and NFiR capacities, which are essential for industrial transformation in the African Maghreb countries. However, even in this case, in addition to profound changes in the international economic landscape, most of the limitations observed for the AACP countries apply. Hence, nothing short of radical re-engineering is needed.

12.5.2.1 Limitations of the EU's model of co-operation with developing countries

Indisputably, despite decades of formalised economic co-operation with the comparatively more advanced states of the EU, most countries in Africa have been growing slowly for a long time. Instead of setting on a process of upward convergence that is expected from such an association, the African countries have seen themselves falling back in comparison to not only advanced countries, but also to other developing countries. Predominance of pre-industrial economy, and de-industrialisation for substantial periods of time are some of the defining features.

Thus, measured by results, particularly the industrial developmental impact, the African–EU co-operation appears to be still anchored in the global orthodoxy. It appears to still manifest the out of date *triad doctrine* global economic order, in which the EU as part of the trilateral powers is the centre and African countries – both from SSA and the Maghreb – are part of the periphery.

The performance of African economies provides strong evidence of the limitations of subsequent co-operation frameworks between the EU and the African, Caribbean and Pacific (ACP) group of nations, which have guided partnership between the AACP and EU. The same applies for co-operation between the EU and the Arab Maghreb African states of North Africa. Due to their design, those models have been incapable of delivering development dividend for Africa.

A ATTEMPTS TO PIN-POINT THE SHORTFALLS

Many empirical studies did attempt to identify and analyse the limitations of the ACP–EU co-operation model. In one such study, Matambalya (1997, 1999) basing his arguments on a review of several studies (cf. AWEEPA 1992; Stevens *et al.* 1993; Reinhart and Wickham 1994; Gonzales 1996; Grynberg 1996; Kappel 1996) classified the shortfalls into two major groups: deficits of the instruments through which preferences are granted to ACP countries, and existence of adverse environment for economic development in ACP countries.

According to the author, the concrete *inherent deficits* associated with the instruments through which preferences are granted to ACP countries include the following:

a   *Redundancy and erosion of the margins of the presumed trade preferences largely to the incoherence of policies.* The incoherence was manifested through several restrictive policies that existed alongside the trade regime, including: rules of origin, clauses to safeguard EU interests, quotas, provisions of the Common Agricultural Policy (CAP), reference prices (which due to their rigidity and high levels may contribute towards the reduction of marginal demand), and the high transportation costs of the mainly bulky agricultural and mineral raw materials exports to the EU (cf. Stevens *et al.* 1993: 96–97; Grynberg 1996; Matambalya 1999: 193, 200).

b   *Limits characterising EU demand of products from the ACP countries.* The concrete concerns pointed out included: perpetuation of export portfolio dominated by a few typically primary products, surge in global supply of commodities, fall in demand of commodities due to emergence of synthetics, fall in demand for commodities as a result of fall in the intensity of use triggered by technological advancement, and high level EU's self-satisfaction in many typical export products of ACP countries, and the smallness of the EU market (cf. Stevens *et al.* 1993: 91–93; Reinhart and Wickham 1994: 21; Matambalya 1999: 117, 171–172, 201–202).

c   *Management challenges of the co-operation arrangement.* The problematic issues identified included the complexity of the arrangements themselves, which embrace a labyrinth of instruments and provisions captured in a lot of paperwork, lack of information, and limited knowledge about the arrangements in the ACP countries beyond a small group of people (cf. Matambalya 1999: 203–220).

d   *Lack of clarity on the distribution of trade preferences margins.* The arrangement did not clarify how the margin should be shared amongst the producer, exporter, importer, and user. As a result, a larger part of the margin tended to be captured by stakeholders from the stronger participant in the party to the agreement, i.e. EU (Matambalya 1999: 204).

e   *Uncertainties regarding the allocation of resources.* There have been no viable criteria for ranking countries or sectors for the purpose of allocating aid money. Also, the allocation of the aid into programmable and non-programmable assistance was not based on scientific criteria. The overall impact of these weaknesses is that some countries got over-proportional allocations, while others got under-proportional allocations (AWEEPA 1992: B6; Gonzales 1996: 11–12; Kappel 1996: 32–33; Matambalya 1999: 192, 204–205).

In a recent review of EU development co-operation vis-à-vis ACP countries, Sindzingre (2012) also identifies several inherent weakness. Arguably, the Economic Partnership Agreements (EPAs) are characterised by intrinsic discrepancies between *ex ante* objectives and *ex post* outcomes. The questions, which the EPA model of development co-operation does not answer convincingly, include the following: how conceptually appropriate are Free Trade Areas (FTA) as instruments to guide Africa–EU co-operation?, how will the limitations associated with South–South arrangements due to their suboptimal character be overcome, what does the proliferation of regional economic communities (RECs) imply, how will the model tackle the lack of inter-country complementarities within EPA groupings, what is the impact going to be on the distorted export structures of Sub-Saharan African countries (which remain strongly commodity-dependent, with narrow industrial bases), what will the impact of the model be on the unbalanced trade relationships between African countries and the EU (cf. Sindzingre 2012).

Imperatively, the features of EPAs erode the prospects for achieving the *ex ante* objectives or goals. Therefore, the author came to the verdict that, with such economic structures, reciprocal trade arrangements between the EU and African countries entail risks (Sindzingre 2012).

B THE RESPONSE

In spite of the evidenced weakness as portrayed in Matambalya (1997, 1999) and several other research works, little attention was paid to the real limitations of the EU development co-operation model, in the design of the Cotonou Agreement.

12.5.2.2 Changed realities in the international system

Since the inception in the Treaty of Rome, of the idea of ACP–EU co-operation largely driven by trade, major changes have taken place in the international system. The economic and political power relations in the international system have shifted and continue to do so at an alarming pace. The EU is still an important player in the global economy, however, it is no longer the solid centre of gravity – a central pole in the international economic system organised according to the triad doctrine – it used to be. Economic power – and with it economic growth and prosperity – are being increasingly more widely shared by nations, i.e. beyond the traditional centres of power propagated by the triad doctrine. The 'new kids on the bloc' – the new players, like China, India, Brazil, etc., are no longer on the horizon, but have already arrived at the scene of global economic action and wield significant and rising economic power.

It should also, in particular, be noted that the ACP–EU co-operation model has lost its uniqueness. In today's post-cold war world, the ACP–EU network of relationships is, by any measure, just one in the crowd (cf. Smith 2004). To underlie this, the EU countries are no longer the leading economic partners of the African countries.

Implicitly, in its current form, the EPA model of development co-operation might not be the best option for African countries to pursue. In order to salvage the long-standing partnership between Africa and the EU, it is necessary to thoroughly assess the provisions of the co-operation agenda between these two partner groups of nations, and to align them to the new realities.

12.5.2.3 Clear rationale for a change of course

All these considerations mean that the AACP–EU partnership must be re-engineered, and, in this context, be refocused to fulfil the following goals:

a   *Make industrial co-operation the fulcrum of AACP–EU co-operation.* Ideally, this should be reflected also in the outcomes of the negotiations for EPA between the EU and the various EPA configurations with the ACCP group of nations. Moreover, it should be a mandatory goal of the forthcoming review of the Cotonou Agreement, which is scheduled for 2020.

b   *Set the achievements of the Japanese-led industrialisation of East Asia as the minimum threshold to be achieved by a reformed AACP–EU industrial co-operation agenda.* Imperatively, the new AACP–EU industrial co-operation agenda should emulate the 'flying geese' model (Kazushi and Rossovsky 1968; Kim 1983; Xing 2007; cf. also Chapter 11 of this book).

c   *Emulate the positive lessons from China's 'bamboo capitalism' model.* The intention should be to follow the impact of '*bamboo capitalism*' in developing industrial productive capacities in East Asia (Xing 2007; cf. also Chapter 11 of this book).

d   *Emulate the positive lessons from China's industrial co-operation with African countries.* The intention should be to emulate the impact of positive lessons of China's engagement in Africa, in terms of developing industrial productive capacities in East Asia.

12.5.3 Putting partnerships between Africa and the key economies in proper contexts

Co-operation between African and other major economies of the world should also clearly seek to stimulate its industrial transformation. This can be achieved through:

a   Increasing the share of FDI flows to manufacturing.
b   Increasing R&D activities by Transnational Corporations (TNCs) in host African economies.

12.6 Economic transformation agenda centred on investment-led growth

Many, if not all, African countries are stuck in a consumption-led growth model that does not emphasise investment in productive capacities. As observed in the report *Industrial and Economic Cooperation between the European Union and*

Developing Countries on past industrialisation strategies in Africa, 'Production of consumer goods has been geared towards luxury items consumed by a small minority of the population...' (EC 1995: 7).

In contrast, one defining aspects of East Asian countries has been their ability to gear their economic growth agenda toward high rates of investments, which also targeted the productive capacities (Singh 1995; Akyuz and Gore 1996; Naughton 2007). Unlike in many other developing countries where consumption (instead of investment) is the most significant driver of growth, East Asian countries on purpose adopted policy frameworks to ensure that consumption growth lagged behind income growth. This, in turn, enabled them to raise the rate of savings and investment, and thus accelerate capital accumulation and growth. This 'catch-up' approach to growth management stresses building productive capacities, which are essential for meaningfully engaging in all stages of economic activities: from investments, to production, to trade.

The investment-led approach also has clear implications for infrastructure provision, as East Asian countries consistently built infrastructure (e.g. roads, airports, harbours, and electricity generation) ahead of demand. Although such an approach is often associated with wasteful, inefficient allocation of capital that leads to industrial over-capacity and over-heating, it is also necessary insofar that it creates the latent capacity that can be used later, thus smoothing the bottlenecks and delays that can impose large costs on the rest of the economy.

From the narrative in the previous paragraphs, it is also clear that industrialisation in African countries should be led by investments, rather than consumption. In this regard, an in-depth understanding of innovations adopted by East Asian countries to address macro- and microeconomic constraints that impeded investment-led growth and a dynamic process of industrial upgrading (Evans 1998; Lin and Wang 2008) would be helpful in formulating and sequencing diverse measures to guide a shift from consumption-led to investment-led growth.

12.7 Right anchoring of the industrial transformation agenda: a country-focus

No country has been able to industrialise by hiding behind 'collective efforts', such as regional programmes or multilateral programmes. Instead, the record of experiences clearly shows that all successful industrialisation campaigns have focused at creating the necessary conditions at country level in the first place. These necessary conditions at the country level created the essential capacities, which subsequently heaved the countries in question into a position to become meaningfully active in the global economic activities at all stages of the value chain: investment, production, and trade. The capacities we refer to here are those which enable a country to effectively harness its potential, as well as to utilise opportunities provided by the international economic system, for its industrial transformation. In this chapter and elsewhere in this book, these capacities have been referred to as FiR capacities and NFiR capacities.

Imperatively, sub-regional, regional, and pan-African and multilateral initiatives to support Africa's industrialisation, though important and useful complements to national efforts, cannot be substitutes for specific country agenda. The utility of measures undertaken at higher levels (e.g. within the contexts of regional integration schemes, and other forms of international partnerships) for a country's development process should be measured through their real contribution towards enabling the given country to meaningfully participate in global industrial economic activities.

Notes

1 The term 'resource curse' refers to a phenomenon in which there is a paradoxical situation where countries with an abundance of non-renewable resources experience stagnant growth or even economic contraction. However, one has to bear in mind that 'resource curse', as observed in colonised countries, is not a universal phenomenon, as literally all European countries used their resource endowment for their own development, and continue to do so. Instead, resource curse should be understood as a manifestation of a special relationship – to be precise, a disconnect – between the system for harvesting and commercial utilisation of the resources on the one hand, the concerns for local economic development of the country in which the resources are concerned on the other hand. It underlines the poor management of resources by the countries in which they are found.
2 The term 'Dutch disease' refers to the negative impact on an economy of anything that gives rise to a sharp inflow of foreign currency. Typical empirical examples have been the discovery of large oil reserves, which triggered a process of de-industrialisation. Like the 'resource curse', the 'Dutch disease' is not a natural phenomenon, as evidently many countries used their resources for development, and continue to do so. Instead, the phenomenon should also be attributed to poor management of resources by the countries in which they are found.
3 EOI is also referred to as export substitution industrialisation (ESI), or export-led industrialisation (ELI).
4 Invariably, industrialisation efforts are hugely constrained, if the developing country does not possess favourable characteristics (e.g. being a substantial market) to make it attract foreign investments, and if it does not have it the essential resource capacities of its own.

References

Akyuz, Yilmaz and Charles Gore (1996). The investment-profits nexus in East Asian industrialization. *World Development* 24(3): 471–470.
AWEEPA (1992). *South African accession to the Lomé Convention: the background issues and questions*. In Central Europe and Southern Africa in Transition. AWEEPA Conference Document. Vienna. October.
Balassa, B. (1988). The lessons of East Asian development: an overview. *Economic Development and Cultural Change* 36(3): S273–S290.
EC (1995). *Industrial and economic co-operation between the European Union and the developing countries*. Directorate General for Development. European Commission. Brussels.
EC (2010). *An integrated industrial policy for the globalisation era putting competitiveness and sustainability at centre stage*. Communication from the Commission to the

European Parliament, the Council, the European Economic and Social Committee and the Committee of the Regions. COM(2010) 614. Brussels.

Evans, Peter (1998). Transferable lessons? Re-examining the institutional prerequisites of East Asian economic policies. *Journal of Development Studies* 34(6).

Gonzales, A. (1996). *Caribbean-EU relations in the post-Lomé world.* Paper presented at a Conference organized by the Friedrich-Ebert-Foundation and the European Centre for Development Policy Management, Maastricht on 12–14 June 1996.

Grynberg, R. (1996). *The Pacific ACP States and the end of the Lomé Convention.* Paper on the 'Future of Lomé' presented at a Conference organized by the Friedrich–Ebert-Foundation and the European Centre for Development Policy Management, Maastricht on 12–14 June 1996.

Kappel, R. (1996). *Europäische Entwicklungspolitik im Wandel – Perspektiven der Koopeation zwischen der Europäischen Union and den AKP-Ländern.* INEF Report. Heft 17/1996. Gerhard–Mercator Universität Gesamthochschule Duisburg.

Kazushi, O. and Rossovsky, H. (1968). Postwar Japanese growth in historical perspective: a second look. In L. Klein and K. Ohkawa (eds), *Economic Growth – The Japanese Experience Since the Meiji Era.* Homewood: R. D. Irwin, pp. 3–34.

Kim, I. (1983). *Jukyo Bunkaken No Chitsujo to Keizai* (The Order and Economy under the Influence of Confucian-Based Culture). Nagoya: Nagoya University Press.

Lin, J. and Wang, Y. (2008). *China's integration with the world: Development as a process of learning and industrial upgrading.* Policy Research Working Paper 4799. Development Economics Vice Presidency & World Bank Institute, Finance & Private Sector Development Division. World Bank. December.

Matambalya, F. (1997). *The Merits and Demerits of EU Policies Towards Associated Developing Countries: An Empirical Analysis of the EU-SADC Trade and Overall Economic Relations within the Framework of the Lomé Convention.* Bern/Frankfurt/New York/Paris/Vienna: Peter Lang Science Publishers. First edition.

Matambalya, F. (1999). *The Merits and Demerits of EU Policies Towards Associated Developing Countries: An Empirical Analysis of the EU-SADC Trade and Overall Economic Relations within the Framework of the Lomé Convention.* Bern/Frankfurt/New York/Paris/Vienna: Peter Lang Science Publishers. Second revised edition.

Mazzucato, M. (2013). *The Entrepreneurial State: Debunking Public vs. Private Sector Myths.* The Institute Blog. Institute for New Economic Thinking. 13 June (available at: http://ineteconomics.org/blog/inet/entrepreneurial-state-debunking-public-vs-private-sector-myths?page=3).

McCarthy, S. (2003). *Industrialisation, the financial sector, diasporas and the European Investment Bank (EIB).* Dossier. The Courier ACP-EU No. 196 January–February, pp. 50–52.

Moreira, M. (1996). Industrial success and government intervention: searching for the links. *Revisita economia politica* 16(1): 107–127, January.

Naughton, B. (2007). *China's state sector, industrial policies and the 11th Five Year Plan.* Testimony before USCC hearing on 'The Extent of the Government's Control of China's Economy and Implication for the United States'. 24 May. (available at: www.uscc.gov/hearings/2007hearings/written_testimonies/07_05_24_25wrts/07_05_24_25_naughton_statement.pdf).

Reinhart, C. and Wickham, P. (1994). *Commodity prices: Cyclical weaknesses or secular decline?.* IMF Working Paper. Washington DC: International Monetary Fund.

Rodrik, D. (2001). *Development strategies for the next century.* Annual World Bank Conference on Development Economics. Washington DC: World Bank.

Sindzingre, A. (2012). *The limitations of European Union's interregionalism*: The example of the Economic Partnership Agreements in the Sub Saharan Africa. UNU – CRIS Working Papers, W-2012/1.

Singh, A. (1995). *How did East Asia grow so fast? Slow progress towards an analytical consensus*. UNCTAD/OSG/DP/97. No. 97. February.

Smith, K. (2004). The ACP in the European Union's network of regional relationships: still unique or just one in the crowd? In K. Arts and A. Dickson (eds), *EU Development Cooperation: From Model to Symbol*. Manchester and New York: Manchester University Press.

Stevens, C., Kennan, J., and Ketley, R. (1993). EC trade preferences and post-apartheid South Africa. *International Affairs* 96(1).

Van Dijk, M. and Marcussen, H. (1990). Industrialization in the Third World: the need for alternative strategies – Introduction. In M. Van Dijk and H. Marcussen (eds), *Industrialization in the Third World: The Need for Alternative Strategies*. London: Frank Cass Co.

Xing, L. (2007). *East Asian regional integration: From Japan-led 'flying-geese' to China-centred 'bamboo capitalism'*. Centre for Comparative Integration Studies. CCIS Research Series. Working Paper No. 3.

Zepeda, E., Caliari, A., Canuto, O., Kassaja, M., Kiiru, J., Mattar, J., Mckinley, T., and Mermet, L. (2009). *Export-led growth as a tool for financing development: Is the financial crisis revealing its limits?* Carnegie Endowment for International Peace. 29 June (available at: http://carnegieendowment.org/2009/06/29/export-led-growth-as-tool-for-financing-development-is-financial-crisis-revealing-its-limits/1cub).

Part VI

Harnessing Africa–European Union partnership for Africa's industrialisation

Policy implications and way forward

13 Reengineering Africa–EU partnership for industrialisation

Beacons of an Integrated Industrial Development Agenda for Africa

Francis A.S.T. Matambalya

Considering the central features of the industrialisation process, this chapter reflects on the beacons of a strategy that would lead the efforts to harness African–European Union (EU) development co-operation to promote and achieve tangible and competitive industrial transformation in both the Sub-Saharan Africa (SSA) countries and African Maghreb countries. It highlights a background where despite industrialisation being a highly desired development objective, there are serious barriers towards achieving it. It also alludes to the broad scope of innovation of the industrial development agenda. It then proposes general purpose measures as well as special purpose (targeted) measures of a holistic agenda to promote industrial transformation in a typical African country.

13.1 The scenarios

13.1.1 Industrialisation: a 'most wanted' development in African countries

One of the main challenges facing almost all African countries today is how to speed up their development by critically improving their performances in the global economy. Because of this, industrialisation is a 'most wanted' development in literally all African countries.

African countries require to industrialise in order to achieve fundamental transformations in relation to economic growth and development. As demonstrated in other chapters in this book, both theoretical postulations (cf. Chapter 2) and lessons from the history and contemporary scenarios of economic transformation (cf. Chapters 3 and 4) strongly support the rationality that industry has been the catalytic sector – it has stimulated and driven the process of structural economic transformation and sustainable development. In this connection, literally each case of successful economic transformation was achieved through a strategy that systematically expanded and diversified the country's production of industrial goods, particularly manufactured goods, and tradable services.

Imperatively, sustainable industrial development in Africa will only be achieved if the industrial sectors of the economies of the concerned countries will be able to steadily catch up with the industrial sectors of the economies from other regions along the entire value chain of the industrial economic activities: industrial investments, industrial production, and industrial trade. In this regard, besides upward integration into the global value chains through investment, production, and trade, the industrial sectors in African countries must diversify their portfolios of industrial products.

13.1.2 Barriers to industrialisation: highest and most pervasive in Africa?

Africa's industrialisation efforts are restrained by a multitude of factors. Generally, the situation in many countries is made less conducive for industrialisation by limitations related to the various legal and *regulatory frameworks* as well as the other *direction-giving* frameworks that lead the process, Financial Resource (FiR) capacities, and Non-Financial (NFiR) resource capacities. These basic challenges are exacerbated by the domestic market characteristics.

Derived from this general characterisation, in concrete terms, the long list of constraints include: weaknesses related to policies, weaknesses related to strategies, lack of resources to finance the process, lack of industrial knowledge and skills, lack of appropriate physical infrastructure, lack of industrial technological capacities, small and fragmented markets, poor markets, etc. This crowd of capacity constraints are logically clustered and discussed in detail in Section 13.3, alongside the feasible intervention required to redress them.

In explicit terms, this means that the scope of innovations that should be devised and implemented in order to set Africa on the industrialisation trajectory, is quite broad. The architecture of an *Integrated Industrial Development Agenda (IIDA)* for each African country (cf. also Chapter 4 of this book) would, in effect, constitute an attempt to answer many questions that are pertinent to the industrial development. They include, *inter alia*, the following:

a   Which FiR capacities (diverse sources from which financial resources can be mobilised, financial resource intermediation institutions like banks and non-bank financial institutions, and diverse financing instruments) are needed to facilitate the process of industrialisation?
b   Which NFiR capacities (entrepreneurial capacities, knowledge and skills capacities, organisational or institutional capacities, physical infrastructural capacities, and technological capacities) are needed to facilitate the process of industrialisation?
c   How can international co-operation be harnessed for national industrialisation?
d   Which role(s) should the state play in the industrialisation process?: in relation to the development of specific capacities (e.g. entrepreneurship and enterprise development, financial resources, knowledge and skills, organisations or institutions, physical infrastructure, technology, etc.), and relation of providing the right policy guidance?

The scope and content of the proposed innovations, which include general-purpose measures, and special-purpose measures are outlined in the following sections.

13.2 Scope of innovations of the industrial development agenda

13.2.1 Straight answers to perennial questions?

To the extent that Africa's feeble performance is associated with the status of development of its industrial sector, two of the most nudging questions are:

a   Can African countries shed their peripheral role in the global economy?
b   Can the African countries shift the centre of gravity of their economies from low value added economic activities in the primary sector[1] to higher value added economic activities in manufacturing and tradable services?[2]
c   If Africa can industrialise, what will it take to do so?

Surprisingly, the answers to these questions appear to be as straightforward as they are simple. First, like any other regions of the world, Africa can industrialise. Indeed, African industrialisation success stories exist in the case of South Africa and, to an acceptable extent, also in the case of Mauritius. However, to be able to achieve continent-wise mass industrialisation, individual African economies will have to develop a viable agenda for industrial transformation, while bearing in mind the pertaining situation in relation to access to essential natural resource inputs for economic production, and productive resource capacities – both domestically and in the global economy. The FiR capacities and NFiR capacities alluded to in this book, as productive resources capacities are, in effect, *acquired resources* that alongside *natural resource capacities* form vital inputs into the economic production process. Also, from the foregoing discussion, we know that a country's resource potential (both acquired and natural) can play a decisive role in catalysing industrial transformation, though such a role is neither automatic nor exclusive.

Second, there is no magic or hidden formula as such, behind the industrial achievement of countries. All information that we need to know about a *recipe* for industrialisation is well-documented and publicly available. The only challenge is that it might be fragmented and strewn across a multitude of theories and empirical studies. *To industrialise, African countries have to (at last) do what other countries did to achieve this feat.* In literally all successful economic transformation stories, sustained growth was achieved through an agenda based on developing essential productive capacities, which in turn led to rapid expansion of the production of industrial goods, particularly manufactured goods, and tradable services. For resource rich countries (e.g. Germany, USA, etc.), the productive capacities enabled them to harness their own natural resources, as well as to effectively use those other resources that could be accessed from international resource markets, to expand and diversify their manufacturing production and the provision of tradable services. However, own natural resources do not seem to be even a necessary condition for industrial transformation. Notably, since natural resource-poor countries (e.g. Japan, South Korea, Taiwan, Thailand, etc.) can access the required resources from international resource markets, the acquired productive capacities enabled them as well, to expand and diversify their manufacturing production and the provision of tradable services.

13.2.2 A not very mysterious route to success?

A viable strategy for spearheading structural change and transformation process – the shift of specialisation from economic activities at the lower level of the value chain to economic activities at higher levels of the value chain – is a key driver of industrialisation-inspired economic growth and development.

Therefore, there is an apparent and urgent need to improve Africa's development prospects through more effective industrial development agenda, and the IIDA is supposed to engrain that solution. As elaborated further in Section 13.3, to be able to address the various development needs of the country concerned (in terms of the particular productive capacity gaps and development needs), IIDA would essentially be an ideologically neutral, hybrid agenda. It should, on the premises that both private sector initiative and collective action through public sector are required for successful industrial transformation, be an unavoidable truism. It should, therefore, pick the best ideas from each ideological orientation, and apply them in an open economic regime. By default, it should blend structuralist and market measures, commensurate with the political economic realities of our time.

The diverse FiR and NFiR capacities are the proximate causes of industrial transformation. However, the process can only take place if policies and other aspects of the governance framework are conducive. Also, the process can benefit from international co-operation.

Therefore, as depicted in Figure 13.1, the various provisions of a viable industrialisation strategy, capable of guiding effectively the efforts for upgrading industrial productive capacities, can be divided into in five clusters (or sub-strategies) as follows:

a   Three core sub-strategies of such a hybrid strategy are: *a strategy to enhance the conduciveness of governance framework, a strategy to develop essential NFiR capacities for industrialisation at country-levels, and a strategy to develop essential FiR capacities for industrialisation at country-levels.* These three strategies underline the essence of the country-focus of any initiative intended to put it on an industrial transformation path.

b   Two complementary sub-strategies, *making multilateral co-operation agenda work for industrialisation of the African countries,* and also *making international partnership work for the industrialisation of the individual countries.* These two sub-strategies recognise the interdependence of national economies through increasing globalisation, and seek to harness the virtues of such a process to promote broadly shared industrialisation.

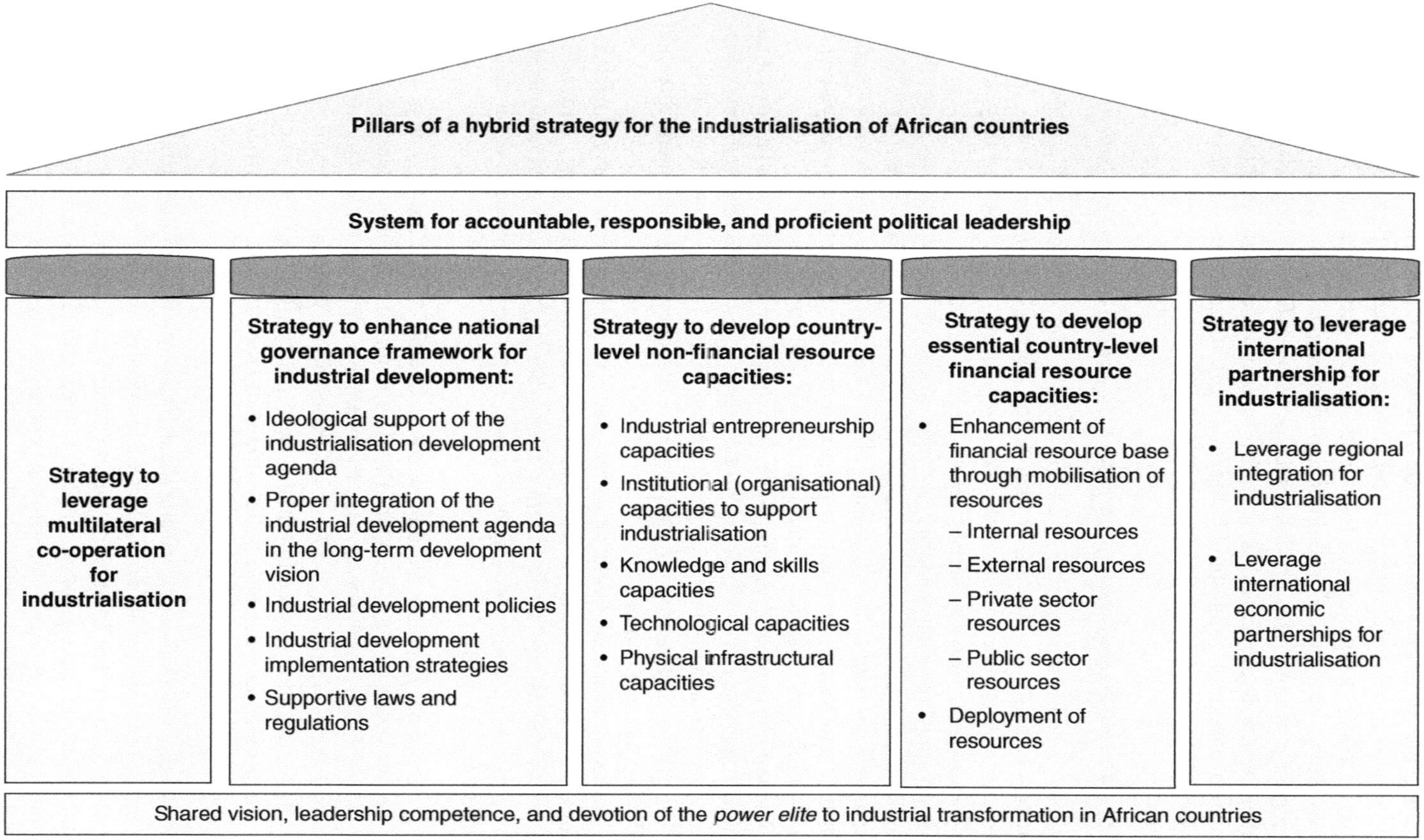

Pillars of a hybrid strategy for the industrialisation of African countries

System for accountable, responsible, and proficient political leadership

Strategy to leverage multilateral co-operation for industrialisation	Strategy to enhance national governance framework for industrial development:	Strategy to develop country-level non-financial resource capacities:	Strategy to develop essential country-level financial resource capacities:	Strategy to leverage international partnership for industrialisation:
	• Ideological support of the industrialisation development agenda	• Industrial entrepreneurship capacities	• Enhancement of financial resource base through mobilisation of resources	• Leverage regional integration for industrialisation
	• Proper integration of the industrial development agenda in the long-term development vision	• Institutional (organisational) capacities to support industrialisation	– Internal resources	• Leverage international economic partnerships for industrialisation
	• Industrial development policies	• Knowledge and skills capacities	– External resources	
	• Industrial development implementation strategies	• Technological capacities	– Private sector resources	
	• Supportive laws and regulations	• Physical infrastructural capacities	– Public sector resources	
			• Deployment of resources	

Shared vision, leadership competence, and devotion of the *power elite* to industrial transformation in African countries

Figure 13.1 Elements of a hybrid agenda for creating conditions for industrialisation in African countries (source: Author).

Overall, the strategy should provide guidance to countries' industrialisation efforts, and harness international co-operation to achieve this goal. It must be capable of addressing many issues simultaneously and effectively. Moreover, the development interventions should be applied sustainably, i.e. consistently over a long period of time. This explicitly means that an Africa–EU development partnership of the future should be moulded around the elements highlighted in the previous paragraph, and should therefore seek to augment the developmental impact of the various components of the hybrid agenda.

13.2.3 Circumstances surrounding the policy space as the real challenge?

Arguably, *power elites* play a crucial role in the development process of a country. Usually, the success of their actions is built on *shared vision, leadership competence, and devotion to a development process*, in which they are not only leaders, but also key beneficiaries.

Analogous to what happens in other parts of the world, at least three important groups of *power elites* play key roles in the development of African countries: *political elite* (highest political leaders); *corporate elite* (major domestic and foreign corporate owners and directors); and (3) *civil service elite* (high-ranking civil service leaders) (cf. Mbeki 2005).

Given their overt and covert power, they have the de facto mandate to set the political agenda, run government affairs, devise and implement business strategies, and dominate the intellectual discourse in general. In short, they call shots in everything that profoundly influences the economic development direction and prospects of a country.

However, in a real world situation – and in particular in today's Africa – things are not organised as easily as portrayed in the preceding paragraphs. Central to this is how the different *power elites*, like African governments and strong global (usually foreign) businesses, relate to one another. As noted by Hartmann (2012: 10):

> ...there are international organizations like the WTO, the IFIs or powerful donors such as the US, Japan, Britain and many more that shape the policy space of developing countries by imposing conditionalities (for example, structural adjustment), enforcing agreements or their internal policies (such as the common agriculture and fishery policy of the EU) or implementing their externally-oriented policy strategies (for example, the African Growth and Opportunity Act by the US).

Thence, the real challenges causing the debacle of efforts to industrialise African countries does appear to lie in lack of knowledge and information about what needs to be done, but in rather in the circumstances surrounding the management of the industrial and economic development agenda. There is a basic challenge of erosion of policy space – hampering the entire management (from implementation to design). The African *power elites* are not the masters even on their home turf.

Which means: a system of international partnership, based on shared vision, leadership competence, and devotion of the *power elite* to industrialise African countries is crucial. It must promote accountable, responsible, and proficient behaviour of the power elite.

13.3 General-purpose measures

13.3.1 Enhancement of the national governance framework

13.3.1.1 Conceptualising governance framework

Generally, countries must develop broad (integrated) frameworks to provide conducive environments for the emergence, flourishing, and consolidation of industrial economic activities. Usually, most countries would have sector-specific policies, intended to promote industrial development defined in a narrow sense, i.e. embracing manufacturing, mining, quarrying, and building and construction. Accordingly, the focal policies in question would usually be those related to such pertinent issues, as land, investments, manufacturing, mining, quarrying, and building and construction.

However, even within this narrow definition of industry, in reality, beyond stipulations in the primary 'policy frameworks' that directly or indirectly impact manufacturing, mining, quarrying, and building and construction; the pertinent provisions that give direction to the development of the various industrial activities would tend to be spread in a wide range of other documents or 'other frameworks'. Typically, those other documents, which give direction and guidance to industrial development efforts (henceforth also loosely referred to as other elements of an extended policy framework; and treated as *quasi* policy frameworks) would bear different names. Common designations include: action plans, codes (of conduct), declarations, directives, instruments, laws and regulations,[3] strategies, etc. Also relevant in this classification are two key frameworks that provide the overall direction and guidance to a country's development efforts in general: ideology stance, and long-term development vision. For instance, a clear ideological direction (and the clear political stance usually associated with it), are essential safeguards against frequent changes of direction.

The frameworks described in the preceding paragraph are useful in bridging the gaps in the basic policy documents (henceforth policy gaps[4]): provisions lacking in basic policy documents may be included in other relevant frameworks, e.g. sector-specific or cross-sectoral strategies.

Another reason why frameworks related to manufacturing, mining, quarrying, and building and construction do not express everything that impacts industrial development is that industrialisation, defined in a broad sense, embraces essentially all sectors of the economy, because the main issue of interest is *developing industrial (as opposed to pre-industrial) modes of economic production* in all sectors of the economy – primary, to secondary, to tertiary, etc.

A further reason why documents labelled policies do not express everything that impacts industrial development is the fact that a good number of pertinent issues are sorted out in international *fora* – rather than at the country level. Invariably, matters involving more than one country are usually contained in relevant international frameworks, e.g. international agreements, international codes of conduct, international norms, international protocols, international treaties, roadmaps, etc. These frameworks are propagated by different institutions: Regional Economic Communities, International Financial Institutions (IFIs), United Nations (UN) special agencies, other types of international organisations like the Organisation for Economic Co-operation and Development (OECD), etc. Imperatively, the international frameworks referred to here could be of bilateral nature, multilateral nature, or plurilateral nature.

Why bother to discuss all this? The bother is worthwhile, due to the implication of this proliferation of frameworks. What does all this mean? It means that, the provisions impacting industrial development can be defined as elements of an *Integrated Industrial Development Governance Framework* (IDGF).

The measures, which will be included in the various *direction-giving frameworks*, are essential for enhancing a country's FiR and NFiR capacities needed to drive industrialisation. The measures that need to be clearly articulated include, among other things, those needed to:

a   Promote the development of a comprehensive regime of bank industrial financing, as well as industrial financing through Non-Bank Financial Institutions (NBFIs).
b   Promote industrial entrepreneurship. This should target both Large Scale Industrial Enterprises (LSIEs), and Small and Medium-Sized Industrial Enterprises (SMIEs).
c   Promote institutions and inter-institutional linkages. Examples of institutions are capacity development institutions, R&D institutions, etc. Examples of linkages are those related to effective forms of Public–Private Partnership (PPP); linkages amongst business, R&D, academia, and governments; linkages between local and foreign institutions, etc.
d   Promote physical infrastructural and human resources capacities needed to adhere to various industrial standards (processes, products).
e   Promoting technological capacities through knowledge generation and acquisition. This should include the generation, acquisition, and commercial utilisation of Intellectual Property Rights (IPR) through R&D and other feasible means.
f   Strengthen industrial statistics to support the Monitoring and Evaluation (M&E) function.
g   Leverage international partnerships for industrialisation, etc.

Figure 13.2 provides further insights about this conception at national level. A predictable environment for industrial development requires the existence of coherence provisions at various levels, and dynamic complementarities amongst them (i.e. the provisions at the various levels).

Tier 1: Broad development philosophy = ideology

- Gives general direction to guide the industrial development process
- Takes the form of an ideology (e.g. capitalism, socialism, etc.), on the basis of which 'concrete' development models are derived (e.g. 'social democratic' capitalism model as practiced in the Nordic countries, the 'liberal capitalist model' that is popular in anglo-saxony countries, etc.)
- Its overriding significance is underlined by the fact that it defines the roles of the state and private sector in managing and contributing to the development process
- Ideology should be supportive of the industrial development agenda

Tier 2: Long-term development vision

- Gives general direction to guide the industrial development process
- Intends to provide the right direction in bridging the present with the future, i.e. establishing where the entity wants to be (e.g. with regard to industrial development) in the future
- Takes the entity (e.g. region, country, organisation) out of the present, and focuses it on the future
- The industrial development agenda must be clearly and properly integrated in the long-term development vision

Tier 3: Policies

- Concretises the direction to guide the industrial development process
- Broad statements of intent
- Includes macro and sectoral development policies and/or strategies
- Derived from and should be in harmony with a country's 'long-term development vision', commensurate with the 'broad development philosophy'
- Sometimes, policies and strategies are subsumed in the same document

Tier 4: Strategies

- Concretises the direction to guide the industrial development process
- Specify concrete development action plans, targets, benchmarks, and monitoring and evaluation framework (with input, output, outcome, and impact indicators)
- Includes macro and sectoral development policies strategies
- Derived from and should be in harmony with a country's policies (and therefore, 'long-term development vision', and 'broad development philosophy')
- Sometimes, policies and strategies are subsumed in the same document

Tier 5: Laws and regulations

- Gives direction and provides the legal and regulatory framework for the industrialisation process
- Effective enforcement of laws and regulations facilitate the translation of policies and/or strategies into concrete socio-economic activities and actions

Figure 13.2 Architecture of the governance framework pillar of a hybrid strategy for creating the right conditions for African industrialisation (source: Author).

The IDGF should articulate the long-term industrial development perspective. Moreover, in order to serve as a blueprint for sustainable industrial transformation, its management should be de-politicised and put above party politics. As a framework carrying the philosophy of development of the country, it should be implemented by any government in office.

13.3.1.2 Strategy to develop an integrated governance framework for African countries

In African countries, however, there are obvious gaps in the governance frameworks. These are manifested by lack of complete systems of coherent frameworks at the national level[5] and related frameworks at the international level[6] to guide industrialisation efforts. Another characteristic of these frameworks is that due to their proliferation and existence at various levels (national, bilateral, regional, plurilateral, multilateral), they are vulnerable to inconsistencies: as provisions in one framework may contradict provisions in another.

In the area of national policy, literally all African countries have at one time or another made reforms to improve their macroeconomic environments. These reforms have largely focused on structural adjustments, and obsessed with the urge to roll back the role of the state.

At another level of conceptualisation, most African countries have developed national visions that call for achieving a middle-income status by about 2025. To realise this dream, Africa's economies will need profound changes in their economic structures. However, in contrast to this aspiration, as shown in Chapter 4, Africa's growth performance cannot be positively associated with structural transformation (cf. also Arbache *et al.* 2008). Instead, the continent's growth performance appears to be driven primarily by new discovery of new mineral resources, rising commodity prices (Arbache *et al.* 2008; Arbache and Page 2010). The absence of structural change implies that growth is unsustainable, casting candid doubt on the ability of most countries to achieve the ambition of becoming middle-income economies.

Thus, further innovations to guide industrial development are necessary in most African countries. They need innovative 'industrial development governance frameworks', properly related to their long-term development visions and ideological stances (Figure 13.2). As an integral element of IIDA (cf. Figure 13.1), the IDGF should enable the governments to provide more effective guidance to the private sector and other economic operators. Among other things:

a   *The framework should stimulate rational and optimal allocation of investments.* This can be achieved by the following:

  i   Channelling the resources into exploiting the economic potentialities of the country as a whole, but also taking into account the intra-country regional particularities, so as to achieve spatially balanced industrialisation;

 ii Channelling the resources into developing the essential NFR capacities;

 iii Focusing on developing competitive product diversification along the entire value chain (i.e. diversification away from the primary sector).

b *The framework should define Local Industrial Development (LID) thresholds.* Notably, time and again, the essentiality of policy to stimulate LID has been pointed out. To cite Prebisch, for instance:

> A vigorous policy for industrialization is required as an inevitable complement to technical progress in primary production.... While the contribution of foreign enterprises to development is highly valuable, it is essential for the promotion and consolidation of free enterprise to encourage the ability and initiative of the Latin American entrepreneurs as well.
>
> (Prebisch 1959: 269)

Thus, it is vital that the IDGF should, as a minimum requirement, ascertain that both local and foreign investments contribute towards the achievement of certain LID thresholds, and provide adequate incentives to economic actors (entrepreneurs) to work towards the goal.

Access to and use of local natural resources should be treated as a central economic right, and be legally safeguarded within the human rights pillar. Hence, maximum thresholds of foreign investments targeting the exploitation of local natural resources, such as minerals, natural gas, ores, etc., should be set. A reasonable indicative threshold would be to guarantee local content and investment participation of at least 70 per cent. This will make such negative measures as Resource Rent Tax (RRT) unnecessary, which is good because businesses need profits. Local investors referred to here can be governments, private sector, or both.

In association with the investment affirmative measures referred to in the previous paragraph, minimum thresholds for value addition locally (i.e. within African countries) of agricultural and mineral raw materials should be set. The bottom line should be to achieve 100 per cent domestic value addition to precious stones, and substantial levels of domestic beneficiation for all other types of minerals.

In addition, incentives, such as subsidies for targeted activities (worker training, technology transfer, investment in local R&D, subcontracting local firms, LSIEs subcontracting SMIEs, etc.) can be used to promote the achievement of these goals. Subsection 13.4.6 elaborates further how these thresholds can be determined.

c *The framework should guarantee political accountability and responsibility (PAR) and Corporate Social Responsibility (CSR).* This is because economic crisis in Africa often highlights, at least in part, deep-rooted governance failures. The values tied to PAR and CSR, though absolutely necessary for the achievement of inclusive, sustainable, and competitive economic transformation processes, are still illusive goals in the African context.

The poor performance of many African countries in the Transparency International's global corruption index (cf. Table 13.1) bears testimony to the underlying challenges.

They mean that eliminating rent seeking and corporate and political corruption should be a high priority of the IDGF. This is because while economic crisis in Africa often highlights, at least in part, deep-rooted governance failures, corporate and political corruption are the two key actors in a system that causes the glaring gap between resource potential and economic performance. Measured on a scale of one (least corrupt) to five (most corrupt), *business/private sector* and *public officials/civil servants* score rather high in terms of being perceived to be corrupt (Transparency International 2013: 35–38).

13.3.2 Strategy to develop essential country-level non-financial resource capacities

The *governance framework* (e.g. broad development policy, public policy, strategies, and laws and regulations),[7] influence the evolution of economic activity, and consequently the country's positioning in the global economy relative to other countries.

Table 13.1 Perception of corruption by business/private sectors and public officials/civil servants in selected African vis-à-vis global average

	Business/private sector	*Public officials/civil servants*
Global	3.3	3.6
Algeria	4.1	3.8
DR Congo	3.7	4.3
Egypt	3.3	4.0
Ethiopia	2.6	2.8
Kenya	2.7	3.6
Libya	2.6	3.3
Madagascar	3.2	4.2
Malawi	3.8	4.3
Mozambique	3.2	4.0
Nigeria	3.0	4.0
Rwanda	1.7	1.7
Senegal	2.9	3.7
Sierra Leone	3.3.	3.4
South Africa	3.5	4.1
South Sudan	3.8	3.3
Tanzania	3.4	4.1
Uganda	3.0	4.0
Zambia	3.6	3.8
Zimbabwe	3.7	4.0

Source: Based on Transparency International (2013).

Notes
DR Congo = Democratic Republic of Congo.

However, having in place an appropriate governance framework is just the first step. Success of an industrialisation strategy is subject to addressing several other factors that hinder the transformation process, and usually reflect country-specific factors. One group of these factors can be discussed under the catchword of NFiR capacities and include: entrepreneurial capacities, knowledge and skills capacities, organisational or institutional capacities to support industrialisation, technological capacities, and physical infrastructural capacities.

13.3.2.1 Developing industrial entrepreneurship capacities

How can we measure the type of entrepreneurial activity most needed for a successful industrialisation process? The answer to this question can also be found in the history of industrialisation. The history of industrial revolution is also a history of captains of industry. The USA, for instance, had its Andrew Carnegie, John D. Rockerfeller, John Pierpoint Morgan, Leland Stanford, and many others. Thanks to, *inter alia*, the business acumen and prowess of its industrial captains, between 1865 and 1890, the country catapulted into the position of the world's greatest industrial power (cf. www.wisegeek. org/what-is-a-captain-of-industry.htm; www.newbedford.k12.ma.us/srhigh/calnan/Industrialists.htm).

The African countries have the smallest populations of industrial enterprises, and most local firms tend to crowd in the commercial sector or elsewhere – and in any case not in the industrial sector. Therefore, many measures are necessary, in order to address the industrial entrepreneurship capacity gaps:

a   Despite inter-country diversity of perceptions, education does presumably help to develop a sense of entrepreneurial spirit. This underscores the need for the integration of entrepreneurship in the education curriculum.
b   The state should use policy incentives to encourage industrial business start-ups, and consolidate the existing industrial businesses.
c   As underlined by historical experiences in different countries, and more recently by the success of China's 'bamboo capitalism' economic model, the state should not shy away from undertaking entrepreneurships activities. Where it is the most feasible 'entrepreneur of choice', the state should 'engage' entrepreneurially, as the major or minor shareholder. Many cases in Africa would require the state as an 'entrepreneur of choice'. Examples include investments involving huge cash outlays, such as required for mineral extraction and beneficiation, large scale agribusiness and agro-industrial undertakings, large scale financial institutions like the ones needed for 'development finance' (e.g. national infrastructure finance banks, national industrial finance banks, national development banks).
d   The relevant measures should embrace devising techno-entrepreneurship and enterprise development programmes and the related skills development, institutional development, and provision of specialised Business

Development Services (BDS) for this category of firms. The existing national capacities should be exploited to meet this goal, and strategic partnerships with external institutions be developed for the same purpose.

13.3.2.2 Developing institutional capacities to support industrialisation

African countries should enhance or establish institutions to provide critical support services and backstop the process of industrialisation. Institutions must be developed to spearhead the provision of support services in each key 'capacity' areas: industrial entrepreneurship, industrial knowledge and skills, industrial technology, physical infrastructure, and industrial finance. Table 13.2 presents an overview of required institutions to support industrial development.

The wide range of institutions that are needed to meet the institutional capacity requirements include among other things: industrial vocational training schools, universities of technology and engineering, industrial colleges, institutions for the provision of management or technical advisory services on industrial development, local industrial enterprise networks, institutions for the provision of extension services to industrial enterprises, etc.

Also, to support the evolvement of inter-firm linkages (local to local and local to foreign), it is necessary to proactively provide information to prospective partner institutions (local and foreign) through Enterprise databases (SMIEs, LSIEs, and supporting institutions), organise official intermediation efforts, and – as already mentioned – use incentives to promote subcontracting (between local firms as well as between domestic and foreign firms).

13.3.2.3 Developing industrial knowledge and skills capacities

To the extent that lacking industrial knowledge and skills impede Africa's productive potential, the upgrading of related capacities is a matter of strategic significance. To ascertain the industrial knowledge and skills needs in a country, a comprehensive needs assessment should be made. The lead question here is: which institutional capacities are required for the facilitation of industrial transformation? Implicitly, some of the pertinent issues that must be addressed relate to the relevance of education and training for industrial development, labour market for professional industrial workforce, and institutional co-operation platforms to develop industrial knowledge and skills. Figure 13.3 presents an overview of the key issues in the mobilisation of knowledge and skills capacities for the industrialisation to be considered by African countries.

In the areas of knowledge and skills development, for example, amongst the concrete education and training programmes that need to be developed or enhanced are those related to: industrial entrepreneurship skills development for entrepreneurs, technical knowledge and skills for industrial employees, quality certification, industrial enterprise monitoring and evaluation, etc.

Table 13.2 Required institutions to support industrial development

Area where support services are needed	Types of institutions to be enhanced and/or developed

Competitive industrial entrepreneurship	• Entrepreneurship knowledge generation and entrepreneurship skills development institutions
	  • Education and training institutions
	  • Specialised entrepreneurship centres
	• Business sector development institutions:
	  • IDPOs
	  • Industrial sector advocacy organisations (e.g. industrial sector local organisations, industrial sector national apex organisations)
	• Quality management institutions or organisations,
	  • Standards organisations
	  • Quality control organisations
	  • Metrology organisations
	  • Testing organisations

Industrial knowledge and skills	• Knowledge generation and dissemination institutions
	  • Education and training institutions
	  • Specialised R&D institutions
	• Institutional arrangements for 'learning-by-doing'[1]
	  • Internships
	  • Fellowships
	  • Twinning arrangements

Industrial technology	• National technology intermediation organisations • Specialised national R&D institutions
Physical infrastructure	• Communication infrastructure • Energy infrastructure • Transport infrastructure, etc.
Industrial finance	• Diverse types of banks to strengthen bank financing • Diverse types of NBFIs to complement bank financing
Cross-cutting	National Centres for Development of Industry

Source: Author.

Notes
1 The process of learning is more than just acquiring knowledge and skills through formal education. 'Learning-by-doing' is important because of the role it plays in the transformation of tacit knowledge (i.e. knowledge that is difficult to transfer to another person by means of writing it down or verbalising it, and therefore requires 'learning-by-doing' e.g. learning a language, ability to use an equipment requirements, etc.) into codified knowledge (i.e. knowledge that can be stored transferred as information).
R&D = Research and Development; IDPOs = Industrial Development Promotion Organisations; NBFIs = Non-Bank Financial Institutions.

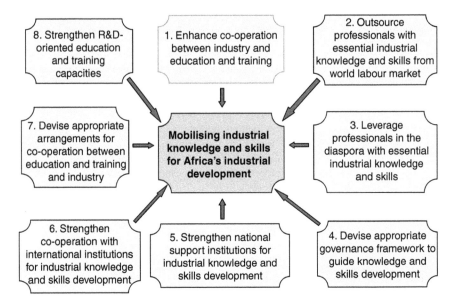

Figure 13.3 Mobilising knowledge and skills capacities for industrialisation (source: Author).

A MEASURES RELATED TO EDUCATION AND TRAINING

Being able to attract and retain industrial investments depends on the existence of qualified labour force. However, as a region, Africa ranks lowest in terms of the size and quality of industrial workforce across all industrial subsectors, as well as in other important sectors of the economy. Thus, there is an urgent need to improve the quality of the labour force. This underlines the need for a revolutionary approach in education and training. The purpose should, *inter alia*, be the following:

a   Put greater emphasis on *higher education* and *research-oriented education.* Higher education and training institutions should be encouraged to devise programmes that adequately respond to the needs of industrial development, including industrial knowledge, industrial skills, and industrial R&D. Producing more graduates at the Master's and Doctoral degrees levels, for instance, will also increase the domestic base of professional personnel. Besides, it will raise the prospects for carrying out R&D in African countries.

b   Integrate in the programmes and make strategic use of appropriate arrangements, to develop the necessary industrial knowledge and skills on a sustainable basis. This can use various forms of and *pre-job training* arrangements, such as internships, fellowships, etc. Similarly, it can use different forms of *on-the-job job training* arrangements, such as fellowships, twinning arrangements, etc.

Achieving the objective implied by the proposed measures shall require close co-operation between education and training institutions on the one side, and industry on the other, in the areas of both programme design and programme delivery. Genuine international partnership can prove very handy in this.

B MEASURES RELATED TO LABOUR MARKET

Appropriate measures should be developed, to leverage both skilled foreign labour, and skilled African labour in the Diaspora for Africa's industrialisation. In this connection:

a   The liberalisation of the labour market should help to attract and retain foreign skilled industrial labour force. Where this is necessary, the African governments should relax restrictions on foreign workers and simplify the application procedures in recruiting skilled workers from overseas. Moreover, governments could regularly organise overseas recruitment missions, to help private enterprises recruit foreign professionals.

b   Over the past decades, African countries have been losing a significant amount of their meagre skilled manpower resources to the developed and developing world. The primary significance of these Africans in the Diaspora for their countries lies in their human capital.[8] Thus, needs assessment studies should help to identify where Diaspora knowledge and skills would be most useful for industrial development. Also, building on international experiences and best practices, *research-informed Diaspora engagement policies* must outline the package of incentives for full or partial return to Africa.

C INSTITUTIONALISING INTERNATIONAL CO-OPERATION PLATFORMS
TO DEVELOP INDUSTRIAL SKILLS

The African countries should leverage international co-operation, to address the gaps in industrial knowledge and skills. Schemes involving both North–South (e.g. involving African countries and their EU partners, Japan, South Korea, USA, etc.) and South–South international co-operation (e.g. involving Africa with countries like Brazil, China, India, Russia, South Africa, Turkey, etc.) in knowledge and skills development should be enhanced and/or established.

In order to put the envisaged international co-operation on a strong institutional base, an African country and its foreign partners should establish an organisation, such as National Centre for the Development of Industry (NCDI). The relevant institution should be given the mandate and adequately empowered with resources, so as to perform the following functions:

a   Conduct industrial knowledge and skills needs assessment of African countries on regular bases.

b   Scout for and prepare catalogues of essential industrial knowledge and skills, which can be sourced from the partner foreign countries.

c   Devise and regularly revise industrial knowledge and skills development programmes to address the identified gaps in African countries.
d   Identify strategic partner institutions (e.g. business enterprises, sector management organs), both in African countries and in the partner foreign countries, which can 'host' the developed knowledge and skills development programmes.
e   Use appropriate tools to facilitate knowledge and skills development: foundation education at undergraduate and postgraduate levels, short duration training, internships, fellowships, on-the-job-training, study tours, twinning arrangements, etc.
f   Devise the component of the Monitoring and Evaluation (M&E) framework, to be used to monitor and evaluate the process and results of the co-operation arrangements.

Imperatively, an NCDI shall serve as technical organ for co-ordinating the broad agenda for the development of a country's industrial productive capacities. It should gather, document, and disseminate global best practices to promote industrial development. By design, it shall develop mutually beneficially co-operation arrangements with partners within and beyond the country.

13.3.2.4 Developing technological capacities for industrial transformation

Technological capacities are conspicuously important for international competitiveness. History reveals that industrialisation, wherever it has occurred, has been aided by various innovations that have changed and improved the way of doing things, and, in the process, also reduced the business transaction costs. Literally, everything that defines our high standard of life today is attributed to (usually multiple) innovation: reliable availability of such energy as electric power, running water in our homes, fast ways of travel and transport and communication, etc.

Moreover, as demonstrated by the recent industrialisation success stories, such as in the case of China, an effective strategy for developing domestic technological capacities must support:

a   The diversification, by embracing low-tech as well as high-tech.
b   The modernisation of the industrial sector, by facilitating transition. In the current and future context, this would involve, among other things, the facilitating of the creation and sustenance of low-carbon resource-efficient economies.[9]

Furthermore, as international value chains are becoming increasingly interlinked, there is increasingly strong competition for scarce energy and raw materials. Therefore, futuristic technological capacity development strategies must also take into account the need for transition to low-carbon and resource-efficient industrial economic activities (cf. EC 2010).

In future, the promotion of sustainable industrialisation in Africa will require also concerted effort to mobilise (through own research and development activities, or acquisition through technology market) and diffuse new technologies in various areas, like agribusiness and agro industries, mineral beneficiation, renewable energy systems, and pollution control, etc.

In order to strengthen their technological capacities and technological development dynamics, African countries need workable programmes intended to achieve the following goals as a minimum: ascertain the needs in technological capacities, institutionalise systems for building technological capacities, mobilise intellectual property assets and leverage them for industrial development, and build R&D capacities (cf. Figure 13.4).

In summary, this means that African countries need to conduct technology needs assessments, create national institutions to co-ordinate efforts to develop technological efforts, work with national and international intellectual property institutions to mobilise intellectual property assets and leverage them for industrial development.

A ASCERTAINING NEEDS IN TECHNOLOGICAL CAPACITIES

A workable programme should aim at ascertaining technological needs and establishing institutional mechanisms to manage innovation and technology

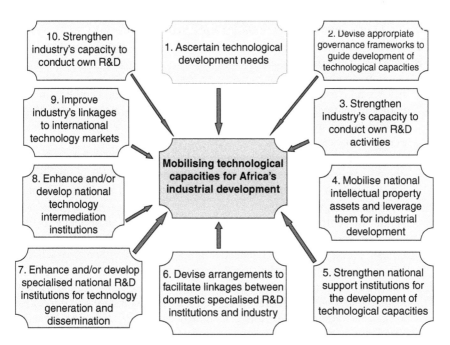

Figure 13.4 Mobilising technological capacities for industrialisation (source: Author).

Notes

R&D = Research and Development.

development process. Appropriate measures should facilitate generation, transfer, absorption, diffusion, and use of technology.

A needs assessment is, among other things, necessary in order to match a country's technological needs and requirements, to the supplies of technologies (i.e. technologies that can be sourced locally, as well as from strategic external partners). Also, it should help to identify priority products, (production) tasks, sectors, enterprises, and institutions, for possible support.

On the bases of the findings of the assessment, feasible measures should be devised to institutionalise comprehensive systems for building technological capacities, and strengthen the protection of IPRs as found appropriate.

B INSTITUTIONALISING A SYSTEM FOR BUILDING TECHNOLOGICAL CAPACITIES

The building of technological capacities is a complex and demanding undertaking, which needs well-co-ordinated efforts of many actors (private and public sectors, domestic and foreign actors). Therefore, the establishment of institutional mechanisms to facilitate the process is essential.

Hence, a country should establish an appropriate institution, such as an NCDI, and mandate and empower it to take the lead in mobilising the necessary technologies by performing the following functions:

a   Conduct technological needs assessments on a regular basis.
b   Scout for essential technologies in Africa's potential partner countries, and prepare a catalogue to document them.
c   Develop appropriate arrangements to serve as bases for co-operation between an African country and its potential partner foreign country, in promoting technological capacities. The feasible options include: internships, fellowships, on-the-job-training, study tours, technical assistance, twinning arrangements, etc.
d   Devise and regularly revise concrete technological capacity development schemes, intended to use the twinning arrangements to link up institutions (e.g. enterprises, sector management organs, etc.) from an African country its partner foreign countries.
e   Identifying strategic partner institutions (e.g. education and training institutions, enterprises, R&D institutions, sector management organs) in an African country, and in its potential foreign partner country, which can 'host' the programmes to develop technological capacities.
f   Using appropriate tools to facilitate generation, transfer, absorption, diffusion, and mastering the use of technologies: internships, fellowships, on-the-job-training, study tours, technical assistance, twinning arrangements, etc.

C MOBILISING INTELLECTUAL PROPERTY ASSETS AND LEVERAGING
THEM FOR INDUSTRIAL DEVELOPMENT

The institution responsible for developing a country's technological capacities, such as such as an NCDI, should conduct an intellectual property audit, to identify resources that can be leveraged for industrial development in African countries. This exercise can be designed and conducted in collaboration with such competent institutions, World Intellectual Property Organisation (WIPO), Africa Regional Intellectual Property Organisation (ARIPO), *Organisation Africaine de la Propriété intellectuelle* (OAPI), and national Intellectual Property Offices (IPOs).

Also, in order to ensure a smooth link to intellectual property markets as platforms for the transfer of essential technologies, an NCDI preferably in collaboration with its partners (WIPO, ARIPO, OAPI, IPO) should jointly conduct a comprehensive study, to explore the existing models of technology transfer, with a view to designing appropriate measures for African countries to mobilise technological capacities. In a joint undertaking of this nature, the United Nations Industrial Development Organisation (UNIDO) should also be brought onboard, to provide counsel on technical matters associated with technology transfer (e.g. skills needed by recipient countries to absorb technologies) for general and sector-specific industrial applications.

The process should produce a catalogue of practical measures for supporting a country to mobilising Intellectual Property (IP) assets and access IP and leveraging them for industrial development.

D BUILDING INDUSTRIAL RESEARCH AND DEVELOPMENT CAPACITIES

At present, most of the global R&D effort is located in developed countries. Also, in quite a number of developing countries, the gap to developed countries in various technological capacities is narrowing, partly because of their increased involvement in industrial R&D. In contrast, the African countries continue to play trivial roles in this connection.

African countries therefore must work, individually and jointly, as well as in collaboration with their international partners, to build up their capacities to generate technologies. The creation and enhancement of infrastructure for R&D is a precondition to achieve this goal. African countries, with their bilateral or multilateral partners, could share the burden by establishing joint R&D institutions, and design and implement joint R&D projects. The co-operation should facilitate access to and equitable sharing of the technologies developed.

13.3.2.5 *Physical infrastructural capacities*

Commensurate with practical observations, it is widely acknowledged that an enabling infrastructure is an essential requirement for the stimulation of investments into industry, including the attraction of Foreign Direct Investment (FDI). Today, one of the factors used in the ranking of countries' attractiveness for FDI is enabling infrastructure, which in the contemporary context includes transport infrastructure,[10] energy infrastructure,[11] and tele-communication[12] (UN 2012: 30).

The ability of Africa to build competitive industrial value chains has been hindered by poor infrastructure. Therefore, the development of Africa's industry to competitiveness levels will crucially depend on the quantity and quality of its physical infrastructure, including energy infrastructure, communication infra-structure, transport infrastructure, etc.

Overall, the consolidation and upgrading of these infrastructures are essential. Among other things, energy infrastructure (e.g. energy networks) must be upgraded and modernised to incorporate smart grids, facilitate the integration of renewable energy, ensure fully functional internal energy markets, and improve energy security of supply. Transport networks need to be improved to facilitate linkages to domestic and international supply and product markets.

The consolidation and upgrading of these infrastructures are essential ele-ments of any industrial development programme. For instance, transport and communications networks need to be improved to overcome bottlenecks and improve cross-border connections.

13.3.3 Strategy to develop essential country-level financial resource capacities

Achieving the requirements for NFiR capacities that are necessary for establish-ing solid industrial bases in African countries would require concerted action to mobilise and prudently deploy huge amounts of FiR. Therefore, an integrated plan to develop the pertinent capacities for industrialisation is necessary. The elements of this plan are depicted in Table 13.3.

A basic requirement of the industrial financing strategy should be to diversify the sources of funding. Useful insights about the possible sources of funding for Africa's industrialisation are contained in the '*Financing and Resource Mobil-ization Strategy*' (FRMS) developed as Annex A of AIDA – the '*Action Plan of the Implementation Strategy for the Accelerated Industrial Development of Africa*' (cf. UNIDO 2010).[13] Accordingly, Figure 13.5 provides an overview of these sources. The diverse sources build on the following contemplations:

a   In an open economic environment, commensurate with the global economic system in which the African countries operate, the needed FiR injections would ideally come from both internal and external sources.
b   In view of the complementary roles of state and markets in promoting the industrial development agenda, the resources will come from private as well as public sectors.
c   Establishing solid industrial bases in African countries and the infrastructure on which they rely, would require substantial investments in industrial production activities from different sources: both public and private capital, both local and foreign investments.

d   In the African context, concerted efforts must be made to mobilise the required resources from diverse sources of industrial financing (e.g. venture capital markets). In this connection, given the perennial deterioration in the state of public finances in many African countries, new and innovative solutions – new financing institutions – should be explored. These include (the establishment of) national Sovereign Wealth Funds (SWF) as well as similar funds at regional and pan-African levels, Structural Funds (national, regional, pan-African), African Regional Development Fund (ARDF), and the African Cohesion Fund (ACF), etc.

In terms of FiR deployment, the industrial financing should be targeted to stimulate business startups, financing dynamically growing firms, financing industrial R&D that often cannot be financed out of the cash-flows of enterprises, etc. It is also essential to align public funding and incentive mechanisms with the strategic national industrial transformation targets.

Besides the improvement of physical infrastructure (communication, energy, transport, clean water, waste water management, etc.) and infrastructure

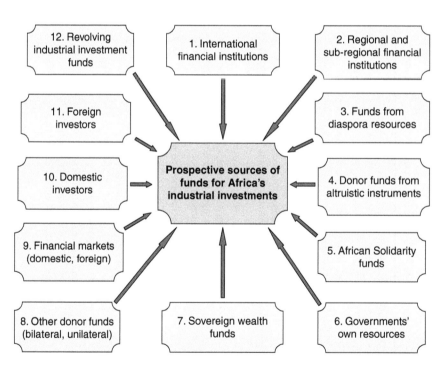

Figure 13.5 Overview of broad categories of funding sources for the implementation of AIDA (source: UNIDO (2010: Figure 4)).

Notes
AIDA = Action Plan of the Implementation Strategy for the Accelerated Industrial Development of Africa.

Table 13.3 Some restraints to industrialisation in African countries – logical clustering of FiR capacity limitations and development requirements

Restraining factor	Manifestations	Development requirements
1 Lack of properly integrated direction-giving and regulatory frameworks to guide industrialisation	*Labyrinth of potentially incongruent frameworks:* • Lack of system of coherent national *legal and regulatory frameworks* (laws and regulations) and other *direction-giving frameworks* (ideological framework, strategies, policies, development visions) and to guide the industrialisation efforts • Influence of the industrial development agenda by international frameworks (e.g. international agreements, codes of conduct, declarations, instruments, policies, protocols, rules, strategies, treaties, etc.) • Frequent changes of direction of industrialisation efforts (prompted by changes in ideological stance, national development visions, etc.)	• Creation of country IIDGF • Align international frameworks to national frameworks and vice versa • Provide safeguards for the course of industrial development agenda against frequent changes

2 Market structure	*Dominance of the financial sector by banks*
	• *Underdevelopment of the banking sector:*
	• Small number of banks
	• Non-existence of certain types of banks, e.g. development finance banks
	• High market share concentration in a few banks
	• *Underdevelopment of NBFIs:*
	• Small number of NBFIs
	• Non-existence of certain types of NBFIs
	• High market share concentration in a few NBFIs
		• Use incentives to drive development of NBFIs
		• Use incentives to drive growth of banking sector by easing:
		  • Market entry
		  • New domestic business start-ups
		  • FDI inflows
		  • Development of different types of banks
		• Use incentives to drive growth of NBFIs sector by easing:
		  • Market entry
		  • New domestic business start-ups
		  • FDI inflows
		  • Development of different types of NBFIs

| 3 | Limited and restrictive financing instruments | Underling shortfalls of financing instruments include the following:
• Typically, financing instruments restricted to short-term finance
• Loan amounts do not take into account the heavy capital outlays of industrial investments | Use following to promote industrial investments:
• Subsidised commercial bank loans for targeted firms
• Credit guarantee system
• Equipment leasing
• Enterprise credit information system |
| 4 | Rigidity in the use of criteria to determine the creditworthiness of potential borrowers | • Lack of information to FIs on the commercial viability of potential industrial borrowers
• Non-existence of certain types of banks, e.g. development finance banks | • Devise industrial enterprise creditworthiness evaluation and advice system suited to country particularities |

Source: Author.

Notes

IIDF = Integrated Industrial Development Governance Framework; FDI = Foreign Direct Investments; NBFI = Non-Bank Financial Institutions; FIs = Financial Institutions.

maintenance and service quality, many specific and targeted measures can be included in the governance frameworks (e.g. policies), and used to promote the inflow of industrial FDI in a given African country, including:

a   *Tying incentives to a list of priority industrial activities and products.* The incentives should seek to promote domestic value added activities, in order to promote local agribusiness and agro-industries, domestic mineral beneficiation, and the development of domestic manufacturing in general.

b   *Using diverse measures to disseminate information about the FDI attractiveness of a country.* This includes maintaining a well-elaborated website, conducting regular investment promotion seminars and missions, effectively using embassies abroad for FDI promotion, using local and foreign exhibitions and trade fairs to attract investors, etc.

c   Establishing industrial estates, such as specialised industrial parks, with sufficient infrastructure and essential business support services.

d   *Undertake flanking measures, in order to reduce the transactions costs for industrial investors.* These could include such labour support measures as education and training, matching for ease of recruitment, housing, commuting/transport, health care, etc.).

e   *Use an 'anchor firm' strategy.* This involves targeting and inviting a firm (or firms), and providing it (them) with required conditions, so that it forms (they form) the hub of development of a certain branch (or certain branches) of industry (e.g. agribusiness and agro-industries, mineral beneficiation).

13.4 Special-purpose measures

13.4.1 Devising special financing mechanisms for small scale industrial enterprises

Even in developed countries, such as the EU, Small and Medium Scale Enterprises make up some two-thirds of industry's employment and a large share of EU industry's growth and jobs potential is to be found in its lively and dynamic SMEs. Promoting the creation, growth, and internationalisation of SMEs thus is the core of the new EU integrated industrial policy (cf. EC 2010).

The need for special support for SMEs from African economies is even greater!

13.4.2 Addressing financing needs of large scale industrial enterprises

Africa's industrial transformation will not take place without the involvement of LSIEs. Large scale private investment projects and infrastructure investment also rely on well-functioning financial markets. They can attract private and public capital from outside Africa, including FDI (e.g. from SWFs). It is essential that FDI operates in an open investment climate and adheres to certain standards with regard to transparency and governance, in line with the best practices.

13.4.3 Strategy to harness regional integration agenda for African industrialisation

The sequential pattern of gradation to industrialisation by the countries of East Asia, and the successful industrialisation of the backward EU countries provide two cases of strong proof that practical (as opposed to just policy-biased) regional integration is a strong tool for promoting industrialisation (cf. Chapter 11 in this book, and Xing 2007).[14]

Through the Cotonou Agreement, and Economic Partnership Agreements (EPAs) that are supposed to spawn from them, the African countries, which belong to the African, Caribbean, and Pacific (ACP) group of countries (AACP) and EU countries already have relatively solid frameworks in place to harness regional integration for Africa's industrialisation. However, for these frameworks to deliver, two things must happen:

a   They must be re-engineered to put industrialisation at the centre of co-operation.
b   They must emulate the many useful lessons from East Asia.
c   The industrial co-operation provisions included in them must be seriously implemented.
d   There should be serious Monitoring and Evaluation (M&E) of the implementation process and results of the industrial development co-operation.

13.4.4 Strategy to harness multilateral agenda for Africa's industrialisation

In order to more comprehensibly tackle the challenges of investment and capacities in developing countries, UNIDO decided to establish a new system of institutions. Thus, it has launched a programme for South-South Industrial co-operation, through which UNIDO Centres for South-South Industrial Co-operation (UCSSIC) are established in some of the more advanced developing countries. The centres in China and India are already operational. Their programmes are funded by the host country and UNIDO.

The development of the UNIDO South-South Industrial Co-operation Programme, and its specific realisation through the UCSSIC presents a viable platform of co-ordinated responses to the technological needs of Least Developed Countries (LDCs). It is an opportunity that can be used to harness the multilateral agenda for Africa's industrialisation.

13.4.5 Strategy for meaningful harnessing of natural resource endowments

In a bid to leverage the natural resource endowment for industrialisation:

a   The national industrialisation initiatives must be properly linked to agricultural transformation and rural development efforts. This underlines both:

   i   The need to develop agribusiness and agro-industries, in order to have an advanced agricultural value chain, which will free African countries from being mere exporters of agricultural raw materials to the rest of the world.

   ii   The need to transform the rural character of Africa's population by changing the structure of the economies. This will be achieved by creating more jobs in the value adding activities, a key objective and feature of industrial development.

   China provides some useful insights about linking industrialisation to rural development. Despite not being perfect institutions that therefore need further improvements (McDonnell 2004), the country's 'Township and Village Enterprises' (TVEs) have nonetheless made outstanding contributions to the industrial development efforts and the overall economic growth, by supporting agribusiness and agro-industries (He Kang 2006).

   The transformation of the rural character of the economy should involve also the establishment of industries at the sources of industrial (agricultural and mineral) raw materials, as well as establishing industries in less developed areas.

b   The national industrialisation efforts must also be geared towards enabling African countries to more meaningfully exploit their mineral wealth, by developing more complete mineral-based industrial value chains. Africa's mineral wealth is indisputably evident. For instance, on the basis of currently available data, the Southern African region alone contributes to world production of major metals and minerals about 53 per cent of vanadium, 49 per cent of platinum, 40 per cent of chromite, 50 per cent of diamonds, and 20 per cent of cobalt (Adam 2013).

   And yet, most African countries draw limited benefits from their mineral wealth, due to their wrong positioning in the global value chain, which is attributed to lack of industrialisation. Therefore, as in the case of agriculture, *mineral beneficiation* (i.e. processing and adding value to minerals – thus transformation of mineral raw material into a more finished product) is essential.[15] Its achievement will free many African economies from just being exporters of mineral raw material to the rest of the world.

13.4.6 Setting thresholds for local industrial participation and performance

The agenda to promote industrial transformation in African countries should involve setting LID thresholds, in order to achieve three important industrial development milestones:

a   Raising the contribution of the industrial sector to the economy.
b   Meaningful participation for indigenous and local enterprises in the industrial economy.
c   Internationally competitive industrial performance by the domestic industrial sector.

Local industrial participation should be defined in relation to investments in subsectors of industry. In this connection, investments in the exploitation of a country's natural resources (e.g. minerals, ores, petroleum, gas) should have a mandatory local participation (i.e. local content). The same should apply for land-based investments such as FDI in basic agricultural production (as opposed to investments in agricultural processing).

To begin with, the eight sub-indices contained in the UNIDO Competitive Industrial Performance (CIP) Index can be used as bases for determining the target performance thresholds for a country. The indices, which are discussed in detail in *Competitive Industrial Performance Report 2012/2013* (cf. UNIDO 2013) and also introduced in Chapter 4 of this book, include:

a   Manufacturing Value Added per capita (*MVApc*).
b   Manufactured Exports per capita (*MXpc*).
c   Medium- and High-tech manufacturing Value Added share in total Manufacturing Value Added (*MHVAsh*).
d   Manufacturing Value Added share in total GDP (*MVAsh*).
e   Medium- and High-tech manufactured Exports share in total manufactured exports (*MHXsh*).
f   Manufactured Exports share in total exports (*MXsh*).
g   MVA as a share of World MVA (*impWMVA*).[16]
h   Impact of a country on World Manufactured trade (denoted as *imWMT*).[17]

In this connection, Table 13.4 provides dynamically determined *indicative thresholds* that must be met in order to set African countries on the pathway to catching up in industrialisation. These indicators are dynamic, in the sense that they are always computed on the basis of current data, and therefore the base data for their calculation change from time to time. Though any threshold would tend to be arbitrary, the proposed ones have been informed by the performance of African economies, and the performance of other countries during periods of successful industrial drives. Because of the need to catch up, a country's concrete thresholds (to be derived from those in Table 13.4) should be aligned to those of the best performing economies.

Table 13.4 Setting thresholds for industrial performance by African countries based on CIP Index

Index	Indicative threshold	
	Minimum	*Desired*
1 *MVApc*	*WMVApc*	*MVApc > WMVApc*
2 *MXpc*	*WMXpc*	*MXpc > WMXpc*
3 *MHVAsh*	*WMHVAsh*	*MHVAsh > WMHVAsh*
4 *MVAsh*	*WMVAsh*	*MVAsh > WMVAsh*
5 *MHXsh*	*WMHXsh*	*MHXsh > WMHXsh*
6 *MXsh*	*WMXsh*	*MXsh > WMXsh*
7 *impWMVA*	*POPsh*	*impWMVA > POPsh*
8 *imWMT*	*POPsh*	*imWMT > POPsh*

Source: Author.

Notes
CIP Index = Competitive Industrial Performance Index; MVApc = country's Manufacturing Value Added per capita; MXpc = country's Manufactured Exports per capita; MHVAsh = country's Medium- and High-tech manufacturing Value Added share in total Manufacturing Value Added; MVAsh = country's Manufacturing Value Added share in total GDP; MHXsh = country's Medium- and High-tech manufactured Exports share in total manufactured exports; MXsh = country's Manufactured Exports share in total exports; impWMVA = MVA as a share of World MVA; imWMT = Impact of a country on World Manufactured trade; WMVApc = World Manufactured value added per capita; WMXpc = World Manufactured Exports per capita; WMHVAsh = World's Medium- and High-tech manufacturing Value Added share in total Manufacturing Value Added; WMVAsh = World's Manufacturing Value Added share in total GDP; WMHXsh = World's Medium- and High-tech manufactured Exports share in total manufactured exports; WMXsh = World's Manufactured Exports share in total exports; POPsh = country's share of World population.

The other desirable targets can be developed in relation to indicators that though not yet forming part of the UNIDO composite CIP Index, provide viable measures of industrial performance. They include:

a   Country's total investments in Manufacturing sector per capita (*INVMpc*).
b   Country's FDI inflows in Manufacturing sector per capita (*MFDIpc*).
c   Country's FDI inflows in manufacturing sector as share of total FDI inflows (*MFDIsh*).
d   Country's FDI inflows in Medium- and High-tech manufacturing sub-sector as a share in total FDI inflows (*MHMFDIsh*).
e   Country's FDI inflows in Medium- and High-tech manufacturing sub-sector per capita (*MHMFDIpc*).
f   Country's number of manufacturing establishments per 100,000 people (*CNME*),
g   Country's number of employees in manufacturing sector as a percentage of total number of employees (*EMPMsh*).
h   Country's Industry Gross Fixed Capital Formation as a share of World Gross Fixed capital Formation (*imWIGFCF*).
i   Country's Investments in manufacturing sector as a share of World Investments in Manufacturing (*imWINVM*).

j Country's Investments in Medium- and High-tech manufacturing sub-sector as a share of World Investments Medium- and High-tech manufacturing sub-sector (*imWINVMHM*).

k Country's *number of manufacturing employment per 100,000 people as a ratio of World Manufacturing employment per 100,000 people* (*imWNME*).

In this case, Table 13.5 provides indicative thresholds that must be met in order to put the African countries on a development trajectory that will lead them to catch up in terms of industrialisation. The indicators presented in Table 13.5 are also dynamically determined.

Table 13.5 Other recommended thresholds for industrial performance by African countries

Index	Indicative threshold	
	Minimum	Desired
INVMpc	*WINVMpc*	*INVMpc > WINVMpc*
MFDIpc	*WMFDIpc*	*MFDIpc > WMFDIpc*
MFDIsh	*WMFDIsh*	*MFDIsh > WMFDIsh*
MHMFDIsh	*WMHMFDIsh*	*MHMFDIsh > WMHMFDIsh*
MHMFDIpc	*WMHMFDIpc*	*MHMFDIpc > WMHMFDIp*
CNME	*WNME*	*CNME > WNME*
EMPMsh	*WEMPMsh*	*EMPMsh > WEMPMsh*
imWIGFCF	*POPsh*	*imWIGFCF > POPsh*
imWINVM	*POPsh*	*imWINVM > POPsh*
imWINVMHM	*POPsh*	*imWINVMHM > POPsh*
imWME	*POPsh*	*imWME > POPsh*

Source: Author.

Notes
INVMpc = Country's total investments in Manufacturing sector per capita; MFDIpc = Country's FDI inflows in Manufacturing sector per capita; MFDIsh = Country's FDI inflows in manufacturing sector as share of total FDI inflows; MHMFDIsh = Country's FDI inflows in Medium- and High-tech manufacturing sub-sector as a share in total FDI inflows; MHMFDIpc = Country's FDI inflows in Medium- and High-tech manufacturing sub-sector per capita; CNME = Country's number of manufacturing establishments per 100,000 people; EMPMsh = Country's number of employees in manufacturing sector as a percentage of total number of employees; imWIGFCF = *Country's Industry Gross Fixed Capital Formation as a share of World Gross Fixed capital Formation*; imWINVM = Country's Investments in manufacturing sector as a share of World Investments in Manufacturing; imWINVMHM = Country's Investments in Medium- and High-tech manufacturing sub-sector as a share of World Investments Medium- and High-tech manufacturing sub-sector; imWME = Country's number of manufacturing employment per 100,000 people as a ratio of World Manufacturing employment per 100,000 people; WINVMpc = World investments in Manufacturing sector per capita; WMFDIpc = FDI inflows in Manufacturing sector per capita; WMFDIsh = World FDI inflows in manufacturing sector as share of total FDI inflows; WMHMFDIsh = World FDI inflows in Medium- and High-tech manufacturing sub-sector as a share in total FDI inflows; WMHMFDIpc = World FDI inflows in Medium- and High-tech manufacturing sub-sector per capita; WNME = World number of manufacturing establishments per 100,000 people; WEMPMsh = World number of employees in manufacturing sector as a percentage of total number of employees.

These indicators presented in Tables 13.4 and 13.5 should form part of the Monitoring and Evaluation (M&E) Frameworks of the industrialisation of African countries.

13.5 Conclusions

The ultimate test of the aptness of any statistics on Africa's economic achievements is in the effect of such observed development trends on the well-being of the African people. More efficient economies will have high levels of productivity, and participation will provides the means to deliver higher incomes to broad sections of societies. This will translate into higher standards of living and more equitable societies. If the dynamics of the societal transformations of the past are anything to go by, then industrialisation is a *sine qua non* for achieving these aspirations.

The previous sections of this chapter have dwelt on many pertinent issues, including demonstrating Africa's needs for industrial transformation. Both the mobilisation of critical amounts of FiR and NFiR, and their prudent deployment, count high amongst the key considerations for promoting industrial transformation in African countries. Moreover, the obligation for managing Africa's economic transformation through industrialisation lies with the African countries themselves. As argued, there is a lot these countries can do in order to set on the path to industrialisation: pragmatic architecture of the industrialisation agenda and harnessing own potential for industrialisation are basic requirements.

Also, as highlighted in this analysis, co-operation between more advanced and less advanced economies can and has been leveraged in practice, to ignite and propel industrial transformation in the latter group of countries. Therefore, African countries should seek to exploit the option, in which case the EU countries as Africa's traditional partners may have a significant role to play.

But, considering the little accomplishment by African countries through centuries of economic ties to Europe, achieving Africa's industrial development by leveraging co-operation with the EU will require a major effort in order to change the European mindset about Africa. In this connection, the political will of the EU will be as much essential as the will of corporate EU, in devising and implementing mutually beneficial economic relations with the African countries.

Finally, it is obvious that African countries must seek to achieve their development objectives within new, and in fact more favourable realities. They must set their development agenda on industrialisation, and undertake concrete measures to revise and broaden their international partnerships for industrialisation, with particular emphasis on co-operation with emerging economies and South-South co-operation in general.

Achieving the considerations highlighted above requires concerted action of the state and non-state actors in every African country, to mobilise and prudently deploy huge amounts of FiR. The NCDI proposed in this chapter should serve as the hub and technical organ for co-ordinating the agenda for developing these capacities and undertaking necessary measures to ascertain their effective deployment.

Notes

1 The primary sector-based economies of most African countries are customarily domi-nated by basic agriculture and mining activities.

2 The higher value added activities referred to industrialisation-driven manufacturing or the production of tradable services. This is done by adding value to the resources – which many of the African countries have in abundance, or can purchase from global resource markets.

3 The laws and regulations bear particular significance, as beyond direction to industrial development, they provide the legal and regulatory framework that guides the process.

4 The term policy gaps, as used in this book, refers to a situation where some sectoral and cross-sectoral policy frameworks would be missing from the policy regime. Although even in a developed country situation, it might be impossible to have a fool-proof policy regime without gaps; such gaps are more common in a typical develop-ing country situation.

5 Typical frameworks at the national level which are referred to here include: broad development philosophy (usually expressed in terms of ideological stance), develop-ment visions (usually expressed as national development vision), strategies, policies, and laws and regulations.

6 In accordance with the terminology used, the typical frameworks referred to here include: agreements, codes of conduct, declarations, instruments, development visions (e.g. development visions of regional economic communities), policies, strategies, treaties, etc. The frameworks in question can be of a bilateral, regional, multilateral, or plurilateral nature.

7 For further articulation about the concept of governance framework, cf. also Chapters 4, 5, 6, 11, 12, and 14.

8 Presumably, their entrepreneurial ventures and sources of capital are essentially negli-gible relative to the economic development requirements of their home countries.

9 Competitiveness in the international value is a dynamic phenomenon. It is driven by a strong competition for scarce resources, including agricultural raw materials, mineral raw materials, and energy.

10 This includes: *road density* (measured in kilometres of road per 100 square kilometres of land area), *percentage of paved roads* in total, *rail lines total route* (measured in kilometres), liner shipping connectivity index (UN 2012: 30).

11 This is measured in electric power consumption.

12 This is measured in: telephone lines/100 inhabitants, mobile cellular subscriptions/100 inhabitants, fixed broadband Internet subscribers/100 inhabitants.

13 The FRMS was developed by the author of this chapter, during the time he spent at the Africa Programme of the UNIDO Headquarters in Vienna, as a Senior Inter-national Industrial Development Consultant.

14 Moreover, the phenomena of industrial development, trade, economic growth, and economic development are closely interrelated. Imperatively, the building of indus-trial (productive) capacities will enable African countries to exploit the opportunities resulting from the international trading system. Without capacities to produce prod-ucts that matter on markets, it is impossible to become a competitive player on domestic and foreign markets.

15 The four beneficiation stages are: (a) mining and producing ore or concentrate, (b) converting concentrate into metal or alloy, (c) transforming these metals and allows into a semi-fabricated product, and (d) making a finished product (Adam 2013). Typically, the mining economic activities in AACP countries are restricted to (a), after which their products are exported to be processed and create jobs and wealth in other parts of the world – many of them are EU countries.

16 Computed as a country's MVA as a share of World MVA.
17 Computed as a country's manufactured Exports (ME) as a share of World Manufactured trade.

References

Adam, S. (2013). *Madini Africa Brings About Investment in African Mineral Beneficiation*. 26 May (available at: http://africaoil.ning.com/profiles/blogs/madini-africa-brings-about-investment-in-african-mineral).

Arbache, J. and Page, J. (2010). How fragile is Africa's recent growth? *Journal of African Economies* 19(1): 1–24. January.

Arbache, J., Go, D., and Page, J. (2008). *Is Africa at a Turning Point?*. Policy Researching Paper 4519. The World Bank. Washington, DC

EC (2010). *An Integrated Industrial Policy for the Globalisation Era Putting Competitiveness and Sustainability at Centre Stage*. Communication from the Commission to the European Parliament, the Council, the European Economic and Social Committee and the Committee of the Regions. COM(2010) 614. Brussels.

Hartmann, S. (2012). *The Conceptual Flaws of the New EU Development Agenda from a Political Economy Perspective, or Why Change is Problematic for a Donor-Driven Development Policy*. Österreichische Forschungsstiftung für Internationale Entwicklung. Vienna. October.

He Kang (Chief Editor). (2006). *China's Township and Village Enterprises*. Foreign Language Press, Beijing.

Mbeki, M. (2005). *Underdevelopment in Sub-Saharan Africa: The Role of the Private Sector and Political Elites*. Foreign Policy Briefing No. 85. CATO Institute. 15 April.

McDonnell, B. (2004). Lessons from the rise and (possible) fall of Chinese Township-Village Enterprises. *William and Mary Law Review* 45(3), Article 5.

Prebisch, R. (1959). Commercial policy in underdeveloped countries. *American Political Science Review* 49(2): 251–273.

Transparency International (2013). *Global Corruption Barometer 2013*. Transparency International, Berlin.

UN (2012). *World Investment Report 2012: Towards a New Generation of Investment Policies*. United Nations Conference on Trade and Development, New York and Geneva.

UNIDO (2010). *Financing and Resource Mobilisation Strategy and Monitoring and Evaluation Framework for the Implementation Strategy of the AU Action Plan for the Accelerated Industrial Development of Africa*. Background Paper. African Union and United Nations Industrial Development Organization, Vienna. March.

UNIDO (2013). *Competitive Industrial Performance Report 2012/2013*. United Nations Industrial Development Organization, Vienna.

Xing, L. (2007). *East Asian Regional Integration: From Japan-led 'Flying-geese' to China-centred 'Bamboo Capitalism'*. Centre for Comparative Integration Studies. CCIS Research Series. Working Paper No. 3.

14 Reengineering Africa–EU partnership for industrialisation

Implications for the management of the development agenda

Francis A.S.T. Matambalya

In view of the indispensable need to reengineer Africa–EU partnership for industrialisation, this chapter summarises the implications of such a shift in the modalities of co-operation for the management of the development agenda. It underscores the fact that the realities under which the development agenda will be managed will be new, and therefore necessitating the refocusing of the agenda itself. Imperatively, while focusing on industrialisation, the new agenda would have to be broadened (to comprehensively address the various capacity needs of the African countries).

Moreover, it would be essential for African countries to adopt development models that actively promote co-operation between markets and states, and to broaden their international partnerships for development by reaching out to other partners (e.g. China, India, Brazil, South Korea, etc.).

Equally important, there is a need to redefine the roles and relations in partnerships for development. African countries must strive to have sovereignty over their development agenda – and hence decouple the prototypical donor-driven agendas that have characterised the relationships between African modern nation states since their establishment, and their foreign and international partners. To achieve industrialisation and real development, a change of the mindset, from the *triad doctrine*, in which Africa is just a periphery serving the interests of the centre, is timely and long overdue. The changed power structure in the international economic landscape offers the African countries a rare opportunity to make this happen.

Finally, there is need to redefine the practices for managing the development agenda. Political and corporate leadership must be more responsible, while systems for monitoring and evaluation of the delivery of the development agenda must be developed, introduced, and seriously adhered to.

Thus, in order to assist its industrialisation endeavours, every African country needs a national Integrated Industrial Development Agenda (IIDA) embedded in the framework proposed in this book.

The following sections provide the details about these contemplations.

14.1 Management of the development agenda under new realities

Given their levels of development, all African countries need an agenda for sustainable and economic growth and development through industrial transformation in order to achieve their ambitions to generate wealth, raise incomes, alleviate poverty, etc. The change towards a new model for economic growth and development in African countries, based on industrialisation-driven economic transformation, would go a long way towards achieving this ambition.

However, the new realities ushered in by the changes will also entail profound implications for the management of the development agenda. The new realities include the following:

a   *Refocusing of the agenda.* This would ideally embrace adopting a development agenda centred on industrialisation, broadening the agenda to guide industrial transformation beyond policies, pragmatic partnerships between markets and states, broadening international partnership for Africa's industrial development.
b   *Redefined roles and relations in the management of the partnerships for development.* This would involve lead roles for African countries in their industrialisation processes, decoupling a from donor driven agenda, and change of mindset away from triad doctrine.
c   *Changed approach to management.* One of the essential characteristics of a changed approach to management should include making corporate and political leadership accountable. The other one will be adopting continuous Monitoring and Evaluation (M&E) as a tool of Results-Based Management (RBM).

14.2 Refocused agenda

14.2.1 Centre the development agenda on industrialisation

As shown in other chapters in this book (e.g. 1, 3, and 11), there are close associations between industrialisation on the one hand, and economic growth and development on the other. Indeed, as has long been argued from classical development economics theory, manufacturing is an engine of growth in the industrialisation era, due to its ability to facilitate economies of scale (with increasing returns to scale) and economies of scope. Visibly, where properly developed, the manufacturing sector clearly serves *as a central joint*, linking economic activities at the lower levels of the value chain (i.e. in the primary sector) with those at the higher levels of the value chain (i.e. economic activities in the tertiary sector, quaternary sector, quinary sector, etc.).

Also, as alluded to in several chapters in this book (e.g. Chapters 2, 3, 4), the strategic role of industrialisation for development is usually associated with the impact it has on various factors that signify development. These factors include, inter alia: higher economic productivity and increasing returns to scale, technology and spill-over effects; high capital intensity; diversification through forward and backward linkages of the various sectors of the economy; demand consideration; and creation and diversification of employment. Accordingly, these factors have been used – in a variety of combinations – to explain the mechanisms behind industrialisation-led theories of economic growth and development. The credibility of industrialisation as a necessary stage of economic development, and as an objective of the development process by itself, is partly based on this.

It is partly in view of these considerations that the development partnership between the African countries belonging to the African, Caribbean, and Pacific (ACP) group of countries (AACP) and their European Union (EU) partners should make industrialisation in African countries a priority.

14.2.2 *Broaden the agenda for guiding industrial transformation*

In the past few decades the global business and economic environment has changed radically. The new global business and economic landscapes pose both challenges and opportunities for African industrial transformation ambitions. On the one hand, any emergent industries in African countries are poised to brace for competition with both established industrial economies (e.g. North America, Europe, East Asia), and emerging industrialised countries (e.g. Brazil, Russia, India and China (BRICS)) in all types of products and along the entire value chain. On the other hand, the global spread of industrial development means that African countries have more partners with whom they can work to achieve their own industrial transformation aspirations.

A fresh approach to industrial development is necessary. An innovative agenda to guide the industrial development of African countries should be based on a properly articulated IIDA, which was introduced in Chapter 13 of this book and contains the following core components:

a Strategy to enhance national governance framework (cf. also Chapters 4, 5, 6, 11, 12, and 13 for the clarification of the concept) for industrial development:
b Strategy to develop essential country-level Non-Financial Resource (NFiR) capacities for industrialisation.
c Strategy to develop essential country-level Financial Resource (FiR) capacities for industrialisation.
d Strategy to leverage international partnership for industrialisation. This one seeks to leverage regional integration, as well as other forms of international economic partnerships for industrialisation
e Strategy to leverage the multilateral co-operation agenda for industrialisation.

14.2.3 *Encourage entrepreneurial partnerships between markets and states*

The debate on the role of the state in any economic setting (i.e. regardless of ideological stance), and how it should relate to markets has been greatly distorted – causing serious and costly confusion. As argued several times in this book, it is crucial for Policy Managers to realise that:

a   The State is not nearly as dreadful an economic actor as many contemporary proponents of Markets would like to make everyone believe. In contrast, it is a necessary and strategic actor now, as it has been in other epochs of development. Ours is still a world in which the way the economy functions is determined not only by Markets, but also by deliberate actions of Nation-States. The latter act through *legal and regulatory frameworks* and *other frameworks* that give direction to and guide the development process (i.e. codes of conduct, development visions, ideological stance, policies, strategies, declarations, instruments, etc.) – and in this way provides guidance to the private sector. From experience, we know that there is a plethora of such frameworks – which can be unilateral, bilateral, plurilateral, and multilateral. These frameworks create the environment within which market forces operate – as through them, States set the rules that entrepreneurs must follow.
b   Many circumstances justify the necessity of States being entrepreneurs – and in some cases 'entrepreneurs of choice'. This explains why States are active entrepreneurs, not only in China and Russia, but also in countries with a long capitalist tradition and irrespective of the version of capitalism:

    i   From the *Anglo-Saxon capitalist model*[1] (UK, USA, Canada, Australia, New Zealand, Ireland, etc.);
    ii   To the *orthodox capitalist model*[2] of continental Europe (e.g. Germany, France, Italy, etc.);
    iii To the *social democratic welfare capitalist model*[3] (e.g. Denmark, Finland, Norway, Sweden, etc.).

    The need for the engagement of the states in entrepreneurial activities under certain circumstances – such as those surrounding industrial investments – is even more urgent in African countries where the local private sector is generally still very weak.
c   The relationship between the State and Markets is not one way – in practice, Market forces would tend to influence the content of the frameworks referred to here, and vice versa.
d   A feasible development agenda – whether targeting the industrial sector or the economy as a whole – necessitates intellectual integration of measures intended to harness the benefits of the States and the Markets.

14.2.4 Broadened international partnership for Africa's industrial development

Within the realm of international co-operation, African countries must be conscious of the fact that the international economic system has changed dramatically over the past 50 years, creating new opportunities. Most notably, the EU is not the only contender in taking up the role of a strategic partner for industrial transformation in the continent. True, the EU remains a potentially viable partner for Africa. However, the African–EU relations are by no means easy. Africa is a junior partner in lopsided relations. The situation is further complicated by the perceived 'colonial baggage' and 'complex superiority mindset' of Africa's traditional Western European partners or their foreign off-shoots, which invariably make them fail to accept African countries as equal partners.

In contrast, such countries as China, India, Russia, South Korea, Japan, etc., do not have a 'colonial baggage' and 'complex superiority mindset' and might be better placed to take over the role of strategic partnership with African economies. Another strong argument in favour of these countries (especially, China, India, and Russia) is that they have a lot of extra FiR capacities, which can be invested in the development of Africa's productive capacities, as well as in real industrial production activities. Moreover, China, for instance, can reach back to and greatly benefit from its experiences of involvement in both the 'flying geese' and 'bamboo capitalism' models of East Asian economic transformation. These models are renowned for forging mutually beneficial economic ties between the less advanced and the more advanced countries (Xing 2007).

Likewise, Russia does not have a history of building mercantilist ties with African countries. Unlike the European integration process, the Eurasian Economic Community (EAEC), which Russia spearheads, and which originated from the Commonwealth of Independent States (CIS), does not involve the stronger economies wholesale taking over the assets and resources of the weaker economies under the disguise of liberalisation and privatisation. This is surely an evolving egalitarian model of economic co-operation, which African countries need to closely study and learn from.

Exposing the Africa–EU partnership to the kind of strong international competition proposed herewith will make the EU change its stance towards Africa, and engage in truly mutually beneficial co-operation, including through contributing to Africa's industrialisation efforts.

14.3 Redefined roles and relations in partnerships for development

14.3.1 Lead roles of African countries

The ultimate test of the aptness of any statistics on Africa's economic achievements is in the effect of such observed development trends on the wellbeing of the African people. More efficient African economies will have high levels of productivity, and genuine participation and inclusiveness will provide the means to deliver higher incomes to broad sections of societies in the continent. This will translate into higher standards of living and more equitable societies. If the dynamics of the societal transformations of the past are anything to go by, then industrialisation is a *sine qua non* for achieving these aspirations in African countries.

The previous chapters have dwelt on many pertinent issues, including demonstrating Africa's needs for industrial transformation. The mobilisation and prudent deployment of sufficient amounts of FiR and NFiR, count high amongst the key considerations for promoting industrial transformation in Africa.

The obligation for managing Africa's economic transformation through industrialisation lies with the African countries themselves. As argued, there is a lot these countries can do in order to set on the path to industrialisation: pragmatic architecture of the industrialisation agenda and harnessing own potential for industrialisation are basic requirements.

14.3.2 Decoupling from donor-driven agenda

One of the characteristic features of North-South development co-operation models (bilateral and otherwise) has been that they are essentially donor-driven and therefore articulating more the concerns and interests of the donors (e.g. EU countries), than the recipient countries (e.g. African countries). This tends to be true irrespective of whether a co-operation arrangement is dubbed a 'partnership' or carries a neutral name.

For instance, the Economic Partnership Agreements (EPAs) between the EU and the ACP group of nations is designated as a 'partnership'. The EPAs between the EU and specific regional groupings in the ACP regions spawn from the Cotonou Agreement, which in turn spawned from the EU's Green Paper (with petty revisions to the text during negotiations with the ACP group), but nevertheless retained the term 'partnership' in its title. However, in reality this is far from a partnership. It is an agreement which has been largely architectured and is driven by the EU.

Besides, several documents prepared by Development Agencies from developed countries are purported to be rooted in the idea of partnership, though in actual fact they are internal documents of the 'donor' countries.

The temptation to produce donor-driven agendas and use them to guide development co-operation is still very much of a problem, as pointed out by Hartmann (2012). In the analysis of the EU's flagship development policy document, the Green Paper on the Agenda for Change (EU 2011), the author notes that only 11 of the 240 responses (equivalent to 4.6 per cent) to the consultation process on the Green Paper came from recipient countries. By any standards, this makes the agenda essentially a donor-driven one (cf. EC 2010; EU and HTSPE 2010; Hartmann 2012: 3).

14.3.3 Change of the mindset away from triad doctrine

That co-operation between more advanced and less advanced economies can and have been leveraged to ignite and propel industrial transformation in the latter group of countries, is a significant fact for the management of the development agenda of African countries. In a strategy signifying a new era and the end of the treatment of Africa as a periphery whose position in the global economic order is in the lower (primary) stages of the value chain, the EU can and should be ready and willing to play a key role in substantive industrial transformation in African countries.

Considering the little accomplishment on the side of the African countries through centuries of economic ties to Europe, achieving Africa's industrial development by leveraging co-operation with the EU will require a major effort in order to *change the European mindset* about the position of African countries in the global economy – *away from the triad doctrine*. In this connection, the political will of the EU will be as much essential as the will of corporate EU in devising and implementing mutually beneficial economic relations with the African countries, in which case they can borrow a leaf from the Japanese-inspired 'flying geese' model of international cooperation, or the Chinese-inspired 'bamboo capitalism' model of international economic partnership.

14.4 Redefined management practices

14.4.1 *Making corporate and political leadership accountable*

Many African countries are not effectively leveraging their potential to achieve critical masses of domestic economic transformation. That these countries repeatedly miss the opportunities to set on a sustainable industrial development path, and instead retain the status of suppliers of agricultural and industrial raw material to the rest of the world, is also due to the malaise befalling corporate and political leadership. Apparently, as has been mentioned in many accounts, these countries, individually – and severally – continue to be deprived of political leadership capable of designing, and overseeing the implementation of development models that adequately respond to specific country development concerns and interests.

Imperatively, African countries need, as one of the key pillars for sustainable development, to develop systems of accountable, responsible, and proficient political leadership. The system should produce leaders who are capable of overseeing the design and implementation of a strategy for industrial transformation, comprising of: an effective integrated governance framework, as well as the programmes for the development of FiR capacities and NFiR capacities.

14.4.2 *Continuous monitoring and evaluation*

Creating an enabling environment for industrialisation is crucial for the success of the process. This is achieved though the design of an appropriate governance framework, and the development of diverse FiR capacities, as well as diverse NFiR capacities (cf. Chapter 12 and 13).

However, for given inputs to support industrial transformation, the achieving of the desired outputs and results (i.e. outcomes and development impact) and the ensuring of sustainability requires being alert all the time. Hence, it is necessary for each country to undertake continuous Monitoring[4] and Evaluation[5] (M&E) of the process and results of the entire development agenda.

Imperatively, the success of the industrialisation agenda requires also the development and deployment of adequate capacities for the M&E of the implementation of the agenda, as well as its results. The intention of M&E is to continuously generate and incorporate lessons learned from the implementation process into the decision making for new actions.

Therefore, a carefully designed M&E system should enable the assessment of both the *implementation stage* and *post-implementation stage* (i.e. *results*) of the undertaking. In accordance with contemporary practices, the M&E framework uses four types of performance indicators. Two sets of indicators measure how successfully the undertaking is implemented. These are the input indicators and output indicators. Another two sets of indicators are associated with the post-implementation stage of the undertaking, i.e. they measure the results. They include the outcome indicators, and impact indicators. Figure 14.1 illustrates the clustering of M&E indicators.

To facilitate monitoring and evaluation, *concrete action plans* should be developed, identifying clearly the planned activities and inputs for each major pillar of the IIDA – the hybrid agenda for the industrialisation of African countries introduced in Chapter 4 of this book:

a   Action Plan of the strategy to enhance national governance framework for industrial development.
b   Action plan of the strategy to develop essential country-level NFiR resource capacities for industrialisation.
c   Action plan of the strategy to develop essential country-level FiR capacities for industrialisation.
d   Action plan of the strategy to leverage international partnership for industrialisation.
e   Action plan of the strategy to leverage the multilateral co-operation for industrialisation.

The M&E should provide a tool for continuously checking the cumulative input of these pillars, on a country's industrial transformation.

14.6 Concluding remarks

For any African country, a national IIDA is rightfully a core component of the overall economic growth and development. It would embrace all the essential

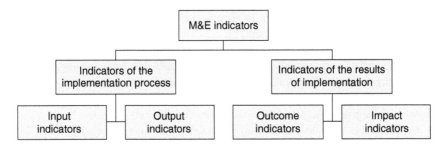

Figure 14.1 Classification of M&E indicators (source: Author).

elements to spearhead industrialisation-driven economic growth and development: an integrated governance system to provide strategic direction to and guide industrial transformation, industrial entrepreneurship capacities, effective organisations or institutions to support industrialisation, adequate industrial finance system, well-developed and maintained physical infrastructure, appropriate and adequate technological capacities, and quality cadres of human personnel (cf. Chapter 13 of this book).

With a successful implementation of IIDA, industry should become the driving force for economic growth and development. The strategic approach should be to grow those industrial sectors with the best potential for maximum contribution of manufacturing value added, and to closely align them with the objectives of export development and deepening integration into the global economy. The expectation is that African countries that will be able to meaningfully engage and leverage the EU and other international development partners (e.g. China, Japan, USA, etc.) for industrialisation, shall have attained and occupied sufficient niche positions in medium and high technology activities within 20 years.

However, the kind of international partnerships that every single African country needs today and will need tomorrow, is one where the balance of domestic and international forces permits the realisation of an African economic emancipation through an organic industrialisation process. The process should leverage Africa's potential for Africa's development. The best model to provide dividends is surely not the *hub-and-spoke model* that has even been officially promoted to guide Africa–EU co-operation, or the *triad doctrine's centre-and-periphery model* that has generally shaped the relationship between the West and the developing world. The *Japanese led-flying geese model*, and in particular the *Chinese-led bamboo capitalism model* are a lot more superior and are instruments of genuine partnership. Therefore, in view of these facts, Africa–EU development partnership should be reengineered accordingly. This change is the only way to salvage the historical linkages between these two groups of nations, save for use of force and coercion, which cannot work in the current context of international relations. Failure to do this will see Africa tilt away from the EU.

Notes

1 The economic model is characterised by (i) less regulated markets (e.g. financial markets, labour markets), and (ii) heightened free-market tendencies.
2 The economic model tends to (i) be more state-controlled, and (ii) more pronouncedly focus on wealth redistribution.
3 The underlying economic model is characterised by comprehensive social welfare policies (and therefore focus more comprehensively on wealth redistribution).
4 Monitoring refers to

> the regular collection and analysis of information to assist timely decision-making, ensure accountability and provide the basis for evaluation and learning. It is a continuing function that uses methodical collection of data to provide management and the main stakeholders of an ongoing project or programme with early indications of progress and achievement of objectives.

(IFAD 2002: A-7)

5 Evaluation refers to

a systematic (and as objective as possible) examination of a planned, ongoing or completed project. It aims to answer specific management questions and to judge the overall value of an endeavour and supply lessons learned to improve future actions, planning and decision-making. Evaluations commonly seek to determine the efficiency, effectiveness, impact, sustainability and the relevance of the project or organisation's objectives. An evaluation should provide information that is credible and useful, offering concrete lessons learned to help partners and funding agencies make decisions.

(IFAD 2002: A-5)

References

EC (2010). Green Paper. *EU Development Policy in Support of Inclusive Growth and Sustainable Development: Increasing the Impact of EU Development Policy.* COM(2010) 629final). Brussels. 10 November.

EU (2011). *Increasing the Impact of EU Development Policy: An Agenda for Change.* (COM(2011) 637final). Brussels.

EU and HTSPE (2010). *Report on the Consultation on the Green Paper on EU Development Policy in Support of Inclusive Growth and Sustainable Development – Increasing the Impact of EU Development Policy.* Project No. 2010/252309 – Version 1.

Hartmann, S. (2012). *The Conceptual Flaws of the New EU Development Agenda from a Political Economy Perspective, or Why Change is Problematic for a Donor-Driven Development Policy. Österreichische Forschungsstiftung für Internationale Entwicklung.* Vienna. October.

IFAD (2002). *A Guide to for Project M & E: Glossary A – Glossary of M & E Concepts and Terms.* International Fund for Agricultural Development. Rome.

Xing, L. (2007). *East Asian Regional Integration: From Japan-led 'Flying-geese' to China-centred 'Bamboo Capitalism'.* Centre for Comparative Integration Studies. CCIS Research Series. Working Paper No. 3.

Appendix 1

Comparable growth of GDP and value added by economic activity, 1970–2010

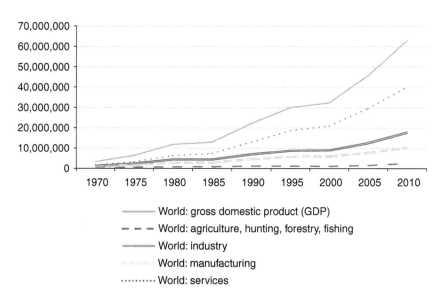

Legend:
——— World: gross domestic product (GDP)
– – – World: agriculture, hunting, forestry, fishing
——— World: industry
– – – World: manufacturing
·········· World: services

Appendix 1a Growth of GDP and value added by economic activity for the world, 1970–2010, selected years.

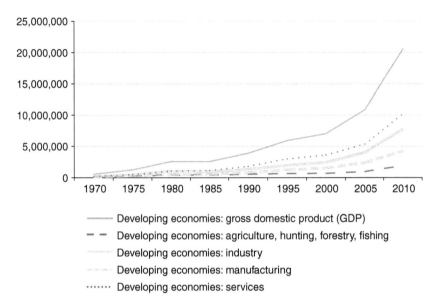

Appendix 1b Growth of GDP and value added by economic activity for developing economies, 1970–2010, selected years.

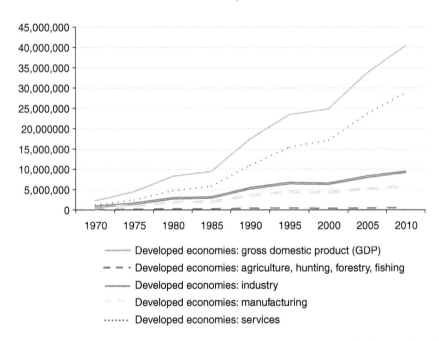

Appendix 1c Growth of GDP and value added by economic activity for developed economies, 1970–2010, selected years.

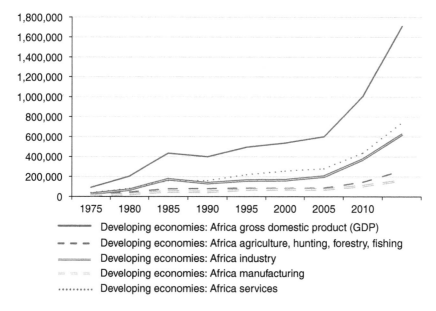

Appendix 1d Growth of GDP and value added by economic activity for African developing economies, 1970–2010, selected years.

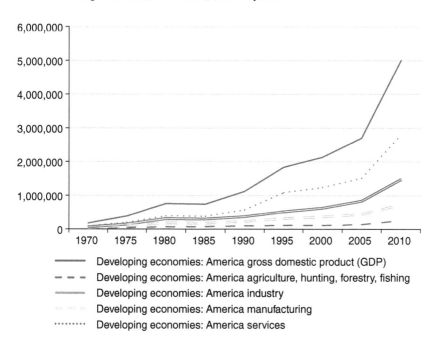

Appendix 1e Growth of GDP and value added by economic activity for American developing economies, 1970–2010, selected years.

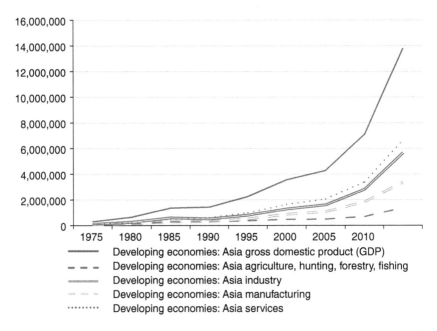

Appendix 1f Growth of GDP and value added by economic activity for Asian developing economies, 1970–2010, selected years.

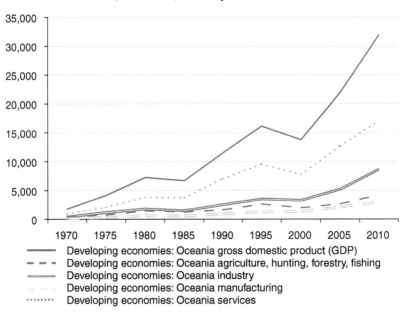

Appendix 1g Growth of GDP and value added by economic activity for Oceanian developing economies, 1970–2010, selected years.

Source: Author's computations based on UNCTAD (2012). UNCTADstat (available at: http://unctadstat.unctad.org/UnctadStatMetadata/Documentation/UNCTADstatContent.htm).

Appendix 2

Comparable structures of merchandise exports

Appendix 2a World structure of merchandise exports, selected years (%)

Product group	1995	2000	2005	2010
All food items (SITC 0+1+22+4)	8.97	6.69	6.53	7.40
Agricultural raw materials (SITC 2 less 22, 27 and 28)	2.68	1.87	1.57	1.55
Ores and metals (SITC 27+28+68)	3.29	2.87	3.37	4.45
Fuels (SITC 3)	7.33	10.47	14.09	15.55
Pearls, precious stones and non-monetary gold (SITC 667+971)	1.22	1.24	1.28	1.89
Manufactured goods (SITC 5 to 8 less 667 and 68)	72.72	73.35	70.37	65.63
Subtotal	96.22	96.50	97.22	96.47

Source: Author's computations based on UNCTAD (2013). UNCTADstat (available at: http://unctadstat.unctad.org/UnctadStatMetadata/Documentation/UNCTADstatContent.htm).

Appendix 2b Structure of merchandise exports in developing countries, selected years (%)

Product group	1995	2000	2005	2010
All food items (SITC 0+1+22+4)	10.00	6.77	6.03	6.75
Agricultural raw materials (SITC 2 less 22, 27 and 28)	2.74	1.61	1.30	1.34
Ores and metals (SITC 27+28+68)	3.71	2.87	3.58	4.51
Fuels (SITC 3)	15.08	19.74	22.70	21.44
Pearls, precious stones and non-monetary gold (SITC 667+971)	1.45	1.34	1.51	2.35
Subtotal	98.87	99.27	99.22	99.22

Source: Author's computations based on UNCTAD (2013). UNCTADstat (available at: http://unctadstat.unctad.org/UnctadStatMetadata/Documentation/UNCTADstatContent.htm).

Appendix 2c Structure of merchandise exports in developed countries, selected years (%)

Product group	1995	2000	2005	2010
All food items (SITC 0+1+22+4)	8.67	6.76	6.98	8.09
Agricultural raw materials (SITC 2 less 22, 27 and 28)	2.57	1.93	1.67	1.65
Ores and metals (SITC 27+28+68)	2.92	2.61	3.04	4.28
Fuels (SITC 3)	3.38	4.77	6.68	7.95
Pearls, precious stones and non-monetary gold (SITC 667+971)	1.16	1.22	1.16	1.62
Manufactured goods (SITC 5 to 8 less 667 and 68)	76.77	78.02	76.67	71.06
Subtotal	95.46	95.32	96.19	94.65

Source: Author's computations based on UNCTAD (2013). UNCTADstat (available at: http://unctadstat.unctad.org/UnctadStatMetadata/Documentation/UNCTADstatContent.htm).

Appendix 2d Structure of merchandise exports in African developing countries, selected years (%)

Product group	1995	2000	2005	2010
All food items (SITC 0+1+22+4)	16.17	10.20	7.41	9.06
Agricultural raw materials (SITC 2 less 22, 27 and 28)	5.18	3.68	2.44	2.16
Ores and metals (SITC 27+28+68)	7.92	6.83	6.67	9.85
Fuels (SITC 3)	36.79	51.52	60.69	56.45
Pearls, precious stones and non-monetary gold (SITC 667+971)	5.01	5.78	4.48	4.25
Manufactured goods (SITC 5 to 8 less 667 and 68)	28.89	21.34	17.49	17.49
Subtotal	99.95	99.35	99.17	99.25

Source: Author's computations based on UNCTAD (2013). UNCTADstat (available at:http://unctadstat.unctad.org/UnctadStatMetadata/Documentation/UNCTADstatContent.htm).

Appendix 2e Structure of merchandise exports in American developing countries, selected years (%)

Product group	1995	2000	2005	2010
All food items (SITC 0+1+22+4)	22.28	14.93	16.05	18.63
Agricultural raw materials (SITC 2 less 22, 27 and 28)	3.72	2.18	2.01	2.05
Ores and metals (SITC 27+28+68)	8.97	6.16	9.15	13.22
Fuels (SITC 3)	14.26	17.59	21.02	19.73
Pearls, precious stones and non-monetary gold (SITC 667+971)	1.15	0.72	1.03	2.61
Manufactured goods (SITC 5 to 8 less 667 and 68)	49.04	57.70	49.91	43.25
Subtotal	99.43	99.28	99.17	99.48

Source: Author's computations based on UNCTAD (2013). UNCTADstat (available at:http://unctadstat.unctad.org/UnctadStatMetadata/Documentation/UNCTADstatContent.htm).

Appendix 2f Structure of merchandise exports in Asian developing countries, selected years (%)

Product group	1995	2000	2005	2010
All food items (SITC 0 + 1 + 22 + 4)	6.71	4.47	3.82	4.38
Agricultural raw materials (SITC 2 less 22, 27 and 28)	2.23	1.26	1.02	1.12
Ores and metals (SITC 27 + 28 + 68)	2.09	1.68	2.08	2.38
Fuels (SITC 3)	13.01	17.19	18.87	18.19
Pearls, precious stones and non-monetary gold (SITC 667 + 971)	1.11	1.03	1.26	2.08
Manufactured goods (SITC 5 to 8 less 667 and 68)	73.56	73.64	72.19	71.02
Subtotal	98.71	99.26	99.24	99.18

Source: Author's computations based on UNCTAD (2013). UNCTADstat (available at:http://unctad-stat.unctad.org/UnctadStatMetadata/Documentation/UNCTADstatContent.htm).

Appendix 2g Structure of merchandise exports in Asian developing countries, selected years (%)

Product group	1995	2000	2005	2010
All food items (SITC 0 + 1 + 22 + 4)	18.42	17.13	19.52	18.57
Agricultural raw materials (SITC 2 less 22, 27 and 28)	11.84	7.09	8.41	8.09
Ores and metals (SITC 27 + 28 + 68)	16.45	13.21	16.83	24.62
Fuels (SITC 3)	11.54	13.33	14.53	12.91
Pearls, precious stones and non-monetary gold (SITC 667 + 971)	8.65	10.86	11.26	19.78
Manufactured goods (SITC 5 to 8 less 667 and 68)	17.26	37.29	27.28	15.25
Subtotal	84.17	98.91	97.83	99.22

Source: Author's computations based on UNCTAD (2013). UNCTADstat (available at: http://unctadstat.unctad.org/UnctadStatMetadata/Documentation/UNCTADstatContent.htm).

Appendix 3

Trends in MVA as a percentage of GDP, 1991–2007, selected groups of countries

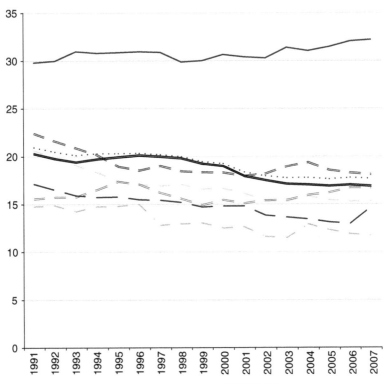

— EAP: East Asia and Pacific
NV.IND.MANF.ZS
Manufacturing value added (% of GDP)

— · LAC: Latin America and Caribbean
NV.IND.MANF.ZS
Manufacturing value added (% of GDP)

— · MNA: Middle East and North Africa
NV.IND.MANF.ZS
Manufacturing value added (% of GDP)

— NOC: High income
nonOECD NV.IND.MANF.ZS
Manufacturing value added (% of GDP)
(NV.IND.MANF.ZS)

— OEC: High income
OECD NV.IND.MANF.ZS
Manufacturing value added (% of GDP)

— · SAS: South Asia
NV.IND.MANF.ZS
Manufacturing value added (% of GDP)

— SSA: Sub-Saharan Africa
NV.IND.MANF.ZS
Manufacturing value added (% of GDP)

····· WLD: World
NV.IND.MANF.ZS
Manufacturing value added (% of GDP)

Source: Author's computations based on ECONSTAT (available at: www.econstats.com/wdi/wdiv_717.htm). The cited source further cites 'World Bank national accounts data and OECD National Accounts data files'.

Appendix 4

World exports by main product categories, in US$ million

Year	Total exports	Primary goods	Manufactured goods	Services
1995	6,341,619.9	1,140,000	3,730,000	1,222,088.2
1996	6,685,963.4	1,230,000	3,900,000	1,307,821.44
1997	6,940,842.3	1,230,000	4,100,000	1,358,876.47
1998	6,869,043.6	1,080,000	4,160,000	1,396,617.42
1999	7,115,349.2	1,130,000	4,300,000	1,432,570.7
2000	7,930,132.6	1,390,000	4,670,000	1,521,680.81
2001	7,671,778.5	1,340,000	4,520,000	1,527469.27
2002	8,065,316.2	1,370,000	4,770,000	1,645,292.44
2003	9,366,185.7	1,640,000	5,500,000	1,888,169.64
2004	11,379,659.5	2,090,000	6,620,000	2,291,594.9
2005	12,937,705.2	2,680,000	7,360,000	2,560,162.15
2006	14,888,810.4	3,220,000	8,370,000	2,897,624.99
2007	17,368,451.1	3,790,000	9,570,000	3,483,555.27
2008	19,867,660.4	4,880,000	10,500,000	3,911,137.7
2009	15,889,984.5	3,450,000	8,340,000	3,483,815.17
2010	18,946,756	4,410,000	9,980,000	3,830,900.9
2011	22,355,563.5	5,670,000	11,500,000	4,236,860.9
Total	200,620,822	41,740,000	111,890,000	39,996,238.37
% of total for the period	21	56		20

Source: Author's computations based on UNCTAD (2013). UNCTADstat (available at: http://unctadstat.unctad.org/TableViewer/tableView.aspx?ReportId=24739).

Index

Page numbers in *italics* denote tables, those in **bold** denote figures.